HISTORICAL STUDIES OF
CHANGING FERTILITY

FORTHCOMING VOLUMES IN THE MSSB SERIES
Quantitative Studies in History:

Demographic Processes and Family Organization in Nineteenth-Century America
The History of American Electoral Behavior
International Trade and Internal Growth

PUBLISHED:

Essays on a Mature Economy: Britain After 1840 (Princeton, 1971)
The Dimensions of Quantitative Research in History (Princeton, 1972)
Race and Slavery in the Western Hemisphere: Quantitative Studies (Princeton, 1975)
The New Urban History: Quantitative Explorations by American Historians (Princeton, 1975)
The History of Parliamentary Behavior (Princeton, 1977)
Historical Studies of Changing Fertility (Princeton, 1978)

Historical Studies of Changing Fertility

EDITED BY

Charles Tilly

CONTRIBUTORS

Lutz K. Berkner - Rudolf Braun - Richard A. Easterlin
Ronald Lee - Franklin F. Mendels - Charles Tilly
Maris A. Vinovskis - Etienne van de Walle
E. A. Wrigley

PRINCETON UNIVERSITY PRESS

This material was prepared with the support of
National Science Foundation Grant No. GS-3256.
Any opinions, findings, conclusions, or recommendations
expressed are those of the authors and do not
necessarily reflect the view of the National
Science Foundation.

Library of Congress Cataloging in Publication Data will
be found on the last printed page of this book

Printed in the United States of America by
Princeton University Press, New Jersey

Series Preface

THIS volume is one of a series of "Quantitative Studies in History" sponsored by the Mathematical Social Science Board (MSSB) and published by Princeton University Press. Other volumes in the series are listed on p. ii. The Mathematical Social Science Board was established in 1964 under the aegis of the Center for Advanced Study in the Behavioral Sciences "to foster advanced research and training in the application of mathematical methods in the social sciences." The following fields are each represented on MSSB by one member: anthropology, economics, history, geography, linguistics, political science, psychology and sociology. The three methodological disciplines of mathematics, statistics and computer science are also represented. Members of MSSB are appointed, subject to the approval of the Board of Trustees of the Center, for a term of four years. At the present time the members of MSSB are:

MSSB has established advisory committees to plan its activities in the various substantive fields with which it is concerned. The current members of the History Advisory Committee are:

Richard Easterlin, Department of Economics, University of Pennsylvania, chairman

Robert Fogel, Departments of Economics and History, Harvard University

Ronald Lee, Department of Economics, University of Michigan

Gilbert Shapiro, Departments of History and Sociology, University of Pittsburgh

Stephan Thernstrom, Department of History, Harvard University

Charles Tilly

Supported by grants from the National Science Foundation, MSSB has organized five major classes of activities:

(1) Training Programs, have lasted from two to eight weeks during the summer, and have been designed to provide young pre- and post-Ph.D.s with intensive training in some of the mathematics pertinent to their substantive field and with examples of applications to specific problems.

(2) Research and Training Seminars, which have typically lasted from four to six weeks, have been composed of both senior scientists and younger people who have already received some training in mathematical applications. The focus has been on recent research, on the intensive exploration of new ideas, and on the generation of new research. The training has been less formal than in the Training Programs; the research and training seminars have had the apprentice nature of advanced graduate work. At present MSSB is not conducting training programs or training seminars, because of lack of funds for that purpose.

(3) Advanced Research Workshops typically last from four to six weeks, and are almost exclusively restricted to senior scientists. They are devoted to fostering advanced research. They afford the possibility of extensive and penetrating contact over a prolonged period, among scholars who are deeply involved in research.

(4) Preparation of Teaching Materials. In some areas, the absence of effective teaching materials—even of suitable research papers—is a very limiting factor in the development of research and teaching activities within universities. The Board has therefore felt that it could accelerate the development of such materials partly through financial support and partly through helping to organize their preparation.

(5) Special Conferences. Short conferences, lasting a few days, are organized to explore the possibilities of the successful development of mathematical theory and training in some particular area that has not previously been represented in the programs, or to review the progress of research in particular areas when such a review seems warranted.

MSSB has played an important part in recent historical research. The Board, for example, regularly sponsored the meetings during the 1960s at which the newly-active importers of econometric methods into economic history forged their agreements, identified their disagreements, and worked out agendas for their inquiries. More recently, MSSB has sponsored a number of activities in demographic history: conferences and seminars on nominal record-linkage, behavioral models in historical demography, family structure in urbanization, models of the family cycle, and others including the seminar from which the papers in this volume took their start. Some earlier volumes in the MSSB-sponsored Quantitative Studies in History, such as Leo Schnore, ed., *The New Urban History* and Stanley Engerman and Eugene Genovese, eds., *Race and Slavery in the Western Hemisphere*, included substantial demographic analyses. This is the first book in the series to deal mainly with demographic questions. With this momentum, the Board may be able to play the same sort of role in demographic history that it earlier played in economic history. I hope it will.

The authors of this book are grateful to Carl Kaysen and the Institute for Advanced Study for the opportunity to meet in gracious, convenient surroundings. Virginia High served efficiently as secretary for our seminar. At the University of Michigan, Chantal Bancilhon, Judith Blanshard, Anne Dolinka, Pamela Hume, Karen Metrick, and Kathryn Tilly helped produce the book. In addition to the National Science Foundation's support of the seminar through the Mathematical Social Science Board, NSF and the Horace Rackham School of Graduate Studies, University of Michigan, indirectly subsidized the seminar through support of my work on population changes in western Europe.

Charles Tilly, Chairman, History Advisory Committee, MSSB

Ann Arbor, Michigan.
August, 1976

Contents

HISTORICAL STUDIES OF CHANGING FERTILITY

1

The Historical Study of Vital Processes

CHARLES TILLY

OVER the last two centuries, almost all western countries have experienced large declines in fertility: the rate at which their female populations bear children. The decline has been more or less continuous. It has often seemed irreversible. Little of the world outside Europe and the areas settled mainly by Europeans has experienced the massive, continuous decline of fertility. During the same period, the same Europe-centered world has undergone industrialization and urbanization to a degree almost unparalleled elsewhere.

The fertility decline, the industrialization and the urbanization have accompanied each other closely enough to encourage the idea that industrialization and urbanization *cause* fertility to decline. We have plenty of ideas to make such a relationship plausible: the idea that urban-industrial families have less need and less desire for the labor of children than agrarian families do, the idea that contraceptive techniques and information improve as a consequence of advances in communication and in scientific knowledge resulting from industrialization, and so on. The problem is that we have too many explanations which are individually plausible in general terms, which contradict each other to some degree, and which fail to fit some significant part of the facts.

An examination of the prospects for a worldwide fertility decline stated: "Negotiating a transit from high fertility to low fertility levels could prove easier for today's underdeveloped countries than it was for present-day developed countries, some of which required over half a century to move from fairly high to low level. . . . Today contraceptive methods are far more advanced, often have the active endorsement of the state, and are strongly opposed by cults and ideological groups only in some countries. Moreover, high fertility combines with low infant and child mortality to impose a heavier dependency burden on adults than was the case in the West in the nineteenth century, when children required less education and entered the labor force earlier. Urbanization also feeds the revolutionary change in man's aspirations now underway in much of the world (Spengler 1974: 17)." [1]

---

[1] The omitted material shows that fertility levels in the poor parts of today's world are higher than they were in most European countries when those countries

3

Now, this statement deals with opportunities rather than established regularities. Nevertheless, its plausibility rests on a series of causal arguments: (1) that the efficiency of available contraceptive technology, the moral and political support for contraception and the extent of dependency all accelerate the decline of fertility; (2) that the worldwide "change in man's aspirations" reduces people's desire or willingness to have many children; and (3) that these changes in goals and in the means available to the goals are the chief factors in the decline of fertility. In such an argument, urbanization and industrialization affect fertility through their impacts on general aspirations, attitudes toward children, burdens of dependency and contraceptive technology.

The connections are plausible. Yet, at present, it is debatable whether the connections are strong or consistent, and whether they are the chief connections between urbanization and industrialization, on the one hand, and fertility change, on the other. In an authoritative collection of essays on fertility and family planning, Simon Kuznets speaks of the "insensitivity of fertility levels to wide differences in economic and social factors despite the marked contrast between the [less developed] and [more developed] groups, each taken as a whole, with respect to both social factors and fertility" (Behrman, et al. 1969: 159–160). In the same volume, Ansley Coale concludes: "Perhaps we shall through a stroke of insight or good fortune discover a grand generalization that will provide a compact and widely valid explanation of the decline of marital fertility in Europe. But at the moment it appears that the process was more complex, subtle, and diverse than anticipated; only an optimist would still expect a simple account of why fertility fell" (Behrman et al. 1969: 19). Furthermore, demographic historians have accumulated ample evidence that fertility rose and fell repeatedly before the industrialization of the nineteenth century, and have even turned up some indications of a widespread rise of fertility in the eighteenth century. Both in accounting for the contemporary distribution of high and low fertility in the world and in accounting for the pattern by which fertility fell in the West, then, we have a surfeit of interesting partial hypotheses and a dearth of successful general formulations.

In this book, we look hard at some portions of the western experience. By studying particular experiences closely, we hope to get a sense of the actual process by which fertility changed and to start ruling out a few of the available hypotheses. By turning to historical material, we hope to find rich, continuous documentation over the sub-

began their nineteenth-century fertility decline. Citations in this form refer to the Bibliography at the end of this book.

stantial blocks of time which major fertility changes require. By being explicit and punctilious about the models and methods we employ, we hope to link what we learn about particular experiences in Europe or North America both with comparable experiences elsewhere and with general arguments—other people's and our own. The book contains a series of general arguments, a number of historical illustrations of the arguments, a body of systematic evidence drawn from the historical experience of western Europe, and a smaller body of evidence drawn from the United States. Each of the elements is incomplete. Nor do all of them fit together perfectly.

Our subject matter, the historical study of populations, is now in something like the state that characterized the quantitative economic history of the 1950s. Although much of the quantitative work underway is sophisticated, it is also largely descriptive. Measurement problems form the bulk of the technical literature. We have a shortage of general theories and of specific models. Where the analysts do have fairly determinate arguments and relevant data, they present a surprising amount of their evidence by visually matching curves or comparing maps with each other or linking descriptive tables via verbal arguments. The statistical work which gets done tends to have an inductive cast: searching for patterns rather than determining whether expected patterns exist. Demographic historians like to justify their emphasis on description and measurement in terms which are congenial to their allies the demographers: you have to get the facts right before you can explain them. On the whole, they dislike the obvious counter: in order to know which facts matter, you need to have a theory.

The parallel with the economic history of the 1950s is imperfect in three ways: First, almost all of demographic history involves some quantification of the material; large expanses of the earlier economic history consisted of non-quantitative narratives of particular firms, entrepreneurs, localities, industries, or forms of trade. Second, econometric history now exists, and the econometric historians have themselves edged into demographic problems when dealing with such matters as the economics of slavery or changes in the labor force. Third, the econometric historians turned easily to existing economic theory (especially, as it happens, to neo-classical economics) for plausible arguments which had often already been given mathematical formulations. The demographic historian draws on theoretical resources which are more disparate and less well developed: some economic theory, some sociology, some anthropology, some demography, and a good deal of reformulation of existing historical arguments. Neverthe-

5

less, today's demographic history resembles the economic history of two decades ago in being ripe for a shift from description to the formulation and testing of determinate models.

Demographic history is actually an old enterprise. John Graunt, William Petty, Thomas Malthus, and Adolphe Quételet were all, in their ways, historical demographers. Yet workable theory has only built up very slowly in the field. For instance, the most widely used theory of large-scale population change—the theory of the demographic transition from high, unstable fertility and high unstable mortality in pre-industrial populations to low, fluctuating fertility and low, stable mortality in mature industrial populations—now seems to raise more problems than it solves. There are few efforts to frame general arguments, to specify relationships, to formulate, to estimate, and to test models of population processes. There are, instead, many efforts to get the descriptions of particular populations, places, and processes right: How widespread was deliberate fertility control in eighteenth-century Europe? Did life expectancy decline in nineteenth-century cities as they industrialized?

Not that a concern with description and measurement is improper, or the work being done second-rate. On the contrary. Some of the freshest and most important work done anywhere in history over the last few decades has been done by demographic historians. As a result of the work done by Louis Henry and his collaborators in France, for example, we are beginning to see that preindustrial Europe differs greatly from its traditional static portrait and that Europe is alive with population movement; it responds quickly to changes in opportunities; it compensates for its population losses in famine or pestilence with surprising spurts of marriages and births. The outcomes of these and other inquiries are forcing us to rewrite social and economic history. Via studies of ideas concerning death, birth, and family structure, and via studies of the impact of population changes on national power and the making of states, they are even beginning to touch the distant preserves of intellectual and political history.

The contributors to this volume have played a part in the renewal of demographic history. Richard Easterlin has linked America's present with its past by analyzing the baby boom after World War II as a logical extension of population processes which were already in operation long before the war, E. A. Wrigley has traced the ups and downs of vital rates in English villages (notably the now-classic case of Colyton, Devon), over centuries, Franklin Mendels has identified the curious and often self-defeating demographic response of rural populations to the expansion of cottage industry, and so on down our roster.

6

The contributors are a varied lot: some seated firmly in economics, some eminently historical in their orientations, some strongly influenced by contemporary sociology and demography.

We sought the variety. From the start of our planning of the seminar which eventually led to this volume, Wrigley and I wanted to bring together three kinds of expertise: (1) historical knowledge of particular populations which had experienced substantial demographic change; (2) formal demographic analysis and (3) formulation, estimation, and testing of mathematical models of social processes. Hardly anyone anywhere is expert in all three areas. Our aim was to form a group which was collectively expert in all three fields, and in which at a minimum each individual was expert in one regard, knowledgeable in another, and interested in the third.

Wrigley and I had several premises in mind. First, we thought that the historical study of fertility change in rural and small-town populations might be ready for a provisional synthesis, both because interesting new ideas and models were emerging and because good local studies were multiplying. Second, we thought that a fruitful synthesis would have to provide some means of dealing simultaneously with variations in kinship, household composition, sexual behavior, economic opportunity and demographic constraints, all in ways which would permit the matching up of detailed local studies with general models and large-scale analyses. Third, we thought it would be good for historical demography in general if model-builders and close observers of particular populations could devise arrangements for working in collaboration. Working from these premises, we arrived at this sort of plan: A small group of specialists in different aspects of fertility change prepare papers on overlapping topics, circulate, and study them in advance, then meet for a sustained period of discussion, criticism, mutual education, and reworking of the papers. That is more or less what happened.

We announced the topic of the seminar as "early industrialization, family structure and changes in fertility." By industrialization we meant the processes producing a net movement of the labor force (1) out of agriculture into the production of services and manufactured goods and (2) into larger and more complex organizations. By "early" we meant the period before factories began to dominate manufacturing. We made it clear that we were strongly interested in the changes within agriculture and in rural areas that accompanied early industrialization. (As readers will see, the content of and the character of the seminar actually shifted the balance away from the analysis of industrialization and toward the analysis of the impact of a variety of economic changes on family structure and fertility.) Having stated the broad problem,

7

we approached scholars who had already done significant work on some aspect of the problem, and who as a group covered the necessary range of historical, demographic and mathematical expertise. We asked each scholar to propose a specific topic related to the broad problem.

We began recruiting participants and commissioning papers in mid-1971. We were fortunate in getting most of the people we sought. They were: Lutz Berkner, a historian (U.C.L.A.) who has worked on the organization and demography of rural populations in Austria and France; Rudolf Braun, a historian-sociologist (Zürich) who is best known for his studies of the transformation of Zürich's hinterland over the whole span of industrialization; Richard Easterlin, an economist-demographer (University of Pennsylvania) who has done extensive quantitative studies of the demographic impact of economic changes in the United States; Ronald Lee, another economist-demographer (University of Michigan) whose work up to that point concentrated on the econometric analysis of demographic changes in England; Franklin Mendels, an economic historian (then of U.C.L.A.) whose major work up to then had been a study of the demographic con-comitants of early industrialization in Flanders; Charles Tilly, a sociologist-historian (University of Michigan) who had done consider-able work on urbanization in Europe and North America; Maris Vinovskis, a historian (then of the University of Wisconsin) under-taking large-scale statistical analyses of American population changes before the twentieth century; Etienne van de Walle, a demographer (then of Princeton University) who had just completed a major re-constitution of fertility changes in nineteenth-century France; and E. A. Wrigley, an economic historian and historical demographer (Cambridge University) who was known both for his synthetic essays and for his detailed long-term local studies of population changes in England and western Europe. Each of these people agreed to prepare a paper linking his particular interest to the general problem of the seminar.

Although we had the usual problems meeting deadlines, the partici-pants did have a chance to study most of the papers before the group assembled. The seminar met for three weeks in June and July 1972 at the Institute for Advanced Study (Princeton, New Jersey). We assem-bled for sustained discussions of individual papers for several days at the beginning of the three weeks, and again at the end. In between, we held special sessions on particular topics which had excited curi-osity or concern during our general discussions (e.g., a presentation of the logic of cross-spectral analysis by Ronald Lee); we met as a group with outside experts (e.g., Ansley Coale of Princeton University, John Durand of the University of Pennsylvania); we tried further analyses on a computer terminal installed for the seminar; smaller groups of us often got together for discussions of our common problems; individually, we read, thought, and wrote more on our special topics. At the end, we decided we had gotten far enough to assemble revised versions of our papers in a published volume. It took fifteen months for all the revisions to come in, a year beyond that for me to edit the papers into the volume, another long year for outside reviews and further revisions of the completed collection. Here is the product of our work.

The purpose of this first essay is to provide a context for the other chapters, to specify some of the ways in which they are incomplete, and to identify some points of contact among them. It is sweeping and speculative where they are prudent and precise. The purpose is still the same: to make connections between western historical experience and alternative general ideas about the determinants of changes in fertility.

I

Vital Processes and Collective Biography

The basic vital processes are fertility and mortality: the beginning and end of life. Vital statisticians center their attention on fertility and mortality. They cannot, however, avoid dealing with three other fundamental demographic processes: migration, social mobility, and nuptiality. Migration enters into analyses of fertility and mortality because the movement of people into or out of a locality affects the liability of the population to conception and its liability to death; in the most obvious case, a large in-migration of young men and women tends to elevate a population's birth rate and depress its death rate. Social mobility—that is, the movement of people from category to category rather than place to place—similarly affects who is at risk to conception or to death in any particular category; furthermore, since categories of people vary in their propensity to family planning, in their access to medical services, and in many other regards which affect their fertility and mortality, a large shift of people from one category to another sometimes alters the vital characteristics of the population as a whole. Nuptiality—the movement of people into and out of marriage—significantly affects fertility, since the great bulk of human conception, and an even greater share of human childbearing, takes place within marriages.

9

Mortality, nuptiality, and fertility form a kind of hierarchy. The existing level and pattern of mortality set limits on who can marry, at what ages. They also affect the numbers and age distribution of women in the childbearing ages. The level and pattern of nuptiality set limits (not so stringent as in the case of mortality) on the portion of the female population likely to bear children. Over the long run the pattern of fertility helps determine who is there to marry or die. There may also be an effect of nuptiality on mortality because marriage somehow affects one's life expectancy. But in general nuptiality constrains fertility, while mortality constrains both nuptiality and fertility.

Other variables affect the core set. I have already mentioned migration and social mobility. Nondemographic variables also matter. For example, over the range of human history, the relative abundance of food has significantly affected the rates at which people have died, married, and borne children. Despite the situation in the contemporary world (in which food-poor countries have high mortality, but also have high fertility and appear to have high nuptiality as well), the main historical tendency has probably been for food shortage to raise mortality and to depress nuptiality and fertility. Again, the urbanization of a population seems to affect the patterns of birth, death, and marriage, alike.

Births, deaths, and marriages are events happening to individuals, while fertility, mortality, and nuptiality are the resultants of those individual events at the level of a population. At the individual level we have the number of children ever born to a particular woman or the age at death of a particular man. At the level of the population we have a total fertility rate or an expectation of life at birth. The handy thing about the demographic analysis of vital phenomena, in fact, is that it permits us to deal with the individual and the group at the same time: first, by specifying the logic by which the one is aggregated into the other; second, by permitting us to compare the experience of any particular individual with that of the population to which the individual belongs.

Because of the explicitness and precision with which demographic analysis performs this aggregation and disaggregation of events, it provides an interesting model for a wide range of historical investigations. Historians who really want to talk about groups often find themselves surrounded by information about individuals. They have several standard ways of jumping the gap: by concentrating on spokesmen, leaders, or elites within the population at hand; by pulling out "typical" individuals; by relying on the testimony of expert observers of the groups in question; and by reporting and illustrating general impressions from long contact with individual records.

Recently, the effort called "collective biography" has offered a more systematic alternative. Collective biography consists of recording features of the life histories of considerable numbers of individuals in a uniform fashion, then aggregating the individual records into a collective portrait of the group and its structure. The collective portrait may consist mainly of averages: mean income, moves per year, median size of a household. It may consist of measures for which there is no precise individual counterpart: income inequality, net reproduction rate, proportion of the labor force in agriculture. It may involve the sorting of the population into its major subdivisions: old vs. young, rich vs. poor, rural vs. urban. It may even reconstruct the relationships among individuals, for example by placing them within their distinct lineages. As the population under study becomes large, the portrait almost necessarily becomes quantitative. It also becomes more and more advantageous to let a computer do the collating and counting. In general, the payoff from collective biography—as compared with other ways of drawing general conclusions from multiple human experiences—rises as the number of persons increases, as the different records containing information about the same individual multiply, and as the general arguments being made are explicit and precise.

At first view, collective biography seems like a very inductive procedure: plug in the individuals and watch the patterns emerge. In fact, collective biography has proven most valuable to historians where someone has already developed an explicit and interesting model of the phenomenon under examination.

The historical study of social stratification and mobility is a good example. In that field, scholars disagree vehemently about the appropriate models, but they commonly work with explicit models of social hierarchies and of movement within the hierarchies. As a consequence, we have (among other things) a series of roughly comparable analyses of American cities since 1850 which contradict the idea of a great expansion of opportunity in the twentieth century, yet establish both the abundance of minor movements up and down the social scale and the rarity of movements from rags to riches or riches to rags. Other versions of collective biography have yielded interesting results in the historical study of elites, elections, legislative behavior, and political conflict.

II

HISTORICAL DEMOGRAPHY

THE most resounding results, however, have come from historical demography. The discipline of demography began to take shape in the

11

eighteenth century as a way of analyzing historical changes in population sizes and characteristics. Yet by the 1930s the discipline had become largely ahistorical in its concerns and its procedures. After World War II demography moved back toward its historical origins. The increasing desire to compare the current demographic experience of non-western countries with the past experience of the West promoted historical studies. The rising interest in identifying the demographic components or counterparts of the processes vaguely and optimistically called "development" augmented the possible return from studying long, well-documented historical population changes. And a series of technical innovations in demography and history made the demographic analysis of historical materials increasingly feasible and profitable. The innovations included the refinement of stable population models, the elaboration of procedures for making demographic estimates from incomplete data and the development of computer routines for the collation of large numbers of observations. They emphatically included the introduction of collective biography.

Two new practices brought collective biography to the center of historical demography. Both owed a good deal to the French demographer Louis Henry. The first was the use of genealogies to produce demographic estimates for whole populations. The second was the application of essentially the same procedures as had been used to analyze genealogies in the construction of demographic estimates from historical records of births, marriages, and deaths. In Henry's version of "family reconstitution," the investigator cumulated individual registrations of vital events into dossiers which related the members of a nuclear family to each other and grouped together the scattered references to the same individual. For families which remained in the population under observation for long periods, it was then possible to reconstruct such matters as the total childbearing experience of a given woman, the frequency of premarital conception of live births and the age at marriage of a family's children—even where the individual records of vital events lacked those items. Historical demographers began to produce long, fine, fascinating series of demographic indices for periods before the census, before governmental imposition of vital registration, indeed before the emergence of demography itself.

What is more, the results proved important to historians and demographers alike. The historians, for example, not only acquired demographic series to relate to the observations of wages, prices, production, and political change they had long been accumulating, but also discovered that an agrarian world they had considered relatively immobile and isolated was swarming with geographic mobility and

12

quickly responsive to changes in economic conditions. The demographers acquired strong evidence of controls over fertility and nuptiality in periods and places which should, by widely held hypotheses, have displayed high, fairly stable, socially uncontrolled rates. Both historians and demographers gained access to a body of materials and procedures which permitted far stronger tests of their assertions concerning long-run population changes than they had ever been able to manage before.

The important yields from parish registers of births, deaths, and marriages (or, more precisely, of baptisms, burials, and weddings) led historical demographers to search for other documents containing related information. They found them. Three main classes of documents contain information lending itself to systematic demographic analysis: (1) population enumerations; (2) registration of vital events; (3) by-products of private transactions.

The census is the contemporary quintessence of the population enumeration. There are few usable censuses anywhere prior to 1800. For the period before 1800, historians have uncovered an abundant supply of the census' ancestor: the enumeration carried on by a large organization for the purpose of identifying resources available to it. The organizations involved are mainly governments, but they include churches, estates, and others. The resources in question are most often property of some kind, yet they sometimes include labor power and special characteristics of the population as literacy or military experience. Fiscal records—assessment rolls, records of payment, and the like—are the chief variety. Conscription registers, cadasters, rent books, enumerations of the poor all have their place. Sometimes these sources contain not only enumerations of the people to be taxed or drafted but also descriptions of their households and summaries of their health, marital status, and so on. Used in conjunction with other documents, even those which only contain one characteristic of the individual will serve to establish the individual's presence or absence at different points in time.

The registration of vital events became a regular activity of western governments during the nineteenth century. Before then some governments (for example, the Swedish state) registered births, marriages, and deaths, but churches played the larger part in recording them. In particular, the Roman Catholic Church required the maintenance of registers, parish by parish, from the seventeenth century onward. The Catholic registers and their Protestant counterparts have survived in abundance; they have served historical demographers well.

The by-products of private transactions which serve demographic

13

purposes include marriage contracts, testaments, deeds, and the documents resulting from the settlement of an estate. This class of records is more heavily biased toward the rich and powerful than are the population enumerations and registrations of vital events. They have some compensating strengths: (1) they often identify a whole kin group, plus quasi-kin such as godparents, at the same time; (2) there are times and places in which most of the population seals a marriage with a contract or divides up an inheritance by written agreement; (3) where the population under study is, in fact, an elite, the by-products of private transactions supplement the standard demographic observations with ample evidence concerning wealth, personal connections and even quality of life.

The historical sources containing population enumerations, registrations of vital events, and by-products of private transactions are rich. More are coming to light every year. But they are distributed quite unevenly. The existence of repeated demographic observations in more or less comparable form depends very much on the presence of large organizations which persist for substantial periods of time. Churches, governments, and estates are the best historical examples. Business firms become important producers of some kinds of continuous series in the nineteenth century.

Where such organizations are rare or weak, the historical record is correspondingly thin and heterogeneous. On the whole, that means the further back in time we go, the more ingenious and determined we have to be in locating the sources and reworking them into comparable form. It also means that with historical records it is often uncertain to what population the documents refer: Do these tax rolls cover the entire population, for example, or just the portion wealthy enough to pay taxes?

In fact, the population covered is characteristically the clientele of a large organization rather than a population in which demographers would take an immediate interest. The problem is then to reconstruct the behavior of a demographically interesting population—a community, a class, a labor force, or something else—from observations of a large organization's clientele. A significant part of the historical demographer's expertise therefore consists of knowing the conditions under which the documents at hand were produced and reconstructing the operations of the organization involved. A large share of the historical demographer's work consists of estimating or correcting gaps, errors, or distortions in the record before drawing inferences from the observed population to the population of genuine interest.

The abundance and richness of historical records makes it possible to use many of them as one would use current vital registration: to detect class and regional differences in mortality, to sort out the relationship of women's childbearing patterns to their ages at marriage or to the mortality of their previously born children, and so on. In this regard, the records simply bring new and interesting populations to the attention of demographers. But there are some problems for which historical materials have definite advantages over contemporary censuses, special surveys, and vital registration.

To the extent that the demographic processes in question take a long time to work themselves out, the relevant evidence necessarily reaches back into history. If we are to verify or modify theories of the "demographic transition" from high to low fertility and mortality, for example, we have no real alternative to assembling comparable series over periods spanning a great deal of urbanization, industrialization, and demographic change; the comparison of different populations at the same point in time as if they marked successive points in a standard progression can never answer the question of whether such a progression actually exists.

Likewise, if the arguments at hand concern life histories rather than individual events, historical records provide fuller and more reliable evidence than can practically any contemporary source. If the great computerized data banks so many of us fear come into existence, they will compete seriously with the materials of historical demography. In the meantime, the demographer who confines himself to contemporary evidence must use retrospective reports which people give in interviews or offer when registering births, deaths, marriages, and other crucial events. Or he can settle for the thin, incomplete life histories accumulating in the files of existing organizations. For my part, I have serious objections to digging the records of living people out of such files, and even more serious objections to linking the information concerning individuals in one file with the information in another file. (If the procedure for consultation of the records guarantees anonymity, shields the individuals involved from direct consequences of the consultation and/or requires the prior consent of the individuals, my objections diminish.) The methods of collective biography, by contrast, permit the construction of rich, complete, and demographically informative life histories from historical records without invading the privacy of living persons.

Finally, the secular trend is of interest. It is worth knowing when and where the world set off at its present, dizzy pace of population growth, and how many times (if ever) the same sort of expansion has happened before. In the more immediate area of this book, it is important to know whether the nineteenth-century fertility decline of western countries followed centuries of high, stable fertility, came as the largest of recurrent declines in fertility, or followed—as some evidence suggests—an extraordinary eighteenth-century rise in fertility. By the same token, it is useful to have historical time-lines of mortality, fertility, urbanization, and migration with which to compare the recent experiences of the world's rapidly urbanizing countries.

So there are some circumstances in which historical materials are not simply a supplementary source of demographic data, but the principal sources one wants to consult: where one's questions concern long-term processes, where the relevant evidence requires full life histories, where the secular trend is itself at issue. The essays later in this volume illustrate all three circumstances, especially the first.

As our essays also illustrate, historical materials do not serve all purposes equally well; they have some characteristic drawbacks. Where intentions, beliefs, and knowledge figure prominently in the argument, historical records rarely contain the direct testimony on these matters which a skilled interviewer elicits from living respondents. Many details of private life escape the written record. When it comes to contraceptive knowledge, desired family size, sexual practices or aspirations for children's careers, the historical evidence is almost always indirect. In these regards, our understanding of times before the twentieth century depends largely on literary treatments, testimonies of supposedly expert observers, penalties inflicted on transgressors, and inferences from such observable phenomena as child-spacing and intervals between marriages and first births.

III

RECENT WORK IN HISTORICAL DEMOGRAPHY

THE discussion so far has another implication. Most of the last two decade's work in historical demography has been descriptive rather than analytical. It has consisted mainly of locating suitable sources, devising procedures for squeezing reliable demographic estimates from the sources, making the desired estimates, then using the resulting series and cross-sections to formulate or corroborate verbal arguments concerning the populations. It has not consisted of the formulation, estimation and testing of rigorous models.

The description is essential. Before national income analysis could become an effective tool of development theory, economists had to spend several decades conceptualizing national income, devising the necessary measurements, and accumulating reliable series for relevant populations. Historical demographers have been doing the equivalent of that work.

What is more, the descriptions often have proved valuable in themselves. For example, E. A. Wrigley's painstaking reconstruction of vital rates in the village of Colyton established that rural marriages and births responded sensitively to changing economic opportunity for centuries before the age of chemical and mechanical contraception. The accumulating weight of descriptions for European and American populations before the nineteenth century has crushed the idea that a shift from "uncontrolled" to "controlled" fertility came with mature industrialism, while raising acute questions as to the character of the earlier controls. Again, the great rapidity with which European populations turn out to have recouped heavy losses to mortality in plague and famine has made explanations of major population shifts in terms of such catastrophes less plausible than they had been. The descriptive work has established that long before the industrial age a large region of southern and western Europe displayed what John Hajnal (1965) has called the "European marriage pattern": relatively later marriage for females, many people permanently unmarried, many households containing unmarried adults as well as a married couple; this arrangement sets early modern Europe off from the rest of the world, and may well have made the region's permanent shift to low fertility easier to manage. Finally, the descriptive version of historical demography has become a standard tool of historians who have no abiding interest in demographic issues as such; following the lead of Pierre Goubert's studies (1960) of Beauvais and its region, they have the means of incorporating information about the life experiences of ordinary people into accounts of the economic, social, and political transformation of a village, city, or region.

By analytical work I simply mean work which asserts a regular relationship among two or more variables, and attempts to test the asserted relationships by means of reliable evidence. One reason that little of the work in historical demography to date has been analytical in this sense is that the questions which first drew investigators into the effort were largely descriptive: when and where did fertility begin its long-run decline? Did preindustrial cities have high levels of mortality? Another reason is that the data for dealing with several variables simultaneously were slow to produce. And a third reason is that a major part of the empirical work was done by historians and others who were not accustomed to the formal modeling and testing of the relationships which interested them. The arrival of quantitatively

17

trained economists, economic historians, and sociologists on the scene accelerated the analytic work in historical demography.

One simple illustration comes from the work of Dov Friedlander (1969, 1970). Friedlander adopts a version of Kingsley Davis' account (1963) of the demographic transition. He takes from it the idea that a rural population which experiences great population pressure (e.g., as a consequence of declining mortality) tends to respond either by lowering fertility or by accelerating out-migration. The greater the opportunities for out-migration, the longer rural fertility will remain high. Friedlander provides a set of hypothetical calculations showing how the two alternatives would work. Then, using already published data, he argues that the British and Swedish experiences conform to the two alternatives: the British urbanizing early, absorbing plenty of rural population through out-migration, and experiencing relatively late declines in rural fertility, the Swedes urbanizing late, having relatively little rural-to-urban migration while mortality declined in the countryside, and experiencing substantial rural declines in fertility before large-scale urbanization.

Later we shall encounter two related difficulties in this approach. First, if we have the *agricultural* population in mind, the formulation neglects an alternative which often occurred in western countries: the movement of agricultural workers into manufacturing within the countryside. Second, as a practical matter it is very hard to measure "population pressure" independently of the responses it is supposed to produce. Still the Friedlander argument immediately suggests extensions to other parts of Europe—including France, a relatively late urbanizer and a classic case of early fertility decline.

The Friedlander work lies halfway between description and rigorous analysis; although the central model is fairly precise, Friedlander neither estimates its parameters nor tests its fit to the available data. It is nonetheless a useful example; it shows the intersection of theories about the demographic transition, contemporary demographic models and procedures, and historical evidence.

IV

THE "DEMOGRAPHIC TRANSITION" TODAY

THE problem of demographic transition dominates the historical study of vital processes today, as it has for thirty or forty years. In their baldest, nontechnical form, the pressing questions are:

1. How and why did the populations of western countries move from

18

high levels of fertility and mortality before 1750 to low levels of fertility and mortality after 1900, while almost none of the nonwestern world went through the same experience?

2. To what extent is the general process (or, failing that, particular relationships within it) generalizable to populations currently undergoing urbanization, industrialization and intensification of communications flows?

In a classic brief statement, A. M. Carr-Saunders did not regard either of these as greatly problematic. "There is no mystery about the fall in the death-rate," he declared. "It was due to improved sanitary conditions and to advances in the study of medicine" (Carr-Saunders 1925: 40). The decline in the birth rate was, he thought, somewhat more complicated, but "While it is impossible to estimate the prevalence of contraceptive practices and of abstention from intercourse, it is probable that they account for the whole of the decline which the figures show" (Carr-Saunders 1925: 42).

In general, Carr-Saunders argued that increased economic efficiency enabled and encouraged a population to expand through increases in fertility, while signs of diminishing returns from technical innovation led the members of the population to restrict births by one means or another. Although he did not formulate the problem of future population growth in terms of what would happen as new areas of the world industrialized or urbanized, he held out the hope that the same semi-conscious process of adjustment would occur elsewhere.

Over the next two decades, western students of population paid rather more attention to the steadily declining growth rates of their own countries than to the accelerating growth rates of the non-western world. "Inadequately explored in a still-Kiplingesque West," writes Joseph Spengler, "were implications of the fact that while the rate of population growth in a politically fissured Western world was falling, that of underdeveloped lands, containing about two-thirds of the world's people, was incipiently high and potentially rising" (Spengler 1972: 339).

The idea of a regular and general demographic transition crystallized: "Modernization" quickly and decisively depressed mortality, mainly through the improvement of sanitation, nutrition, and medical care, then slowly but no less decisively depressed fertility, mainly through the development and diffusion of (1) new aspirations which were incompatible with the bearing of large numbers of children; and (2) contraceptive knowledge. The debate remained open about which features of "modernization"—urban life, for example, or the opening

19

of individual careers requiring an investment in education—really mattered. However it worked, the consequences were clear: accelerating natural increase during the period in which mortality declined faster than fertility, then declining natural increase as "modernization" proceeded still farther. Presumably the same cycle would occur in the poor parts of the world if they could properly begin the process of modernization.

Since World War II, the terms of the discussion have altered—but not fundamentally. The idea of an early, general mortality decline resulting from technical change has persisted, despite some doubt about the life-saving effects of medical improvements before quite recent years, despite increasing emphasis on a reliable food supply as a life-saver, and despite the realization that in the contemporary world governments were introducing controls over disease in areas which showed no signs of "modernization" in most other regards; the theory made these areas dubious candidates for the next steps of the demographic transition.

Another of the original ideas has persisted: that the transition occurs—if it occurs—through the widespread conversion of married couples to the deliberate, efficient control of births. The major alterations in the discussion since World War II have been: (1) the recognition that levels of nuptiality and fertility are much higher in important parts of the contemporary nonwestern world than they were in most of the West before the nineteenth-century's massive fertility decline began; (2) the growth of the idea that high rates of natural increase (notably those resulting from the deliberate control of mortality in poor, high-fertility populations) in themselves block the economic path to the situation in which increases in production, in the long run, actually depress fertility; and (3) an increasing insistence on government policy as the means to population control. W. D. Borrie has stated: "With regard to the basic requirement of food, the race between Malthus' hare of population growth and tortoise of food production still goes on, with the latter showing some signs at least of catching up a little. The next step, which is now being recognized in the forward planning of high growth regions is to sustain the balance between food production, social investment and industrial investment. Thwarted by their failure to reach this desideratum in face of ever expanding population growth rates, many of the 'developing' countries have now, as we have seen, turned to a new line—in Malthusian terms how to persuade the hare to go to sleep for a while. The limited success so far should not be interpreted as inability to bring about curbs to growth. The experiments now being tried are at most a decade old.

20

The demographic transition of today's 'developed' countries of western and northern Europe and Europe overseas took from fifty to seventy years to accomplish. The trends this century in eastern Europe and Japan are reminders that events can move faster in the twentieth century. The new element in the present situation of the 'developing' areas is the widespread determination of governments to act and to lead their people toward the goal of population control . . ." (Borrie 1970: 294–295). Thus the issue is still whether and how the poor countries of the world can recapitulate the demographic experience of the rich countries. But now the pressing questions for research appear to be *first*, under what conditions do married couples actively restrict births? *Second*, does "modernization" produce those conditions in a reliable, regular way? *Third*, to what extent (and how) is the production of those conditions a feasible object of government policy?

Historical demography is unlikely to produce firm answers to the third question. But it has some capacity to answer the first two. In fact, the two questions have dominated the analytical agenda of recent historical demography. The historical study of fertility has overshadowed the study of mortality, migration, social mobility, and even nuptiality. The recurrent hope of historical demographers has been to develop an account of fertility change which would simultaneously (1) explain fluctuations before the nineteenth century; (2) clear up uncertainties about the western demographic transition; and (3) elucidate the characteristics of the populations of the contemporary world.

V

THE HISTORICAL AGENDA

WHILE historical demographers have concentrated on the demographic transition in general and fertility in particular, other investigators have applied demographic procedures to a much wider range of historical problems. Insofar as this work concentrates on determining what happened in particular times and places rather than describing or analyzing some general demographic phenomenon, we can conveniently call it "demographic history" instead of historical demography. The distinction is not precise, but it is useful.

I shall make no attempt to summarize the history of demographic history. Nor shall I try to prepare a comprehensive outline of its subject matter. Instead, I want to mention some large clusters of historical problems which have already attracted demographic attention. They are likely to attract a good deal more. I concentrate on European experience, with side glances at North America. That concentration

21

ignores excellent work being done in Asia and Latin America, but it allows me to show connections and to work with the material I know best.

The basic question of demographic history is: How did fundamentally agrarian populations turn into essentially urban-industrial populations? The question applies throughout the world. If we want to deal with large populations and nearly completed transformations, however, we must confine our attention to Europe, its extensions, and Japan.

In Europe during the last five centuries or so, the question is more precisely how a predominantly *peasant* population turned into an urban-industrial one. The focus upon peasants matters. Let us employ the term in a strict sense: members of households whose major activity is farming, which produce a major part of the goods and services they consume, which exercise substantial control over the land they farm, and which supply the major part of their labor requirements from their own energies. Nomads, hunters, fishermen, plantation laborers and many other rural workers drop out.

In that narrow sense, the world's major areas of peasant agriculture have been China, Japan, India, and Europe. Occasionally, someone makes a supplementary case for Central America, Indonesia, or parts of Africa. Peasant agriculture in this sense rarely (or never) appears in the absence of cities, extensive markets, and large-scale structures of political control. The narrowing matters here for two reasons: (1) We have reasons to believe that the demographic characteristics of peasants differ significantly from those of other rural populations; and (2) in the case of Europe and its extensions, the distinction of peasants from other members of the rural population helps identify profound alterations in rural social life and in the composition of the rural population which occurred while the population as a whole remained mainly rural.

Both points will receive plenty of attention later in this book. We shall, for example, repeatedly consider the possibility that the European peasant household (or the peasant community, or both) operated as an effective population-control mechanism, closely matching the opportunities for marriage and procreation to the number of persons the land could support. We shall also encounter evidence that rural wage-labor expanded considerably before any substantial urbanization of Europe and its extensions, and that the expansion of rural wage-labor tended to weaken the peasant system of population control. In fact, the arguments of this book suggest an unexpected, paradoxical extrapolation to the contemporary world: that the poor, economically dependent populations of the world are repeating the demographic experiences of the *proletarian* segments of western rural populations under conditions of more complete proletarianization and more thorough penetration of capitalism than occurred in the rural west.

The transformation of peasant into urban-industrial populations is a very old preoccupation of western historians. Demographic historians did not discover it. There are, however, new advantages to stating the problem demographically. First, we are now beginning to accumulate the demographic evidence which can make the analysis of the transformation more than a vague metaphor. Second, the demographic statement of the problem helps specify what there is to explain. For example, it is a long leap from the observation of a net loss of peasants accompanied by a net gain of urban workers to the conclusion that peasants moved off the land into urban factories. If peasants themselves made the move, it is at least possible that they experienced the shock of uprooting, unfamiliar surroundings and unpleasant work routines and responded to the shock with despair, disorganization or rebellion. But the net shift is also compatible with a chain of moves: peasants into rural wage-labor, rural workers into urban services, city-born children of rural migrants into factories, and so on.

Many historians—and even more sociologists, political scientists and economists seeking to build historical support for their analyses of development—have offered the first interpretation. I consider the second more likely. Whether either interpretation is correct, however, does not matter much here. What matters is that demographers almost intuitively ask the essential intermediate questions: What part did differential fertility and morality play in the population shifts under discussion? What was the size and composition of the various flows between industrial sectors and between rural and urban areas? Did the patterns of fertility, nuptiality, and mortality themselves change as a consequence of the flows? The demographer brings to such historical qeustions an accounting framework which helps specify the when, where, and how.

The demographic side of the inquiry into the creation of urban-industrial populations out of peasant populations breaks up into three elements: (1) connections of population growth and economic change; (2) components of growth and compositional changes; and (3) small-scale processes. Let me take up and illustrate each one in turn.

VI

POPULATION GROWTH AND ECONOMIC CHANGE

ANY attempt to generalize about population growth and economic change immediately confronts contradictions. Over the long run, population growth and economic expansion generally accompany each other.

Likewise, economic decline and demographic contraction tend to occur together. In the short run, fertility and nuptiality tend to respond positively, mortality to respond negatively, to upswings in economic well-being. Yet the demographic transition associates declining fertility and mortality—and, eventually, decelerating natural increase—with economic growth. In order to make consistent statements, we have to disaggregate: different rules for different time-scales, no doubt; different generalizations for different vital processes, certainly; perhaps different arguments for different populations and eras as well. Then it may be possible to see that all the regularities result from the operation of the same elementary principles in varying circumstances. At present that is a hope, not a promise.

One common way of disaggregating the problem has been to concentrate on shorter-run fluctuations in vital events: seasonal, annual, or cyclical. Far more of the short-run studies have dealt with fertility and nuptiality than with mortality. Available studies divide into those concentrating on the relationships among strictly demographic variables and those treating demographic fluctuations as possible responses to economic fluctuations. The first is the particular province of demographers. It includes a high proportion of sophisticated theoretical work and another high proportion of painstaking measurement, but not much testing of models.

A characteristic essay in this vein is Roland Pressat's decomposition of births in any particular year into three factors: the age composition of the female population, the lifetime fertility of the various female birth cohorts at risk to have children in that year, and the fertility level attributable to that year as such. Starting from there and using well-known data for white American females, he makes a plausible case that from 1920 to 1930 the annual fluctuations in births included a significant tendency for lifetime fertility to decline from one birth cohort to the next, while during the 1930s the best estimate of the annual change in lifetime fertility is 0 (Pressat 1969).

Again, Gösta Carlsson's analysis of variations in Swedish marital fertility from 1830 to 1879 (Carlsson 1970) deals directly with the impact of nuptiality on fertility fluctuations, then goes on to propose arguments linking short-run rises in marital fertility to economic well-being. The main statistical results are a demonstration that short-run fluctuations in births occur in partial independence of the marriage rate, and a strong suggestion of birth control within Swedish marriages of the nineteenth century. Carlsson does not take the next logical step: the direct modeling and measurement of the relationship of fertility to economic fluctuations.

24

Others do. In one of the most sophisticated and comprehensive demographic treatments of the subject, Henri Léridon concentrates on month-to-month variation in fertility. Once he clears away various statistical obstacles with exquisite precision, he arrives at findings which are mainly negative or uncertain. Definite seasonal patterns appear in series from France and elsewhere, it is true. They are remarkably constant from one year to the next. But the differences among months are small compared to those reported for old-regime Europe or for poor agrarian countries of the contemporary world. Differences in seasonal patterns among countries and among social classes are declining. Once corrected for seasonal effects, month-to-month variation in fertility from 1950 to 1969 shows no significant relationship either to earlier fluctuations in marriage or to economic variables such as industrial production, employment and savings (Léridon 1973).

The last set of findings may surprise people who have been reading analyses of annual and cyclical variations in fertility. Although there is some dissent (e.g. Sweezy 1971), the bulk of the available theorizing and the mass of the available statistical results attribute a significant positive effect on fertility to economic well-being. K. G. Basavarajappa in concisely summarizing his analysis of Australia says, "An analysis of age-specific marriage and age-duration of marriage-specific confinement rates showed that, during the interwar years (1920–21 to 1937–38), the movements in these rates were very closely associated with the movements in economic conditions" (Basavarajappa 1971: 50). In the case of Italy from 1863 to 1964, "in the first seventy-five years . . . the conformity among marriages, births and business cycle is rather high and without trend either in its intensity or in its direction . . . the recent two decades bring an attenuation, rather than a consolidation, of the concordance between business cycle and demographic phenomena . . ." (Santini 1971: 581).

Likewise, Morris Silver follows up his similar analysis of the United States with reports for the United Kingdom from 1855 to 1959 and for Japan from 1878 to 1959: "Births and marriages in the United Kingdom conform positively to ordinary business cycles. The cyclical response of births is not simply a reflection of cyclical fluctuations in marriages; it is, at least in part, a direct response. These conclusions also seem to hold for births in Japan and possibly for marriages. In addition, births in both countries seem to conform positively to Kuznets cycles in national income" (Silver 1966: 315). He finds no evidence that the strength of the cyclic response changed over time.

Like most of the work which boldly relates short-term fertility fluctuations to changing economic conditions, Silver's analysis rests on a rudimentary model: A stream of births moves in response to changing national income, which presumably represents the opportunities and costs impinging on couples capable of having children. He uses relatively simple detrended regressions to estimate the basic relationships. To find work which attempts to specify the entire process connecting fertility to changing economic opportunity, we must turn to theoretical syntheses such as the one Richard Easterlin provides in this volume. Easterlin's own empirical investigations of American fertility fluctuations (e.g., Easterlin 1973), for example, work with incomplete models and only estimate a few of the relationships involved. We shall encounter other efforts to model the economic conditions affecting fertility when we come to the study of the small-scale processes.

We have a longer-run version of the same problem: If growth promotes population increase, how does that happen? Karlheinz Blaschke's massive study of the Saxon population from 1100 to 1843 brings out a contrast, which is now standard in European demographic history, between purely agricultural zones with a limited holding capacity, exporting their irregular natural increase to cities and to industrial regions, and rural-industrial zones of almost unlimited absorptive capacity: "In these areas social differentiation developed early and to an extreme; the especially fast growing segment of their population, moreover, was the people whose basic economic activity was in handicrafts. This segment of the population and these areas in general provided the starting-point for a genuine industrial development in the nineteenth century; the industrial revolution could attach itself without a break to the existing structure (Blaschke 1967: 231)." Blaschke's study has the characteristic strengths and weaknesses of the historical literature: a fine sense of time and place, plus coverage of a great span of change; little specification of the exact demographic mechanisms by which changes occurred. The obvious sequel is a closer study of the interplay of mortality, fertility, nuptiality, and migration in at least some portions of Saxony's 750-year transformation.

Much of the existing work in demographic history works in the other direction, seeking the consequences of population growth instead of its causes. In speaking of eighteenth-century England, H. J. Habakkuk enumerates five ways in which the substantial population increase may have stimulated economic growth: by producing economies of scale, by making cheap labor abundant, by inciting a search for new methods to substitute labor for capital and natural resources, by promoting investment and by inducing extra effort from cultivators (Habakkuk 1971: 47–48). Not all of these strike me as plausible, or consistent with the others. In any case, they cry out for explicit modeling—

26

including the representation of effects in the other direction from economic growth to population increase. The successful modeling and testing of these relationships will be of the greatest interest to students of todays' poor but fast-growing countries.

The same is true of the more rigorous (but no less controversial) argument Ester Boserup has applied to agriculture. Noting the association of high population density and highly productive agriculture, Boserup argues against the basic Malthusian assumptions of an inelastic supply of land with diminishing returns from intensification. More exactly, she argues that under population pressure the inputs of labor (as exemplified by clearing of wastes or introduction of irrigation) tend to increase sufficiently to override the diminishing returns due to the inferior quality of land brought under cultivation. Therefore, population increase stimulates the productivity of agricultural land. By the same logic, however, population increase depresses labor productivity, at least in the short run; to offset the declining product per person-hour of labor, cultivators either eat less or work harder. Boserup theorizes that they commonly work harder. She also holds that rising population density and harder work tend to produce further consequences which do increase labor productivity and thereby promote economic growth. Increasing density, she argues, "facilitates the division of labor and the spread of communications and education" (Boserup 1965: 118). And harder work sometimes promotes the adoption or invention of more efficient work routines.

Coupled with recent arguments (for instance, those of Eric L. Jones) treating agricultural improvement as a stimulus to manufacturing, Boserup's analysis leads to an anti-Malthusian conception of the whole process of economic growth. Indirectly, it therefore raises questions about the supposed swamping of today's poor nations by excessive population growth. The answer could be that the relationship is curvilinear: some middling rate of population increase is most favorable to economic growth, while higher and lower rates are deleterious. Or it could be that Boserup is wrong. However the Boserup thesis comes out, the modeling and measurement of these relationships clearly belong on the agenda of demographic history. Her work has helped place them there.

One important exception to the simple correlation between population growth and agricultural productivity is the case of rural industry. In Europe and the Americas, there was a strong association between the expansion of rural industry and rapid population growth, on the one hand, between rural industrial concentrations and high rural densities, on the other. The causal connections are just as hard to specify in

27

the case of rural industry as in the case of agriculture. In a recent close look at the phenomenon, Arnošt Klíma summarizes Karnikova's findings: "In eighteenth-century Bohemia, population density varied in different parts of the country, being much higher in the mountainous and less-fertile regions. Statistics for 1764 give the average density of population for the whole country as 37.3 per square kilometre: 48 in the mountainous part of northern Bohemia but only 32.4 elsewhere; thus the less-fertile parts had a density almost 30 percent above the average for the country. Towards the end of the century, in 1789, the country average had risen to 54.8 per square kilometre, but that of the linen districts of northern Bohemia rose to 82, while the very fertile regions of Bohemia had no more than 56 per square kilometre" (Klíma 1974: 50; see also Horska 1972, Purš 1965). The observation recalls Blaschke's findings for Saxony. We shall encounter the same contrast in Braun's analysis of the Zurich region, later in this book.

Klíma, Blaschke, and Braun are describing protoindustrialization; the expansion of manufacturing outside the factory system. Franklin Mendels introduced the convenient term into the historical literature; different features of protoindustrialization are well known as cottage industry, the domestic system, the *Verlagssystem*, etc.) It occurs by means of an increase in the number of producing units rather than a change in technology or a shift in the average scale of production. A great deal of European and American industrial expansion before 1850 happened through protoindustrialization. Much of it took place in poor rural areas rather than in towns or cities.

Protoindustrialization has an important place in European and American demographic history. It is a major source of rapid population growth. It deserves special study because it provides a large series of partly independent natural experiments in which dissimilar populations responded to changing economic opportunity by adjusting their patterns of nuptiality and fertility.

If the current drift of scholarly opinion is right, rural industry tended to grow up in regions combining (1) an underemployed land-poor population; (that is a possible consequence of immigration, partible inheritance, enclosures or rapidly declining mortality; in these circumstances, forms of agriculture with relatively inelastic labor requirements, such as dairy farming, favored rural industry over the intensification of agriculture), and (2) access to urban markets for cheap finished goods. To be sure, merchants small and large played a crucial part in linking rural producers to raw materials and to urban markets; but the supply of merchants seems to have been highly elastic everywhere.

Protoindustrialization raises several different demographic problems. First, how regularly, and how, did rapid population growth precede the linking of cheap labor to urban markets via rural manufacturing? Second, is it true that the availability of employment in rural industry tended to lower the age of marriage, increase both legitimate and illegitimate fertility, and reduce the household to the nuclear family without servants? Third, is it true that the process was asymmetrical—expanding employment produced rapid population growth, but contracting employment simply produced misery—and that the resulting industrial population was more vulnerable to the wage-price scissors than the agrarian population was? Part of the problem is to what extent these tendencies are peculiarly true of rural manufacturing rather than landless labor in general. During the eighteenth and nineteenth centuries, the landless increased in both agriculture and industry; whatever the cause and effect, before 1900 the bulk of the rapid population increase resulting from the western demographic transition occurred among the rural landless. Working out the demographic role of proto-industrialization would therefore aid our understanding of the western demographic transition.

Both protoindustrialization and the growth of landless labor in agriculture homogenized the economic experience of the rural population: larger and larger groups of people responded more or less simultaneously to the same fluctuations in prices, wages, and employment. The transformation shows up in the changing pattern of migration. In Europe and America, there is no real evidence that large-scale industrialization greatly increased the frequency with which people changed residence. But the distances they moved increased tremendously.

The reason scholars have thought otherwise is that they have seriously underestimated the mobility of preindustrial rural populations. Demographic historians who look at the subject directly almost invariably come out with high rates of turnover. In an agricultural community of Sweden from 1881 to 1885, for example, Eriksson and Rogers arrive at mobility rates in the range of 0.5 moves per person-year of residence (Ågren et al. 1973: 72). In the town of Eskilstuna and its vicinity, Öhngren computes annual rates of gross migration (in-migration + out-migration) in the range of 200 per thousand population in the 1850s and 1860s. In the period of rapid industrialization which followed, the rates rose to 300 or so. Even then they were often higher than that in the nearby agricultural parishes (Öhngren 1974: 374–375). "In Hallines and Longuenesse (Pas-de-Calais) for the periods of 1761–1773 and 1778–1790," Poussou reports, "we find 51.3 and 36.3 percent of the population leaving, 45.2 and 45.1 percent of the population arriv-

29

ing, in twelve years" (Poussou 1971: 20). In these and other places, the average distance covered by migrants greatly increased as essentially local exchanges of labor gave way to large-scale movements among rural areas and, especially between country and city.

Giovanni Levi (1971) reviewed a number of recent works in French demographic history dealing directly or indirectly with population mobility. He proposed a three-phase summary of migration from the seventeenth century to the early nineteenth: (1) extensive movement but small net flows, dominated by a) circular movements of specialized non-agricultural workers between town and country as well as among towns; b) movements—especially seasonal—of agricultural laborers within the countryside; c) flows of beggars and unemployed workers in all directions, depending on the current geography of hardship; (2) rising long-term migration, increasing net movements from rural to urban areas and to industrializing rural areas, associated with and resulting from the increase of rural landless labor, the formation of large-scale labor markets and the rise of periodic unemployment; (3) large, permanent flows from rural to urban areas resulting from the deindustrialization of the countryside, the growth of large urban industries and the declining demand for labor in agriculture. Levi assumed that the third type of migration moved many people from farming directly into manufacturing. That is probably incorrect. Some of that impression is due to the movement of rural industrial workers into urban industry. The main flow out of agriculture probably went into services. Furthermore, Levi's scheme neglects the large backflows behind the net movements in his second and third phases. Finally, it deals exclusively with labor migration, and therefore neglects such large streams of migrants as young people moving at marriage.

A more adequate model would replace the phases with statements about four sets of variables: (1) the rising scale of labor markets, (2) the conditions under which workers move among labor markets (including markets defined by different industries, whether geographically separated or not); (3) the changing geography of job opportunities; and (4) the ties of residential changes to job changes. Nevertheless, Levi's summary catches the distinctions among circular, chain and career migration (C. Tilly 1974: 288–296). It also gives a sense of the process by which small-scale but fairly regular movements of workers gave way to large-scale, irregular movements. In the process, large segments of the rural population fell into the rhythm of national and international fluctuations in economic activity.

At the extreme, whole regions became the economic dependencies of distant capitals. Their demographic experiences came to depend on the rise and fall of demand for their products in faroff places. For Java, Clifford Geertz has described the process of "agricultural involution": Villages adjacent to foreign-owned plantations sold their labor to the plantations, retreated (often under pressure) from market production to subsistence agriculture, grew rapidly, eventually became dependent and vulnerable. So long as the world market for Indonesian sugar, rubber or tobacco expanded, the villagers multiplied and survived. When the plantations collapsed, the villages sank into misery.

In a broadly similar manner, the grain-growing regions of eastern Europe were becoming dependencies of Amsterdam and the other commercial-industrial centers of northwestern Europe during the sixteenth and seventeenth centuries. The growth of the "second serfdom" in eastern Europe consisted mainly of large landlords' assuming direct management of their properties instead of continuing to live on rents, using the help of the political authorities to coerce labor from their peasants and to fix them in place, and raising wheat on a large scale for export via such commercial centers as Gdánsk (Danzig) or Riga.

A direct chain of credit attached the manors of Poland and Pomerania to the bankers of Antwerp. In his recent synthesis, Immanuel Wallerstein put it this way: "This system of international debt peonage enabled a cadre of international merchants to bypass (and thus eventually destroy) the indigenous merchant classes of eastern Europe (and to some extent those of southern Europe) and enter into direct links with landlord-entrepreneurs (nobility included) who were essentially capitalist farmers, producing the goods and keeping control of them until they reached the first major port area, after which they were taken in hand by some merchants of west European (or north Italian) nationality who in turn worked through and with a burgeoning financial class centered in a few cities" (Wallerstein 1974: 122). There is a demographic side to all this: the argument requires a substantial labor shortage at the beginning of the process. It suggests that the considerable growth of the east European population during the sixteenth century resulted from migration—from deliberate colonization of thinly occupied frontier lands. On the other hand, the scattered accounts now available indicate that the sections of eastern Europe devastated by the Thirty Years' War in the following century recovered their losses quickly through natural increase. Perhaps natural increase also played a significant part in the sixteenth century.

We encounter the possibility that the same sort of saturation process that Geertz attributes to Java under the plantation system occurred in eastern Europe under the hegemony of the great wheat-growing estates. Faint in the background flickers a fascinating possibility: that the

31

high rates of population growth in today's Third World countries will turn out to be less consequences of their own peculiar internal organizations than effects of their economic relationships with the rich countries of the West. The first scraps of information favoring such an interpretation would be discrepancies between results of cross-sectional and over-time analyses of fertility at the national level, evidence of a relationship between fertility and economic dependency (as indexed, for example, by the share of raw-material exports in national income) and signs of strong responsiveness of fertility in Third World countries to fluctuations in the world prices of their primary exports. Several years ago, Nathan Keyfitz (1965) suggested in passing that some such mechanisms were at work in the Third World. So far as I know, neither he nor any other demographer has followed up the suggestion seriously.

Work on population growth and economic change bears on the fundamental problems of western economic history. Assumptions concerning population processes underlie the alternative explanations of the industrial revolution which are now available. Our present state of uncertainty and ignorance concerning those population processes lays down a double challenge to demographic historians: to explicate and test the alternative models now in use, to specify the demographic mechanisms whereby the transformation to an urban-industrial population occurred.

VII

Components of Growth and Compositional Changes

In its simplest terms, the problem is to allocate the changes in size of the major populations under study among three factors: fertility, mortality, and migration. British scholars, for example, are still debating to what extent the substantial eighteenth-century growth of population was due to a rise in fertility or a fall in mortality; a complete account would also allow for in-migration (e.g. from Ireland) and out-migration (e.g. to North America). How the three components changed makes a considerable difference to our interpretation of the period's social and economic history. If declining mortality is the chief contributor, we can imagine the rapid growth as starting without much prior change in the structure of everyday life: People were already receptive to life-saving innovations, and medical or sanitary improvements can begin without substantial prior changes in the average person's daily routines. (It is more difficult, but not impossible, to make the same sort of argument for life-saving improvements in nutrition or food supply.)

If rising fertility or accelerating in-migration make major contributions to growth, on the other hand, almost any model of the change we can fashion will imply large prior changes in the local structure of opportunities. Thus the elementary analysis of population growth into its components sets important constraints on the possible explanations of the growth, and thereby on general interpretations of the period's social and economic history.

Components-of-growth analysis also helps with the details of economic and social history. To illustrate, let me sketch the significance of two overlapping processes: (1) the proletarianization of the population in general; and (2) the changing composition of the rural population.

Proletarianization is a decline in the proportion of the labor force who have effective control over their own means of production, an increase in the proportion who for survival are essentially dependent on the sale of their own labor power. The definition contains several traps. "Effective control" is often hard to judge, for example, in the cases of miners, weavers, or tenant farmers. Yet by almost any standard the proletarian share of the labor force increased enormously throughout the West some time after the fifteenth century. Between 1500 and 1800, the European population increased from roughly 55 million to about 190 million. My own guess at a partitioning of the increase appears in Table 1-1. These are, evidently, only guesses at numbers for which we have but shards of the necessary documentation. An early item on the demographic agenda is to refine and correct them. Yet the guesses are not fantastic. In the case of England, Gregory King guessed in 1688 that there were 1.4 million families, of whom 1.2 million drew their principal income from agriculture. Of the 1.2 million, according to King, 350,000 lived from their own land

TABLE 1-1. ESTIMATED PARTITIONING OF INCREASE IN EUROPEAN POPU-
LATION, 1500–1800

Category	Population in 1500 ($\times 10^6$)	Population in 1800 ($\times 10^6$)	Increase ($\times 10^6$)
Landlords, owners & managers of producing units + their households	0.5–1.5	2–3	1–2
Peasants + their households	25–35	70–90	40–60
Wage workers in cities of 100,000+ & their households	0.5–0.75	4–5	3.5–4.5
Other wage workers & their households	20–30	90–110	65–85
Total population	50–60	180–190	125–135

33

(Pollard and Crossley 1968: 154). In 1831, the census of Great Britain showed 1.8 million persons in agriculture, forestry and fishing; only 20 percent to 25 percent of them were full-fledged farmers (Deane and Cole 1967: 143).

Before the late nineteenth century, most of the increase of landless and land-poor labor occurred outside the factory-based proletariat so dear to twentieth-century Marxists. As Marx himself well knew, the growth of landless labor in agriculture and rural industry created the mass of the European proletariat up to his own time; urban services and small-scale manufacturing accounted for most of the remainder. Factory employment grew later.

The analysis of proletarianization presents a standard, if difficult, components-of-growth problem: To what extent did the class of proletarians grow through its own natural increase and to what extent through movement of people from other categories. Each of these questions leads to others: What were the contributions of changes in fertility and mortality? Among the transfers, how many were (1) changes of position experienced by individuals within their own working careers; (2) movements into the proletariat by the children of nonproletarians; and (3) movements into the proletariat from outside the population under consideration—for example, the enslavement of Africans? (This last category has its own historical interest. Fogel and Engerman [1974], following Curtin, argue that the natural increase of enslaved blacks on the North American mainland was high enough to produce sustained population growth, while life expectancy of their counterparts in the Caribbean was so low that only steady importation of slaves from Africa maintained the population. One probable consequence of this state of affairs would be a much more continuous flow of African culture into the Caribbean. Jack Ericson Eblen's careful estimates for the black populations of the United States and Cuba during the nineteenth century, on the other hand, show a rate of natural increase for the native-born Cuban black population dropping from 20 to 25 per thousand before 1825 to around 5 in the 1870s, and a parallel decline in the natural increase of United States blacks in the decades just before the Civil War. Mortality seems to have risen dramatically in both places during the last years of slavery: Eblen 1974.)

In historical accounts of proletarianization, the usual assumption is that the bulk of the proletariat moved into the class from outside through such processes as enclosure and the absorption of independent craftsmen into the factory system. Those were important processes, no doubt. The studies of the natural increase of landless labor I mentioned earlier, however, raise the possibility that the proletariat multi-plied itself to a large degree. If a careful compositional analysis showed that to be true, it would have profound implications for the political, economic and social history of the western working class. It would, for example, weaken Luciano Pellicani's argument that the "internal proletariat of capitalism" came into being via a process of "total uprooting" (Pellicani 1973: 68). It would diminish the probable role of the "loss of status" as a source of working-class protest. It would increase the plausibility of a distinct, continuous proletarian culture. It would open up the possibility that the change in size and characteristics of the proletariat was the most dynamic element in the western demographic transition.

Another version of that unsettling possibility appears in the changing composition of the rural population. I already have insisted that the rural population of western countries included many nonpeasants. It even included many nonagricultural workers. In the case of France—that quintessentially peasant country—at the beginning of the nine-teenth century about a third of the labor force in rural places was living from services, manufacturing, commerce, and other nonagricultural pursuits. ("Rural" places included all communes with fewer than 2,000 persons in the central settlement.) At that point, rural textile production was the largest category, but woodcarving, smelting, basketry, and even watchmaking all supported important clusters of rural people. Most miners also lived in, if not of, the countryside.

Miners are an informative extreme case. Friedlander has recently presented indirect evidence for the hypothesis that ". . . in coal-mining areas women had little opportunity for employment and could, therefore, contribute only little to the family's income and that men's earnings probably tended to shrink at a relatively early stage of life due to the nature of the special kind of work. This, and the unbalanced age-sex distribution resulting from heavy immigration, may explain . . . the pattern of early marriages and high marital fertility in coal-mining areas (Friedlander 1973: 49)." In Friedlander's analysis, extensive employment opportunities for young unmarried persons and lack of employment opportunities outside the home for adult women both promote high nuptiality and high fertility.

With some modifications, Friedlander's argument may apply throughout the rural population. Let us return to the idea of the peasantry as a self-regulating population. The regulation of numbers occurs through the tying of marriage and the opportunity to procreate to the inheritance of places on the land. When mortality is high, all other things being equal, new places on the land open up more frequently, both nuptiality and fertility rise. (One of the more important questions about this hypothetical system is whether fluctuations in fertility depend mainly on changes in nuptiality, or whether both respond independently to shifts in opportunity—for example, through the estimates of prospective parents concerning future opportunities for their children.)

Let us assume that the basic decision rule of couples in the system runs something like this: marry as soon as you can acquire a permanent livelihood, and adjust your number of children to their chances of survival and the probable return to the nuclear family of different levels of investment per child. Then under a long-run decline in mortality people embedded in the peasant system are likely to shift from relatively high fertility to low fertility. Opportunities for outmigration will presumably slow this response. On the other hand, if attractive but expensive career opportunities for children arise, they should accelerate the process; there will be a movement, in Gary Becker's sardonic terminology (Becker 1960), toward producing children of higher quality.

Something like this shift probably did occur widely among Europe's peasant populations as mortality fell from the eighteenth century onward. It did not show up as a dramatic and general decline in rural fertility, for two main reasons: (1) because the opportunity for outmigration and the opportunity for local employment outside peasant life both provided alternatives to restrictions on fertility; and (2) because the nonpeasant population did not behave in the same way. The first is plausible, but far from proven, in the light of what we know so far. The second is intriguing because the high-fertility behavior of the nonpeasant population could result from following the peasant decision rule under changed circumstances. The rule is still to marry as soon as you can acquire a permanent livelihood, and adjust your number of children to their chances of survival and the probable return to the nuclear family of different levels of investment per child. But for agricultural laborers and rural industrial workers, a permanent (if not a sumptuous) likelihood is available when they are young, some remunerative labor can be squeezed from almost any member of the household, and a heavy investment in one or two children would be risky. The result is high nuptiality and high fertility.

David Levine's study (1974) of two Leicestershire villages from 1600 to 1851 reveals something like this system at work. Shepshed became the site of intensive rural industry in the eighteenth century. Bottesford remained entirely agricultural, but shifted toward labor-intensive dairying in the nineteenth century. In both places, as job opportunities which were detached from the inheritance of places on the land opened up, age at marriage went down and completed family size went up. In the industrial village, as an impoverished population crowded on the land, mortality eventually rose. Increases in fertility due mainly to the earlier start of childbearing made major contributions to the boisterous growth of Shepshed in the eighteenth century and the sedate growth of Bottesford in the nineteenth. Although it would take comparisons of different types of workers *within* the villages to clinch the case, the Leicestershire evidence supports the idea of significant fertility differences between peasants and rural proletarians.

The hypothesis of a fundamental difference in the fertility behaviors of peasant and nonpeasant rural populations is intriguing for another reason. It could help account for the gross regional differences in European fertility before the declines of the nineteenth century. The relatively low premodern fertility levels of Italy, France, Spain, and Portugal could result from relatively high proportions of peasants in the total. The great block of high fertility in eastern Europe could be a consequence of the early proletarianization of the rural population on great estates. We would thereby circle back to the hypothesis linking high fertility to economic dependency. Let me insist that this is a chain of reasoning, not a chain of evidence. Part of the task of this book is to confront that reasoning, and its alternative, with evidence.

One more question raised by this line of reasoning is how fertility could ever have declined in the countryside. The answer is that the opportunities for rural wage-labor declined. It happened earlier in rural manufacturing than in agriculture, but it happened in both. On the whole, the European "rural exodus" followed the appropriate sequence: rural industrial workers relatively early, agricultural wage-laborers somewhat later, peasants (or, at least, agricultural workers who controlled their own land) the last to go in large numbers (Merlin 1971). If the peasants had been gradually restricting their fertility as mortality declined, but the nonpeasants had been responding asymmetrically to employment opportunities, the net effect of this pattern of departure would be to produce a massive, rapid decline in rural fertility followed by a long, low plateau. Although the opportunities for out-migration and for social mobility complicate both the argument and the evidence, something like this pattern occurred widely in Europe. Again, part of this book's task is to set limits on that sort of reasoning.

If my summary is correct, however, a new problem becomes salient: in the days of rural exodus, what happened to the fertility of the rural wage-laborers and their urban descendants? To produce the large, continuous declines observable in European fertility, we need some combination of escape from the Malthusian trap in the countryside and transformation of behavior coincident with migration to the cities. I suspect the change was slow in the country and fast in the city—and that the crucial difference was the availability in the city, at a high price, of opportunities to help one's children move up in the world. In the short run, the decision rule remains the same, but the difference in available opportunities transforms the behavior. In the longer run, however, the situation alters so much as to produce a new decision rule.

VIII

SMALL-SCALE PROCESSES

The arguments I have just been sketching rely on assumptions about the behavior of individual households. Moreover, they contradict a good deal of common sense and a great many portrayals of premodern fertility by treating procreation as the outcome of a more or less rational weighing of alternatives. So risky a notion deserves direct attention. It requires the study of processes at a smaller scale than we have been considering so far: at the level of the individual, the household, and the kin group.

In the last decade, economists have been developing models of household behavior—including what they like to call "the production of children"—which operate at the small scale and incorporate assumptions of rational choice. Marc Nerlove has summarized the major features of the theory most commonly employed in recent work as ". . . (1) a utility function with arguments which are not physical commodities but home-produced bundles of attributes; (2) a household production technology; (3) an external labor-market environment providing the means for transforming household resources into market commodities; and (4) a set of household resource constraints. . ." (Nerlove 1974a: 537). Most of the work done within this framework, as Nerlove observes, has been static in character; it has given little attention to such problems as the effects of changing household composition, the investment of one generation in the welfare of succeeding generations, or the causes and consequences of long-run shifts in vital rates. Furthermore, the framework depends on some very demanding assumptions. Perhaps the most important for our purposes is the existence of a common utility function for the household. Gary Becker has sought to make the transition from individual to household through the notion of "caring": each individual's building into his own utilities the benefits received by other members of the household. Zvi Griliches comments: "What parents care for is not the utility that their children receive, but the utility function that the children have and the resources that they control. Parents care about the consumption basket of their children; they have preferences over actual actions, not just their subjective outcomes. . . In any case, a common utility function cannot explain either the growth of households or their dissolution, or indicate the point at which it pays for the young to opt out of it" (Griliches 1974: 546). In addition to their novelty and complexity, these weaknesses of the economic approach to household behavior help explain the small impact the approach has had on historical work. That is unfortunate, for a number of arguments elaborated in the recent economic literature converge on an hypothesis of great interest for historical analysis: that "a rise in the cost of mother's time for the family will cause a substitution away from time-intensive goods such as children and toward those requiring more inputs of market-purchasable commodities" (Nerlove 1974a: 537).

Nerlove makes three suggestions which could connect this line of argument with the general pattern of the demographic transition: that the effect of declining child mortality is to generate a greater demand for children (since the cost of achieving a given family size declines while the discounted sum of satisfactions per child increases); that declining child mortality produces an offsetting decline in the cost of child quality relative to the cost of numbers of children; that over the course of economic development the value of a unit of human time tends to rise as a consequence of increasing investment in human capital, with the consequence of "reinforcing the tendency to fewer children of ever-higher quality" (Nerlove 1974a: 544).

The second and third suggestions dovetail with the arguments and findings presented elsewhere in this book. At first glance, the first— that declining child mortality increases the demand for children— contradicts a major theme of the chapters. Although Easterlin builds direct satisfaction from the presence of children into his analysis (and although none of our authors denies that the sum of such satisfactions per child tends to rise as child mortality declines), others stress the importance of desires to transmit household wealth to successive generations without fragmenting it. The household itself is the major unit of production among peasants, artisans and many varieties of merchants, manufacturers, and service workers. Where it is, the double desire to maintain and to transmit household wealth is likely to be strong. To the extent that this is the dominant incentive for procreation, the effect of declining child mortality on completed family size will be negative, not positive.

Yet we have good reasons for further reflection on Nerlove's hypothesis. The "demand" for children in question is actually two dimensional: quantity x quality. Just as a shift from many small, tough steaks to fewer large, succulent steaks can represent an increase in the poundage (not to mention the dollarage) of steak demanded, a move toward smaller numbers of healthier, better-educated children can, in this formulation, reflect an increased demand for children. We might modify Nerlove's statement to say that declining child mortality tends to increase the demand for healthier, better-educated children faster than it depresses the demand for large numbers of children. The notion deserves historical attention: Did parents begin to worry less about the sheer survival of their heirs, and more about the personal characteristics of those same heirs, as mortality declined? Philippe Ariès' explorations of changing orientation to life and death suggest they did.

The quantity x quality formulation, for all its surface crassness, raises another historical puzzle. Under what conditions and why do parents become concerned about either the continuity of their households or the success of their children or both? Perhaps the taproots of concern for children run so deep that we have no hope of drawing the fundamental answer from historical material. Yet parents—including whole populations of parents—do vary in their apparent readiness to sacrifice for their vision of their children's welfare. They certainly vary in the *way* they are prepared to sacrifice. (I remember a radio interview with the parents of a Greek-American soprano who had just made her national opera debut. *Interviewer:* "I suppose you really had to sacrifice to get your daughter her musical training." *Immigrant Mother:* "Yes, we could have bought three apartment houses with the money.") Furthermore, continuity of the household and success of the children sometimes coincide and sometimes compete: staying on the family farm versus going off to school. There, parents make choices; historical research should help us understand the rules, implicit or explicit, they use in making the choices.

The earlier discussion of proletarianization provides some hints as to what is going on. Proletarianization dissolved the nexus among employment, household position, marriage, procreation, inheritance, and the maintenance of household continuity. As the nexus weakened, so probably did the pressure to conserve and transmit household wealth. Hence the resulting constraint on fertility weakened as well. As the opportunities for employment of children outside the household expanded, the possibilities of enjoying them both for themselves and for the wages they brought to the household increased. The diminished pressure for household continuity probably also allows more room for what Philip Neher calls the "pension motive": "Parents invest in their children by bearing their rearing costs in anticipation of retirement when their children, in turn, will support them" (Neher 1971: 380). It may be, then, that Nerlove's formulation applies to today's essentially proletarian populations, but lacks a significant variable when applied to populations in which the household is the fundamental unit of production as well as of consumption, or to households which exercise collective control over substantial capital. The missing variable is the pressure to conserve family property.

Why do parents worry about the conservation of the family property or the household enterprise beyond their own lifetimes? Part of the answer resides in the general motivations for having children at all, part of it has to do with guaranteeing returns within the parents' lifetimes, and part of it remains puzzling yet profoundly important. On the first count, Zvi Griliches suggests three interdependent motives: "(1) economic security (current labor and old-age provisions), (2) the production of reciprocal caring, and (3) an attempt at immortality via one's offspring" (Griliches 1974: 547). Griliches' list just misses another motive which is implicit in most recent writings on the economics of fertility: the vicarious feeling of worth—call it a sense of craftsmanship —that accrues to parents whose children turn out well, whatever the prevailing standards of wellness.

Parents do not know when they will die. They often act on the hidden assumption that they will live a very long time. Children will be more likely to satisfy their parents' childbearing motives during the parents' lifetimes if the children themselves receive contingent guarantees of return from the family property or the household enterprise. As a result, the parents' provision for satisfactions in their own estimated lifetimes amounts to a provision for a portion of their children's lifetimes. In order to fashion this line of reasoning into a general explanation, however, I suspect that we would have to set many parents' estimates of their own life expectancies at several centuries. Perhaps that is the "immortality" Griliches mentions. More likely important variables are still missing.

Speaking of missing variables, a reader from outside economics is likely to be amazed that these arguments attach so little importance to sexual desire and satisfaction. As Richard Easterlin remarks later in this volume, the economics of fertility is a "notably sexless subject." As a reaction to the crude Malthusianism which has underlain so much previous writing on fertility, it is useful to have an approach which

41

stresses the nonsexual calculations behind fertility. Yet people do enjoy sexual intercourse; they sometimes pursue it in apparent disregard of costs and risks. Unwanted children are born both in and out of wedlock. Abortion and infanticide occur frequently enough to make us think that the decisions leading to sexual activity and to childbearing are at least partly separable.

The diagnosis suggests the remedy. We need an analysis of decisions to engage in intercourse, a separate analysis of decisions to have children, and an analysis of the constraints one sets for the other. The constraints will include the whole series of contingencies between intercourse and childbirth: the extent and effectiveness of contraception, the fecundity of the sexual partners, the likelihood of fetal loss, and so on. In seeking to synthesize the economics *and* sociology of fertility, Easterlin is making exactly that effort to relate arguments concerning sexual behavior to arguments concerning fertility.

Historians and sociologists have commonly finessed the problem in one of two ways. Sometimes they have treated the one set of decisions as dominant, the other as derivative: The essential decisions govern the frequency of sexual intercourse, while the probabilities of conception and birth are basically technical matters; or the essential decisions govern marriage and childbearing, while within the limits set by those decisions sexual activity varies too little to matter. The second finesse is to postulate a massive change from one system to the other: from "uncontrolled" to "controlled" fertility.

Under uncontrolled fertility, in this way of thinking, the essential variable governing fertility is the age structure of marriages. Who can marry when is a function of economic opportunities, the supply of potential spouses and social pressure. Thus fertility responds strongly but indirectly to changing social conditions. (In the baldest Malthusian arguments, however, even that response is weak or nonexistent; uncontrolled fertility simply means fertility approaching the human capacity.) Controlled fertility, in such a formulation, appears when couples acquire the individual freedom and the technical means to detach fertility decisions from sexual ones. Modernization provides the freedom and the means.

The idea of *natural* fertility is a special version of uncontrolled fertility. The idea has two uses: as a baseline model and as an historical hypothesis. The baseline model most commonly represents the rate at which a given group of women would bear children under current economic conditions, marital arrangements, and sexual behavior, but in the absence of any deliberate control of conception and birth. If the model can be given some independent plausibility, then deviations from the model in real populations provide evidence of the extent and character of controls those populations are exercising over conception and birth. Thus Louis Henry offers a baseline of a population in which age-specific fertility is independent of number of children previously born, while Rudolf Andorka and Hans Christian Johansen propose the less stringent baseline of a population in which age-specific fertility is independent of years of marriage. In this book, Richard Easterlin builds a natural fertility baseline into his general model of fertility behavior. The use of Hutterite fertility patterns as a baseline by Ansley Coale and his associates has some similarities to these other approaches—and the advantage of an empirical referent—but deviations from Hutterite fertility may result either from deliberate controls or from differences between the Hutterites and the populations under observation with respect to fecundity, customary practices affecting the frequency of coitus, and so on.

As a historical hypothesis, the idea of natural fertility essentially makes the baseline model into the relevant behavioral model for most of the world up to the last century or so. According to the hypothesis, before the end of the eighteenth century only a few special groups in western countries had the knowledge and the will to restrict births deliberately. Such fluctuations in fertility as occurred resulted mainly from alterations in fecundity, female mortality, and nuptiality; changes in sexual activity unmotivated by any deliberate plan to control births, according to the hypothesis, played a sometime contributory role. Around the time of the French Revolution, runs the argument, the people of a few rural areas began the deliberate control of births. During the nineteenth century the practice spread rapidly and irreversibly through much of Europe, the era of natural fertility ended, and the demographic transition began.

The hypothesis of natural fertility has the great attraction of focusing the search for explanations on deliberate, and presumably dramatic, changes in the behavior of well-defined populations some time after 1750. Etienne van de Walle's chapter shows that very inquiry in progress. But his analysis also points up some of the difficulties. For example, he pushes his observations of French fertility patterns back to 1801, yet finds the fertility decline and the characteristic regional differentials in fertility already established at that early date; we have to conclude either that the multiple local studies of eighteenth-century French fertility have so far missed a fundamental change or that the change occurred with surprising swiftness during the last few decades of the century.

The natural fertility hypothesis poses a more general problem. Such

43

long-term studies as E. A. Wrigley's analysis of a Devon village ordinarily show substantial rises and falls in fertility before 1800. Many observers have noticed emphatic short-term rises in fertility following death-dealing famines, epidemics, and wars. In the absence of some sort of fertility control, how could those fluctuations occur? Perhaps changes in fecundity, induced by the Grim Reaper's selective swath or by alterations in nutrition, made their contribution. But the conventional idea has stressed the effect of nuptiality: After a demographic crisis, for example, more places are supposed to be open on the land or in shops. More places, more opportunities for marriage. Therefore earlier and more general marriage. We saw a version of that homeostatic model at work in the earlier discussion of peasant versus nonpeasant fertility. Yet there is more trouble. For analyses such as that of Ronald Lee, in this volume, raise serious doubts whether fluctuations in nuptiality account for the observed fluctuations in fertility—indeed, whether they could do so in principle. The contradictions pose a theoretical challenge, and an empirical one as well.

Another variant of the uncontrolled-to-controlled-fertility argument appears in several of this book's articles. It postulates a shift from socially controlled to individually controlled (or, better, couple-controlled) fertility. In E. A. Wrigley's essay, for instance, we find the distinction between an "unconscious rationality exercised by individuals following the norms set for them by the society in which they live" and a "conscious rationality characteristic of couples in industrial societies where family limitation is widespread" and the hypothesis of a general transition from one to the other. Wrigley points out that declining mortality destroys the "unconscious rationality" of the sorts of fertility strategies which prevailed in preindustrial Europe. He suggests that declining mortality has helped promote the fertility decline wherever it occurred. Elsewhere (e.g., Wrigley 1972) he makes a rough equation between modernization and the spread of conscious, economically maximizing rationality, and hints that it occurred largely as a consequence of the diffusion of new ideologies.

An ironic result follows. We go from a society in which well-defined collective needs explain group-to-group variations in fertility while individual differences are matters of chance, impulse, and inclination to a society in which collective needs set few constraints on fertility but individual calculation governs it very closely (cf. Ariès 1971). It seems to follow that at the level of the individual or the couple the importance of decisions concerning sexual behavior as determinants of fertility declines greatly as modernization proceeds. If that is the case, the further we go back in time, the less well the available economic models of fertility should work. And the more sex should matter.

That extrapolation of Wrigley's argument differs significantly from Edward Shorter's analyses of illegitimacy and sexual behavior in the modern West (Shorter 1971a, 1972). Shorter inserts another stage between the eras of socially controlled and individually controlled fertility. The middle stage has working-class women, liberated from family control by new opportunities for employment outside the home, leading a general move toward individual gratification, including the search for sexual pleasure. At the same time, middle-class women lead the trend toward restriction of births. As the two waves wash in opposite directions, they dissolve the old ties among marriage, birth and procreation. The middle stage therefore begins with rising fertility both inside and outside marriage, as increasingly desirable and permissible sexual activity rises without a corresponding increase in contraceptive effectiveness; it ends with a decline in legitimate and illegitimate fertility, as effective contraception diffuses.

Louise Tilly, Joan Scott, and Miriam Cohen have attacked Shorter's argument both for lack of evidence concerning the hypothetical changes in attitudes and for inconsistency with what is known about the actual patterns of female employment in western countries since 1800 (Tilly et al. 1974; Scott and Tilly 1975). They have pointed out that large numbers of European and American women worked in the company of their parents and siblings, committed their wages to the welfare of parents and siblings, and ceased their wage labor at marriage. They have also pointed out that the bulk of the nineteenth-century increase in female employment outside the home occurred through the expansion of nonfactory occupations which had long employed women and girls. They concede the concomitant rise and fall of both legitimate and illegitimate fertility, and agree with Shorter in stressing the contribution of contraception to the decline. But they deny Shorter's calendar of attitudinal change and attribute the earlier rise in fertility to short-run effects of proletarianization and of declining mortality. Reviewing the American evidence, Daniel Scott Smith (1973) rejects Shorter's calendar even more emphatically, minimizes the attitudinal changes involved in the last century's alterations in sexual behavior, and suggests that the most recent shifts continue a long series of swings up and down in both legitimate and illegitimate fertility.

Three elements of Shorter's analysis do not, I think, stand up well to criticism: the hypothesis of a new, massive, irreversible diffusion of desires for individual gratification starting toward the end of the eighteenth century, the idea of a consequent general alteration of sexual behavior as traditional constraints crumbled, and the explanation of fertility changes as a result of the new self-indulgence. But the debate is not closed. The concomitance of changes in legitimate and illegitimate fertility, as Shorter points out, challenges explanations which focus exclusively on changing family strategies. Likewise, the apparent generality and rough simultaneity of both the rise and the fall in fertility throughout western Europe make it difficult to invoke the immediate effects of urbanization or industrialization, which proceeded at very different paces in different regions. My earlier discussion of proletarianization gives some reasons for seeking a major part of the explanation in the expansion and then the contraction of rural landless labor. Whether that is a false lead or not, checking it clearly belongs on the agenda of demographic history.

The agenda includes the specification and localization of the vital changes to be explained. It includes combing and collating the scattered eighteenth- and nineteenth-century descriptions of sexual behavior and family life. It includes close study of differential patterns of change by occupation, industry, age, family status, wealth, and locality. And it involves modeling the relationships to be expected if the hypothesis of a massive, effective ideological change is correct or if the major alternatives to that hypothesis are correct.

Both this particular line of inquiry and the general problems in household economics discussed earlier lead to another two agenda items we have not yet discussed directly: the determinants of household composition and the causes and effects of labor force participation by different members of the household.

Household composition is problematic in more ways than one. First, the work in household economics generally depends on the assumption of collective decision making by a household in terms of a single utility function. At a minimum, the presence or absence of aged parents, collateral relatives, numerous children, boarders, servants or multiple nuclear families within the same household should affect the shape of that utility function; with complex households, the assumption of a single collective decision maker may work badly. What is more, household composition is a *consequence* of household decision making: decisions to marry, to migrate, to have another child, to take on a hired hand, and so on. Thus decisions at one point in time will reshape the utility function for the next round of decisions.

In addition, households often make deliberate changes in composition as an alternative to altering their fertility patterns or changing their patterns of consumption of goods and services. Some homely examples are sending babies out to nurse (and therefore, quite likely, to die), bringing in a hired hand when the farm family has a short supply of male workers, hiring out a youngster as a servant or an apprentice, doubling up with a sibling's family in times of hardship. All of these were common and crucial in some phases of European history. It may be possible to generalize the economic analysis of fertility into an analysis of decisions concerning household composition. Otherwise, we shall have to graft a new set of arguments about the causes and effects of household composition onto the existing tree.

Peter Laslett (1972) has recently held out hope of avoiding that complexity. He notes the statistical predominance in western countries of households consisting of no more than one nuclear family and no non-family members. Ansley Coale and others had already shown (e.g. in Coale et al. 1965) that for compelling demographic and structural reasons the large "extended family" consisting of a couple, their children and their children's children was likely to be rare even where people held it up as an ideal. Their arguments did not rule out the possibility of compounding through the co-residence of married siblings, the employment of servants, the taking in of lodgers, and so on. Working mainly from nominal census lists, Laslett and collaborators laid out long runs of evidence for the rarity of these arrangements in England, France, Italy, the Balkans, the Low Countries, and the United States.

In a searching critique, however, Lutz Berkner shows that the evidence is not overwhelming: it is dubious whether the enumerations analyzed do distinguish households in a uniform and theoretically meaningful way, the statistical predominance of nuclear households at any one point in time is quite compatible with arrangements in which households normally have a compound phase, and in any case the ethnographic accounts provided by Laslett's collaborators document the widespread existence of compound households. Berkner states: "Despite their focus on the small nuclear family, what do these studies actually indicate about family structure in the past? First, that a large proportion of the households in many regions included an extended family phase. This is true in southern France, Tuscany, Corsica, and of course Serbia and Japan. Second, that there is a great deal of regional variation which can be explained by social and economic differences. In Tuscany, households were more complex in the rural villages than in the cities, in the Netherlands they were more complex on arable than livestock farms, and in Japan complexity and size reflected commercial isolation. Third, that the complexity and size of peasant households is directly related to their wealth. This is the case in rural Lancashire, Corsica, and Tuscany. Fourth, that inheritance and succession rules are crucial variables. They explain the high incidence of household complexity in Japan (through adoption) and Serbia, and

47

might explain the difference between southern and northern France or between Holland and Overijssel" (Berkner 1975: 737–738). It looks as though students of small-scale demographic processes will not be able to avoid dealing with household composition.

The same goes for the causes and effects of labor force participation by different members of the household. The problem is already on the agenda in the form of discussions of tradeoffs or conflicts between female employment and fertility. The general version of the problem concerns the disposition of the household's entire supply of labor. That includes the labor of children and old people. Following Chayanov (1966), a number of students of the European peasantry have looked closely at the labor requirements of different types of farms, and have seen peasant households as carrying on a continual negotiation between their own age-sex composition and the work to be done (see Thorner 1964, Wolf 1966). The demand for labor on most peasant holdings is relatively fixed. Over the longer run, goes the hypothesis I mentioned earlier, peasants adjust their fertility to that demand for labor. Peasants respond to short-run discrepancies between the supply and the demand on their own holdings by farming out their own youngsters or taking in youngsters from other farms, by renting additional land or renting out land they cannot handle themselves, by hiring land-poor laborers, and so on. (In this volume, Berkner and Mendels, Braun, and Wrigley all discuss different features of these adjustment processes.) The availability of piece-work and wage-work in rural industry and agriculture provide an alternative to the tuning of household composition to the labor requirements of the individual holding; however, it also provides means and incentives for the departure of wage-earners from the household.

Permanent employment outside the household and long-distance migration often begin as simple extensions of these local adjustment processes: a region of Switzerland comes to specialize in the supplying of mercenaries to European armies, and their remittances keep the family economy going; what was once a few years of domestic service before a girl married becomes a lifetime as a maid, and so on. In another variant of the process, whole households come to be engaged in rural industry—first carding, spinning, weaving and so on within their own dwellings, then transferring the same division of labor into the early factories. The earliest promoters of "child labor," as Neil Smelser insisted some time ago, were the parents of the child laborers. They brought the children with them into the shop, received remuneration for the household as a team, and had to hire someone to fill the children's roles if they had no offspring of their own to do the job.

48

Historically speaking, the problem of labor force participation links directly to the problems of household composition and of proletarianization. In rural households, the connections between employment opportunities for children and fertility seem at least as important as the connections between employment opportunities for married women and fertility.

The current theoretical challenge in the study of small-scale vital processes is to see whether economic models such as those proposed by Nerlove and Easterlin can accommodate these new contingencies or whether we shall require new models incorporating multiple utility schedules, changing household composition, partially independent determination of sexual activity and fertility, varying loci of control over fertility, and multiple opportunities for employment of the household's labor supply.

IX

THE AGENDA

THE historical study of vital processes, it turns out, has an agenda which is rich, distinctive, and significant. Parts of the agenda belong to demography as a whole; historical materials are simply a convenient source of data for them. That is true, I would say, of the decomposition of year-to-year vital changes into cohort, compositional, and annual effects. Other parts of the agenda are of great interest to historians, but matter little to demography itself. Most of the components-of-growth analyses I discussed earlier fall into that category. Yet there is an important remainder: fundamental problems which are at once historical and demographic. The damaged theory of demographic transition will not be repaired without close analysis of long series of changes in fertility and mortality. The extent to which peasant populations are self-equilibrating—and, if the extent is large, how the equilibrating processes work—matters to western economic history as well as to contemporary analyses of population control. The related question of whether proletarianization has a strong, consistent tendency to promote high rates of natural increase (and if so, how) applies to a wide range of situations both historical and contemporary. The tangled ties of population growth, labor supply, consumer demand, and economic growth require sorting. How much, how effectively, and how out-migration, employment in wage-labor, restrictions on marriage, and control of fertility itself acted as alternatives to each other in the western historical experience deserves the closest demographic attention. Finally, it will take a great combination of historical and demo-

49

graphic expertise to determine where, when, and how the durable nineteenth-century decline of fertility occurred in Europe and America: Did something crucial happen in the cities? Did the proletarians' acquisition of property and of opportunities for mobility help them escape the Malthusian trap? Did some sort of attitudinal revolution rapidly revise people's approaches to sexuality and child-bearing?

These strands of provocative questions braid into two: (1) In the parts of the world which are now predominantly urban and industrial, by what demographic process did the transformation of an agrarian into an urban-industrial population occur? (2) What caused the long-run changes in the fertility level and in the determinants of fluctuations in fertility within those same areas? Other questions concerning mortality, nuptiality, migration, and social mobility are also worth asking. Some of them come up inevitably on the way to answering the two master questions. But the general inquiries into the creation of urban-industrial populations and the determinants of fertility changes will surely dominate the agenda for some time to come.

In each case, we have two groups of theories to choose from. The first postulates a sharp discontinuity between the old system and the new one, and thereby requires us to formulate three subtheories: one concerning the dynamics of the "traditional" or "preindustrial" demographic system, another concerning the dynamics of the "modern" or "industrial" system, and a third concerning the transition between them. In the case of the creation of an urban-industrial population, the typical components are a model of the labor requirements of an agrarian economy, a model of the labor requirements of large-scale industrial production, and a model of a modernization process: diffusion, capital accumulation, entrepreneurship, organizational innovation, technological change in some combination or other. In the case of fertility change, the typical components are a model of "natural," "socially controlled" or "traditional" fertility behavior; a model of "controlled," "individually controlled" or "modern" fertility behavior; and a model of the process by which one replaces the other: a primarily ideological process, a primarily technical process, or something else.

The second group of theories treat both long-run and short-run dynamics as outcomes of the same fundamental regularities, and thereby stress the continuities between past and present. In the case of the creation of an urban-industrial population, we have technical innovation, capital accumulation, investment, organizational transformation, and changes in population composition accelerating or decelerating together as a consequence either of their own internal dynamics or as a function of exogenous changes in mortality, in communications, or in institutions of property and political control. In the case of fertility change, we have individuals or households maximizing in accordance with a set of utilities which change very little and which are relatively uniform from one group to another, but under constraints which vary importantly from population to population and which shift significantly both in the short run and the long.

The choice between discontinuity theories and continuity theories is familiar. Every problem of "modernization" or "development" poses the same choice. It is not merely a matter of emphasis; the compromise "Some things change, while others remain the same," will not resolve it. What is at issue is not whether the values of crucial variables remain the same, but whether the *relationships* among variables change so radically from one domain to another that we need a new theory for each domain. Advocates of continuity theories tend to treat this as partly an empirical question (How well does a model which operates effectively in one domain work in the next?) and partly a question of convenience (At what level of generality is it currently easiest and/or most effective to argue?); they hope to subsume the best stage formulations into their own general models. Advocates of discontinuity theories tend to consider proposed general models as much more bound to their times and places or origin than their advocates admit, and to attack the fit of their assumptions, their categories, and their empirical implications in the new domain; Karl Polanyi, for example, argued long and hard that the market was an historically specific development, that economic theories built around market mechanisms could not and did not fit most agrarian economies (Polanyi et al. 1957).

As is probably obvious in the earlier discussion, my own sympathies lie with the attempt to build general models. Nevertheless, I would like to see models which take time itself seriously. In general, I mean models in which what has happened before constrains what happens next. Developmental models which portray essentially the same set of changes as recurring in essentially the same manner within population after population violate the prescription by treating each case as more or less autonomous.

The formation of national states (to take an example outside the present discussion) was an historically specific process which began in earnest in western Europe some time around 1500, which lead to the creation of a state-system encompassing almost the entire world by the middle of the twentieth century, in which the states in existence at any given point in the process strongly affected the statemaking activities and outcomes of the newcomers at that point in time, and in which the

51

states and protostates involved continuously shaped each other through war, diplomacy, and economic activity. Yet we have abundant theories of political development which propose a recurrent process happening (or failing to happen) in country after country more or less autonomously.

The same confusion prevails about capitalism: an historically specific system of property relations which likewise originated in Europe and likewise came to dominate the entire world. It makes relatively little theoretical sense to label some countries of the contemporary world as capitalist and others as noncapitalist when all are embedded in an international system in which the market sets the price for all the factors of production. It makes almost no sense at all to analyze the development of capitalism country by country as if it were a standard, recurrent, autonomous process. Instead of developmental theories, in this sense of the word, we need historical theories: theories which relate the experience of any particular population to historically specific processes involving a number of different populations at the same time.

The inclusion or exclusion of time matters because it affects the possibility of our generalizing from historical studies. Where a well-defined and self-contained developmental process actually does exist, on the analogy to the life-cycle of an organism, we can conveniently neglect time, and predict or even promote the recurrence of that same process in a new setting. That has been a sustaining hope of development theorists in economics, sociology, and politics. To the extent that a process is larger than any particular population we may care to analyze and/or is changing significantly over time, the analogy from past to present will be faulty. That does not mean there is no way to generalize from the past; it means the generalization will have to include an adjustment for the time of its application, and may have to include specific allowances for the relations between the population in question and the rest of the world.

How does my polemic apply to historical studies of changing fertility? Mainly by warning against the effort to derive a standard sequence for the demographic transition from the experiences of single western countries and to apply it directly to the poor countries of today's world, by drawing attention to possibilities such as the larger and larger role proletarianization plays in the whole world's population processes as the economic interdependence of different parts of the world increases, and by suggesting that the form and extent of a population's dependence on others should become major variables in our models of urban-industrial transformation as well as our models of fertility change. In short, by giving preference to continuity theories, but with time built in.

52

The authors in this volume have no obligation to honor my preference. In fact, they vary considerably in their theoretical preferences. Consider the contrast between a continuity theorist such as Ronald Lee, who aspires to capture the entire evolution of the English population in a single set of equations, and a discontinuity theorist such as Rudolf Braun, who insists on the cultural distinctiveness of a Swiss world of preindustrial times whose regularities the expansion of industry simply swept away. Compare Easterlin's portrayal of households maximizing under changing constraints with van de Walle's stress on the diffusion of new ideas and information. The purpose of my long commentary on the existing literature has been to pace out the space and help the reader see where my collaborators stand within it, not to herd them all into the same corner of the space.

We have arranged our papers in a rough descending order of generality. We begin with Richard Easterlin's synthesis of economic and sociological ideas about fertility. The treatment is abstract, the scope the entire world. E. A. Wrigley discusses the impact of different mortality schedules on the survival of households or communities exhibiting various patterns of fertility. He concerns himself mainly with preindustrial European populations, but explores in general terms in what sense such populations could be, and were, self-regulating. Ronald Lee fashions a series of economic models of the determinants of temporal fluctuations in vital rates. He estimates the models by means of long series from England before the nineteenth century, using techniques ranging from simple regression to spectral analysis. The paper by Etienne van de Walle reports some of the findings of a massive region-by-region study of fertility changes in nineteenth-century France. More so than in other reports of the study, van de Walle examines (and makes preliminary tests of) arguments concerning the diffusion of contraceptive practice in France. Lutz Berkner and Franklin Mendels undertake the systematic analysis of a problem which has produced a good deal of folklore, but few clear results: the relationship among the system of inheritance, the composition of households and the patterns of nuptiality and fertility in western Europe before the twentieth century. In particular, they try to determine whether the inheritance system—especially the distinction between partibility and impartibility —has an independent effect on demographic patterns. Maris Vinovskis actually presents a substantial discussion of vital trends in New England during the first half of the nineteenth century as well as the large cross-sectional analysis. Using the fertility ratio as the primary dependent variable, Vinovskis alternates between establishing the strength of regional variations and measuring the relationships between his fertility indexes and a number of characteristics of the local popula-

53

tion. Finally, Rudolf Braun draws on his long historical studies of the transformation of Zurich's hinterland as cottage industry rose and fell. In this essay, he emphasizes the contrasting demographic behavior of rural households in agriculture and in industry, and sketches the demographic mechanisms by which the industrial population increased.

I take up the contents and implications of the seven chapters in the conclusion. Here I want simply to forecast some of their common themes.

As compared with the existing literature and as compared with the agenda this group set for itself at the beginning of the inquiry, the chapters attribute relatively little importance to industrialization as such. That is partly because of their concentration on "preindustrial" populations. (The word is misleading because of the extensive small-scale manufacturing which went on in rural Europe before the nineteenth century.) It is partly because much of their work goes into inserting other variables—especially demographic variables—in between industrialization and fertility change. But it also reflects a growing doubt that exposure to large-scale manufacturing and its concomitants reliably transforms the patterns of nuptiality and fertility in the populations involved.

On the demographic side, our inquiries increased our appreciation of the effects of changing mortality. The theoretical discussions (for example, in the chapters by Wrigley or Berkner and Mendels) stress the importance both of the turnover in adult positions due to mortality and of the highly variable life expectancy of children. The empirical analyses (e.g., in Lee and van de Walle) consistently reveal strong associations between levels of fertility and mortality. In compensation, several of the studies (notably Lee's) question whether variations in opportunities to marry acted as quite the regulator of fertility that Malthus and many after him have thought. In preindustrial and industrial populations alike, fertility regulation within marriage comes out as the primary adjustment mechanism.

That line of inquiry leads a number of the papers—most explicitly, Wrigley's—back to the hypothesis of a self-regulating system which roughly matched the procreative tendencies of preindustrial populations to the carrying capacities of their environments. Not that the system was gentle: In all our portraits, it depended on life expectancies at birth of less than forty years. In several of the analyses, it was compatible with long periods of declining real wages. And our general arguments make the system vulnerable to the increasing dependency of the local population on employment governed by demand in distant markets.

Nevertheless, a picture of self-regulation short of utter misery emerges from our varied explorations of the agrarian West. By implication, our findings give grounds for both optimism and pessimism about the population problems of the contemporary world. Cautious optimism: We end up with some confidence in the capacity of human populations to regulate themselves. Pessimism: We end up doubting that the high fertility of the Third World results from the fact that its populations have not yet begun to restrict births—but will somehow begin to do so automatically as modernization proceeds.

2

The Economics and Sociology of Fertility: A Synthesis

RICHARD A. EASTERLIN

THIS chapter presents an analysis, the main outlines of which were first sketched in 1970 in a paper prepared for the United Nations Population Division (Easterlin 1970). A much fuller statement was presented in 1972 at the Princeton seminar whose proceedings comprise the present volume. The chapter constitutes almost a complete redrafting of that paper, presenting the analysis in more formal terms.

A chapter with such a long history necessarily places the author in debt to so large a number of individuals that adequate acknowledgment is impossible. I can list here only a few from whose comments I have particularly benefitted in way or another, with apologies to those omitted: Glen G. Cain, John D. Durand, Stefano Fenoaltea, Henry A. Gemery, Adrienne Germaine, Ralph B. Ginsberg, Michael R. Haines, Allen C. Kelley, Ronald Lee, Peter H. Lindert, Jay R. Mandle, George S. Masnick, Karen O. Mason, William H. Newell, Robert A. Pollak, Robert Summers, Riad B. Tabbarah, Etienne van de Walle, Michael L. Wachter, and Barbara Wolfe. General acknowledgment should also be made of the helpful contributions of my colleagues in the Princeton seminar, and of several classes of graduate students in my course on economic-demographic interrelations. Finally, I want especially to acknowledge the help of my research assistant, Gretchen A. Condran, with whom I had continuously profitable discussions over several years, and assistance in production of the paper of Dana E. Lightman, Cynthia E. Schneider, and Betty A. Rippel. Lydia F. Christaldi drew the charts. The research on which the paper is based was supported in part in NICHHD grant 1 RO1 HD-05427 and NSF grant GS-1563.

After decades outside the fold, population has become in recent years a legitimate subject of economic analysis. Nowhere is this change more exemplified than in the study of the causes of human fertility. There was a time when economists perfunctorily abandoned this subject to sociologists and demographers. Since Becker's seminal article, however, recognition has grown of the possibility of incorporating this area

57

of human behavior into the theory of household decision making (1960: 209–231). Both theoretical and empirical work have increased at a respectable, if not overwhelming, rate.

Sociologists and demographers have viewed this incursion with mixed feelings. On the one hand, the possibility is enhanced of clarifying the persistently troubling problem of the role of economic considerations in human fertility. On the other hand, there is dismay at the tendency of economists to disregard the conceptual and empirical contributions of noneconomists, and by implication to assert the primacy and universality of what might be called the "economic theory of fertility," stemming from Becker's work.

Indeed, there are well-grounded empirical observations which must give pause to even the boldest exponent of the household decision-making approach. In Africa, for example, there are wide differences among populations in marital fertility, with some societies approaching levels of completed fertility as low as those observed in developed societies (Clark 1967: 24). A matter of differences in the demand for children due to cost or income factors? Of differential knowledge of methods of fertility control? It seems doubtful. There is little or no evidence of conscious efforts by most households to regulate fertility in these societies. How then can these differences be viewed as a matter of household choice?

The African data exemplify a more general conclusion that has emerged in recent years regarding fertility in premodern societies. As Bourgeois-Pichat has observed, it used to be thought that fertility in such societies was universally high and that modernization resulted in the emergence of noticeable fertility differences among societies. The evidence now becoming available, however, suggests that fertility differences among preindustrial societies are vastly greater than those among modernized societies (Bourgeois-Pichat 1967b: 160–163).

There is evidence too of significant short and long term fluctuations in fertility in premodern societies (Wrigley 1969: ch. 3). Moreover, sizeable and reliably documented increases in fertility have been observed during what might be called "early modernization" in places such as Jamaica, British Guiana, and parts of Africa (Hurault 1965: 801–828; Mandle n.d.; Olusanya 1969: 812–824; Roberts 1957: 262–285, 1969: 695–711). Similar increases may have occurred in the earlier experience of today's developed countries (cf. Shorter 1971a). An effect of rising income on the demand for children? Possibly. But in some of these places there appears to be little evidence of noticeable income change among the mass of the population when fertility was rising (Mandle n.d.: ch. 8).

There are other reservations one may have about the economic analysis of fertility. For one thing, it is a notably sexless subject. This is not a mere quibble, for this omission has logical consequences for the theory. Without reference to sexual intercourse one is hard put to explain why households would engage in the "production" of children once the desired number is reached, and consequently why excess fertility would ever occur (Easterlin 1969: 136). Similarly, there is a notable scarcity in the economic analysis of fertility of references to physiological or biological factors that may influence fertility. There is also inadequate consideration of the nature of and evidence on the ways in which fertility is actually regulated.

Doubtless these omissions reflect in part the empirical reference implicit in most economists' work, namely, fertility behavior in the more advanced nations. But even for these nations, fertility among certain population subgroups, as well as nonmarital fertility, might well require reference to such considerations. When economists turn to less developed nations, fertility analysis does sometimes touch on matters such as fecundity. But such considerations are treated much less systematically than the core variables of price and income.

In contrast, sociologists start with what might be called the production side of fertility. The analysis typically proceeds from discussion of frequency of intercourse and the reproductive capacity of a population to specific methods of fertility regulation, such as abstinence, contraception, and abortion, by which births are kept below the biological maximum. Beyond this, the discussion moves on to motivational and other factors, but the framework becomes much less uniform from one writer to another.

It seems reasonable to suppose that an analysis which integrated the approaches of both sociologists and economists might clarify their relationship and help foster beneficial exchanges between scholars in the two disciplines. It might also have wider empirical applicability than either approach taken alone. Accordingly, this chapter proposes a framework which would combine the economics and sociology of fertility. In an earlier article, I made a start in this direction, emphasizing the contribution that sociology might make to the economics of fertility, chiefly through clarifying the process of taste formation (Easterlin 1969: 127–156). In retrospect, this argument, though valid, underrates the role of sociology, because it omits the extensive sociological literature dealing with supply considerations. The present treatment, I feel, represents more nearly a marriage of equals, though partisans of either discipline will doubtless come away feeling shortchanged.

59

A valuable step in the direction of reconciling the two disciplines is provided by Riad Tabbarah's contribution (Tabbarah 1971: 257–277). In developing the present analysis, Michael L. Wachter's contribution (1972) has played an important part. Wachter's article was especially helpful in suggesting a formal and readily comprehensible expository framework. Other work that has been drawn on substantially includes that of Bourgeois-Pichat and Henry on natural fertility (Bourgeois-Pichat, 1965: 383–424, 1967a: 68–72, 1967b: 160–163; Henry, 1961a: 625–636, 1961b: 81–91, 1963: 333–350) and those of Freedman (1961–1962: 35–68), Davis and Blake (1956: 211–235), and Petersen (1969) on the sociology of fertility. Mention should be made too of Ansley Coale's framework for fertility analysis (Coale 1971: 193–214, 1967: 205–209; 1969: 3–24, 1973). While Coale's approach is not included in the present scheme, which focuses on marital fertility, extension of the present framework to incorporate the Coale approach is both possible and desirable, as shall be shown later.

First, the analysis presents the "simple" economics of fertility, and then the "simple" sociology of fertility. In such brief compass, it is not possible to do justice to either of these substantial subjects, and the treatment is necessarily heuristic and selective. Then the formal synthesis is discussed. Throughout these first three sections, the concepts and form of the framework are developed with a view to maximizing links to the empirical literature. To this end, reference is frequently made to relevant data both for developed and less developed areas. The concern is with marital, not total fertility. Following the theoretical exposition, the usefulness of the framework is illustrated by applying it to the interpretation of some real world situations—fertility behavior in premodern societies and the effect of modernization on fertility (the demographic transition). The chapter concludes by noting various qualifications and needed extensions of the analysis.

I

THE SIMPLE ECONOMICS OF FERTILITY: A DEMAND APPROACH

AMONG economists, Becker's analysis of the demand for children based on tastes, prices, and income is the common ground from which fertility analysis starts (Becker 1960: 209–231, 1965: 493–517). Beyond this (or recent variants thereof), differences start to appear.[1] The prin-

[1] Among recent contributions to the economic theory of fertility are those by Cain and Weininger (1967), Kelley (1976), Leibenstein (1957, 1973), Namboodiri (1972: 185–206), Robinson and Horlacher (1971: 1–39), Sanderson and Willis (1971), T. P. Schultz (1969: 153–180, 1971: 148–174), Silver (1966: 302–315), Simon (1974), Spengler (1966: 109–130), and Tabbarah (1964: 187–196, 1971:

cipal idea, stemming from the theory of consumer choice, is that the demand for children is based on the household's balancing of its subjective tastes against externally determined constraints of price and income in a way that maximizes its satisfaction. Considerations of fecundity and contraception enter in regard to the possible "overproduction" of children, but the primary emphasis is on demand factors, and these other concepts, along with child-spacing concerns, are not as systematically integrated into the theoretical framework.

The basic reasoning is as follows. Suppose households view children as a type of consumption good, yielding satisfaction like economic goods in general. Household desires for children can be conceived in terms of an indifference map with number of children on one axis and goods consumed by the parents on the other (see the I_1, I_2, and I_3 curves of Figure 2–1a). Any given point on the map expresses the degree of satisfaction attaching to that particular combination of children and commodities. An indifference curve embraces all combinations that yield the same amount of satisfaction—curves further from the origin correspond to progressively higher levels of satisfaction. Formally, the indifference map for an individual household may be expressed by

$$U = f(G_p, C), \qquad (1)$$

where U is the utility of the parents,

C is the number of children surviving to adulthood, and
G_p is the quantity of goods consumed by the parents.

One can think too of a price tag attaching to children. This would consist of the appropriately discounted cost of the various expense items required to have and raise children, including the opportunity cost of the time devoted to child care, due allowance being made for the offset constituted by the work done by children. Together with household income and the prices of goods consumed by the parents, this establishes the household's budget constraint (the ef line of Figure 2–1a). The budget constraint describes the set of combinations of G_p

257–277). Kelley (1976), Robinson and Horlacher (1971: 1–39), and Simon (1974), include valuable bibliographies of recent economic studies. A special issue of the *Journal of Political Economy* (Vol. 81, No. 2, Part II [March/April 1973]) entitled "New Economic Approaches to Fertility" was published shortly before a revised draft of this paper was completed. In a paper presented at the April 1973 meeting of the Poulation Association of America, Michael and Willis apply an approach like that presented here to recent American experience (Michael and Willis 1973).

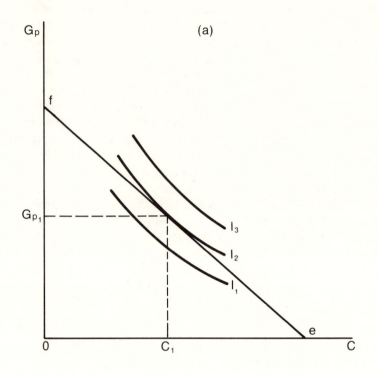

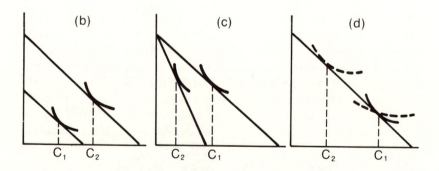

Figure 2–1 A Simple Economic "Demand" Model of Fertility Determination

and C constituting the outer limit of those within financial reach of the household. Analytically, the budget constraint is given by:

$$Y = p_g G_p + p_c C, \qquad (2)$$

where Y is the potential lifetime income of the household,
and p_g and p_c are the prices of goods and children, respectively.

For simplicity, it is assumed that the household makes a single decision at the start of the reproductive union based on the discounted values of income and prices expected over the course of its life cycle. Given the limit to its choices imposed by the budget constraint, the household selects the combination of children and goods that will yield the largest subjective satisfaction. In Figure 2–1a, this is the combination G_{p1}, C_1, given by the tangency of the indifference curve I_2, the outermost curve attainable, with the budget line ef. If the basic taste, income, and price determinants remained unchanged, and the estimates of them were correct, the household's reproductive career would consist of the implementation of this decision.

Observed behavior with regard to family size is thus the result of balancing subjective preferences against an externally imposed constraint based on prices and income. Variations in these basic determinants will cause differences in behavior among households at a given time or for a given household over time. If the level of the household's expected income were higher, the equilibrium combination would include both more children and more goods (assuming as is customary that children are "normal" goods), though the increase would not necessarily be proportionately the same (Figure 2–1b). If the relative price of children were higher, for example because, the price of child care items rose more than the average price of goods generally, the optimal combination would shift toward more goods and fewer children (Figure 2–1c). Finally, if subjectively the attractiveness of commodities rose relative to that of children, a similar shift would occur (Figure 2–1d). Thus, the number of children parents have would be expected to vary directly with household income and with the price of goods relative to children, and inversely with the strength of desires for goods relative to children. Changes in the basic determinants might occur in the course of the reproductive cycle of a household and lead to altered decisions and fertility behavior.

The dependent variable in the economic analysis of fertility is surviving children: parents are ultimately interested in grown offspring, not births. Birth behavior is linked to the demand for children through

63

the rate of infant and child survival. For households to achieve a given number of surviving children, the necessary number of births would be higher the lower the level of infant and child survival. Thus, we have for a given household

$$B = \frac{C}{s}, \qquad (3)$$

where B is the total number of births,

C is as defined in (1) above, and

s is the probability of survival of a live birth to adulthood, say, age 20.

Even though tastes, prices and income (and thus C) remain unchanged, birth behavior might vary because of changes in the survival prospects of children. Other things being equal, the higher the survival prospects, the lower the number of births. The high rates of infant and child mortality observed in premodern compared with modernized societies are frequently cited to account for pronatalist practices in the premodern societies—high fertility helps to compensate for high infant and child mortality and thus enhances (but does not guarantee) the prospect of realizing the number of children demanded.

In the economic analysis of fertility, observed birth behavior may differ from that dictated by demand considerations because of a tendency for too many births. Usually this is viewed as caused by inadequate knowledge of contraception or because of inefficiency in its use. Thus contraceptive knowledge and practice eventually enter the analysis, although both the theoretical and empirical treatment of these factors is much less refined than that for the demand variable.

So far the presentation has implicitly assumed (as is usual in consumer demand theory) that the quality of the goods under discussion is given. Thus the decision to have more or fewer children refers to children of a given "quality," that is, embodying a given set of inputs of time and goods. Allowance can be made for child quality by viewing it as an additional good along with number of children and goods consumed by the parents (Wachter 1972). The equilibrium decision would then involve a combination of G_p, C, and child quality. An increase in income would be expected to raise not only the number of children but also child quality, while a rise in the relative prices of inputs required for children would lead to substitution against both child numbers and quality. Also subjective preferences relating to child quality might change. For example, increased concern for the

64

quality of children might occur at the expense of feelings about the number of children, and lead to the selection of combinations in which child quality is more favored relative to child numbers.

While the analysis is straightforward, the concepts involved in the economics of the demand for children are, in practice, far from simple.[2] The income concept, Y, relevant to fertility decisions is the "full income" or "potential income" of the household (Easterlin 1969: 129). This takes account of the earnings potentials of both the husband, wife, and children over the course of the parents' life cycle, as well as any nonlabor income available to the household. The usefulness of actual income observations as an approximation to this concept must be assessed in the light of the problem at hand. The husband's income may be less biased as an indicator of household differences in potential income than family income, which includes earnings of the wife as well as other family members (Easterlin 1969: 155). But even the husband's current income is not necessarily a reliable guide to household differences in potential income, as in the case where the observations relate to an early stage of the life cycle and do not adequately reflect differences in longer term income prospects—differences that would play a part in actual family size decisions.

The price of children, p_c, is a price index which expresses the (properly discounted) cost at any given time of the market-basket of commodities and time required for child-bearing and child-rearing, relative to a price index of the items alternatively consumed by the parents, p_g. The items comprising this market-basket (the quantities included in the index) embrace a child's requirements up to adulthood for such things as food, shelter, clothing, education, and hospital and medical care (including that of the mother associated with pregnancy and birth) plus the labor time required for child-care, net of the child's contribution of time for paid work and household chores. The prices are actual market prices. The relative price of children to a household would be expected to decrease with the number of children, because of influences such as economies of scale in consumption and the possibility of older children caring for the younger, resulting in a budget constraint convex to the origin.

Economists typically value child-care time in terms of the wife's opportunity cost, usually assumed to be proportionate to the full-time rate of earnings of women actually in the work force (Mincer 1963: 67–82). The validity of this assumption is likely to vary with the problem under study. There is some minimum unavoidable amount of time

[2] A number of the following points are discussed and illustrated more fully in (Easterlin 1969).

that a mother must typically give to child-care, and the wife's earning potential is relevant to evaluation of this time. But it is possible to obtain domestic help to cover a substantial part of child-care requirements. There may also be available for this purpose private or public child-care facilities, or elderly relatives and older children living in the household with low market earnings prospects. Another possibility is that mothers with low market opportunities might offer day care facilities for the children of others. In all such cases, use of the wife's wage rate to evaluate all child-care time is likely to exaggerate the cost of children if the wife is above the lowest wage level (see Hill and Stafford 1971 for pertinent data).

In view of the frequent mention of cost considerations in the fertility literature, it is surprising to find that conceptually meaningful estimates of the relative price of children are virtually nonexistent. If the true effect on fertility behavior of prices rather than tastes or income is to be estimated, measured time or space variations in the price of children should arise solely from the prices, and not the quantities in the index of the relative price of children. The extent of measured price variation will differ, of course, depending on the market-basket of quantities by which the prices are weighted, the "quality" of children. This is a common index number problem which may be handled by developing alternative price indexes, each relating to a given quality of children. Any given index, however, should be estimated for a fixed market-basket of child cost items. Otherwise, estimates of the price elasticity of demand for children, based on the co-variation of fertility and prices, would confound the effect of price changes with those of income and tastes, and lead to erroneous inferences, for example, about the likely impact of disincentive policies on fertility. Most data that are labeled "cost of children" are not conceptually appropriate, because they are typically estimates of expenditures on children and thus include the effect of quantity as well as price variations (United Nations 1956). Empirical research by economists has largely focused on a particular component of the price of children, typically the opportunity cost of the wife, or settled for qualitative judgments, for example, based on rural versus urban residence (Mincer 1963: 67–82; Phillips et al. 1969: 298–308). However, recent and ongoing work shows promise of providing new insights on this question (see Cain 1971: unpublished appendix; Espenshade 1972: 207–221; and especially Lindert 1973, which is by far the most thorough inquiry yet attempted). Probably the most defensible generalization at present is that the relative price of children is higher in nonfarm than in farm situations, due to differences in food prices, housing prices, the time children take away from a mother's paid work, and the time contributed by children to the household's activities (Lindert 1973: 37). This would imply that the relative price of children is less in less developed societies than in more developed societies. But there is need for more thorough empirical study of variations in the cost of children in time and space, and among various subclasses of the population.

Relatively little research has been done by economists on preferences or "tastes" for children, in the sense of a preference map expressing the household's estimation of the degree of satisfaction attaching to various possible combinations of children and other economic goods. However, there has been some work which has yielded empirical maps of indifference curves relating to different commodities (shirts versus shoes) and to household attitudes toward male versus female children (and implicitly different numbers of children) (Myers and Roberts 1968: 164–172; Roberts et al. 1971). These studies suggest the possibility of directly measuring tastes as defined in (1) above. In sociology, attitudinal data already available both on goods aspirations and ideal family size [3] throw some light on preferences (Blake 1967: 159–174; Freedman et al. 1959; Ryder and Westoff 1971; Whelpton et al. 1966). Also relevant is research which has made progress toward estimating the respondent's intensity of feeling about different family size numbers (Goldberg and Coombs 1962: 105–129). One interesting result of research done on American attitudes is that for an overwhelming proportion of adults the ideal number is concentrated in the two to four child range (Freedman et al. 1965: 250–275). Families with no children or only one tend to be much less favored. Moreover, it seems possible that a mix of 2 boys and 2 girls represent a satiation point for many Americans.[4]

In the absence of direct measures of tastes, indirect estimation is possible using a model of taste formation. The preference map at any time may be viewed as molded by heredity and past and current environment (Spengler 1966: 109–130). For example, tastes may be taken as a function of such factors as religion, color, nativity, place of residence, education, family economic background, and the number of siblings. These factors may be introduced into the demand function in lieu of direct readings on tastes.[5] Ideally, the treatment of

[3] Of the various queries on family size attitudes, that on "ideal" size probably elicits the least constrained response.

[4] Attitudinal data sometimes reveal strong preferences as to the sex of the children (Freedman and Taskeshita 1969). This consideration may enter as an additional influence on tastes affecting the number of children demanded.

[5] Some work is in progress along these lines (Ben-Porath, unpublished; Condran, unpublished; Wolfe, unpublished).

67

such factors would be based on a tested model of taste formation derived from multivariate analysis of preferences and their underlying determinants.

Despite limited research on preferences, there is reason to think that the preference for children relative to other goods may be greater in less developed societies than in developed. For example, comparing the goods aspirations of survey respondents in developed and less developed countries, Hadley Cantril has concluded: "People in highly developed nations have obviously a wide range of aspirations, sophisticated and expensive from the point of view of people in less-developed areas, who have not yet learned all that is potentially available to people in more advanced societies and whose aspirations concerning the social and material aspects of life are modest indeed by comparison" (Cantril 1965: 202; cf. D. Freedman unpublished papers and 1970: 25–48). On the other hand, expressions of family size preferences yield larger numbers in less developed countries (Glass 1962: 231–261; Mauldin 1965: 1–12). While these differences in response may be partly due to different income and price constraints which are implicitly taken into account, they may also reflect differences in basic subjective attitudes toward children versus goods.

The foregoing discussion of child preferences relates to completed family size, and not the spacing of children. Subsequently, the assumption will be made that prospective parents are not concerned about the spacing of births. The main reason for this assumption is to simplify the exposition, but it is pertinent to note that there is some empirical justification for the present emphasis on completed size, though to neglect spacing considerations entirely is, of course, extreme. For example, criticizing the emphasis that some advocates of family planning in less developed areas place on attention to spacing, Stycos says: "[T]he evidence indicates in various ways that women in the underdeveloped areas are more interested in stopping births. On the whole, women have relatively little interest in fertility control early in the pregnancy history. For reasons of prestige, marital legitimation solidifying otherwise unstable unions, etc., women in cultures where kinship is of special importance want a few children, or at least one or two sons, as soon as possible after marriage. Having discharged their obligation and achieved their status as fertile women, they subsequently become concerned about economic, rearing and health difficulties" (Stycos 1962: 488).

Moreover, even in developed countries, while attention to spacing is more common, spacing preferences may be rather ill-defined. A study of American fertility attitudes and behavior leads Westoff et al.,

68

to the hypothesis that control over child-spacing is not more common because "spacing values are often vague and of low intensity, thereby resulting in a half-hearted practice of contraception, or sometimes dispensing with it altogether," and a comparison of spacing preferences and actual birth intervals shows only a weak association (Westoff et al. 1961: 21–22). In general, it seems that attitudes toward spacing are much less well-developed than are preferences for completed family size, and that the fertility transition accompanying modernization typically involves attention first to limiting family size and only at a later stage to spacing of births. Nor should one exaggerate the precision with which either number or spacing preferences are held. In general, even in developed nations, households probably start with rather general notions of how many children would be desirable, and even rougher ideas, if any, of how far apart these children should be born. These attitudes may well be modified as a result of on-going experience.

Compared with the taste, income, and price variables, the infant and child survival rate, s, is a fairly straightforward concept. Even for this, however, it is necessary to stress a point bearing on all the variables in the economic analysis of fertility, namely, that the relevant magnitude is the value of the variable as perceived by the parents at the time of decision making. This means that the observed real world value may not necessarily correspond to that on which the child-bearing decision is actually based. For example, infant and child mortality may decline, but awareness of this may not come until late in the reproductive period when parents find more children surviving than was anticipated. Indeed, if catastrophic events disproportionately influence people's judgments, then reproductive behavior may be geared to the worst rather than average mortality conditions. Similarly, income or cost considerations may be incorrectly anticipated by the household in a way producing a systematic bias. Because of this, actual empirical estimation of such variables may need to take cognizance of the manner in which perceptions are formed, possible lags between real world changes in fertility determinants and perception of those changes, and the way in which uncertainty may affect behavior as a result of differing attitudes toward risk taking versus risk aversion.

II

THE SIMPLE SOCIOLOGY OF FERTILITY: A PRODUCTION APPROACH

SOCIOLOGISTS, in contrast to economists, start with what might be called the production side of fertility. The analysis typically proceeds from discussion of frequency of intercourse and the reproductive capacity of a population, to specific methods of fertility regulation such as abstinence, contraception, and abortion, by which births are kept below the biological maximum. Good representative presentations are those of Freedman and Petersen (1961–1962: 35–68; 1969). The initial emphasis is on a complete accounting for the immediate factors ("intermediate variables") through which any influence on fertility must ultimately operate. The Davis-Blake (1956: 211–235) framework in one form or another is the usual basis for organizing this discussion.

As one proceeds beyond this, the sociology of fertility becomes less uniform from one writer to another, though not less extensive. Along with other underlying determinants, demand considerations of the sort emphasized by economists are introduced in discussing family size and child spacing attitudes. Such factors, influencing the motivation for fertility regulation, along with knowledge of and access to various methods, are seen as influencing fertility through one or another of the intermediate variables of fertility control. The present treatment of the sociology of fertility places production considerations in the forefront, not because sociologists disregard attitudinal or motivational factors— far from it—but because there is much more consensus in the sociological literature on the framework used in the production aspects of the subject.

The point of departure of the sociology of fertility may be represented analytically by:

$$B \equiv N - R, \qquad (4)$$

where, for a given marital union,

B is the cumulative number of live births,

N is natural fertility, the cumulative number of live births that would occur in the absence of any voluntary control of fertility, and

R is a summary measure of the practice and efficiency of fertility regulation, expressed in terms of births averted.

It holds, definitionally, that observed fertility varies directly with natural fertility and inversely with the effective degree of fertility regulation. Table 2–1 identifies the factors included under natural fertility and fertility regulation classified by stage of the reproductive process. Sociologists will recognize this as a rearrangement and a slight modification of the "intermediate variables" of the Davis-Blake (1956: 211–235) framework. The Davis-Blake variables relating to marriage

70

practices have been omitted, since the concern here is with marital fertility.

The factors in the Davis-Blake framework have been divided between those relating to natural fertility and those relating to techniques of fertility regulation. As will be explained shortly, the critical consideration in this regard is that of motivation of the couple. Only if a couple sees the purpose as that of controlling fertility is a given practice classified as a technique of fertility regulation. Thus abstinence due to a desire to limit numbers falls under column 3, as a technique of fertility regulation, but abstinence due to illness or absence of one spouse from the household, which has an unintended effect on fertility, is classified as a component of natural fertility in column 2. Presumably, this distinction is what Davis and Blake had in mind when using the terms "voluntary" and "involuntary," which have been retained in the presentation in Table 2–1.

As shown in Table 2–1, the principal components of natural fertility are frequency of intercourse, involuntary limits on fecundity, and foetal loss due to involuntary causes.[6] Contrary to what one might suppose, natural fertility may vary widely among real world populations. Hypothetical calculations for a population of women who marry early, complete their fecund period, and practice no fertility regulation suggest a maximum natural fertility averaging about thirteen live births over the whole reproductive period. The largest observed figures are somewhat below this. For example, in the United States among the Hutterites, a devout rural community which makes no effort to regulate fertility, the total number of births over the reproductive period of married women averages somewhat over ten. In many populations, however, natural fertility is considerably less than this, since there can be substantial variation in one or more of the components of natural fertility identified above. One of the foremost authorities on natural fertility, Bourgeois-Pichat, (1965: 383–424) develops on the basis of available data a fifty-six class typology for natural fertility based on varying assumptions as to coital frequency, permanent sterility, proportion of ovulations fecundable, and temporary sterility. (He also has an additional cross-classification in terms of five types of marriage patterns.) He does not give actual estimates for each class, but it seems clear that by combining assumptions adverse to fertility one might

[6] Good summary discussions of natural fertility used in this presentation are given by (Bourgeois-Pichat 1965: 383–424; Clark 1967: ch. 1; Hawthorne 1970; and Sauvy 1969: 348–360). Espenshade (1971: 525–536) has recently proposed a new method of estimating natural fertility for historical populations or contemporary less developed societies.

Table 2-1. Components of Natural Fertility of Married Women and Techniques of Voluntary Fertility Regulation by Stage of Reproductive Process

(1) Reproductive stage	(2) Components of natural fertility	(3) Techniques of fertility regulation
Intercourse	*Coital frequency* (including the effect of involuntary abstinence due to factors such as impotence, illness, fatigue, and unavoidable but temporary separations)	*Voluntary abstinence*
Conception	*Fecundity or infecundity* [a] *as affected by involuntary causes* (e.g., permanent sterility due to disease, variations in proportion of ovulations fecundable, temporary sterility associated with postpartum infecundity)	*Fecundity or infecundity as affected by voluntary causes* (e.g., sterilization, subincision, medical treatment, etc.) *Use of contraception* a.) Mechanical and chemical means (e.g., condom, diaphragm, pill, jelly) b.) Other means (rhythm, withdrawal, simulated intercourse without penetration, other sexual practices)
Gestation and parturition	*Foetal mortality from involuntary causes* (miscarriage and stillbirth)	*Foetal mortality from voluntary causes* (induced abortion)

[a] Infecundity refers to any physiological impairment to a normal rate reproduction (cf. Freedman, 1961–1962: 39).

obtain an average estimate of natural fertility for a society as low as three or four births per married woman.

The available information suggests that natural fertility is typically lower among less developed populations than those which are more developed. Involuntary abstinence tends to be greater and coital frequency correspondingly lower among less healthy and less well-nourished populations. Permanent sterility, as indicated by data on childlessness, is often greater. Temporary sterility is enhanced by the practice of lactation, which is typically more prevalent in poorer societies. To judge from evidence on stillbirths, involuntary foetal mortality is greater in less-developed countries, probably because of problems of health and nutrition.

The concept of "natural" fertility is something of a misnomer, since the name leads one to suppose that natural fertility is entirely a biological or physiological phenomenon. Actually, as the anthropological literature demonstrates, cultural practices may play an important part in determining natural fertility. An example is the belief that sexual intercourse should be avoided while a mother is nursing. Two societies identical in biological and physiological characteristics might differ in natural fertility because this cultural belief led to a higher prevalence of involuntary abstinence in one society than in the other. It seems useful therefore to distingiush two channels of influence on natural fertility—one, biological; the other, cultural. Included under the former would be factors that influence natural fertility through biological or physiological mechanisms, such as genetic influences on fecundity or the effect of disease and malnutrition on coital frequency and the ability to carry a foetus to full term. Venereal disease in particular tends to lower natural fertility by inducing temporary or permanent sterility. Under the latter would be various social customs or events that inadvertently affect coital frequency, fecundity, or foetal mortality. As an example, reference has already been made to a social taboo on intercourse during lactation, which insofar as an end is perceived, is usually justified in terms of the health of the child or mother.[7] In some societies this may be reinforced by the mother's returning to her parents' home while she is nursing. Another example is the custom in India of very young brides remaining in their parents' homes for several years after marriage. Another is the practice of wives returning

[7] As recent research by the van de Walles (1972: 686–701) shows, failure to recognize the existence of this taboo may lead researchers erroneously to ascribe reduced fertility to temporary sterility associated with lactation (a biological mechanism), whereas the true cause is this taboo operating via the frequency of intercourse (a cultural mechanism).

73

to the parents' home or making a retreat to a convent when "hard times" occur. Cultural influences on natural fertility are not confined, however, to social customs. If there are differences among societies in sexual desire (aside from the influence of illness) this would alter natural fertility via its effect on coital frequency. The "desire for coition" (Easterlin 1969: 127–156) thus enters the analysis as a factor influencing N.

Under the cultural head would also be included circumstances which might result in the physical separation of partners, such as wars and the movement of men in response to employment opportunities. Sometimes such factors may affect natural fertility through the biological side as well. For example, wars or natural catastrophes, such as floods or earthquakes, may operate through the physiological side by way of personal injury and through the cultural side via separation of partners.[8]

To turn to R, which measures the scope and efficiency of fertility regulation, techniques for voluntary regulation of fertility may operate at all stages of the reproductive process and on virtually all of the components of natural fertility (Table 2–1, column 3). At the stage of intercourse, coital frequency may be reduced through voluntary abstinence. At the next stage, the probability of conception may be eliminated or reduced by sterilization (i.e., vasectomy) or the use of contraception. At the gestation stage foetal mortality may be increased through induced abortion. The techniques range from time-honored methods which may be assumed to be known to virtually all populations (abstinence, withdrawal, and at least crude methods of induced abortion) to modern and sophisticated ones such as the oral pill and IUD. Some techniques require market transactions, and some do not.[9]

The existence of a practice in a given society which reduces fertility below the biological maximum is not in itself evidence that fertility regulation, as defined here, exists, that is, that R is greater than zero. This is because natural fertility, as we have seen, is affected by social

[8] Because the concern here is with cumulative fertility, the present discussion has neglected the influence of age. Natural fertility varies over the course of the reproductive cycle. Among women in their early teens, the probability is low of conceiving as a result of intercourse, or, if the conception occurs, of carrying a foetus to full term. These probabilities rise from menarche to the twenties and then decline, approaching zero as women reach their mid-forties. Another factor which may give rise to variations in natural fertility over the reproductive cycle is frequency of intercourse, which typically declines with duration of marriage.

[9] Infanticide is excluded from the analysis at present, since it is a method of controlling population increase via mortality rather than fertility regulation. (Statistically, however, it may show up in lower births rather than higher deaths, if birth of the victims is not officially recorded.) An indication of how it might be handled will be given in the concluding section of the chapter.

74

customs and circumstances which may involve practices like those which show up under R. For example, abstinence may be practiced either because of an intercourse taboo during lactation or because a couple wishes to restrict family size. In the first case, it falls under N, in the second, R. As has been noted, the critical issue in determining whether or not a given fertility-affecting practice is included under R is not the existence of the practice, but the intent lying behind its use. If use of the practice reflects a wish on the part of the individual household to regulate fertility, then the practice is classified under R, otherwise it falls under N.[10] The variable R thus relates to practices of fertility regulation which arise from household decisions governed by fertility concerns. This treatment corresponds to the general distinction made by sociologists between the "manifest" and "latent" functions of a given social practice, corresponding roughly to the intended and unforeseen consequences of the practice. In the present case, only if the manifest function of a practice is to control fertility is it properly included in R. A clear-cut distinction between voluntary and involuntary influences is not always possible. Ambiguity arises, for example, in the case of fatigue reducing coital frequency and extended lactation lowering fecundity.[11] As a practical matter, however, the line can probably be drawn in most cases.[12]

As in the case of natural fertility, the measurement of R is itself a current area of research. The most recent efforts on this score are those aimed at quantifying the effectiveness of family planning programs in terms of "births averted" (Ross 1972: 7ff.). In principle, such a measure should, in time, provide a concise summary figure for R as defined here. In the meantime, there is a considerable amount of qualitative evidence on the scope and efficiency of fertility regulation which is informative, even if not as conceptually suited for the present purpose as one might like. This evidence shows wide societal differences in the extent and

[10] A recent paper by Srinavasan (1972) employs the same distinction as that used here. He differentiates between fertility regulation due, on the one hand, to biological and social mechanisms operating through natural fertility, and that due, on the other hand, to "deliberate individual control."

[11] Ambiguity also occurs in the case of infanticide, as, for example, in the case of increased infant mortality due to neglect associated with other family pressures.

[12] The emphasis here on the intent lying behind a given fertility-limiting practice is not an analytical quibble, for it bears on such questions as the prospective efficacy of a family planning program. In the abstinence example above, if the practice arises from an intercourse taboo during lactation (and thus operates via N), the household is not potentially in the market for an improved means of fertility regulation. On the other hand, if the practice is undertaken with the purpose of reducing family size (and thus operates via R), there is an implicit demand for an alternative method of fertility control. Obviously, the response to a family planning program would be different in the two circumstances.

types of fertility regulation practiced (Davis and Blake 1956: 211–235; Nag 1968; Petersen 1969). Thus, Davis and Blake (1956: 233) suggest that primitive and peasant societies tend to have somewhat greater voluntary abstinence than do industrial societies. Sterilization, with a few exceptions, tends to be of limited importance in most societies. Contraception, including both old and new methods, is much more widely practiced in industrial societies. Induced abortion varies considerably among developed societies. In preindustrial societies, according to Davis and Blake (1956: 229), "abortion is widely practiced . . . being the individual's principal means of limiting fertility," but documentation for this is not easy to obtain.

Possibly, some generalizations may be established regarding the pattern of adoption of voluntary fertility control. Thus, Requena (1969: 478–479) suggests a shift in Chile from induced abortion as the principal fertility control technique initially used to a more modern stage of "use of effective contraceptives." Srinivasan offers a challenging and wide-ranging hypothesis regarding "phases of fertility regulation": "Every population undergoing a demographic transition also experiences a transition in the nature by which it regulates fertility. . . . The stages of transition of fertility regulation methods can conveniently be classified into phases. Biological, Natural, Premodern, and Modern" (Srinivasan, 1972: 8).

A limited amount of research has also been done on the efficiency of contraceptive use (cf. Tietze 1962b: 357–369). The usual measure is the failure rate per 100 years of use

$$\frac{\text{number of accidental pregnancies} \times 1200}{\text{total months of use}}$$

(Petersen 1969: 190). Unfortunately, possible generalizations about contraceptive efficiency must be based on data confined largely to the United States, and little can be said about the comparative situation in different societies. Among the more efficient methods (so far as the data go) are the oral pill, IUD, condom, diaphragm, and withdrawal (Petersen 1969: 191). But efficiency also varies depending on the extent to which a household has reached or exceeded the number of children it desires. For households which have achieved desired family size, virtually all methods of contraception are used with considerable efficiency, and differences among methods in efficiency are considerably less than for households which fall short of their family size goals (Ryder and Westoff 1971).

Sociological discussion of the determinants of fertility regulation typically involve three types of considerations—motivation, attitudes,

76

and access. In general, fertility regulation is viewed as varying directly with the degree of motivation, favorableness of attitudes, and extent of access. The motivation for fertility regulation is seen to stem from concerns about having too many children or having them too soon, and leads into discussion of such things as "social norms about what family size ought to be" (Freedman 1961–1962: 35–68) and the appropriate spacing of children. It is at this stage that many of the economist's demand considerations enter the analysis, though in rather different form.

Attitudes toward fertility regulation embrace both very broad notions of the acceptability of family planning in general, as well as feelings about the appropriateness of quite specific practices, such as abortion. In terms of Ronald Freedman's (1961–1962: 35–68) analysis, this subject relates to "social norms about each of the [Davis-Blake] 'intermediate variables.'" The limited practice of voluntary abstinence within marriage reflects the universally high disutility associated with this form of fertility regulation, and illustrates that variations in subjective attitudes toward different methods depend in part on the extent to which use of a method is directly associated with the act of intercourse. One of the arguments for the oral pill as an independent stimulus to greater fertility regulation is that the act of taking the pill is independent of the time of intercourse. Attitudes may also be affected by the reversibility of a method and whether it involves surgical procedures, as in the case of sterilization. Variations in attitudes reflect too the social acceptability of different methods (e.g., induced abortion may be condoned in one society and not in another; among Catholics only the rhythm method of contraception is approved, and so forth).[13] Thus both personal and social conditions enter into the formation of atttiudes toward fertility regulation.

The question of access pertains to the availability (including cost) of contraceptive knowledge and supplies, including abortion services. These are the considerations emphasized by advocates of family planning services when attributing inadequate contraception among, say, the poor, to "lack of access" to effective contraception.

On most of these matters, some survey research evidence is available. Motivation is inferred from statements on the extent to which households "want no more children" or "have more children than they want" (Berelson 1966: 655–668; Freedman 1963: 220–245; Freedman and Takeshita 1969; Mauldin 1965: 1–12). (Another approach that has been

[13] The discussion by Davis and Blake (1956: 211–235) of considerations affecting the relative prevalance of abstinence, contraception, and abortion in less developed societies touches on a number of factors affecting fertility control attitudes.

77

used in demographic analysis is to difference data on total births, adjusted for mortality, and reports on family size desires.) Some comparative data on excess fertility concerns in the period around 1960 have been brought together by Parker Mauldin (1965: 7; see also Nortman 1971: 1–48). The figures are for percentages of persons reporting they do not want more children and cover fourteen countries—eleven in Asia, plus Puerto Rico, Jamaica, and Hungary. Commenting on these data, Mauldin observes: "The most striking thing . . . is the large proportion of people in every society who want to limit family size. This is particularly true for those already having a moderately large family, for example, 4 or more living children. Even in developing countries, typically, two-thirds or more of the persons having 4 or more living children say that they do not wish to have more children" (Mauldin 1965: 6).

Data relevant to attitudes are obtained in response to questions as to whether respondents "approve" or "disapprove" of fertility regulation in general and of each of a number of specified methods of fertility regulation (though such questions suffer from not ascertaining the intensity with which these feelings are held). Since the surveys embrace a variety of methods, and knowledge of different methods varies among societies, it is not easy to generalize about intersocietal differences in attitudes. One might suppose that attitudes toward fertility regulation are more positive in developed societies. Yet inquiries in less developed areas into attitudes toward the idea of family planning typically yield surprisingly favorable responses (Mauldin 1965: 1–12). Moreover, in some developed societies, abortion as a method of fertility regulation is frowned on, and this is perhaps less generally true in lower income societies. At present, the extent of intercountry differences in attitudes must be left an open question. There are, of course, wide differences in the practice of fertility regulation, but this does not necessarily imply corresponding differences in attitudes; attitudes may be equally favorable in two societies, but differences in other factors may lead to greater practice of fertility regulation in one.

With regard to access, surprisingly little comparative evidence on costs is available: the price of condoms and oral pills, the costs involved in fitting a diaphragm or inserting an IUD, or the price of an induced abortion or vasectomy. Family planning programs, of course, typically operate via subsidized or free provision of one or more methods of fertility regulation. It is possible that in some societies induced abortions may be much cheaper (though perhaps riskier) than in others.

In contrast to the situation regarding costs, there is, in the case of knowledge about fertility regulation, a fair amount of information from sociological surveys. In general, the state of knowledge is better in more developed societies, particularly with regard to contraception. "[T]ypically it is assumed, and with reason, that in developed countries almost everyone has some knowledge about birth control methods. . . . In the developing countries when questions about knowledge of contraceptive methods are asked, the numbers of persons giving answers that show they know about contraceptives is often so low that almost any vague answer is accepted as positive information" (Mauldin 1965: 6). On the other hand, it would be a mistake to suppose that there is no knowledge whatsoever of contraception in these societies. Traditional methods such as coitus interruptus are generally assumed to be widely known. The extent to which such practices appear to have been adopted during the demographic transition in now-developed societies supports this assumption.

III

SYNTHESIS

THIS section integrates the economic and sociological analyses of the two preceding parts. The discussion is framed in terms of the individual family, the "representative household," so to speak. The dependent variable is the completed fertility of a married couple. To simplify the exposition, the following assumptions are made: (1) There is only one technique of fertility regulation; (2) prospective parents are not concerned about the spacing of births; (3) there is no child adoption market; (4) no techniques are available for enhancing fertility; and (5) there is no uncertainty about the independent variables over the planning horizon. The quality of children and the work/leisure allocation of time are also taken as given, so that the problem of choice focuses on number of children versus goods for the parents. By the latter is meant how well off the parents themselves can live materially, considerations of children aside. These assumptions and their implications will be taken up subsequently, especially in the concluding section.

The approach adopted is that employed in static economic analysis. Given the values of the basic fertility determinants, the problem is first to determine the equilibrium solution for the number of children (C) and births (B) over the reproductive cycle of the household, and, then, the effect on the equilibrium of changes in the basic determinants. As will be seen, the extent of fertility regulation (R) and the amount of excess fertility (X) are simultaneously determined along with C and B.

The analysis builds on the concepts developed earlier, including

79

formal counterparts of the sociological notions regarding fertility control of motivation, attitudes, and access, just discussed. As is usual in economic analysis, the basic determinants are viewed as relating to the perceptions of the decision makers, and are conceived in an *ex ante* (forward-looking) rather than *ex post* (realized) sense.

Equilibrium determination of C, B, R, and X. We can take as given at any point in time the subjective preferences of the parents for goods and children (their utility function), along with their perceptions of their potential income (Y), the relative price of children (p_c/p_g), the prospects for child survival (s), and their natural fertility (N). In keeping with the economic analysis of fertility, one may draw up an indifference map and budget constraint of the type discussed in connection with Figure 2-1. These are shown in Figure 2-2 as, respectively, the broken line set of indifference curves, I_1, I_2 . . ., and the budget constraint line ef. The shape of the indifference curves would embody "social norms about what family size ought to be," as discussed in the sociological literature (Freedman 1961–1962: 39). To this we now add provision for the production side of fertility behavior, based on the foregoing discussion of the sociology of fertility. This may be done by transforming natural fertility into its counterpart in terms of number of children:

$$C_n = sN, \qquad (5)$$

where C_n is the number of surviving children the parents would have in the absence of any voluntary control of fertility, and s and N are defined in (3) and (4) above.

For example, if N were 12 and two out of three babies survived to adulthood ($s = \frac{2}{3}$), then $C_n = 8$. In Figure 2-2, a vertical line is erected at C_n to represent the parents' perception of the production side of the decision. C_n is therefore a production constraint much like the income constraint represented in the household's budget line.

Before proceeding to the next step, where formal allowance will be made for the factors influencing the adoption of fertility regulation, it is instructive to contrast two equilibrium positions representing opposite extremes. One is the situation in which no fertility regulation is practiced, because, let us suppose, the economic cost is prohibitively high. In this case the equilibrium outcome would be given by the intersection of I_1 and C_n, and parents would have the maximum possible number of children. The other is the case of the "perfect contraceptive" society (Bumpass and Westoff 1970: 1177–1182)—fertility regulation is

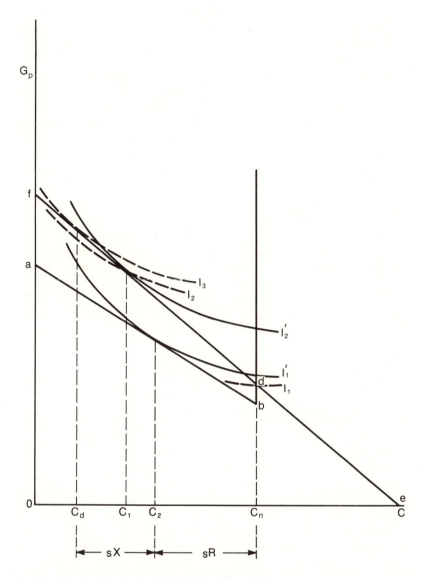

Figure 2-2 An Economic Model of Fertility Determination Incorporating "Output" Variables and Costs of Fertility Control

completely costless, not only as far as market prices are concerned, but also in regard to subjective concerns. Under these circumstances the equilibrium outcome would be C_d, the point at which I_3 is tangent to ef. This value, C_d, probably corresponds roughly to what survey respondents report as "desired family size." Essentially it is the number the children the parents would have if there were no subjective or economic problems involved in regulating fertility. While it is unrealistic to suppose that fertility regulation could ever be completely costless, one can imagine fertility control developments which would progressively reduce the cost to lower and lower levels, with the C_d outcome forming the limiting case.

We are now ready to take explicit account of the considerations influencing the adoption of fertility regulation. The sociologists' concept of motivation is already implicit in the analysis. In terms of economic theory, it is the distance, $C_n - C_d$, the number of unwanted children that parents would have if fertility were unregulated. The consequence of unregulated fertility would be to shift parents downward from the I_3 to I_1 indifference curves in Figure 2–2. It is this prospective loss in welfare attendant upon unwanted children that provides the motivation for regulating fertility. The greater the distance, $C_n - C_d$, the greater the potential loss in welfare, and the higher the motivation for regulating fertility.

Because of obstacles to regulating fertility, it does not follow that parents, even though they have the motivation, would immediately adopt fertility control and go to the equilibrium position, C_d. Let us distinguish, in keeping with the sociological literature, between impediments to fertility regulation deriving from subjective attitudes and those arising from lack of access (inadequate knowledge or high costs).

The subjective costs of fertility regulation, which embody what sociologists term "social norms about . . . the intermediate variables" (Freedman 1961–1962: 39) and are partly captured in their empirical studies of fertility control attitudes, may be conceptualized by rotating the indifference map so that the slope of the indifference curve through any given point is increased (technically, the marginal rate of substitution is raised). The increased slope means that when fertility regulation involves subjective costs, parents will require more goods than before to induce them to have fewer children. This is because having fewer children imposes on parents the psychic costs of fertility control, and an additional goods incentive is now necessary to compensate them for incurring these costs. A simple analytical formulation (analogous to that frequently used by economists in the treatment of embodied technology or inferior quality goods) (Burmeister and Dobell 1971: ch. 3) is

$$U = f(\alpha G_p, C). \qquad (6)$$
$$1 \geq \alpha > 0$$

where α is a summary measure of the disutility attaching to fertility regulation, and

U, G_p, and C are as defined in (1).

If $\alpha = 1$ there is no subjective disutility of fertility regulation and (6) reduces to (1). As α decreases, the subjective disutility of fertility fertility regulation increases, and the indifference map rotates to a position like that shown by the solid I_1', I_2' . . . curves in Figure 2–2. If subjective concerns were the only obstacle to fertility regulation, the equilibrium solution would now be C_1, the tangency of the I_2' curve with ef. Parents would have fewer children than the C_n number of the unregulated situation, but more than the C_d amount they would like if there were no psychic costs of fertility regulation.

The economic costs of fertility regulation embrace the considerations covered in the sociologists' concept of "access." In contrast to the subjective or psychic costs of fertility regulation, which influences the indifference map, the economic costs alter the budget constraint—both by shifting and rotating it. Following Wachter (1972), we may distinguish two types of economic costs—a fixed sum, p_i, representing the outlay initially required to obtain information on how to regulate fertility, and a variable amount, p_b, needed for the actual purchase of supplies or services, including the opportunity cost of the time required to obtain them (for example, loss of wages due to absence from work). The fixed cost, p_i, can be viewed, in effect, as a flat sum reduction in income, and thus a downward parallel shift in the budget constraint. It is represented in Figure 2–2 by the distance db. This amount must be paid if fertility regulation is to be practiced at all, and any equilibrium other than C_n attained. Once this is paid, the maximum goods that can be had with any given number of children is less than before (and correspondingly, for the maximum number of children attainable with any given quantity of goods).

The variable economic costs of fertility regulation have the effect of decreasing the slope of the budget constraint, rotating it counterclockwise about the point b in Figure 2–2. Assuming natural fertility has a fixed positive value, the total variable costs are zero at $C=C_n$, the situation in which no fertility regulation is practiced, and a maximum in the situation of childlessness $(C=0)$. The excess of the vertical distance af at $C=0$ over db at $C=C_n$ represents the total variable cost of fertility regulation necessary to attain childlessness $(C=0)$ and is equal to p_b, the variable cost per child averted, multiplied by C_n, the total number of children averted. When economic costs attach to the practice of fertility regulation, the maximum amount of goods the parents can obtain for themselves is reduced from of to oa. The combination $(G_p=oa, C=0)$ is one extreme on the budget constraint now applicable to the parents' decision. As one moves rightward from this point in Figure 2–2 to combinations involving more and more children (and thus, progressively fewer children averted), the total variable costs of fertility regulation become smaller and the vertical distance separating ab from df correspondingly less. The new budget constraint defining the outer limit of the combinations within financial reach of the household becomes abd and is characterized by a smaller slope than the old budget constraint df.

In sum, in allowing for the economic costs of fertility regulation, the effect of the fixed costs is equivalent to that of a reduction in income, while that of the variable costs is equivalent to a rise in the price of goods. The effect of the variable costs, p_b, thus parallels on the market side that of the disutility of fertility regulation, $\propto$, on the side of subjective preferences. The former raises the economic or market costs of goods, the latter raises the subjective cost of goods.

When account is taken of the fixed and variable costs of fertility regulation, the budget constraint relevant to the parents' decision becomes, formally,

$$Y=p_gG_p+p_cC+p_b(C_n-C)+p_i \qquad (7)$$

where p_i is the fixed (information) cost of fertility regulation ($p_i>0$ for $C<C_n$, and $p_i=0$ for $C=C_n$),

p_b is the variable cost of fertility regulation per child averted, and

the other concepts are as previously defined.

The equilibrium solution, taking account of both the subjective and economic costs of fertility regulation, becomes C_2, the tangency of I_1' with abd. As one might expect, the addition of economic costs of fertility regulation causes parents to have even more children than when there were only subjective costs attaching to fertility regulation, and to be still farther from the desired family size, C_d. The excess of C_2 over C_d is, in effect, the cost parents pay in terms of unwanted children for their reluctance to incur the costs of fertility regulation. The distance $C_1 - C_d$ is the number of unwanted children attributable to subjective costs, and $C_2 - C_1$, to economic costs. The distance between the equilibrium number of children C_2 and the number that would result in the unregulated fertility situation, C_n, is a measure of the scope and effectiveness of the parents' practice of fertility regulation, in terms of the number of children averted.

To this point the dependent variable has been number of children. We can transform these results into births by taking account of the survival rate of babies, as in (3) above. Thus if $C = 4$ and the chance of survival to adulthood is 2 out of 3, six births will be needed. Correspondingly, the measure of unwanted children and of the extent of fertility regulation can be transformed from numbers of children into births. Thus we may define

$$X = \frac{C - C_d}{s}, \text{ and} \qquad (8)$$

$$R = \frac{C_n - C}{s}, \qquad (9)$$

where X is excess fertility, the number of unwanted births,

R is a births averted measure of the scope and efficiency of fertility regulation, and

the other variables are as previously defined.

The graphical representation of these concepts is shown at the foot of Figure 2–2—the distance $C_2 - C_d$ corresponds to sX, and $C_n - C_2$, to sR.

The synthesis is now complete. The basic data are, on the side of subjective attitudes, the utility function for goods and children and the subjective disutility of fertility regulation, $\propto$. These define the two indifference maps, I_1 and I_2 . . . and I_1', I_2'. . . . The budget constraint, if there were no overproduction problem, is ef, and depends on the potential income of the household, Y, and the relative price of children, p_c/p_g. The supply of children if fertility were unregulated is given by natural fertility, N, and the survival rate of infants to adulthood, s. Based on the natural supply of children, the fixed and variable market costs of fertility regulation, p_i and p_b, and the initial budget constraint, a new budget constraint abd is established, which is applicable to the situation of prospective overproduction. The household balances its subjective preferences, including attitudes toward fertility control, against this external constraint to arrive at the equilibrium number of children, C, and, taking account of s, the equilibrium number of births, B. The decision with regard to C establishes at the same time the horizontal distances sX and sR, and, correspondingly, X and R. Unwanted fertility and the practice of fertility regulation, as measured by births averted, are simultaneously determined along with numbers of births and surviving children in the equilibrium outcome. The present analysis thus makes explicit the complementary nature of the economics and sociology of fertility. The sociologist's emphasis on the nature and determinants of fertility regulation (R) by which births are kept below the natural fertility level (N) and the economist's emphasis on the decision to have children, come together to yield as concurrent outcomes of the same forces, the number of children, including unwanted children, and the extent of fertility regulation.

Since the equilibrium situation involves some excess fertility and a correspondingly limited use of fertility regulation, it may seem irrational for households to suffer from unwanted children when the means of birth control are "at hand." But this view fails to take account of the subjective and economic costs that influence the fertility regulation decision. To individuals in a decision-making position, excess fertility is the price that is paid to put off the psychological disquiet and economic costs that are perceived as attending a premature venture into fertility restriction.

One may ask whether it is meaningful to speak of an excess fertility condition prevailing "in equilibrium." Equilibrium means, by definition, that in the absence of change in the underlying determinants, the given outcome will persist through time. In economic theory, an excess supply condition is usually viewed as inconsistent with equilibrium, because it would set in motion corrective market forces that would change the equilibrium outcome. How can one reconcile excess fertility then with an equilibrium condition? The answer is that excess fertility means in this case that there are persons who have unwanted children and who are potential traders with others in an excess demand situation (such as those with problems of sterility and subfecundity). However, there is effectively no market in which those in an excess supply situation can deal with those in a condition of excess demand. A market for baby or child adoption is the one potentially relevant to solving the imbalance. Extension of the present framework to analysis of the adoption market would be possible, and desirable, for the existence of a substantial adoption market would seemingly have profertility consequences. From the viewpoint of explaining real world fertility, however, an adoption market is typically of such limited empirical significance that the most useful working assumption seems to be the present one, namely, that no such market exists. As a result, the usual market adjustment is blocked, and a situation is created in which an excess fertility condition prevails as part of the equilibrium outcome.

The effect of a family planning program. The effect on the equilibrium of changes in the underlying determinants may now be considered. The economic analysis of the effects of changing tastes, incomes, and prices, presented in Figures 1b–1d, would be applicable in the present case as well. The results, however, would be affected by the values of the determinants newly added to the analysis. (For example, the demand curve relating children, C, to their price would be derived in the same way as previously, but shifts in the demand curve would now occur because of changes, not only in Y and the utility function, but also in $\propto$, p_i, p_b, s, and N.) In what follows, the discussion focuses on the effects of the determinants newly added to the analysis. As is customary, the effect of a change in any one determinant will be analyzed on the assumption that all other determinants are held constant.

Family planning programs usually work chiefly in two ways. First, they improve access to the means of fertility regulation by widening and cheapening the provision of various types of fertility regulation and disseminating knowledge about fertility control. Second, they promote more favorable attitudes to the use of fertility regulation by breaking down individual and social taboos. In regard to access, the effect of a new program corresponds to a reduction in the economic costs of fertility regulation, p_i and p_b. Assuming that before the program one were at C_2 in Figure 2–2 and that the program reduced the economic costs to zero, the equilibrium would be shifted from C_2 to C_1. So far as attitudes are concerned, a reduction of subjective costs caused by the program would increase $\propto$, rotating the indifference curves counterclockwise. At the extreme, in which there were no subjective or economic costs, the equilibrium would be that of a "perfect contraceptive" society, C_d, in Figure 2–2.

The effect of a family planning program is thus seen to be to reduce the number of children people have, C, concurrently increasing the practice of fertility regulation, R.[14] As illustrated so far, C_d is unaffected by the program, and the reduction in C takes place at the expense of excess fertility, X, with unwanted children becoming, at the

---

[14] A qualification to this statement is brought out in the subsequent discussion of Figure 2-3.

extreme, zero. This is the predominant view as to how such programs operate, and it is the interpretation stressed by Kingsley Davis (1967: 730–739) in his skeptical appraisal of the ability of family planning programs to solve the "population problem." In terms of our framework, Davis' argument is that family planning programs reduce C by reducing X, but do not make a dent on C_d. Since, according to Davis, existing evidence on family size desires in many less developed countries implies rather high fertility and thus high population growth rates, there is need for policies that would operate also on C_d—his own emphasis appears to be on influencing C_d by raising the relative price of children p_c/p_g.

However, as Davis recognizes, it is not entirely correct to assert that family planning programs have no effect on C_d. Some programs do include as part of their "educational" budget, a component which aims to publicize the desirability of small families. If effective, this would alter utility functions in a way that would lower C_d, thereby increasing $C_n - C_d$, the motivation for fertility regulation. With the supply prices of family planning services given, the rise in motivation would increase R and lower C. Thus C_d would no longer be a fixed floor setting the minimum level to which fertility can fall. In this case, the contrast often drawn between family planning programs, on the one hand, and motivation, on the other, as influences on the adoption of fertility regulation is blurred, since the program affects motivation as well as the supply of services and attitudes toward them. The likely effectiveness of expenditures on motivation is, of course, often questioned (though adequate research is lacking), and in practice the bulk of family planning expenditure is actually focused, not on family size attitudes (C_d), but on the provision of family planning services (working through p_i and p_b) and attitudes toward fertility control ($\propto$).

The effect of an innovation in fertility regulation. A new method of fertility control such as the oral pill or IUD would affect fertility along the lines typically attributed to a family planning program, and therefore requires only brief mention. By providing new information about fertility regulation or through its impact on outlays directly needed for fertility control, a new method would reduce p_i, p_b, or both. Also, a new method may in various ways influence subjective attitudes, raising $\propto$. It provides a new option to the public that may meet objections to current methods (for example, by separating the act of fertility control from that of intercourse). It also increases general publicity about fertility control, and may make for a reassessment of some of the existing methods.[15] With the state of motivation ($C_n - C_d$) given, a new

[15] A somewhat related phenomenon is the effect of experience with one method

method, through one or more of these channels, would tend to increase the extent and/or efficiency of fertility regulation, R, and correspondingly lower both actual and excess fertility, B and X.

Ordinarily, one would expect a new method not to alter family size desires, C_d, but simply to make it easier for parents to come closer to realizing those desires by avoiding unwanted children. In a recent paper, however, Larry L. Bumpass argues that the oral pill and more recent fertility control innovations in the United States are likely to affect family size norms (1973: 67–69). He argues that for the typical American woman, motherhood is no longer inevitable, because of the greatly increased efficiency of fertility regulation. She is thus free as never before to consider childlessness as a realistic possibility, and hence is more likely to choose this course. This argument provides an example of how an innovation in fertility regulation might alter C_d by shifting the utility function in a manner unfavorable to children.

The demand curve for fertility regulation. The relation between the price of fertility regulation, p_b, and its use, R, may be formalized in terms of a demand curve, following procedures analogous to those used in deriving the demand curve for children. A reduction in p_b increases the slope of the budget constraint ab in Figure 2–2. The result is to shift the equilibrium position leftward, reducing C and X, and correspondingly increasing R. Holding the other determinants constant, one may thus generate a series of observations on p_b and R, measured in births averted, by rotating the ab curve clockwise. This yields a demand curve of the typical negatively sloping type, showing that the consumption of fertility control would increase, other things being held constant, as the price of fertility control declined. In principle, one may calculate from this a price elasticity of demand for fertility regulation. One may also conceive of shifts in the demand curve for fertility regulation, arising from changes in the other determinants. For example, more favorable attitudes toward fertility regulation (an increase in $\propto$), would lead to greater consumption of fertility regulation at any given price, shifting the demand curve to the right. A similar result would follow from an increase in the motivation for fertility control, $C_n - C_d$, due to changes in one or more of the factors lying behind either C_n or C_d. To the extent that a family planning program or innovation in fertility regulation cheapened the direct outlays required per child

---

in causing more favorable attitudes toward others. It is frequently reported, for example, that women who give up the IUD tend not to abandon fertility regulation, but to switch to another method. This could be due in part to reduced reluctance, as a result of the actual experience of fertility regulation, to try a method which was formerly resisted.

averted (that is, lowered p_b), consumption of fertility regulation would be increased by a downward movement along the demand curve. To the extent these developments resulted in more favorable attitudes or increased motivation they would shift the demand curve to the right, increasing consumption at any given price.

The effect of an increase in natural fertility. So far the analysis has implicitly assumed that the number of children in a natural fertility regime would exceed the number desired; that is, C_n would be greater than C_d. Brief reference was made, however, to the possibility that because of sterility or subfecundity, a household might be unable to realize its family size desires. This situation of "excess demand," that is, more children wanted than can be produced, might actually typify a society if there were a high incidence of involuntary sterility due, for example, to venereal disease. Very high family size desires would also enhance the possibility of an excess demand condition. In considering the effect of variations in natural fertility on the equilibrium outcome, it is instructive to start with a situation in which the number of children that would be produced if fertility were unregulated falls short of the number desired. To simplify the graphical presentation, it will be assumed throughout this section that there are only economic costs of fertility regulation, and no subjective costs (that is, that $\alpha = 1$).

Figure 2–3a shows the effect of excess demand conditions. Let us suppose that initially the number of children, if fertility were unregulated, would be C_{n_1}, less than the desired number C_d yielded by the tangency of the I_2 indifference curve and the budget constraint, ef. In this situation the best the household can do is have C_{n_1} children, which will put it on the I_1 indifference curve. Any smaller number of children would leave the household on a lower indifference curve, making it even worse off. Any larger number of children up to C_d would increase the household's welfare, but it is unable to reach such positions because it cannot produce any more than C_{n_1}. The situation shown is analogous to that of the effects of rationing, which forces households to accept welfare positions inferior to the free market solution.

In this situation there is no point to modifying the budget constraint for the economic costs of fertility regulation, since there is no motivation for the household to reduce fertility. On the contrary, the situation shown is one which would lead to a demand for ways of raising fertility or to adopt children. To the extent such options existed they would raise the equilibrium outcome, but they are disregarded in the present analysis on the grounds that they are typically quantitatively unimportant. This situation illustrates the one described by Tabbarah where a family planning program would meet with no response be-

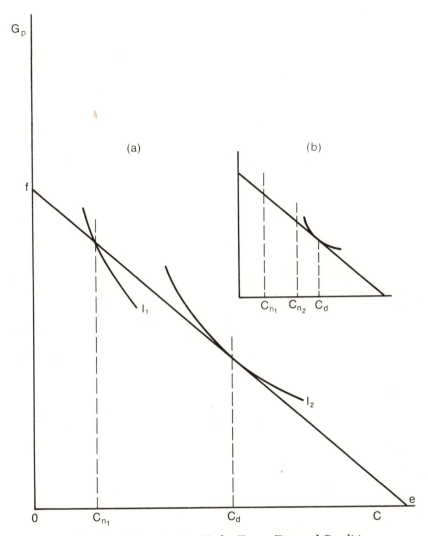

Figure 2–3 Fertility Determination Under Excess Demand Conditions

cause of lack of motivation (1971: 274; see also Tabbarah 1964: 187–196). Surveys might find attitudes seemingly favorable to the idea of family planning and even actual knowledge of a method, but no practice. Obviously, positive motivation (C_n greater than C_d) is a necessary (but not sufficient) condition for a family planning program to be effective.

Formally, the equilibrium outcome for the situation where $C_n < C_d$

91

is given by:

$$C = C_n = sN, \text{ and} \qquad (10)$$

$$B = \frac{C}{s} = N. \qquad (11)$$

Note that in this case the birth rate is the same as the natural fertility rate.

Variations in natural fertility will produce corresponding changes in C and B, as long as C_n remains less than C_d. For example, as shown in Figure 2–3b, if increased natural fertility shifts C_{n_1} to C_{n_2}, then the equilibrium number of children will change in the same way, and births will move proportionately, the exact numerical change in B depending on the value of s. Moreover, the effect of changes in the variables of income, prices, and tastes which operate through C_d by shifting the budget constraint or indifference map is uncertain. If C_d continues to be greater than C_n after these variables change, then fertility will remain unaffected. It is only when C_d falls below C_n that changes on the demand side will tend to influence C. Even in this case, whether C will be affected depends on the magnitude of the excess of C_n over C_d, and the costs of fertility regulation. However, the conclusion that fertility may be unaffected by movements in the budget constraint depends upon the C_n function being a vertical line of the type shown in Figure 2–3. Subsequently, in applying the framework to premodern fertility, a more realistic form of the C_n function is recognized, where changes in the budget constraint do affect observed fertility (see Figure 2–5).

To return to Figure 2–3b, let us imagine that C_n continues to rise beyond C_{n_2}, with the other fertility determinants remaining unchanged, until it reaches a level greater than the desired number of children, C_d. We have now shifted from an excess demand to an excess supply situation—if fertility were unregulated, the number of children would exceed the number desired. Under these circumstances, will measures necessarily be taken to regulate fertility?

The answer to this question is no. Whether fertility control will voluntarily be adopted depends, on the one hand, on the strength of the motivation (the excess of C_n over C_d), and, on the other, on the costs of fertility regulation. The lower the motivation and the higher the costs, the less likely it is that fertility control will be adopted in an excess supply situation.

Figure 2–4 illustrates two possibilities—one in which regulation is

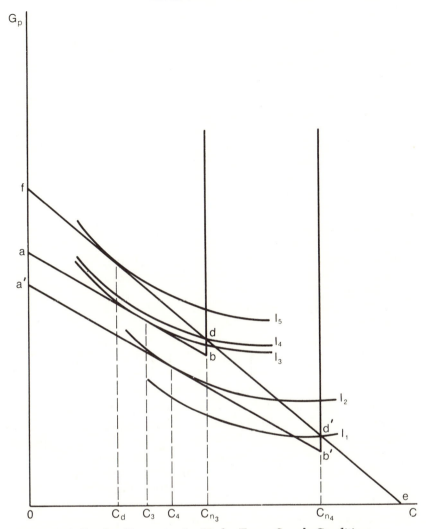

Figure 2–4 Fertility Determination Under Excess Supply Conditions

not adopted, even though C_n is greater than C_d, and one in which it is. The nonadoption case is that in which natural fertility would produce C_{n_3} children. Because motivation for fertility regulation exists, the relevant budget constraint is abd, as in Figure 2–2. This budget constraint is tangent to the I_3 indifference curve at C_3 children. This is the best situation attainable for the household if it regulates fertility. The household has the option, however, of not controlling fertility at all, in which case it would have a larger number of children, C_{n_3}, and end up on the I_4 indifference curve. The latter represents a more satisfactory welfare situation than the I_3 curve, and hence would be preferred by the household. Thus the existence of motivation for fertility regulation is logically consistent with nonadoption. Even though unwanted children reduce the household's welfare (thereby providing motivation for fertility regulation), the costs of regulating fertility may be so great that adoption of fertility control would leave the household even worse off, despite the fact that it would have fewer children. In the present case, the costs are by assumption wholly economic costs. The existence of subjective costs would provide an additional offset to the motivation to adopt fertility control.

If C_n continues to rise, with the other fertility determinants unchanged, we can imagine a situation emerging in which natural fertility would produce C_{n_4} children, and the relevant budget constraint is a'b'd'. In this situation the household's best outcome, if fertility were regulated, is C_4 children. This would place the household on the I_2 indifference curve, a position superior to the outcome under unregulated fertility, C_{n_4}, which would put the household on the I_1 indifference curve. The prospective overproduction of children is now so great as to portend a loss in welfare exceeding that associated with the costs of fertility regulation—the motivation to control fertility exceeds its costs. The equilibrium solution becomes C_4 children, less, not only than C_{n_4}, but even than the C_{n_3} outcome of the previous natural fertility situation.[16]

Reviewing the successive equilibrium solutions as natural fertility increases so that the potential output of children grows from C_{n_1} to C_{n_4}, other things constant, one observes the following. At first, the equilibrium number of children would increase, but beyond some point fertility control would be induced and the equilibrium number would fall. The rise in natural fertility is thus partly self-correcting. As long as an excess demand condition exists, the rise in natural fertility results in a corresponding increase in the equilibrium fertility rate. As natural fertility continues to rise, however, a potential excess supply of children develops and eventually mounts to a point at which the motivation to regulate fertility outweighs its costs.

Note that the correct measure of the motivation to regulate fertility is $C_n - C_d$, the number of unwanted children the household would have

[16] The C_n function can not intersect the X-axis to the right of point e, since this would imply that parents with no goods for themselves would be able to produce children. A representation of the C_n function which takes account of this appears subsequently in Figure 2-5.

94

if fertility were unregulated, not $C - C_d$, the number of unwanted children the household actually has. The latter is the excess fertility measure typically reported in population surveys. In Figure 2–4 the motivation to adopt fertility regulation is greater in the C_{n_4} than in the C_{n_3} situation, and this is correctly reflected in a $C_n - C_d$ measure. A measure of how many unwanted children people actually have would incorrectly imply lower motivation in the C_{n_4} situation ($C_4 - C_d$ is less than $C_{n_3} - C_d$).

The point at which fertility control is induced as C_n continues to increase might be thought of as a "threshold," separating the unregulated from the regulated fertility situation (Kirk 1971: 123–147; United Nations Department of Economic and Social Affairs 1965). However, different combinations of the basic fertility determinants might establish the same threshold. For example, high natural fertility and a high C_d due, say, to a low relative price of children, might yield the same $C_n - C_d$ threshold as low natural fertility and a low C_d due to a high relative price of children. There is no particular value of a fertility determinant, therefore, which necessarily corresponds to the threshold situation from one society to another—the threshold situation depends on how any one determinant combines with the others to establish the value of $C_n - C_d$.

One can see too how the values of the costs of fertility regulation ($\propto$, p_i, and p_b) would affect the threshold level. The more nearly a society's initial conditions approach a perfect contraceptive society the sooner would adoption of fertility regulation occur as potential excess fertility ($C_n - C_d$) mounted, and the lower would be the actual values of excess fertility (X) that occurred. In contrast, suppose a society were initially in an excess demand situation with no extant practice and high costs of voluntary fertility regulation. If a rise in C_n were to shift such a society from an excess demand to excess supply situation, adoption of fertility regulation would occur more slowly than in the preceding case. One argument for family planning programs is that the introduction of such services in this situation would result in more rapid adoption of fertility regulation by lowering costs, and correspondingly yield lower observed values of C and X. The rise of C_n above C_d would create a demand for fertility regulation, which the introduction of family planning services would aim to satisfy.

This analysis also brings out the possibility of interdependence between the N and R variables of the sociology of fertility. A change in R—that is, the adoption of fertility regulation—is in the case illustrated in Figure 2–4 caused by a change in N. As a result, an increase

95

in natural fertility, rather than raising observed fertility as would be predicted if the possibility of interdependence were overlooked, may actually lower it by inducing the adoption of fertility control.

The effect of an increase in the probability of survival to adulthood. The foregoing discussion of the effect of a change in natural fertility is also relevant to that of an improvement in mortality conditions. The immediate factor through which a change in natural fertility exercised its effect was C_n. The shifts in C_n that were analyzed in Figures 2–3 and 2–4 could have been due to an increase in s as well as to an increase in N. The argument then would be that in an increase in the probability of survival to adulthood occurring under excess demand conditions would raise the equilibrium value of C. However, as the increase continued and excess supply conditions emerged, a threshold would eventually be crossed, beyond which fertility regulation would be induced and C would decline.

There is one respect, however, in which the effect of a change in s differs from that of a change in N or, indeed, in any of the other fertility determinants. Because s enters the analysis not only as a component of C_n (equation 5) but also as the link between C and B (equation 3), a change in s does not have the same proportionate effect on C and B, as do the other determinants.

A numerical example based on the analysis of the preceding section may illustrate the point. Suppose that N increases from 4 to 16, while all other fertility determinants (including s) are constant. If one assumes a shift from the excess demand to excess supply condition following the sequence in Figure 2–3 and 2–4, the course which C and B might follow would be as follows:

	(1)	(2)	(3) C_n (1)×(2)	(4)	(5)	(6) B (5)÷(1)
	s	N		C_d	C	
C_{n_1}	.5	4	2	4	2	4
C_{n_2}	.5	8	4	4	4	8
C_{n_3}	.5	12	6	4	6	12
C_{n_4}	.5	16	8	4	5	10

Note that C and B move up and down in the same proportion.

Now let us imagine that s increases in a way that produces the same sequence of C_n values, while the other fertility determinants (including N) remain unchanged. In this situation one would expect the successive equilibrium values of C to be the same as previously, as shown below:

	(1)	(2)	(3)	(4)	(5)	(6)
			C_n			B
	s	N	$(1)\times(2)$	C_d	C	$(5)\div(1)$
C_{n_1}	.20	10	2	4	2	10
C_{n_2}	.40	10	4	4	4	10
C_{n_3}	.60	10	6	4	6	10
C_{n_4}	.80	10	8	4	5	6.3

Both columns 3 and 5 are the same in the two cases. However, column 6 is noticeably different. As shown in the first two lines, in a situation of excess demand and consequently unregulated fertility, a rise in survival rates would increase C, thus narrowing the shortfall of actual children compared with the desired number of children, but would not alter the birth rate. Furthermore, an increase in the survival rate which pushed the household across the adoption threshold (lines 3 and 4) would result in a larger proportionate decline in B than C. This is because the downward pressure which the increase in s exerts on C through raising motivation (increasing $C_n - C_d$) is, in the case of B, further enhanced by the fact that the increase in s reduces the number of births needed to achieve any given number of children. Thus, while s and N tend to have the same effects on C, they influence B somewhat differently. In an excess demand situation, an increase in natural fertility leads to a rise in both C and B, but an increase in s leads only to a rise in C, and not in B. As the situation changes to one of excess supply, increases in N and s operate to induce declines in both C and B, but the effect of s on B is greater.

Sometimes public programs to improve health and mortality conditions are viewed as aggravating the "population problem" and draining resources that might otherwise go into family planning programs to reduce fertility.[17] The present analysis brings out the complementary nature of health and family planning programs. On the one hand, health programs, by shifting households into an excess supply situation, create the motivation for fertility regulation, without which a family planning program would be ineffective. On the other hand, as was pointed out earlier, given the motivation, fertility regulation is likely to be more rapidly adopted if family planning services are present, lowering the costs of fertility control.

A problem in explaining recent declines in fertility in places such as Taiwan and Korea is to determine how much family planning programs have actually contributed to the fertility decline vis-a-vis other factors, such as an increase in s, which have raised the motivation for fertility

[17] See the discussion of this issue in (Taylor 1968: 4).

regulation (Freedman and Takeshita 1969). A similar issue is posed by Gösta Carlsson in his well-known article on the historical experience of Sweden, "The Decline of Fertility: Innovation or Adjustment Process?" (1966: 149–174). The "adjustment process" which Carlsson has in mind is the response that occurs when a drop in infant mortality pushes households across (or further to the right of) a fertility control threshold as in Figure 2–4. He contrasts this with an explanation of the fertility decline in terms of "innovation," presumably in methods of fertility regulation—in our terms, of changes in p_i, p_b, or $\propto$. Carlsson argues that the evidence for Sweden favors an interpretation of that country's fertility decline as an adjustment process resulting from an increase in s, rather than one arising from an innovation on the side of fertility regulation.

Summary. Table 2–2 brings together the relationships developed in this part, and lists the definitions of the concepts, the empirical counterparts of which were indicated in the two preceding parts. As has been seen, determination of the equilibrium values of C and B differs according to whether C_n is greater than C_d (an excess supply situation), or is less (an excess demand situation), and the table is divided accordingly. The absence of demand equations for the excess demand case in panel II does not mean that demand conditions are irrelevant. The value of C_d, which together with C_n, establishes whether the situation is one of excess demand or supply, depends upon demand considerations. Moreover, as will be seen shortly in the discussion of premodern fertility, if a more realistic shape of the C_n function is recognized, the budget constraint plays a more important role than panel II suggests.

IV

Application to Interpretation of Premodern and Modern Fertility

So far we have considered the theoretical effects of a one-time change in a given fertility determinant on observed fertility, all other factors held constant. Real world problems of fertility explanation rarely involve only one fertility determinant. Rather they reflect the concurrent operation of a number of factors sometimes working in opposing directions on fertility. In this section, the theoretical analysis is further illustrated by applying it to the interpretation of premodern fertility and the transition to modern fertility levels. An important implication of the analysis is that the dominant factors in fertility explanation may be different in premodern and modern circumstances.

98

Table 2-2. Summary of Basic Relationships and Concepts

	Reference
I. $C > C_d$	
$U = f(\alpha\, G_p, C) \qquad 1 \gtreqless \alpha > 0$	Eq. (6)
$Y = p_g\, G_p + p_c\, C + p_b\,(C_n - C) + p_i$	Eq. (7)
where $p_i = 0$ for $C = C_n$	
$\qquad\quad p_i = k > 0$ for $C < C_n$	
$C_n = sN$	Eq. (5)
$B = \dfrac{C}{s}$	Eq. (3)
$R \equiv N\text{-}B = \dfrac{C_n - C}{s}$	Eq. (4), (9)
$C_d = C$ for $\alpha = 1,\ p_i = p_b = 0$	text
$X = \dfrac{C - C_d}{s}$	Eq. (8)
II. For $C \gtreqless C_d$	
$C = C_n = sN$	Eq. (10)
$B = \dfrac{C}{s} = N$	Eq. (11)

III. Concepts

U is the utility of the parents;

C is the cumulative number of children surviving to adulthood;

G_p is the number of goods consumed by the parents over their lifetime;

α is a summary measure of the disutility attached to the principle of fertility regulation, in general, and to specific regulatory practices;

Y is the potential income of the household;

p_g and p_c are the prices of goods and children, respectively;

p_i is the fixed (information) cost of fertility regulation;

p_b is the variable cost of fertility regulation per child averted;

N is natural fertility, the number of live births that would occur in the absence of any voluntary control of fertility;

s is the probability of survival of a live birth to the age of 20;

C_n is the number of surviving children the parents would have in the absence of any voluntary control of fertility;

B is the cumulative number of births;

R is the scope and efficiency of fertility regulation, measured in terms of births averted;

C_d is the desired number of surviving children in a perfect contraceptive society;

X is excess fertility, the excess of the actual number of births over the desired number.

99

In the present exposition, for simplicity, primary attention will be given to C, the number of surviving children, as the dependent variable. The fertility determinants are grouped into three sets—those affecting C_n, the number of surviving children parents would have in an unregulated fertility regime; those affecting C_d, the desired number of children in a perfect contraceptive society; and those affecting the costs of fertility regulation, both subjective and market. A critical issue is whether C_n exceeds C_d; that is, whether there is a prospect of unwanted children and hence a motivation to regulate fertility.

Premodern fertility. As one reads through the literature on fertility in premodern societies, the impression grows that in many of these societies there is little evidence of the conscious practice by the population of methods to limit family size (Henry 1961b: 81–91; Lapham and Mauldin 1972: 29–52; Mauldin 1965: 1–12; Nag 1968; Srinivasan 1972). This does not mean that fertility is at its biological maximum; on the contrary, there are usually various practices that have the latent or indirect function of regulating fertility. But from the viewpoint of the individual these practices are not motivated by concern about family size. In these societies both mortality and fertility are high and fluctuate widely. Under these circumstances, the primary concern of the typical household regarding reproduction is whether it will be able to have as many children as it wants, not whether it will have too many. Surveys of attitudes toward family size in Africa, for example, frequently show preferences for larger families than those actually realized (Caldwell 1968; Pool 1970: 12–17).

In terms of the present analytical framework, the situation tends toward that illustrated in Figure 2–3. The household is unsure whether the potential output of surviving children, C_n, will be equal to the number desired, C_d, and its situation thus approximates one of excess demand rather than of excess supply. There is little or no motivation to limit fertility; rather, the primary interest (the "rational" concern) in regard to family size may be in ways of raising fertility. Under these conditions, completed family size will depend on potential output, C_n, and will vary with changes in the underlying determinants of C_n. To the extent this is so, the explanation of premodern fertility movements and differentials calls for inquiry primarily along the lines followed by sociologists and other students of the social and biological determinants of natural fertility.

Consider, for example, the striking fertility differentials in Africa, mentioned at the start of this chapter. One factor which has gained prominence as an important cause is the differential incidence of veneral disease and associated sexual promiscuity. For example,

100

Romaniuk concludes from a study of the data for districts of the Congo: ". . . [T]he evidence points definitely to the existence of a sequence of events one would logically expect to occur. The birth rate is low because of the high incidence of sterility; the latter is caused by venereal disease, the incidence of which varies with the degree of sexual promiscuity" (Romaniuk 1968: 214–224; see also 1968: 241–339). If this is correct, we see here an illustration of a fertility differential ascribable to the natural fertility variable, N.

Another example of the real world influence of natural fertility conditions is provided by Knodel's study of three parishes of Bavaria in the late nineteenth century (1968: 297–318). In this case differences in natural fertility arise, among other things, from differences in the practice of lactation. In a parish where breast-feeding is practiced, the fertility of women who marry young is lower than in the two parishes where there is little resort to breast-feeding. There is no evidence that differences in lactation are due to differences in the desire to regulate fertility. Rather, differences in the use of lactation appear to have their roots in cultural traditions passed on from one generation to the next.[18]

In discussing Figure 2–3, it was pointed out that if C_d exceeds C_n and the C_n function is a vertical line, then variations in the taste, price, and income determinants emphasized in the theory of household choice would not affect fertility behavior. However, it is unrealistic to suppose that C_n is unaffected by the parents' living level, as is implied by a vertical C_n function. A more plausible shape is shown in Figure 2–5. The C_{n_1} function in this figure implies that below some minimum level of parents' consumption, natural fertility would be zero.[19] Starvation conditions, for example, would drastically lower frequency of intercourse and heighten the likelihood of spontaneous abortion if conception did occur. As the parents' living conditions improved from very low levels, natural fertility would progressively increase, though the increments would become gradually less until eventually a point were reached at which further living level changes left natural fertility unaffected. This is the relationship portrayed by the C_{n_1} curve of Figure 2–5. Starting with a positive intercept on the Y-axis, it shows an initial positive relation between C_n and G_p, but eventually reaches a vertical phase in which C_n is unaffected by further advances in G_p.

Given the C_{n_1} function, observed fertility would then depend on the

[18] Cutright's analysis (1972: 24–31) of the uptrend in United States teen-age illegitimacy since 1940, discussed in the next part, provides an example of the possible operation of natural fertility factors in contemporary America.

[19] For simplicity, the present discussion is couched in terms of the natural fertility variable, N, rather than C_n, with the infant survival rate, by implication assumed constant.

101

position of the budget constraint, as shown by the ef and e'f' lines in Figure 2–5. Formally, the determination of completed family size would depend on two relationships:

the natural fertility function, $C = f(G_p)$,

and the budget constraint, $Y = p_g G_p + p_c C$.

The budget constraint is written in the form given in (1) above rather than (7), because fertility control costs are irrelevant in an excess demand situation. Given the income and price parameters, one may solve for the values of G_p, the parents' living level, and C, completed family size. Changes in the income or price parameters would change completed family size—an increase in income or a reduction in the cost of children, other things being constant, would increase observed natural fertility and completed family size. A change in tastes would not affect fertility unless C_d fell below C_n.

The budget constraint and C_n function of Figure 2–5 would produce a positive income-fertility relationship. However, this relationship and the underlying mechanisms differ from that discussed in the usual economic analysis of fertility behavior. The usual relationship relates to how many children people want and is shown by the dotted line "expansion path" in Figure 2–5, which traces the course of the tangencies between the budget constraint as income rises and the (given) indifference map. In contrast, the present relationship relates to how many children a household can produce and reflects the effect of income, not on the demand for children, but on the potential supply. Failure to recognize this could lead to a mistaken interpretation of an observed income-fertility association as a demand relation (the expansion path) rather than a supply relation (the C_n function). In the supply case, the underlying mechanisms are such things as the effect of nutrition on reproductive capacity or the operation of the social custom of young wives returning to their parents' home when "times are hard." Similar supply circumstances might underlie a positive association between income and fertility at a point in time within a premodern society. To cite one such possibility, higher income may be associated with greater reliance on "wet nursing." As a result, the typical higher income wife would have a shorter period of temporary sterility and higher natural fertility, giving rise to the observed positive association. Clearly, while it is important to establish the nature of the empirical association between income and fertility, as Ronald Lee does in the present volume, it is also desirable to ascertain the mechanism re-

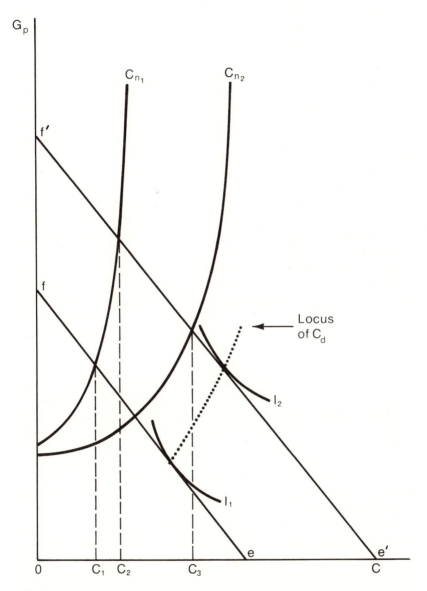

Figure 2–5 "Output" Compared With "Demand" Interpretation of a Positive Income-Fertility Relationship

sponsible for it. If it is the demand mechanism emphasized in the economic analysis of household behavior, then there is an implicit demand for fertility regulation, whereas, if it is a supply mechanism, there is no such implicit demand.

The attention given in the last few paragraphs to the income-fertility relationship in premodern societies is not intended to imply that income or, more generally, a society's economic condition, is the only or even predominant factor determining natural fertility. As is clear from the earlier discussion of natural fertility, there are many factors potentially relevant. In Figure 2–5 the effect of such factors would be reflected in shifts in the C_n function. For example, given the e'f' budget constraint, a shift from C_{n_1} to C_{n_2} due, for example, to better health resulting from new medical knowledge, would raise fertility from C_2 to C_3. Observed behavior can thus be thought of as a composite of shifts in the C_n function, on the one hand, and movements along the C_n function due to changes in income or prices, on the other. In either case observed fertility would correspond to natural fertility, and the primary task of research would be to determine the factors underlying changes in natural fertility, economic or noneconomic. While a more realistic treatment of the C_n function leads to recognition of fertility movements due to changes in the budget constraint, the original conclusions still hold about the importance of research on natural fertility in premodern societies and the difference from modern societies in the process of fertility determination.

The present discussion has focused upon the typical household, that representative of the mass of the population. At any given time there would be differences among individuals and groups in a society in the demand and supply situation regarding children. A high status group, for example, might be in a position of excess supply, while the bulk of the population were in a situation of excess demand. The present suggestion that conditions in premodern societies tend in an excess demand direction applies, of course, primarily to the situation of the population in general.

The shift to modern fertility levels. The leading extant interpretation of the shift from high to low fertility in modernizing societies is the theory of the demographic transition (Notestein 1953; for recent evaluations, see Coale 1973; Durand 1967: 32–45). In this scheme, a shift to low fertility follows with a lag a similar shift to low mortality levels, and is associated in a general way with the process of urbanization and industrialization.

The present framework suggests a more comprehensive view of the factors influencing the movement to lower fertility levels. In this inter-

104

pretation, the demographic transition model appears as one of various possible real world patterns. The emphasis here is on the numerous possible channels through which the process of modernization may shift the representative household from a situation under premodern circumstances approximating an excess demand for children to one in a modern society of excess supply. This shift engenders within the household a new type of concern in regard to reproduction, that of limiting numbers, and a corresponding motivation to regulate fertility.

The presentation below first sketches various hypothetical ways in which the motivation for fertility regulation might emerge in the course of modernization, and illustrates the interaction to determine completed family size of the three sets of fertility determinants mentioned above—those affecting C_n, C_d, and the costs of fertility regulation. It then states more fully the nature of modernization and develops explicitly a number of possible channels through which modernization principally impinges on reproductive behavior. Finally, mention is made of the way in which the principal determinants may vary from one real world situation to another.

Figure 2–6 charts some hypothetical trends during modernization in the equilibrium values of C_n, C_d, and other variables, as determined in the manner described in the preceding part.[20] In the figure the solid C_d curves refer to the desired number of surviving children of the representative household in a perfect contraceptive society, as determined by tastes, prices, and income; the broken line C_n curves, to the number that parents would have in a natural fertility regime, as a result of the underlying biological and cultural determinants, and the state of infant and child mortality; and the dotted C curves to the actual number of surviving children. In all of the diagrams, the progress of economic and social modernization is assumed to be correlated with time, and corresponds to a rightward movement along the X-axis. The diagrams represent only the general nature of the possible relationship during modernization; no implication is intended regarding specific magnitudes.

As we have seen, the motivation for fertility regulation varies directly with the algebraic difference between the number of children parents would have in a natural fertility situation and the number they would like to have if fertility regulation were costless, in effect, on the prospective number of unwanted children, the excess of C_n over C_d. In the upper panel of Figure 2–6, this is shown by the solid line at the bottom of each diagram; in the lower panel this line has been omitted

[20] I owe the idea for this form of presentation to Riad Tabbarah (1971: 257–277), who used a chart similar to Figure 6c in a seminar presentation of his analysis.

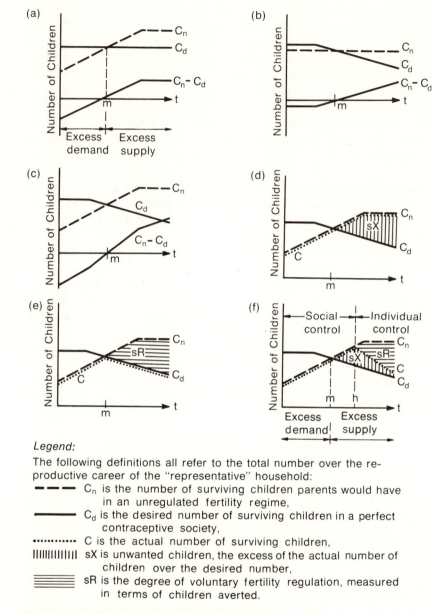

Legend:

The following definitions all refer to the total number over the reproductive career of the "representative" household:

▬ ▬ ▬ C_n is the number of surviving children parents would have in an unregulated fertility regime,

▬▬▬ C_d is the desired number of surviving children in a perfect contraceptive society,

•••••••••• C is the actual number of surviving children,

|||||||||||| sX is unwanted children, the excess of the actual number of children over the desired number,

≡≡≡ sR is the degree of voluntary fertility regulation, measured in terms of children averted.

Figure 2–6 Hypothetical Trends in Fertility Variables Associated with Economic and Social Modernization

to simplify the presentation—the applicable one in Figures 2–6d–2–6f is that shown in Figure 2–6c. In all of the diagrams in Figure 2–6, the initial situation, that on the Y-axis, is one in which there is no motivation for fertility regulation, because parents are unable to produce as many children as they would like to have. More generally, all positions to the left of point m are excess demand situations. In these circumstances there would be a demand, not for ways of reducing fertility, but of raising it, and also for children to adopt. This representation is thus generally in keeping with the premodern circumstances just discussed, but it is, of course, vastly over-simplified. For example, a more realistic diagram might show C_n fluctuating widely in premodern conditions and the early stages of modernization, and then trending upward as the fluctuations dampen. The average level of C_n might even exceed C_d, but because of the sharp fluctuations in C_n there would be sufficiently frequent intervals of deficient output of children to create a general state of uncertainty among the bulk of the population as to the likelihood of realizing desired family size.

Figures 2–6a–2–6c illustrate alternative ways in which the motivation to regulate fertility might emerge and grow in the course of modernization, causing the $C_n - C_d$ curve to cross the X-axis and move upward to the right. Figure 2–6a shows a situation in which the moving force is a rise in natural fertility (due, for example, to improved health of mothers), while desired family size remains constant. Figure 6b illustrates the contrasting situation in which C_n is constant but desired family size shifts from above to below C_n (as a result, for example, of an increase in the relative cost of children), leading to the appearance of unwanted children. Figure 6c shows a shift from excess demand to excess supply conditions due to changes in both C_n and C_d.

As has been noted, while motivation is a necessary condition for fertility regulation, it is not a sufficient condition. Whether in a given excess supply situation fertility control will actually be used depends on the strength of the motivation compared with the subjective and market costs of fertility regulation. Figures 2–6d and 2–6e illustrate the two extremes with regard to costs of fertility control. In both diagrams, to the left of point m parents are not able to have as many children as they would like to have. As a result, in this range the actual number of children they have, shown by the dotted C line, is equal to the maximum amount they can produce, as indicated by the C_n curve, and rises as potential supply increases. We have here the premodern circumstances of fertility determination described above. As one moves to the right of point m in both diagrams, a problem of unwanted children emerges, creating the motivation to regulate fertility. In Figure

107

2–6d, it is assumed that the costs of fertility regulation are prohibitive. Thus the actual number of children continues to follow the potential output curve, C_n, and unwanted children increase. The number of unwanted children is shown by the vertical distance between C and C_d, marked sX. Figure 2–6e, on the other hand, represents the perfect contraceptive society—subjective and market costs of fertility regulation are zero. As soon as the motivation to regulate fertility occurs, parents immediately do so. The actual number of children falls short of the maximum possible, and follows the C_d curve, turning downward in the case shown. The extent of fertility regulation, measured in children averted, is shown by the vertical sR distance between C_n and C.

In any real world situation, fertility control costs would be neither zero nor prohibitive. The likely course of the actual number of children for a given level of fertility costs is shown in Figure 2–6f. Initially as the potential output curve, C_n, edges above the desired number of children, C_d, to the right of point m, the motivation to regulate fertility is not great enough to offset the costs, and the actual number of children continues to be governed by the C_n curve, with unwanted children increasing as shown by sX. As the rightward movement continues, however, a point is reached at which the loss in welfare due to unwanted children begins to exceed that associated with the costs of fertility regulation. In effect, a threshold of fertility regulation as discussed in connection with Figure 2–4 above is reached. This threshold is labeled h in the diagram. Fertility control is introduced and the C curve turns downward in the direction of the C_d curve, with fertility regulation practiced to the extent shown by the vertical distance sR. As long as costs of fertility control are positive, however, there will continue to be some unwanted children, indicated by sX. Given the C_n and C_d curves, the effect of a reduction in the costs of fertility regulation would be to shift point h leftward, and for any given excess of C_n over C_d, to reduce unwanted childen, sX, and increase the amount of fertility regulation, sR.

Links between modernization and the principal fertility determinants. We have, then, a general representation of the manner in which fertility regulation as a common practice may emerge in the course of modernization, and the way in which the principal fertility determinants interact. But what are the specific modernization developments affecting C_n, C_d, and the costs of fertility regulation?

Modernization, as used here, refers to the transformation in economic, social, and political organization and in human personality observed in a growing number of nations chiefly, but not exclusively, in the West, since the mid-18th century (Coleman 1968: 395–402; Easterlin 1968a: 395–408; Kuznets 1966; Lerner 1968: 386–395). Among the complex of changes embraced by modernization, several seem especially important in bringing about the shift to modern conditions of child-bearing. Historically, these have been: (1) innovations in public health and medical care; (2) innovations in formal schooling and mass media; (3) urbanization; (4) the introduction of new goods; and (5) per capita income growth. More recently in a few countries another aspect of modernization—family planning programs—has perhaps also played a noticeable role in influencing reproductive behavior.

Table 2–3 presents a summary view based on the present framework of the channels through which reproductive behavior is influenced by these various aspects of modernization. The aspects of modernization are listed on the left hand side, and the supply and demand factors immediately relevant to fertility determination, at the top, as column headings. An entry in a cell indicates that the specified item on the left influences the fertility determinant at the top in the direction shown. For example, the negative sign in column 1 of row 4a indicates that, other things being equal, the introduction of new consumer goods during modernization tends to reduce the strength of preferences for children relative to goods. In drawing up Table 2–3, an attempt has been made to identify on the basis of the literature what seem to be the most important links between modernization and reproductive behavior rather than all hypothetically possible connections. Thus the absence of an entry in a cell does not necessarily mean that no relation whatever exists, but simply that it is probably not of very great quantitative importance.

The reasoning underlying the specific cell entries is as follows. Improved public health and medical care in the course of modernization impinges on the reproductive situation of the family by tending to increase the potential supply of children in two ways. First, it is likely to increase the natural fertility of women, because, for example, healthier women are more likely to carry a fetus to full term (Bourgeois-Pichat 1967: 68–72). Second, even if natural fertility were unchanged, infants are more likely to survive to adulthood and the potential supply of children would be correspondingly increased. These relationships are indicated in Table 2–3 by the positive signs in columns 4 and 5 of row 1.

Also, better public health and medical care may raise per capita income, because a healthier, more energetic population is likely to be more productive (Malenbaum 1970: 31–54). Increased per capita income, in turn, influences a number of fertility determinants over and

109

Table 2-3. Direction of Effect of Various Aspects of Modernization on Indicated Determinants of Completed Family Size

	(1)	(2)	(3)	(4)	(5)	(6)	(7)
	\[Factors through which family size is influenced\]						
	Demand for children, C_d			Potential supply, C_n		Costs of fertility regulation	
	Tastes $[U = f(G_p, C)]$	Income (Y)	Prices (p_z/p_c)	Natural fertility (N)	Survival prospects (s)	Subjective (α)	Market (p_l, p_b)
1. Better public health and medical care [a]				+	+		
2. Growth in formal education and mass media [a]	−		−	+	+	−	−
3. Urbanization [a]	−		−		−	−	−
4. New goods							
a. Consumer goods	−						
b. Fertility control						−	
5. Per capita income growth	−	+		+	+		−

[a] To the extent this item also increases per capita income, additional effects as shown in row 5 would occur.

beyond the effects of better health just mentioned. However, to simplify the table, only the effects directly attributable to public health and medical care improvements are shown, not those that might indirectly be induced through the effect of better health on per capita income. As indicated in footnote a to Table 2–3, a full accounting for the effects of improved public health and medical care would take account as well of the indirect consequences via per capita income growth shown in row 5. The same treatment has been followed in Table 2–3 with regard to the next two aspects of modernization, improved education and urbanization, each of which may raise per capita income as well as influencing reproductive behavior directly. The effects shown in the row for each of these factors exclude any indirect consequences they may have via increased per capita income. Correspondingly, in principle the full range of effects of each of these factors comprises, not only that shown on its respective row but also that shown in row 5 for per capita income growth.

The growth of formal education and associated expansion in mass media, even disregarding any effects via per capita income growth, is one of the most pervasive factors influencing completed family size. As shown in Table 2–3 it operates on all three of the principal fertility determinants—demand, supply, and the costs of fertility regulation. The impact on potential supply may be touched on first, since the reasoning is much like that in regard to the effect of public health and medical care improvements. Formal education and expanded mass media may improve health conditions by diffusing improved knowledge with regard to personal hygiene, food care, environmental dangers, and so on. They may also break down traditional beliefs and customs and thus undermine cultural practices, such as an intercourse taboo, which have had the latent function of limiting reproduction. In these ways they tend to enhance the potential supply of children by raising natural fertility and/or increasing the survival prospects of babies; hence the positive signs in columns 4 and 5 of row 2.

Education and the mass media also tend to lower the costs of fertility regulation, as shown by the negative signs in columns 6 and 7. They may provide information not formerly available on various means of fertility control, reducing the expense in time and money previously required, and may alter cultural norms adverse to the use of fertility control, thus lowering the subjective costs of fertility regulation by challenging traditional beliefs and encouraging a problem-solving approach to life.

Finally, formal education and the expansion of the mass media tend to reduce the demand for children by shifting tastes in a manner

111

unfavorable to children and decreasing the price of goods relative to children (row 2, columns 1 and 3). With regard to the relative price of children, if better education improves the income-earning possibilities of women, then the alternative cost of the mother's time required in child-rearing is increased. While some offset to this may be available, for example, through the help of domestics or older family members, there is doubtless some net positive effect on the cost of children and thus a tendency toward a reduction in desired family size. In addition, compulsory education may increase the relative cost of children by reducing the possible contribution of child labor to family income.[21]

Tastes for children, more specifically, the intensity of the desires for children relative to goods, are affected negatively by education because children, and the life style associated with them, are essentially an "old" good, while education and the mass media present images of new life styles competitive with children. In a recent survey in Taiwan, Deborah S. Freedman (unpublished paper: 17) has found that "the more a couple has been exposed to modern influences, as indicated by their education and exposure to mass media, the more likely it is to want modern goods and services" (cf. also 1970: 25–48). Another possibility, receiving much emphasis today, is a "liberated" life style for women, involving greater market work and less family activity. Education and mass media may lead to higher standards with regard to child-care and child-rearing, creating greater emphasis on the "quality" of children at the expense of numbers. (Note that this is a taste, not a "cost" effect, since it works through a change in subjective attitudes and not in market phenomena). In these ways, education and the mass media increase the subjective attractiveness of expenditures competitive with having more children, and thus tend to lower desired family size.

These developments are part of a more general shift in attitudes that takes place during modernization. This shift is brought about not only by education and the mass media, but also by the population's increasing urbanization and participation in other modern institutions like the factory and agricultural cooperative. A valuable summary description of this development is provided by Inkeles: "We believe our evidence . . . shows unmistakably that there is a set of personal qualities which reliably cohere as a syndrome and which identify a type of man who may validly be described as fitting a reasonable theoretical conception of modern man. Central to this syndrome are: (1) openness to new

[21] Schultz and others have particularly stressed the cost effects of education (see Schultz 1971: 148–174).

experience, both with people and with new ways of doing things such as attempting to control births; (2) the assertion of increasing independence from the authority of traditional figures like parents and priests and a shift of allegiance to leaders of government, public affairs, trade unions, cooperatives, and the like; (3) belief in the efficacy of science and medicine, and a general abandonment of passivity and fatalism in the face of life's difficulties; and (4) ambition for oneself and one's children to achieve high occupational and educational goals. Men who manifest these characteristics (5) like people to be on time and show an interest in carefully planning their affairs in advance. It is also part of this syndrome to (6) show strong interest and take an active part in civic and community affairs and local politics; and (7) to strive energetically to keep up with the news, and within this effort to prefer news of national and international import over items dealing with sports, religion, or purely local affairs" (Inkeles 1969: 210). Among others, Ronald Freedman (1963: 220–245; cf. also 1961–1962: 35–68, 1965: 417–444; Ryder, 1967: 26–36) has emphasized the fertility implications of these attitudinal changes, citing involvement with "the ideas and institutions of a larger modern culture" as a basic factor in the transition to lower fertility.

The process of economic modernization requires a redistribution of population from rural to urban areas, and this is largely accomplished by a vast increase in rural-urban migration. Sociologists have traditionally stressed the implications for reproductive behavior of this aspect of the modernization process, and Kuznets too has assigned an important role to this factor (Kirk 1946; Kuznets 1973; Lorimer 1954). Urbanization, like education, reduces the demand for children by lowering tastes and lowering the price of goods relative to children (row 3, columns 1 and 3). (We continue to set aside possible effects via per capita income change.) The effect via tastes has been touched on immediately above. With regard to costs, the available evidence indicates that the relative price of children of a given "quality" is usually higher in urban areas than in rural (Lindert 1973: 37). A variety of factors are responsible for this. The price of food is higher in urban areas than in rural. Also farm children take less time away from a mother's paid work and contribute more time toward family work than do urban children. In both cases, this would raise the relative cost of children in urban areas compared with rural. Thus, the effect of urbanization of the population is increasingly to place the population in an environment where goods become relatively less expensive than children, and other things being equal, correspondingly more attractive.

In regard to the supply of children, urbanization is probably a nega-

113

tive influence, tending in itself to lower the survival prospects of children (row 3, column 5). The reasoning here is that concentration in densely populated areas increases exposure to disease and tends, other things being unchanged, to raise mortality. The result would be a lower number of surviving children from a given number of births. (This effect may be less applicable under the more modern public health and medical conditions in urban areas in many of today's less developed nations than in the historical experience of the developed countries).

Finally, urbanization tends to reduce both the subjective and market costs of fertility regulation, in ways much like those of formal education and expanded mass media (row 3, columns 6 and 7). In higher density urban situations, access to fertility control knowledge is likely to be greater, and market costs consequently reduced. Subjective costs too are likely to be less, because of the role of the urban environment in breaking down traditional attitudes, among them the reluctance to try new ways of doing things.

Another facet of economic modernization is the continuing introduction of new goods (Rosovsky and Ohkawa 1961: 476–501). The association between increased consumption of modern goods and reduced fertility has been noted in recent studies of Taiwan (D. Freedman unpublished paper; R. Freedman and Takeshita 1969). In terms of the present framework, the introduction of new goods tends to lower the demand for children by shifting tastes in an adverse manner, as shown by the negative sign in row 4a, column 1. In general, the enjoyment of new goods tends to require life styles other than those centering on children, since new goods are typically substitutes for, rather than complementary with, children. Thus, holding other factors constant, the relative strength of household desires for goods unrelated to children is increased, and desired family size, decreased. At any given level of income, households would tend to shift expenditure toward new purposes and away from old goods, including in the latter, having and raising children.

Among the new goods associated with modernization are some specifically related to fertility control. Historical examples are the modern condom and improved methods of induced abortion; more recently, the oral contraceptive pill and IUD. Such developments typically reduce the market costs of fertility regulation by providing cheaper methods. They may also lower the subjective costs of fertility regulation by providing less objectionable options to the household. For example, an advantage claimed for both the pill and IUD compared with most other methods is that they separate the contraceptive act from that of inter-

114

course. Allowance for the effects of new methods of fertility control is made in Table 2–3 by the negative signs in columns 6 and 7 of row 4b.

We come finally to the effects of per capita income growth, whether due to the aspects of modernization in rows 1–3 of Table 2–3, or other factors, such as the adoption of modern techniques of production. In economic analyses of fertility the effect of per capita income change typically stressed is a positive effect. On the assumption that children are normal goods, one would expect, other things being equal, that higher income would encourage households to want more children, just as higher income encourages greater consumption of goods generally. This influence is shown by the positive sign entered in row 5, column 2.

But there is another and counteracting effect of per capita income growth on the demand for children, operating via tastes, as shown by the negative sign in row 5, column 1 (Banks 1954; Easterlin 1969: 127–156; Leibenstein 1973). Because of the substantial upward trend in living levels during economic development, each generation typically comes from a more prosperous background than that of the preceding generation. Because of this, the views of each successive generation as to the material requisites of the "good life" tend to be progressively higher. Goods which to one generation may have been luxuries become necessities to the next—the automobile is a case in point.[22] This "inter-generation taste effect," as it might be called, tends to raise the minimum living level which parents feel is necessary before they can "afford" to have children. In terms of Figure 2–2, there is a floor to the curvilinear indifference map at the minimum required living level. Below this floor the indifference lines become horizontal, signifying that welfare depends only on the parents' goods and having children adds nothing to satisfaction.[23] With the progress of economic growth this "subsistence" floor shifts upward and the marginal rate of substitution decreases at any given point above the floor, indicating that children are becoming less attractive relative to goods. In effect, a third ("subsistence level") constraint is added to the analysis of Figure 2–2 along with the budget line and production constraints.

Thus while per capita income growth increases the resources available to households, it also affects the consumption aspirations which individuals acquire in their economic socialization. Moreover, since the escalation in consumption aspirations is itself a reflection of actual income growth, this means that the adverse taste effect of such growth

[22] See the evidence on goods aspirations in developed and less developed countries in Hadley Cantril's book (1965: ch. 10) cited earlier.

[23] This treatment is like that used in linear expenditure systems with minimum requirement levels (see McElroy 1969; Stone 1954: 511–527).

115

tends to be strong enough, on the average, to wash out the positive income effect. This effect operates within generations as well as between them. Some empirical evidence is provided by Deborah S. Freedman's analysis of Taiwan: "In sum, the findings of this study suggest that the emergence of non-traditional family goals—namely, the achievement of new modern consumption standards—which may conflict with supporting a large family, influences couples to desire fewer children and can have an appreciable influence on the use of contraception to achieve family size goals. The steadily increasing income levels in Taiwan have not encouraged couples to have more children. Instead, these higher incomes have served to develop new wants—particularly for the new kinds of goods and services development has made available and these new wants, in turn, have encouraged couples to take positive steps to limit family size" (Freedman unpublished paper: 39–40).

The foregoing effects of per capita income growth operate via the demand for children. As has been noted, per capita income growth may also affect the potential supply of children, especially in the early stages of modernization. In terms of personal consumption experience of the population, per capita income growth typically comprises, among other things, substantial advances in food, clothing, and shelter. The consequent improvement in resistance to disease and reduction in exposure to disease is likely to raise the fecundity of women and increase prospects of infants surviving to adulthood. These influences are shown in Table 2–3 by the positive signs entered in columns 4 and 5 of row 5.

The discussion above suggests a number of ways in which modernization may produce trends in C_n and C_d of the sort shown in Figure 2–6, and a decline in the costs of fertility regulation. By way of summary, Figure 2–6f provides a convenient basis for illustrating how these influences may come together to induce a shift to low fertility levels.

The supply influences in columns 4 and 5 of Table 2–3 are reflected in Figure 2–6f in the upward movement of the C_n curve, which eventually levels off as modern health and living levels are established. It is assumed that the several factors in Table 2–3 operating to increase C_n outweigh in the long run the one tending to decrease C_n.

The demand influences in columns 1–3 of Table 2–3 are shown by the downward movement of the C_d curve in Figure 2–6f. The net balance of the demand influence is taken to be negative, despite the positive sign for the income effect, since as was noted, the latter tends to be balanced out, on the average, by the inter-generational taste effect. In the diagram, the C_d curve is initially horizontal while the

116

C_n curve is rising. This might occur in a society where, for example, the introduction of public health measures substantially preceded the other aspects of modernization.

As one moves to the right in Figure 2–6f the balance of supply and demand forces gradually shifts from one in which the typical family produces less children than it wants to one (as point m is passed) where it produces more. As the excess of potential supply over demand continues to mount, the motivation to limit fertility grows. Eventually, it outweighs the given level of fertility control costs. At this point the fertility control threshold h is crossed. Actual family size, C, which has previously been moving upward with the potential output curve now turns downward, as intentional prevention of births is initiated. The extent of fertility control, measured in terms of number of children averted, is shown by the vertical distance sR, while the number of unwanted children is given by the vertical distance sX.

The reduction in fertility control costs during modernization shown in Table 2–3, columns 6 and 7, would, other things being equal, shift the threshold point h to the left, increasing fertility regulation and reducing the number of unwanted children at any given time t. In a perfect contraceptive society with zero fertility control costs, the threshold point h would be identical with point m, that is, prevention of births would occur immediately on the emergence of excess supply conditions, and the C curve beyond point m would be identical with the C_d curve, as shown in Figure 2–6e.

As noted previously, until the threshold of fertility regulation has been reached, completed family size is governed solely by the factors determining C_n, specifically natural fertility and child survival prospects. Since modernization typically exerts a positive impact on each of these factors, there is consequently a tendency for actual family size to increase during the early phases of modernization (Collver 1965; Hurault 1965: 801–828; Mandle n.d.; Olusanya 1969: 812–824; Roberts 1969: 695–711 1957: 262–285; Shorter 1971). In this early stage of modernization, while desired family size and the costs of fertility regulation may be changing in a negative direction, these factors are unlikely to influence actual family size, because the typical household has not yet felt a motivation for fertility control sufficient to overcome the costs. Here is an example of the situation in which the establishment of a family planning program would meet with little or no response, because there is insufficient motivation among the public to regulate fertility (Tabbarah 1964: 187–196; 1971: 257–277). Nevertheless, decreases in desired family size and the costs of fertility control would move the threshold of fertility regulation closer.

Eventually, as modernization progresses, the typical family moves across the threshold of fertility regulation, and fertility turns downward. In part, as just noted, this may be due to a gradual reduction in desired family size and in the costs of fertility regulation. In part, it is caused by the increase in potential supply itself, which increases motivation for fertility control by raising progressively the family's prospective number of unwanted children. In this sense, developments raising the supply of children are partly self-correcting, since, as they continue, they tend eventually to induce the adoption of fertility regulation and thereby a reduction in family size. Moreover, with regard to the effect of an increase in child survival prospects, a downward influence on fertility is exerted over and above that working through completed family size. For households to achieve a given number of surviving children, the necessary number of births would be lower, the better the prospect of infant and child survival. Because of this, one would expect the downward movement in fertility due to increased child survival prospects to be proportionately greater than that in completed family size once fertility regulation is adopted, as shown in the numerical illustration of the preceding part.

The variability of experience. The foregoing sketch attempts to bring together the variety of factors operating to induce a fertility decline during modernization. There is, of course, no necessity for these factors to operate simultaneously or with equal force in all situations. Indeed, by making different assumptions regarding changes in the basic fertility determinants, it is possible to generate with the present framework a variety of patterns of change from high to low fertility. For example, the typical demographic transition pattern—a shift from high to low mortality preceding a corresponding movement in fertility—may be most simply generated, if, with other fertility determinants given, one assumes mortality is sharply reduced in a situation of initially high mortality and fertility. The accompanying increase in child survival prospects, and perhaps also in natural fertility of mothers due to better health, would raise C_n, shifting the typical household into an excess supply situation of the type shown to the right of point m in Figure 2–6a. As the prospect of unwanted children continued to grow, the typical household would, in time, reach and cross the fertility control threshold h, and fertility rates would start to move downward, thus following with a lag the decline in mortality.

Other patterns of fertility decline can be generated by assuming different changes in the underlying fertility determinants. Coale has remarked on situations in which the fertility decline accompanied or preceded the mortality decline (1969: 3–24). Such a pattern might arise from changes in the economic and social structure which give rise to

118

unwanted children by shifting C_d below a given C_n, in the manner shown to the right of point m in Figure 2–6b.

As these examples show, there is no necessity for any one aspect of modernization such as mortality decline to exhibit an invariant timing pattern in relation to actual fertility. Coale, (1967: 205–209; 1969: 3–24; 1973) Durand, (1967: 32–45), and many others have emphasized that the fertility movements actually observed as different countries modernize are highly variable, and for good reasons.[24] The initial premodern conditions, such as levels of vital rates and fertility control costs, differ among countries. So too may the historical trend in a particular aspect of modernization, such as the rapidity with which the movement toward universal elementary education takes place. Again, the various factors may come together in different combinations; for example, in one case economic development may substantially lead to social modernization, and in another, the opposite may be true. Also the period of history plays a part—in today's less developed nations there are influences which were absent from the earlier experience of the now-developed nations.

The traditional generalization about the "demographic transition," with its emphasis on the underlying role of urbanization and industrialization, is based largely on the particular modernization experience of northwestern Europe. Even for this area, as the careful work of Coale (1969: 3–24; 1973) and his associates (Livi Bacci 1971; van de Walle and Knodel 1967: 47–55) is now showing, the generalization is not well-founded. It is even less valid for the overseas areas settled by Europe. For example, early mortality conditions in the United States were quite different from and more favorable than those in northwestern Europe (Greven 1970; Lockridge 1966: 318–344). Moreover, the movement to low fertility in the United States was especially due to declines in the fertility of the rural population (Easterlin 1972: 121–183; Grabill et al. 1958: 17). Eastern Europe, an area deserving much more study, exhibits yet another contrast with northwestern Europe, starting with much higher vital rates, and exhibiting marked declines among low literacy peasant populations before World War II. (The possible role of land scarcity in inducing rural fertility declines in both the United States and Austria-Hungary has been noted (Demeny 1968: 502–522; Easterlin 1972: 121–183; Yasuba 1962). In a number of today's less developed nations, advances in public health and education are occurring at an earlier time in relation to economic

[24] Attempts to establish typologies of the demographic transition are common. See, for example, Cowgill (1956: 125–134), Mackensen (1967: 37–46), and Pavlik (1967: 56–59).

119

modernization than was true of the now-developed nations. More-over, new influences are at work that were previously absent, for exam-ple, government family planning programs, mass media in the form of television, and new modes of fertility regulation such as the IUD (Tabah 1967: 999–1030; van de Walle and Knodel 1967: 47–55). To judge from the data presented by Freedman and his associates, the fertility decline so far in Taiwan is largely attributable to the factors underlying the potential supply of children and the costs of fertility regulation, rather than to changes in desired family size (Freedman 1972: 281–296; Freedman and Takeshita 1969). Perhaps this will prove to be representative of the early phases of the fertility adjustment in today's less developed nations, due to the special timing of social modernization relative to economic development.

Substantial differences in historical patterns of fertility change may arise, not only from variations in the long term trends, but from differential fluctuations as well. In premodern conditions substantial variations in fertility occur in connection with movements in natural fertility due to epidemics, famines, and similar events (Wrigley 1969 and ch. 3 below). As has been noted, the establishment of modern health conditions and living levels may give rise to a temporary surge in actual fertility as fecundity rises. In modern societies, pronounced fluctuations have been observed in conjunction with migration move-ments and economic conditions. In regard to the latter, it has been observed that while the taste and income effects of income growth may cancel out over the long term, they do not necessarily do so over shorter periods, and disparities between the two may be responsible for the post-World War II baby booms observed in the United States and elsewhere (Easterlin 1968b, 1973; Simon 1969: 327–341).

One must recognize too that at any given time various groups in a society are in different circumstances, and different factors may be responsible for changes in their fertility. For example, whereas the effect of an increase in the survival prospects of children might be especially felt by those in the older reproductive ages, a change in the factors underlying desired size might have a greater effect on those in the younger ages.

Instead of the demographic transition model, what is needed, there-fore, is an analytical framework sufficiently flexible to accommodate explanation of the wide variety of historical and ongoing trends, fluc-tuations, and differentials in the shift from premodern to modern fertility levels. The present framework is an attempt to supply this need.

Rationality and the changing nature of fertility determination. A

120

number of scholars have argued that modernization results in a fundamental change in the mechanisms determining fertility. For example, Bourgeois-Pichat states: "Fertility in preindustrialized societies seems to be strongly determined if not controlled in the sense we give to this word today. It is determined by a network of sociological and biological factors and when the network is known, the result can be predicted. Freedom of choice by couples is almost absent. The couples have the number of children that biology and society decide to give them.

"One of the main features of the so-called demographic revolution has been precisely to change not only the level of fertility but also change its nature. Having a child has been becoming more and more the result of free decision of the couple. And this change in the nature of fertility may be more important than the change in its magnitude. Fertility has left the biological and social field to become part of behavioral science. . . .

"For fertility we had for a long while a lot of customs carefully molded in the course of time which almost completely determined the size of families. These customs are still there but they are for the most part useless, as fertility is now under the will of people." (Bourgeois-Pichat 1967: 163). A similar distinction is that made by E. A. Wrigley (1969: 192) between "social sanctions" which operate to restrict fertility in a preindustrial situation and "family sanctions" which operate in a modernized society. K. Srinavasan's (1972) classification, previously mentioned, of fertility regulation into phases of biological and social controls, on the one hand, and "deliberate individual control," on the other, provides another illustration.

While there are doubtless differences between the view presented here and those underlying such statements, the present analysis lends general support to the idea of a basic change in the nature of fertility determination during modernization. Although the framework for fertility analysis given here is equally applicable to premodern and modern conditions, the principal determining factors are different in the two situations. The threshold point h in Figure 2–6f may be thought of as the dividing line between premodern and modern fertility determination. To the left of point h, fertility is "regulated" by a variety of social and biological mechanisms working through natural fertility. It is not yet viewed by the household as involving a potential problem of unwanted children, and is in effect outside the standard household decision-making calculus. The modernization process, which shifts the typical household to a position to the right of point h, creates a fundamental change in the circumstances of family reproduction, moving the

121

household from a situation where child-bearing is a matter "taken for granted" to one posing difficult problems of individual choice regarding the limitation of family size. To the left of point h, although there is a demand for children, the usual demand mechanisms emphasized in the economic theory of fertility are typically not operative. As we have seen, however, fertility may be affected by economic variables operating through supply conditions. The explanation of fertility in such a situation calls for inquiry along the lines followed by sociologists and other students of natural fertility. To the right of point h, the household decision-making approach comes into its own. Even here, of course, sociology still has an important part to play, particularly in the investigation of taste formation. To dramatize this contrast, the sections to the left and right of point h in Figure 2–6f have been labeled respectively "social control" and "individual control," following Bourgeois-Pichat's terminology. Such sweeping distinctions are never fully satisfactory. Social sanctions are operative in both premodern and modern circumstances, while the idea that there is no individual choice whatsoever in a premodern society is too strong. Moreover, no society shifts en masse at a single point of time from the "social" to "individual" control situations. The real world process would inevitably be characterized by timing differences between various groups in the population.

The proposition that there is a change in the basic nature of fertility determination should not be confused with the notion that modernization leads to the emergence of rationality in the area of human reproduction. In the present analysis, premodern reproductive behavior is rational in the sense that the means are appropriate to the end. Given a conception of the problem as one of having enough surviving children, maximization of output within the existing set of biological constraints and established social practices makes sense. The process of modernization alters not the rationality of the individual, but the nature of the problem from one of having too few children to one of having too many. Perception by individual households of this change in the nature of the problem and the devising of means of cope with it would hardly be expected to be instantaneous—hence the persistence of high fertility under circumstances where it is no longer needed. But this lag in the adjustment of fertility is a temporary one and is understandable, given the turn-around that has taken place in the nature of the problem, and is no evidence of irrationality.

It is possible that the emergence of a pressure for fertility limitation is one of the first forms in which modernization comes to impinge directly on the mass of the population. The appearance of a problem

122

that had not previously existed—that of limiting family size—and thereby of a need for decision making of an entirely new sort, creates a pressure for attitudinal changes in a fundamental and immensely personal area of human experience. From this viewpoint the "population problem" may have positive consequences, by contributing to modernized attitudes that may more generally favor economic and social development. The presence of appropriate family planning services may facilitate this shift and ease the psychological pressures on individuals by increasing the likelihood of resort to "modern" techniques of fertility regulation rather than cruder traditional methods.

V

EXTENSIONS OF THE FRAMEWORK

IN this section, we note some limitations of the framework developed here. The discussion focuses first on the need to move from analysis of marital fertility to the fertility of all women, by extending the framework to include nonmarital fertility and marriage behavior. It then notes some needed extensions of the marital fertility analysis itself, along with a few more general research implications.

The components of the fertility rate of all women. The foregoing analysis relates to the fertility of married women. The cumulative birth rate of all women is a weighted average of the fertility rates for married and unmarried women, where the weights are the relative proportions of married and unmarried women. The recent and ongoing studies of Ansley Coale (1971: 193–214; 1967: 205–209; 1969: 3–24; 1973; Livi Bacci 1971; van de Walle and Knodel 1967: 47–55) and his co-workers have provided valuable data on these three components of fertility (in somewhat different form) for a number of European nations and their political subdivisions. Their work points up the need for a general theory of marriage and fertility that will provide a basis for systematic analysis of these data.

For this purpose the present framework needs to be extended to cover the explanation of nonmarital fertility and the distribution of women by marital status. Nonmarital fertility can be analyzed with essentially the same framework as that developed here for the study of marital fertility; marital status, however, involves new considerations. No attempt will be made to go thoroughly into either of these here, but a few observations may be made. While the present remarks relate to a simple twofold classification by marital status, for some purposes a more elaborate scheme might be desirable. For example, for Latin American countries the proportion of consensual unions and the fertility rate for this class might be distinguished as separate categories of analysis, as is done by G. W. Roberts (1969: 695–711).

Nonmarital fertility. With regard to the explanation of nonmarital fertility, the framework developed for marital fertility is applicable but with some shift in analytical emphasis. In the case of natural fertility, one would expect the role of social taboos, particularly as they relate to extramarital sexual relations, to be of greater importance relative to biological factors for nonmarital than for marital fertility, and correspondingly to merit even greater analytical attention. For example, the rise in teen-age illegitimacy rates in the United States since 1940 is popularly attributed to greater frequency of intercourse among young unmarried persons due to a "sexual revolution" that has vastly relaxed social constraints on premarital intercourse. Certainly, in explaining the universally low levels of nonmarital fertility in the world, the underlying importance of such taboos in one form or another is important (Davis 1956: 214–215). This does not mean, however, that biological factors can be neglected. In fact, in regard to the uptrend in United States teen-age illegitimacy, Phillips Cutright (1972: 24–31) has presented data indicating that biological aspects of natural fertility have been important.[25]

A second respect in which the analysis of nonmarital fertility differs in emphasis from that of marital fertility is that the desired number of children is likely to be zero. Actually, as will be noted subsequently, this is too strong an assertion, but let us suppose for the moment that it were correct. Then, in terms of Figure 2–6, the C_d line would be horizontal at a value of zero, coterminous with the X-axis, and the trend in observed nonmarital fertility would depend on the C_n curve and the trend in subjective and market costs of fertility regulation. The C_n curve would presumably be at a much lower level than for marital fertility, because of the operation of social taboos on extramarital intercourse. The simple economic analysis of the demand for children which works through C_d would be irrelevant to the explanation of nonmarital fertility.

This, in fact, is the position taken in a valuable recent study by Shorter, Knodel, and van de Walle of the long term decline in nonmarital fertility in Europe since the nineteenth century. The authors note the close parallel between the trends in marital and nonmarital fertility, and argue that the economic pressures sometimes cited to account for the decline in marital fertility cannot be used to explain the trend in nonmarital fertility: "J. A. Banks' explanation of the decline in marital fertility as a consequence of rising middle class stan-

[25] Tietze (1972: 6) has raised some questions about Cutright's analysis.

124

dards of living and of simultaneous greater educational aspirations of parents for their children is much less plausible when applied to the decline in nonmarital fertility. It is unlikely that higher incomes moved unwed mothers to curb their illegitimate fertility so as to plan better the educational future of their bastards on hand. Possibly improvements in the standard of living during the last quarter of the nineteenth century restricted illegitimate fertility through some other mechanism. But an ad hoc rummaging about for alternate linkages to an 'economic prosperity' model is unlikely to result in any generalizable kind of explanation" (Shorter et al. 1971: 393). The authors suggest that the decline in nonmarital fertility was due to "obscure changes in the attitudes towards reproduction, and in the knowledge and acceptability of contraception and abortion," and that there is little evidence that the decline was due to a reduction in the frequency of nonmarital sexual activity during this period, the factor through which changing social constraints would have operated (1971: 382, 393). In terms of our framework, the emphasis is on changes in the costs of fertility regulation, and not C_n, the factor reflecting frequency of intercourse.

However, this view minimizes too much the possible relevance of economic considerations. For one thing, the argument regarding nonmarital fertility is used to question the bearing of economic factors on the trend even in marital fertility. Speaking of the declines in both marital and nonmarital fertility, the authors state: "Perhaps quite different and independent circumstances lay behind the drop in each, so that arguments explaining fertility limitation among married couples need not apply to a similarly successful limitation among unmarried couples. But in view of the extraordinary parallelism in the movement of these two facets of general fertility, this seems unlikely" (Shorter et al. 1971: 392). The present framework, however, suggests a mechanism whereby economic factors might cause a decline, not only directly in marital fertility but also indirectly in nonmarital fertility as well. Suppose, for example, that a decline in the demand for children among married couples due, for example, to the reasons given by Banks, generated a greater demand for fertility regulation, and in response to this, a substantial expansion occurred in the supply of abortion services, lowering their market cost and increasing their social acceptability. The reduced costs of fertility control would make it easier for unmarried as well as married women to terminate pregnancy, and thereby reduce nonmarital fertility. Thus a decline in nonmarital fertility might arise from the same basic circumstances that caused a decline in marital fertility. This argument does not contradict the emphasis that the article's authors place on the costs of fertility regulation in explaining

125

the nonmarital fertility decline, but shows that changes in these variables might ultimately be linked to demand considerations bearing on *marital* fertility. This is not to argue that this was in fact the case, but merely to illustrate how the present framework lends itself to analysis of nonmarital fertility and to clarification of the possible channels through which economic factors may exert their influence.

When account is taken, therefore, of the possible interdependence between marital and nonmarital fertility, the factors emphasized in the economic theory of fertility may prove to be relevant to the explanation of nonmarital fertility. Economic circumstances may also assume more importance when another type of interdependence is recognized, that between nonmarital fertility and the distribution of women by marital status. There is evidence that some unmarried persons initiate intercourse in the expectation of eventually getting married (Kanter and Zelnick 1972: 9–18). If pregnancy occurs, and if at the same time young men are suddenly confronted with adverse economic circumstances, then marriage expectations may not be realized and the illegitimacy rate may consequently rise. With regard to American experience, it is possible that economic pressures may have operated to discourage marriage somewhat in the 1960's, and in this way have contributed to the rise in illegitimacy (Easterlin 1973). But whether or not this was the case, this example illustrates another way that economic factors may influence nonmarital fertility through the interdependence between nonmarital fertility and other fertility components.

Distribution by marital status. In view of the empirical evidence on the importance of variations in marriage behavior in fertility differences, and the fact that marriage constitutes an area of decision making largely separate from fertility, it is surprising how little effort has been devoted to the theory of marriage behavior (Coale 1971: 193–214; 1967: 205–209). The present comments can do no more than note briefly a few of the considerations, economic and noneconomic, that need inclusion in such an analysis. It is obvious, however, that the lack of a theory of marriage behavior is one of the biggest gaps in the explanation of human fertility patterns.

Economic factors, in some respects similar to those included in the analysis of fertility, are relevant to marriage behavior. In his impressive documentation of the comparatively late marriage patterns of Western Europe, Hajnal (1965: 133–134; cf. also Davis and Blake 1956: 215–218) speculates that the rate at which land became available for the founding of new families may have been a controlling factor. Included in his discussion is the idea that some "typical" level of support is necessary for marriage and family formation. Thus the explanation of marriage behavior involves a question of the earnings potential of young men relative to desired living levels, a conception similar to that advanced to explain fertility changes in nineteenth-century Britain and the recent swing both in marriage and fertility behavior in the United States (Banks 1954; Easterlin 1973).

Noneconomic factors are also relevant to explaining marital status. The type of kinship organization in a society may be important. Davis and Blake (1956: 215) suggest, for example, that a joint household system is more conducive to early marriage than an independent nuclear family organization, because "marriage is in no way made contingent on the possession of separate property by the newly married pair." There are also important differences among societies in social customs relating to remarriage of those whose spouses have died.

Mortality conditions play a part in shaping the distribution by marital status. The practice of early marriage is sometimes attributed to concern over high and variable mortality. "Early marriage . . . represents the maximum possible hedge against the threat of failure in population replacement" (Davis and Blake 1956: 215). Coale (1967: 207) has pointed out that in India the decline in mortality has reduced the incidence of widowhood. The consequent shift in the marital status distribution of women would tend to raise fertility, other things being equal.[26]

An analysis of marriage behavior must also take account of interdependence between marriage and other components of fertility. The previous discussion noted a possible connection between nonmarital fertility and marriage. Matras, Coale, and others have suggested a link between marital fertility and marriage behavior. The argument is that as knowledge and acceptance of various practices of fertility regulation became common in twentieth-century Europe, this diminished the pressure for deferring marriage and contributed to a tendency toward earlier marriage (Coale 1967: 207; Hawthorne 1970: 25; Matras 1965: 349–362). It is possible that in Ireland religious constraints on family limitation within marriage contributed to the development of an unusually late marriage pattern even by Western European standards. Factors such as these need to be integrated in a framework that will lay a basis for systematic interpretation of observed marriage behavior.

Extension of marital fertility analysis. The present analysis was developed on the basis of assumptions especially chosen with a view to focussing attention on the interrelations among desired family size, the potential output of children, and the costs of fertility regulation. Exten-

---

[26] See also Sauvy (1969: 359) for an indication of the possible importance to fertility of the lessened dissolution of marriages due to the death of one partner.

sion of the analysis would require relaxing these assumptions, though this would necessarily involve an increase in complexity. Only brief enumeration is needed here of a few possibilities for future work.

1. Considerations regarding the spacing of children may be incorporated in the analysis both on the supply side, based on natural fertility considerations, and on the demand side, deriving from taste, income, and price variables (cf. Tabbarah 1971: 257–277). As a result there would be a distribution over the life cycle of the motivation to regulate fertility, typically increasing with time as desired family size is approached. When balanced against the costs of fertility regulation, this would lead to a life cycle pattern of adoption of fertility control, which itself might change as the underlying determinants change.

2. Sex preferences may be taken account of in the utility function for children. Some promising investigations along this line are those by Myers and Roberts (1968: 164–172) and Ben-Porath and Welch (1972).

3. Decisions regarding number of children are interdependent with those regarding quality and also the allocation of the wife's time between leisure, work at home, and work in the market place. Much recent economic research on fertility has been especially devoted to taking account of the simultaneous determination of these variables (see, e.g., Schultz 1969: 153–180; Schultz 1971).

4. The present analysis assumed there was only one technique of fertility regulation, though the general discussion at times departed from this position. Formally, account may be taken of the availability of a variety of techniques by associating different subjective costs ($\propto$), and market prices (p_i, p_b) with each.

5. The determination of natural fertility requires more formal development, possibly along the lines suggested by Bourgeois-Pichat (1965: 383–424) and others. In this connection, explicit differentiation of the role of biological factors from cultural conditions is especially desirable.

6. The present framework treats the infant and child survival variable, s, as involuntarily determined, as is usually done in the analytical literature. However, the framework lends itself to recognition of the possible practice of infanticide, and thus to the role of voluntary influences on s. Unwanted children may be eliminated, not only through restricting fertility, but through exposure or neglect of an infant, and by this means the supply of children may be brought more into balance with demand. While there is historical evidence of the practice of infanticide in some societies, there is some ambiguity regarding its contemporary importance.[27]

[27] Thus Hawthorn (1970: 48) states that "[i]nsofar as any certainty is possible

128

7. Instead of the "representative" household, one may deal explicitly with the population of households, taking account of the variation in circumstances among them. Not only would this facilitate analysis of fertility differentials at a point in time, but it lends itself to recognition of the concurrent existence of a demand for ways of increasing fertility as well as of limiting it, and to formal analysis of a child-adoption market.

8. The previous observation starts to go beyond marital fertility as such. In conclusion, one further research possibility of this sort may be noted. In many models of economic growth, population and human fertility are treated as independent of the process of economic development. According to the view sketched above, voluntary fertility regulation tends to be induced by the pressures of modernization. Once this adaptive mechanism is recognized, models of the effects of population on economic growth which treat fertility as exogenous are called into question. According to the present analysis, a more realistic representation would treat fertility as an endogenous variable in the model, and recognize that economic growth has feedback effects on population change.

VI

Summary

This chapter presents an analytical framework that integrates the approaches to fertility analysis of economists and sociologists, thus fostering mutual understanding and a more common conception of the subject, and of the needs for research and the potential contributions of both disciplines. While the chapter is primarily conceptual in nature, the empirical counterparts of the various concepts are discussed, and the use of the framework is illustrated by applying it to the interpretation of premodern fertility behavior and the transition to modern fertility levels. One implication of the discussion is that the dominant factors in fertility explanation and the underlying mechanisms may be different in premodern and modern circumstances.

The framework developed here is an expansion of the usual economic framework for fertility analysis to take fuller account of subjects particularly stressed in sociology, especially the production side of fertility

---

when assessing the frequency of contraceptive methods, it is certain that infanticide is no longer an important method of fertility control." On the other hand, Carl Taylor (1968: 2–7) speaking of today's less developed countries, expresses the view that "[i]n many rural groups differential care favoring boys produces a signficantly higher mortality of girl babies, a highly effective population control method."

behavior, and attitudes toward and access to fertility regulation. More formal treatment of the production of children, including the possibility of shifts in output independently of demand conditions, is one of the principal innovations of the framework. The analysis relates to marital fertility, the principal dependent variable being the cumulative number of children surviving to adulthood (C), and, for simplicity, is expressed in terms of the "representative" household.

The determinants of fertility are seen as working through one or more of the following: (1) desired family size (C_d), the number of surviving children parents would want if fertility regulation were costless; (2) the potential supply of children (C_n), the number of surviving children parents would have in an unregulated fertility regime; and (3) the costs of fertility regulation, including both subjective (psychic) costs and objective costs, the time and money required to learn about and use specific techniques. The immediate determinants of desired family size are income, Y; the price of children relative to goods, p_c/p_g; and tastes (the utility function for children and goods), the factors chiefly discussed in economic analyses of fertility. It is through tastes or subjective preferences that some of the attitudinal considerations and measures stressed by sociologists operate such as norms regarding family size and the "quality" of children (that is, standards of child care and rearing). Economists, for the most part, pay less attention to tastes, and emphasize in their theoretical and empirical work income and price determinants of the demand for children.

The supply of children in an unregulated fertility regime depends on natural fertility, N, the total number of births parents would have if no conscious effort were made to regulate fertility, and the probability of a baby surviving to adulthood, s. As studies by sociologists, anthropologists, and economic historians show, natural fertility depends on both physiological and cultural factors. The latter comprises household circumstances which unintentionally influence fertility, such as an "intercourse taboo" or physical separation of partners due to such things as civil strife or seasonal migration for employment purposes.

The supply and demand conditions relating to children jointly determine the motivation for fertility regulation. If the potential supply falls short of demand $(C_n < C_d)$, there is no desire to limit fertility. On the contrary, an "excess demand" situation of this type would result in a demand for ways to enhance fertility and for children to adopt, though these possibilities are usually quantitatively unimportant. In this situation, actual fertility would depend on natural fertility.

On the other hand, if the potential supply exceeds demand $(C_n > C_d)$, an "excess supply" situation, parents would be faced with the prospect

130

of having unwanted children and would be motivated to regulate their fertility. The degree of motivation, however, must be weighed against the costs of fertility regulation, which are of two types. There are psychic costs—the displeasure associated with the idea or practice of fertility control. Data relevant to these costs are obtained in sociological inquiries into fertility control attitudes. There are also market costs—the time and money necessary to learn about and use specific techniques, covered under sociological discussions of "access." The costs of fertility control are formalized in the present analysis in terms of α, a summary measure of subjective concerns about fertility regulation affecting the indifference map, and p_i and p_b, the fixed and variable market costs of fertility regulation, which modify the budget constraint.

When account is taken of the costs of fertility regulation along with the factors shaping motivation, an equilibrium value of number of children, C, and births, B, is determined. At the same time the extent and efficiency of fertility regulation, R, which measures the shortfall of actual compared with natural fertility, is determined, as well as X, the excess of the actual number of births over the desired number. The variables R and X are approximated in sociologists' measures of "births averted" and "excess fertility." Thus, in the present analysis, actual fertility, excess fertility, and "births averted" are found to be simultaneous outcomes of the determinants underlying C_d, C_n, and the costs of fertility control. These determinants are, to sum up, the utility function for goods and children, potential income of the household (Y), the price of children relative to goods (p_c/p_g), natural fertility (N), the survival rate to adulthood (s), and the subjective and market costs of fertility regulation (α, p_i, and p_b). It is through these variables that all other influences operate.

In applying this framework to the interpretation of actual experience, it is suggested that fertility conditions in premodern societies more nearly approximate an excess demand situation than one of excess supply. This is because mortality and fertility are high and widely fluctuating in these societies. As a result the principal concern of the typical household is likely to be whether it will be able to have as many children as it wants, not whether it will have too many. In this situation, observed fertility will depend on natural fertility. The economic variables of income and prices subsumed in the budget constraint would affect fertility through their impact on the potential output of children, but not by way of the usual demand mechanisms. Tastes play a part insofar as they help to establish a desired family size as large or larger than potential output, but changes in tastes would not affect

131

fertility behavior unless desired size fell below potential output. With regard to research needs, this implies that inquiry into premodern fertility should be primarily along the lines followed by sociologists and other students of the cultural and biological determinants of natural fertility.

The transition to modern fertility levels occurs because modernization shifts the representative household from a situation approximating an excess demand for children to one of excess supply, thereby generating a motivation to limit fertility and avoid unwanted children. This shift arises from aspects of modernization which tend, on the one hand, to increase the potential output of children, C_n, and, on the other, to reduce desired family size, C_d. Potential output tends to increase because of such developments as improved health of mothers, better education and knowledge of personal hygiene, better nutrition, and reduced infant and child mortality. Desired family size tends to decrease because of changes in taste and costs favoring goods relatively more than children. Also, at the same time that modernization increases the motivation for fertility regulation, it reduces the costs of fertility regulation, through urbanization, education, and the associated expansion of the mass media. These developments reduce market costs of fertility control by increasing access to methods of fertility limitation and they lower psychic costs by legitimizing the practice of fertility control. Modernization also results in innovations in fertility control methods, further lowering the costs of fertility regulation.

Thus while the forces of modernization lead, on the one hand, to greater motivation to limit fertility, on the other, they make fertility regulation easier by lowering its subjective and market costs. Eventually in the evolution from premodern to modern conditions the balance between motivation for fertility regulation and its costs tips in favor of fertility control. A "threshold" of fertility regulation is crossed and family size moves downward. For many reasons, however, the pattern of decline would be likely to be different from one place to another. There are differences in the initial premodern conditions from which societies start, and in the trends in the various aspects of modernization. In today's less developed countries there are influences which were absent from the earlier experience of the now developed nations.

In modernized societies, then, fertility is governed by the interaction of the factors shaping family size desires, the potential output of children, and the costs of fertility regulation. Modernization thus alters the essential nature of fertility regulation. Child-bearing in premodern societies, though "regulated" by a variety of social and biological

132

mechanisms working through natural fertility, is not yet viewed by the household as involving a potential problem of unwanted children. In contrast, in modern societies, fertility poses difficult problems of individual choice regarding the limitation of family size. As long as fertility control costs are positive, there will continue to be some unwanted children in modern societies, but in the course of time, actual family size tends to converge toward desired family size. "Fertility has left the biological and social field to become a part of behavioral science" (Bourgeois-Pichat 1967: 163).

3

Fertility Strategy for the Individual and the Group

E. A. WRIGLEY

THE demography of preindustrial societies was a weighty factor in determining their welfare. It holds a special interest in the period immediately preceding the industrial revolution since the demographic posture of a society has an important bearing on its chances of breaking clear from the curbs upon sustained growth which gave preindustrial economies some of their most distinctive features (Wrigley 1969: ch. 4). But every major aspect of preindustrial demography was itself greatly influenced by social custom and economic circumstance so that there is difficulty in knowing how best to approach the set of relationships as a whole. In what follows I wish to examine briefly a limited number of issues to do with the effect of the size of a family upon the fortunes of its members, and more generally of the fertility levels on the fortunes of a community as a whole.

I

UNCONSCIOUS RATIONALITY

THE central issue might be called that of unconscious rationality. Ever since Darwin's day men have been intrigued by the presence of patterns of behavior in animals which bring an apparent benefit to the species of which the individual members of the population are unaware. What is true of societies of animals may be true equally of societies of men (Wilkinson 1973: ch. 3). Thus the proportions of land devoted to the several main food staples in parts of West Africa are sometimes close to the best possible mix of land use if the aim of the society were to guard itself most effectively against the danger that extremes of weather might result in starvation (Gould 1963: 290–297). Trial and error may be presumed to have produced this by conferring advantages upon individuals or groups who lighted on good solutions, initially perhaps by chance. In much the same way the invisible hand working through competition in the market place is held to cause an optimal allocation of the community's resources in spite of the obtuseness of some or all the individuals concerned. Equally, it is reasonable

135

to argue that practices such as infanticide, periods of abstinence from intercourse, conventions about the circumstances in which a couple may marry and begin a family, which may become accepted by a community for many different reasons, may survive and become rooted in the habits of the group because they serve to alleviate demographic pressures which would otherwise grow acute (and which may indeed have undermined rival groups with higher fertility). In places where high fertility was for any reason beneficial to the community, on the other hand, fertility fostering customs would have the greater value in the "objective" circumstances of the groups in question.

Though the benefit derived from unconscious rationality is usually analyzed in terms of the group, it is clear that it must influence individual behavior if it is to operate at all. Very often, no doubt, it would be reinforced by a conscious rationality, too, as might be the case when a peasant contemplates how best to pass on his holding intact to the next generation without unfairness between his offspring. But equally the individual may be moved by traditional or religious considerations in, say, following a particular weaning custom, though the result may have important demographic results and a bearing upon the overall demographic balance of the community and the interlocking of demographic, economic, social, and other features of the society.

We may approach the essence of the problem more nearly by considering the general constraints within which any preindustrial community had to work. Mean birth intervals of less than 24 months or average completed family sizes larger than 10 were very rare. Natural fertility among people, in other words, is very modest compared with that of most animals. In certain circumstances, indeed, the ceiling set by natural fertility [1] may be lower than the unavoidable minimum mortality, what might be called the basic mortality schedule. There have been many cities, for example, in which the conditions of life caused mortality rates to rise to levels at which without in-migration the population must have fallen. Equally, there were country areas, especially in low-lying marshlands, where population decline would also have been unavoidable but for the steady inflow of new residents. In the majority of preindustrial communities, however, the level of natural fertility was such as to carry the danger that fertility might exceed the basic mortality schedule.

Neither natural fertility levels nor basic mortality schedules were the same in all communities, but the latter probably varied more than the

[1] Natural fertility may be regarded as existing when the likelihood of a birth of rank x within a family is not directly influenced by the size of x; where, in other words, the number of children already born to a couple does not of itself affect the likelihood of a further birth. Natural fertility is thus quite compatible with a relatively low absolute level of fertility.

136

former. The prevalence and virulence of local endemic diseases, the degree of exposure to occasional attack from diseases which were not endemic, the annual and seasonal variations in food supply, and many other factors could all affect the basic mortality schedule (and to some extent the level of natural fertility also). In addition, mortality rates were strongly influenced by population density. Above certain levels of density the basic mortality schedule inevitably started to rise both because it tended to involve increasing difficulty in meeting food needs, and also because the risk of exposure to infectious disease appears to have been related to the density of the population. The effect of increasing density on fertility was less direct but there are several ways in which increasing density might, given the existence of an appropriate social mechanism, cause a fall in fertility (as when marriage is tied to acquiring a holding). Finally, both fertility and mortality rates in all communities were affected by a host of social customs.

Clearly if the basic mortality schedule of a community is lower than its prevailing fertility and there is no significant socially induced mortality (through, say, war or infanticide), population will rise. Many writers of the late preindustrial period interested in population matters, such as Adam Smith and Malthus, took the view that the normal propensity of populations was to rise unless checked by adverse circumstances. They also assumed that if a community's ability to produce expanded, population would tend to rise at least commensurately, though recognizing that the existence of conventional minimum standards of living might prevent populations falling to the lowest subsistence levels.

This is a more restrictive view than that which follows from the hypothesis of unconscious rationality since the latter may produce patterns of behavior which ensure that the overall situation is stable and may even approach an optimum. The demonstration of the existence of such a situation, and particularly of its optimality, presents logical difficulties since it tends to be demonstrable only ex post facto by its power of survival, which carries dangers of circular argument. Nevertheless, it is useful to consider the question of what constituted "rational" behavior for the individual and the group in order to see whether this approach holds out any hope of improving our understanding of preindustrial societies.

II

HEIRSHIP STRATEGY

IT is convenient to begin with what is sometimes called heirship strategy. (Goody 1973: 3–20; see also Wells 1971: 273–282; Le Bras

WRIGLEY

1973: 9–38; Bourdieu 1972: 1105–1127). This is an interesting issue in its own right and will serve to introduce wider questions. The general problem lies in the fact (or prevalent assumption) that a man had to walk a delicate path between danger, on the one hand, that he might be without a male heir at his death, and, on the other, that he might have difficulty in providing for several sons, each with a claim on his resources. Where dowries were substantial, daughters might create similar problems.

The simplest conceivable solution in a society whose resource base was static would be for each married couple to have one son and one daughter to survive and replace them. But such a solution is always unattainable. Some families have many children; others few or none. Some are depleted by death; others are luckier. Some men never marry; others marry several times. To discuss, therefore, the opportunities and handicaps produced by variations in family size can be instructive both when considered in relation to the individual family and to the larger community.

As a first step, let us consider the question of the likelihood that a man at his death will have a male heir to succeed him. In some societies this is of the greatest importance for religious reasons and because stress is laid upon the value of maintaining the patriline, and even where such considerations are absent or of less importance, a man in possession of a holding may be anxious to have a son to succeed him.

If we make the simplifying assumption that the population in question is neither growing nor decreasing, an assumption likely to be approximately true for a substantial proportion of all preindustrial societies, then the likelihood of having a male heir at death is little affected by the combination of fertility and mortality which produces stability in total numbers. Consider, for example, three possible situations. Each embodies assumptions which are oversimple but it is improbable that the results would be greatly modified if a more refined method of calculation had been used. I assume: (1) that the sex ratio at birth at all birth ranks is 100; (2) that the chances of any one child in a family dying are independent of the chances of death of all other children in the family; (3) that the chances of each child dying before the death of his or her father are the same without regard to the rank of the child in the family (in other words each child is treated as if it were born in the same year of life of the father rather than allowing for the fact that the births are distributed about the mean age of father at birth of child); (4) that the chances of any given child being male or female is uninfluenced by the sex of any earlier children in the family; (5) that the life table death rates for children of both sexes are the same; and (6) that every man marries.

Making use of model life tables and appropriate assumptions about average age of father at birth of child, it seems reasonable to consider three possibilities of which the first and last are assumed to represent extremes for preindustrial societies: (1) that a new-born child has a 1 in 3 chance of surviving to the death of his father; (2) that he has a 1 in 2 chance of surviving to the death of his father; and (3) that he has a 2 in 3 chance of surviving to the death of his father.

The method used in calculating the likelihoods of each eventuality shown in the tables is explained in the appendix. It will be obvious that the relative frequencies of families of different sizes shown in the tables are arbitrary sets of figures designed to produce an overall total of children born per 1,000 families sufficient to offset the mortality levels in each population. They show, however, a fair resemblance to the frequencies found in historical populations, rounded to simplify calculation. For the larger family sizes the probabilities involved are rather laborious to calculate, and therefore, in this illustrative exercise, I have considered family sizes 0 to 9, but above this size have considered only the case of the 12 child family. In a more elaborate and exact computer analysis the drastically simplified assumptions used in this essay could easily be relaxed and a wider range of possibilities examined.[2]

As might be expected intuitively the tables show a striking stability in the proportions of families with no heir, a female heir or heirs only, and at least one male heir, in the proportions roughly 2, 2, and 6. Thus it is immediately apparent how difficult it is likely to have been for a family to maintain a direct patriline over any considerable number of generations. The obverse of this same coin is the comparative wealth of opportunity for younger sons, for what appears as a difficulty to one man who is heirless at his death or has only surviving daughters represents an opportunity for another man frustrated by the existence of a brother from access to the main holding of his own family.

III

The Timing of Marriage

Some of the assumptions used in this exercise must be examined further. For example, I have proceeded as if the expectation of life of the father at his mean age at birth of child were not only the period of time over which a birth cohort is depleted by the stated fraction, but also the mean age of male marriage. The first point is obvious and the second should also be approximately true since, if men in the cohort

[2] This has subsequently been done and confirms the validity of the initial exploratory work reported in this chapter.

of sons have already been married for some time on average when members of the older generation die, the number of marriages in the younger generation will be larger than in the older and, given the same distribution of family sizes, this will result in an increasing population. If the average age at marriage is higher than the expectation of life of the father at the mean age at birth of child, the opposite will be the case.

It is instructive to examine the circumstances in which these assumptions are viable. Table 3–4 helps to elucidate the matter. The implicit assumption about age at marriage may be illustrated by considering Population 2 (Table 3–2) in conjunction with the level 6 expectation of life figures in Table 3–4. If we assume a mean age of father at birth of child of about 31 years, his expectation of life will then be about 26 years. Since a birth cohort is depleted by one half over a period of a little more than 26 years in level 6, the pieces fit together neatly. The interval between age at marriage and mean age at birth of child is plausible, bearing in mind that in Population 2 each family has an average of 4 children. From level 6 to, say, level 12 the same basic relationships can be preserved, provided that, as expectation of life improves, a higher mean age at marriage is accepted. For example, at level 12 expectation of life at age 35 is about 29 years. If this were also the mean age of first marriage, about 32 per cent, or nearly one third of the initial birth cohort would have disappeared, and this conforms quite closely to the requirements of Population 1 (Table 3–1).

The range of mortality rates represented by levels 6 to 12 (expecta-

TABLE 3–1. POPULATION 1
(EACH CHILD HAS A ⅔ CHANCE OF SURVIVING UNTIL THE DEATH
OF THE FATHER.)

Family size	Frequency per 1,000 families	No heir	At least 1 female, but no male heir	At least 1 male heir	Total number of children
0	100	100.0	0.0	0.0	0
1	200	66.7	66.7	66.7	200
2	200	22.2	66.6	111.2	400
3	150	5.6	38.9	105.6	450
4	110	1.3	20.4	88.3	440
5	85	0.3	10.9	73.8	425
6	60	0.1	5.2	54.8	360
7	40	—	2.3	37.6	280
8	25	—	1.0	24.0	200
9	20	—	0.5	19.5	180
12	10	—	0.1	9.9	120
Total	1,000	196.2	212.6	591.4	3,055

TABLE 3–2. POPULATION 2
(EACH CHILD HAS A ½ CHANCE OF SURVIVING UNTIL THE
DEATH OF THE FATHER.)

Family size	Frequency per 1,000 families	No heir	At least 1 female, but no male heir	At least 1 male heir	Total number of children
0	85	85.0	0.0	0.0	0
1	125	62.5	31.3	31.3	125
2	125	31.3	39.1	54.6	250
3	125	15.6	37.1	72.3	375
4	125	7.9	31.8	85.4	500
5	125	3.9	25.8	95.4	625
6	90	1.4	14.6	74.0	540
7	75	0.6	9.5	65.0	525
8	60	0.2	5.8	54.0	480
9	40	0.1	2.9	37.0	360
12	25	—	0.8	24.2	300
Total	1,000	208.5	198.7	593.2	4,080

tions of life at birth between 30 and 45) fits the experience of a large proportion of early modern western European populations. Given that late mariage was normal (Hajnal 1965), the rule that each couple on marriage should establish themselves in a separate household could easily be maintained if there was a rough coincidence between the death of a generation of fathers and the marriage of a generation of

TABLE 3–3. POPULATION 3
(EACH CHILD HAS A ⅓ CHANCE OF SURVIVING UNTIL THE
DEATH OF THE FATHER.)

Family size	Frequency per 1,000 families	No heir	At least 1 female, but no male heir	At least 1 male heir	Total number of children
0	70	70.0	0.0	0.0	0
1	70	46.7	11.7	11.6	70
2	70	31.1	17.5	21.4	140
3	70	20.7	19.7	29.5	210
4	70	13.9	20.0	36.2	280
5	70	9.2	19.1	41.7	350
6	70	6.2	17.3	46.6	420
7	70	4.1	15.5	50.4	490
8	70	2.7	13.6	53.7	560
9	280	7.3	47.0	225.7	2,520
12	90	0.6	9.4	80.0	1,080
Total	1,000	212.5	190.8	596.8	6,120

141

TABLE 3–4. EXPECTATION OF LIFE
(MALES MODEL WEST [COALE AND DEMENY 1966])

	Age	Expectation of life	Percentage dying by
Level 1	0	18.0	0.0
	25	24.1	67.6
	30	21.6	71.0
	35	19.2	74.4
Level 6	0	30.0	0.0
	25	30.0	48.9
	30	27.0	52.3
	35	24.0	55.9
Level 12	0	44.5	0.0
	25	36.6	30.0
	30	33.0	32.7
	35	29.3	35.6
Level 15	0	51.8	0.0
	25	39.6	21.4
	30	35.7	23.6
	35	31.7	25.9

sons. And given such a rule, mortality, fertility, and marriage age could fluctuate in relation to each other in such a way as to keep a homeostatic balance in the demography of the community. If mortality improved, marriage was automatically delayed for the average son, but since a higher proportion of each generation reached the later marriage age, a lower average size of family was sufficient to maintain the population. And delay in marriage for men, if paralleled by a similar postponement among women, would reduce fertility by approximately the required amount without additional regulation of fertility within marriage (Ohlin, 1961: 190–197). In practice the behavior of populations was far more complex and other variables, such as the proportion of the population never marrying, were at times of great importance, but the *possibility* of homeostatic regulation of numbers in this way is worth noting.

Mortality levels outside the range just considered produce greater problems in the context of the assumptions made earlier. Take, for example, Population 3 (Table 3–3) and level 1 of the Model West life tables. Level 1 incorporates extremely severe mortality rates and an expectation of life at birth of only 18 years. Yet it still appears possible at first blush to maintain the implicit assumptions of Population 3 (Table 3–3). At age 30, for example, male expectation of life is 21.5 years, and about 65 percent, or two-thirds, of each birth cohort has died by age 21.5. And a mean age at first marriage of 21.5 is consistent with an average age at birth of child of 30 years since family sizes in Population 3 (Table 3–3) are large. But there is a serious difficulty. It lies in the extremely high fertility rates which it is necessary to attain to prevent a steady decline in numbers. That they are very demanding is evident from the family size distribution of Population 3 (Table 3–3). Men and women even in the prime of life are subject to heavy mortality (more than a third of those living at 20 have died by age 40) which reduces the likelihood of having a large family. Moreover, there is very little "play" in the system. Although the mean expectation of life of father at birth of child is so low, the use of a mean tends to conceal the fact that some fathers will live much longer than the average and others much less. In communities with a relatively late average age at marriage the two offset each other more effectively than in a high mortality community with early marriage, for in the former sons whose fathers die relatively young are more likely than in the latter to have reached maturity. This is so because expectation of life at mean age at birth of son is only just over 20 years in Population 3 (Table 3–3) whereas in Population 1 (Table 3–1) it is almost 30 years. The relatively early death of a father in a community with the characteristics of Population 3 (Table 3–3) therefore, is more likely to find his sons too young to marry. They cannot marry until they are, say, 16 while those whose fathers live relatively long will still have to wait to marry. A very early mean age at first marriage is unattainable in these circumstances.

Yet early marriage is a necessity where mortality rates are very high if families are to be sufficiently large on average to prevent a fall in population. A community in these circumstances will need to develop marriage rules which ensure that men (and still more women) marry soon after reaching sexual maturity, regardless of whether their parents are living or not. Population 3 (Table 3–3) is so placed that it is almost inevitable that many men will marry before their fathers' deaths. This in turn means that many men will, in the course of their life-cycle, pass a few years soon after marriage in the household of their parents or parents-in-law. To have a rule that every couple should start married life in a house of their own would imply maintaining a stock of housing substantially larger than is necessary if spending some time in an extended family household is regarded as acceptable.

Low mortality rates, of course, produce the opposite type of difficulty, that of "losing" fertility. Consider level 15 in Table 3–4. Almost three-quarters of each birth cohort reaches age 35 so that fertility must be modest if population growth is not to occur. Early marriage in such a population in any regime of natural fertility would mean rapid popu-

143

lation growth, and early marriage is also inconsistent with the assumption that mean age at marriage and expectation of life of father at birth of child should be the same. The underlying assumptions used in constructing Tables 3–1, 3–2, and 3–3 can still be preserved if a mean age at marriage as late as about 31 or 32 is acceptable and provided that marital fertility is at a fairly low level. Indeed the assumptions can be preserved at even lower mortality levels, but this will imply still higher marriage ages (or a rising proportion of men never marrying [3]). Control of fertility within marriage can solve or alleviate the problem of excessive fertility where men marry young and this alternative to late marriage will be likely to prove increasingly tempting in populations in which expectation of life has risen substantially. Most such populations are relatively wealthy and can afford the extra cost of maintaining a stock of housing large enough to enable them to do without extended family households in the period of overlap between the marriage of sons and the death of fathers.

At both extremes, therefore, sons are likely to marry before their fathers' deaths, though in the one case the reason, so far as fertility is concerned, lies in the importance of maximizing it, whereas in the other, the practice is possible over any extended period of time only because fertility can be controlled within marriage. In between there is a wide band of mortality levels where some association between the death of a father and the marriage of a son is quite a "rational" custom. There is no reason why the marriage of a young man should be linked to the death of *his* father. The death of any father without surviving sons (which Tables 3–1, 3–2, 3–3 suggest will happen in about 4 cases in 10) may create a marriage opportunity for all unmarried young men or for some class among them depending on the marriage rules of the community in question. Where a general pool of opportunities is created by the death of men without male heirs it is easy to appreciate the attraction of customs like Borough English (ultimogeniture), particularly where mortality is relatively low,[4] since older sons are likely to be well on into manhood at the time of a father's death and there will be earlier opportunities of marriage for them to take up.

[3] Postfamine Ireland combining late marriage with high permanent celibacy (and much emigration) is a good illustration of this possibility.

The custom of an elderly father retiring from a holding in favor of a son who can then marry is sometimes noted. It may be consonant with stable numbers but this may increase the likelihood that other men are permanently excluded from marriage.

[4] For example, I assumed earlier in discussing Model West level 12 mortality and Population 1 (Table 3-1) that the expectation of life of a father at mean age at birth of child was 29 years. His eldest son would normally be several years older than this.

In what way is the symmetry between "surplus" sons and vacant niches, apparent in stationary populations considered as a whole, reflected in the best presumptive strategy for individual families? To keep the discussion of a very complex question within bounds I shall continue to concentrate largely on the problem of securing a reasonable certainty of a male heir while avoiding the danger of being burdened with too many sons who might cause the subdivision or overloading of the holding.

IV

Family Formation

It is easy to overlook a simple but vital preliminary point in discussing the strategy of individual families. Children are not born simultaneously but successively, except in the case of multiple births. Therefore it is misleading to argue, for example, that because (in a case like Population 3 [Table 3–3]) the chance of one son surviving until his father's death is only 1/3, the chance of having a son to succeed when two sons are born into the family is only 5/9.[5] This would be true only if the two were twins and the mortality of twins were like that of other children. In other cases when a second son is born either the first is still living or he has died. If the latter, the birth of the second only gives a 1/3 chance of a male heir. If the former, however, the matter is very different since the first son will by then be, say, 4 years old and will have survived the perils of early life. His chance of living until his father's death is now improved (about 64/100 even at level 1), and the combined chance of at least one son surviving is 75/100 at level 1. Within a year of the birth of the second son, assuming the survival of both sons, this chance improves to 84/100. The comparable figures at level 12 are 85/100 (for the first son when the second is born), 95/100 and 97/100.

In these circumstances it might seem that the "rational" man might well pause before running the risk of having a third son whose arrival would not greatly improve his chance of a male heir, but would seriously increase the danger of having to provide for two or even three sons. For example, assuming the two earlier sons both to be living at the birth of a third, the chances of having 2 and 3 sons at death are 47/100 and 17/100 if mortality rates are those of level 1; while at level 12 the chances are 36/100 and 57/100, or a 93/100 chance of at least 2 surviving sons. Inasmuch as the provision of a dowry for

[5] Since each has a ⅔ chance of dying before his father, the combined probability that both will die is ⅔ × ⅔ = 4/9, leaving a 5/9 chance that one or both will survive.

145

daughters may also bring headaches for the thrifty and farsighted, there is a parallel argument applicable to them.

The frequency distributions of completed families available from reconstitution studies show that there were a great many families in European preindustrial village communities which had "overinsured" against the failure of male heirs. In most cases, it is true, the tabulated data do not deal conclusively with the issue since they show numbers ever born to a given marriage rather than the number living at a point in time, and very often they do not indicate sex combinations. More refined analysis of data of this type would be helpful in making it clear whether there is any tendency to arrest family formation when certain combinations of children *still living* are present in the family. However, the point of substance does not seem to be in much doubt. 'Over-insurance' was common. Consider, for example, the frequency distribution of family sizes given for Population 2 (Table 3–2). In it there are a total of 346.2 families per 1,000 which have 3 or more sons.[6] This involves a significant danger of having to provide for more than one male heir combined with a minimal risk of having no surviving son. At level 6 in more than a third of these cases, or in about 1 family in 8 overall, 2 sons will have been still living when the third was born and, of these cases in turn the chances of having 2 and 3 sons surviving to the death of the father are 47/100 and 37/100, a combined chance of 84/100. In addition, of course, many families had exactly 2 sons (207.2 per 1,000 families). In a quarter of these cases both sons would survive the father. In Population 2 (Table 3–2) as a whole the proportion of fathers having at least 2 sons living at their death is 276 per 1,000. Thus well over a quarter of all families in Population 2 (Table 3–2) would have faced such difficulties as may have been involved in providing for more than one son at the father's death.

If it were true that having more than one son to provide for created serious difficulties, therefore, it would be hard to find evidence of "rational" control of fertility in the frequency distribution of family sizes of Population 2 (Table 3–2), itself broadly similar to that of many preindustrial European populations. This is not direct evidence of lack of desire to do so, of course, since such a desire might have been frustrated only by lack of knowledge of effective technique, but at least existing data do not generally seem to support the view that couples acted to control family size for reasons of the sort discussed, or that the same effect was brought about indirectly by the operation of social customs.

[6] The same method used to calculate the characteristics of Populations 1-3 (Tables 3-1, 3-2, 3-3), described in the appendix, can be extended to yield information about the frequency of particular combinations of sons or daughters.

But has the problem been well conceived? For we have already seen that the imbalance between resources and claims upon those resources which is presumed to exist if a man has many sons is not mirrored in the economy as a whole if the population is stationary. The existence of families with several sons is offset by the existence of families without heirs or with daughters but no sons.

Knowledge of opportunities outside the immediate family may work through many institutional forms. The apprenticeship of a son from a large family in the household and workshop of a craftsman who is himself without a son is one possible arrangement, found in many folk tales and fairy stories. In complex economies the balancing out process may be indirect and multiple but knowledge of its operation embodied in the conventional wisdom may relieve parents blessed with large families from serious worry about the prospects of their children later in life.

Often there were opportunities for "surplus" sons close at hand. The averaging out of large and small families which produces a stationary population overall will also be reflected to some extent within any group of kin larger than the nuclear family. Within such a group some redistribution of sons between the producing units may provide either temporary or permanent solutions to the problems of families with many sons and daughters and also help those with few or none. Similarly, the institution of living-in service, based on locality rather than kinship may help to redistribute young people among the productive units in a manner which eases the burdens of fertile parents while at the same time tending to keep the marginal product of labor high.

Looked at in this light it would be reasonable to argue that in a preindustrial population in which numbers were stationary there would normally be no possibility that a rational strategy of heirship would dictate limitation of fertility even when a man had several sons. Limitation of fertility would have entailed, *ceteris paribus,* leaving ecological niches untenanted. In the simple case where each man lives on a separate holding, it would have meant leaving some holdings unoccupied. If population pressure were high, this might bring benefits for a time since the average size of holding would then creep up, but only to the level which represented one man's ability to cultivate land. Beyond that point, further contraction in numbers would bring no benefit.

It may be objected that this is special pleading since a man with many children might be poor as a result of the size of his family whatever the overall position of the economy in which he lived. He would be better off with fewer children. This is a matter which would repay much further study, both empirical and by the building of models

147

incorporating various assumptions about age of entry into the labor force, productivity with rising age, patterns of consumption, wage rates and employment opportunities. It may well be that, provided the population is stationary and not excessive, a large family brings net economic benefit while the children are at home and that the children's longer term prospects of establishing themselves in adult life are not significantly worse if they come from a large family. In any case, the community as a whole often needed "surplus" sons so badly that widespread family limitation would have undermined it.

Once the assumption of a stationary population is abandoned, of course, there may be penalties for excessive fertility which would be absent in a stationary population. The problem might be resolved demographically either by delaying marriage, or by restricting fertility within marriage, or by a rise in the schedule of mortality of sufficient magnitude to prevent further population growth, or by any combination of these changes or their equivalents. It could also be met by increasing production to provide the necessary opportunities for the new generation entering the labor force in larger numbers. Thus parts of Belgian Flanders in the eighteenth century attempted to meet the problem of growing population by expanding rural industry, while much of France met a similar difficulty a little later by demographic restraint rather than economic expansion.

V

Social Control and Individual Choice

When the demographic transition occurred it did not take the form of a move from a situation in which fertility was uncontrolled to one in which it was reduced by the exercise of prudential restraint. Fertility is under constraint in almost all societies, as the comparison of the levels of natural fertility in preindustrial societies clearly shows. The key change was from a system of control through social institution and custom to one in which the private choice of individual couples played a major part in governing the fertility rate. It was a change of profound importance, but the change is not best characterized as a change from lack of control to control. Even though control was not through private choice, it could be very effective nonetheless. Whether private choice is likely to be a solution which a society may countenance will be greatly influenced by its basic mortality schedule. At, say, level 1 Model West a population could hardly allow private choice since it must mobilize maximum fertility if it is to survive at all. At level 6 (where expectation of life for women is 32.5 years and for men 30 years)

148

a Gross Reproduction Rate (GRR) of about 2.00 is needed if the population is to replace itself. Given the certainty that there will be many small families (from the early death of parents and from infertility), and that some men and women in every generation do not marry, there must in this case also be a substantial number of families of large size if population decline is to be avoided (in Population 2 [Table 3–2] there are 290 in 1,000 families with 6 or more children, even though it is assumed that everyone marries). A society in which death rates were at this level for reasons outside its control (that is, from the presence of endemic disease for which no effective treatment was known, and the effects of periodic failure in food supply) would run into great difficulties if any significant proportion of the population was so moved by concern for solving its immediate problems of heirship that it kept family sizes down to a level that appeared rational in the local context of the immediate nuclear family. Its numbers would fall and it would be replaced by a population which was not so inhibited. Within any given preindustrial population of this type, of course, there might well be certain socioeconomic or other groups which could practice family limitation to alleviate concern about provision for the next generation, without endangering the society as a whole, provided that the groups were small enough to leave the overall pattern of family sizes little affected.

The Genevan bourgeoisie may have been a case in point (Henry 1956), and it would not be surprising if further study brings to light similar groups in other western European countries at that time. Particular individuals scattered through a community might do the same without seriously affecting overall fertility. Indeed, in both cases, provided the phenomenon is not widespread, it is also in a sense self-correcting in that a high proportion of the members of the next generation will come from large families and will not have the small family system deeply implanted in their habits of life.

Since there were very many preindustrial communities in which it is reasonable to believe that the basic mortality schedule was at least as unfavorable as level 6, it follows that there were also a large number in which what constituted the best fertility strategy for society as a whole prevailed over any strategy of heirship which might seem to promise benefits for individual families. Where mortality rates were substantially lower than this, however, say at level 12, the GRR necessary to ensure that numbers are maintained is more modest (c.1.45 at level 12) and the higher end of the frequency distribution of family sizes can be curtailed fairly drastically without running the risk of population decline. Expectation of life is now about 45, still not a high

149

figure compared with the present day, though higher than in most pre-industrial communities. Such a figure appears to have been reached, however, in parts of western Europe by the eighteenth century (and even earlier in certain parishes like Colyton, Devon which experienced comparatively low life-table death rates even in Elizabethan times), (Wrigley 1972) and was widespread in parts of North America, such as New England, from the earliest period of settlement.

In communities such as these population will grow quite rapidly given natural fertility within marriage. As long as this presents few difficulties to the society in question because economic opportunity is expanding equally fast, there is no strong stimulus to adopt a new fertility regime, but where this is not the case failure to change will bring penalties with it. For society as a whole, the problem is the familiar one that population is growing faster than productive capacity. Stability can be achieved once more only at the cost of the mortality schedule rising to meet the fertility schedule rather than vice-versa. For the individual family the problem presents itself differently. Since population is rising there will be a fall in the proportion of men dying without heirs or without male heirs. More men will have sons standing by them at their death beds and many more will have several sons rather than one to provide for. Therefore fathers in families with several living sons will face greater difficulties than in the past in assuring their future for them. The best strategy for heirs changes. There is new point to any strand in peasant wisdom about the advantage of avoiding too many sons.

The change in the outlook for "surplus" sons can be violent when mortality improves substantially but fertility remains unchanged. In Population 2 (Table 3–2) 317 men in every 1,000 have 1 son living at death, and 276 have 2 or more living sons. These include 427 "surplus" sons left after assuming that provision can be made for one son by each father. To set against this there are 407 "vacancies" created by men dying without heirs or with female heirs only. This balance between men and opportunities is implicit in the absence of growth in the population.[7]

If, however, the mortality of Population 2 (Table 3–2) is combined with the fertility of Population 3 (Table 3–3), implying a rate of growth of population of about 1 percent per annum, there is a marked change. In this case 298 in every 1,000 men have 1 living son at death, 384 have

[7] The small difference of 20 between "surplus" sons and "vacancies" is due to the nature of the fertility assumptions of Population 2 (Table 3-2) which result in generation $x + 1$ standing to generation x as 2,040 to 2,000, and of this surplus one half is male.

150

2 or more living sons, including a total of 677 "surplus" sons, but now there are only 318 "vacancies," while if the mortality of Population 1 (Table 3–1) is combined with the fertility of Population 3 (Table 3–3), implying a rate of growth of population of about 3 percent per annum, the corresponding figures are 244 (1 son living), 564 (2 or more sons living), 1,242 ("surplus" sons) and 212 ("vacancies"). The last of these is an extreme case, though close to the situation in many developing countries today, but the second case, where the ratio of "surplus" sons to "vacancies" is more than two to one, was approached more and more frequently in early modern Europe. Elizabethan England saw something of this and most of Europe moved toward it in the eighteenth century. It makes for a fluid and unstable society, and demands a rapid and sustained growth in the economy if the younger generation is to find employment and to enjoy standards of living equal to that of their fathers. In this new situation lower fertility within marriage may bring benefit both to the individual and to the community as a whole.

In 1700 there was near uniformity in Europe in maintaining natural fertility within marriage (which is not synonymous, of course, with high fertility). By 1900 there was near uniformity in converging towards the new system of private control of marital fertility, exercised in such a way that the frequency of large families fell away to negligible proportions. In between there was great variety of behavior and trend. From late in the eighteenth-century France made steady progress toward the new system which was already widely present in the regional populations of Normandy and the southwest early in the nineteenth century. In some of the new industrial areas of England and Germany, on the other hand, fertility in marriage remained high or increased, while with the transformation of society in these areas obstacles to early marriage were often much reduced, causing a rise in general fertility rates. But fertility began to fall generally in the late nineteenth century. In some measure, no doubt, the steady rise of average real incomes in the later decades of the nineteenth century and the early part of the twentieth was facilitated by the missing millions who would otherwise have pressed into the labor market.

A rational fertility strategy is much harder to define in an industrial than a preindustrial society since the ability to expand economic production at exponential rates of growth over a long period removes one of the most restrictive features of the older situation. Thus at the societal level it may be a matter of less moment than in preindustrial times to avoid population growth, at least until concern for the environment becomes a major issue. On the other hand, the individual family is relieved of whatever societal pressures are exerted in favor of natural

151

fertility during periods of high basic mortality. Individual choice can operate freely without serious penalty and, in time, in all populations so placed, the large family has been abandoned by the great majority of couples. Perhaps in seeking an explanation for the comparative simultaneity of fertility change across much of Europe in the later nineteenth century, one should have more regard to the independent importance of falls in mortality [8] in creating a situation in which change could occur and less to measures of economic modernity— urbanization, industrialization, literacy and the like.

How far it is sensible to write of unconscious rationality exercised by individuals following the norms set for them by the society in which they live, and to contrast it with a conscious rationality characteristic of couples in industrial societies where family limitation is widespread is debatable. If the notions have value it may be more in defining polar alternatives than as descriptions of particular situations. Men's actions at all times are influenced by their appreciation of their personal interests and by their response to social norms. Nevertheless, it is interesting to examine strategies of family formation as if couples behaved in conformity with these stereotypes of thought and action. In particular it is illuminating to try to define those demographic circumstances in which it will cease to be a matter of small consequence how large a family grows. There is a crossover point to one side of which for society as a whole, and perhaps in most cases for the individual, too, high fertility cannot bring insuperable problems because the ranks of the older generation are thinning fast enough to satisfy the needs of the younger. On the other side of this point excess fertility ceases to be a remote problem and begins to create challenges to which some response must be made. Sometimes the challenge was met only by accepting higher mortality and reduced living standards; sometimes by economic or social changes which restored the lost balance between population and production. In Europe in the eighteenth and nineteenth centuries there was a more fundamental change—the industrial revolution—which permanently altered the terms of the problem and in so doing made possible new demographic structures within society.

[8] Fall in infant mortality has received much attention as the 'trigger' which is alleged to have set off control of fertility in marriage, but the balance between "surplus" sons and "vacancies" is also greatly influenced by mortality in childhood and youth. This deserves equal attention. Much of the argument based on changes in infant mortality has neglected the point made earlier in this chapter about the implications of the fact that births in a family take place successively rather than simultaneously.

152

Appendix

THE method by which the characteristics of Populations 1–3 (Tables 3–1, 3–2, 3–3) were derived may be illustrated by considering a single case, where 5 children are born to a married couple and each child has a 1/2 chance of surviving until the death of the father. There are 6 possible combinations of the sexes of the children in a family of 5: 5 females, 4 females and 1 male, 3 females and 2 males, 2 females and 3 males, 1 female and 4 males, and 5 males. The frequency with which each combination will occur can be determined by binomial expansion $P(r) = \binom{N}{r} p^r q^{N-r}$ (in this exercise I have assumed that the sex ratio at birth is 100).

Suppose that we are interested in establishing the likelihood that at least 1 female but no male heir will survive at the death of the father. This may be calculated for each sex combination and multiplied by the frequency with which that combination occurs. For example, if 2 female and 3 male children were born, the likelihood that at least 1 daughter will still be living at her father's death is 3/4, while the likelihood that all 3 sons will have died is 1/8, and the combined likelihood is 3/32. The likelihood of having 2 female and 3 male children in families of 5 children is 10/32 by binomial expansion. And therefore the overall likelihood of there being at least 1 female but no male heirs in families of 5 where 2 of the children are girls and 3 are boys is $3/32 \times 10/32 = 30/1024$. Similar calculations for each possible type of 5 child family are shown in the table below.

It will be seen from the total figure at the foot of column D that the overall probability in 5 children families of having a female but no male heir is 20.6 percent. When the relative frequency of families of different sizes has been determined, this base figure can be adjusted accordingly. Thus in Table 3–2 the cell in the row for family size 5 which expresses the probability of at least 1 female but no male heir contains the figure 25.8 $\left(125 \times \dfrac{20.6}{100} \right)$.

Parallel calculations are made for each possible family size and then an overall probability for each eventuality may be determined for the population as a whole.

The likelihood of, say, leaving 2 or more male heirs can be calculated similarly, and the statistics of this and other comparable eventualities were derived in the same way.

A Sex combination of children	B Probability of this combination occurring	C Probability of this combination resulting in at least 1 female heir but no male heir at father's death	D B × C
5F 0M	1/32	31/32	31/1024
4F 1M	5/32	15/32	75/1024
3F 2M	10/32	7/32	70/1024
2F 3M	10/32	3/32	30/1024
1F 4M	5/32	1/32	5/1024
0F 5M	1/32	—	—
			211/1024

4

Models of Preindustrial Population Dynamics with Application to England

RONALD LEE

INTRODUCTION

POPULATION size in itself was of no great importance to preindustrial societies, but in relation to resources it affected the productivity of labor on which depended material welfare; because of this, population control was essential.[1] However labor productivity could also vary independently of population size, under the influence of climate, technology, capital, and organization; and mortality could alter population size independently of labor productivity, under the influence of climate and disease. In the face of these dislocating disturbances, preindustrial societies developed institutions which, by regulating fertility and hence population, enabled them, imperfectly and within broad limits, to establish and protect a standard of material welfare.

In this chapter we develop simple models of hypothetical population control strategies, and derive their implications. We then use data from preindustrial England to estimate and test these models. We have two main concerns: first, to determine the structural relations characterizing the population control system and wage determination; second, to analyze the sources of disturbance to the system and allocate responsibility for change.

The chapter has five parts. In the first part we discuss the properties of various hypothesized population control systems, emphasizing the role played by the form of fertility regulation in relation to mortality and wages. We use a simplified model in which all variation in mortality is exogenous, fertility depends on mortality and wages, and wages depend on population size.

I would like to thank Professor Ansley Coale and the Seminar on Early Industrialization, Fertility and Family Structure for their many helpful comments. I am also grateful to Jack Goodman, Lynda Sowers and Andy Mason for assistance with the research and to Carolyn Copley for typing and editing the manuscript and preparing the diagrams. Any remaining errors are my sole responsibility. Preparation of this manuscript in final form was supported in part by NICHD Grant Number HD08586.

[1] We abstract from considerations of military power, the genetic pool, need to staff the social organization, and so on.

155

In the second part we use regression analysis to estimate and test the model using data from eighteenth-century England. Results are compared to those from an earlier paper (Lee 1973) which analyzed English data for 1250 to 1700. The demographic changes of the eighteenth century are explained by the interaction of an unchanged population control system with a steadily increasing demand for labor and fluctuating mortality.

We have so far stressed fluctuations in mortality as a source of exogenous disturbance to the system; but of course there was also an endogenous component of mortality change: the Malthusian "positive check." In the third part we incorporate it in the model, derive its theoretical implications, and analyze its actual operation using various sets of data. We also attempt to assess the relative importance of exogenous change in mortality and the demand for labor.

In the fourth part we consider to what extent the regulation of fertility operated through nuptiality, and to what extent through the control of fertility within marriage.

The fifth part discusses the results of the previous four.

I

MORTALITY AND THE PREVENTIVE CHECK

THE context of variation within which preindustrial population control systems operated presented two problems: responding to changes in the demand for labor and protecting population size from fluctuating mortality. Most analyses have singled out one or the other of these two aspects of fertility control for study, and it will be convenient for us to consider them separately.

A. FERTILITY AND MORTALITY

The problem of maintaining a relatively stationary population in the face of fluctuating mortality may be resolved by tying the level of fertility directly to that of mortality. This may be done by linking age at marriage to mortality, or by linking fertility within marriage to mortality. We consider these two possibilities in that order.

1. *Mortality and Marriage* The most thorough theoretical investigation of the link between mortality and fertility by way of age and frequency of marriage has been provided by Goran Ohlin. He argues that if "marriage is contingent upon access to livelihood" then "One should expect higher mortality to occasion earlier inheritance, earlier marriage, and therefore higher fertility" (Ohlin 1961: 190). Formalizing this model and measuring the quantitative effect of this mechanism,

156

he found that "mortality changes alone would not . . . account for secular movement in population . . ." (Ohlin 1961: 197). In other words, mortality changes would induce offsetting changes in fertility, leaving population growth rates virtually unaffected.

2. *Mortality and Marital Fertility* It has been plausibly argued that family size goals, if they exist, will be formulated and implemented in terms of numbers of surviving children, not of births. Fluctuations in child mortality will therefore induce fluctuations in marital fertility, as couples attempt to replace children who have died. This sort of argument has been made frequently: in the sociological literature by Bogue (1969: 52) and by Freedman (1963); in the microeconomic literature by Becker (1960), Easterlin (see Chapter 2 above), and Schultz (1971); and more generally by Marshall (1965), Heer and Smith (1968), and Rutstein (1971) to list only a few of the many instances. Empirical evidence from developing countries lends qualified support to this assertion (see Rutstein and Schultz cited above).

However, it is not clear that preindustrial European couples *did* formulate and implement family size goals; and if they did not, then this argument cannot apply. The findings of Gautier and Henry (1958) and other historical demographers working with European material indicate that fertility behavior was independent of parity at the family level (which is the defining characteristic of what Henry has called "natural fertility"). This suggests that couples were not aiming for any particular number of children, surviving or otherwise.

When we pass from behavioral considerations to biological ones, the picture is again mixed. On the one hand, child mortality may interrupt lactation and thus stimulate fecundity, as many historical studies have concluded (e.g., Gautier and Henry 1958). On the other hand, both mortality and fecundity are related to general health, but in opposite ways, and this relation to a common variable might induce a negative association between them.

In any case, it is a plausible hypothesis that in preindustrial Europe, a combination of institutional, voluntary, and biological factors operated to produce a positive relation between fertility and mortality, thus affording populations some protection from fluctuating mortality (for a more comprehensive discussion of these points, see Lee, 1974c).

B. The Preventive Check

The problem of establishing and protecting a customary level of material welfare in the face of diminishing returns to labor and fluctuating production relations was met in part by the "preventive check"—a link

157

between fertility and the available means of sustenance. This could, in principle, operate through either nuptiality or marital fertility, and we shall consider these two cases separately.

1. *Marriage and Wages* The view is widely accepted that in pre-industrial Europe, a man could not marry without the means to support a family at a conventional standard of living (Habakkuk 1965; Hajnal 1965). This should not be interpreted as requiring access to a holding, since wage laborers did marry, and since the ability of a given holding to support a family was variable, depending on climate, technology, available crops, stock of capital, and so on. More appropriately we may follow the classical economists and hypothesize a relation between nuptiality and the real wage. The real wage measures the marginal productivity of labor, and therefore relates to the welfare of those who work their own land as well as that of wage earners. Furthermore, it depends in part on the demand for labor, and thus reflects changes in the quantity and productivity of land and capital.

2. *Marital Fertility and Wages* It is also possible that fertility within marriage depended on the real wage, though it is not generally thought to have done so. Such a dependence could reflect conscious control by individual families over the timing of fertility or over completed numbers of children. It also could occur fortuitously: fecundity, dependent on nutrition, may have varied with the real wage; involuntary separations of husband and wife may have been more frequent when times were hard; or the desire for coitus may have been reduced by adversity. In any case, a positive relation between marital fertility and real wages would be quite consistent with natural fertility (in Henry's sense) provided that the reaction of fertility to wages was independent of parity at the family level.

C. A SIMPLIFIED MODEL OF THE GENERAL CONTROL SYSTEM

In order to discuss the implications of these hypothetical aspects of fertility behavior, we develop in this section a rough model of the remainder of the system.

The various possibilities for fertility regulation are expressed in the following equation:

$$f_t = \mu + \alpha \ln(w_t) + \lambda m_t$$

where f_t is the crude birth rate, $\ln(w_t)$ is the natural logarithm of the real wage, and m_t is the crude death rate, all at time t.[2] μ, α, and λ

[2] The use of the logarithm of wages is for later econometric convenience, and of no substantive importance.

invariant parameters characterizing the fertility control system. At this stage we make no distinction between the effects of nuptiality and marital fertility on f_t; later we will analyze these separately.

If $\alpha > 0$, then fertility is positively related to wages, and there is a preventive check; if $\alpha = 0$, then fertility is invariant with respect to wages, and there is none. If $\lambda = 1$, then fertility compensates perfectly for variation in mortality, leaving growth rates unchanged; if $\lambda = 0$, then fertility is invariant with respect to mortality; if $\lambda < 0$, then they are negatively related. When both α and λ equal 0, then fertility is constant; or, more properly, any variation in fertility is exogenous to this simple system.

Now let us consider the relation between population and wages. The wage is determined by the intersection of a labor-supply schedule, which shifts with population size, and a labor-demand schedule, which shifts with time (due to changes in climate, technology, capital stock, trade, and similar factors). We thus write:

$$w_t = \sigma_t P_t^{-\beta}$$

where w_t is the real wage and P_t is the population size, both at time t. The exponent of population size is negative, expressing diminishing returns to labor. σ_t is a scale variable which fluctuates with the demand for labor.

For the present, we assume that there is no positive check; m_t is independent of w_t, and fluctuates exogenously under the influence of climate and disease. This assumption is later relaxed in Part 3.

Finally, we assume that there is zero net migration, so that the rate of population growth (designated P^*/P) equals $f_t - m_t$. We thus have the following simple system:

$$f_t = \mu + \alpha \ln(w_t) + \lambda m_t \tag{1}$$

$$w_t = \sigma_t P_t^{-\beta} \tag{2}$$

$$P_t^* / P_t = f_t - m_t \tag{3}$$

To analyze this simple model, we may begin by deriving the equilibrium values of wages and population size. If σ_t has no time trend, so that there is no steady shift in the demand for labor, then the system will be in equilibrium when population is stationary. This requires that $m_t = \mu + \alpha \ln(w_t) + \lambda m_t$, which leads directly to the equilibrium values:

$$w^E = \exp\{(-1/\alpha)\,[m_t\,(\lambda-1)+\mu]\} \qquad (4)$$

$$P^E = (w^E/\sigma_t)^{-1/\beta} \qquad (5)$$

We note that unless there is a preventive check ($\alpha > 0$), the equilibrium wage and population size do not exist. We also note that unless $\lambda = 1$, the equilibrium values, if they do exist, will depend on the exogenously determined level of mortality. The next section relies heavily on these two conclusions. Finally, while the equilibrium population size depends on the demand for labor, σ_t, the equilibrium wage does not; this expresses the Malthusian conclusion that economic progress cannot benefit the laboring class except temporarily.

If left to itself, such a system would converge to these equilibrium levels and persist in the "stationary state." But in history, and in our model, the system is not left to itself. As we have emphasized, there are two major sources of disturbance: fluctuation in mortality (m_t), and fluctuation in the demand for labor (σ_t). How these affect the system depends on the values of α and λ; this is the topic of the next section.

D. POPULATION CONTROL STRATEGIES

We may now describe fertility control systems in terms of their values for α and λ. We will consider four sets of values representing polar cases.

1. Constant Fertility (CF): One might argue that over the long run, institutions evolved which fixed aggregate fertility at a constant level equal to the average level of mortality. Thus $\alpha = 0$, $\lambda = 0$ and $f_t = \mu = E(m_t)$. Since there is no preventive check ($\alpha = 0$), the system has no equilibrium levels for population or wages. In fact, given any initial level, population size will deviate from it by increasing amounts as time passes.[3] Thus this system provides no control over population size or material welfare, though it does moderate the rates of change of these variables.

2. Constant Population (CP): Suppose there is no preventive check, so that $\alpha = 0$, while fertility compensates perfectly for variations in mortality, so that $\lambda = 1$. In this case there are no equilibrium values for population and wages, although population size will remain at its initial level, independent of fluctuations in mortality or the demand for labor. If population size is somehow changed, it will remain at

---

[3] Formally, $\ln P_t - \ln P_{t-1} \equiv \mu - m_t$. Starting at time 0, after T years, we will have: $E(\ln P_T) = \ln P_0$; $Var(\ln P_T) = T\,Var(m)$.

its new level. Such a system provides no control over material welfare; it merely imparts a great deal of inertia to the status quo.

3. Mortality Dependent Equilibrium Wage (MDEW): If there is a preventive check ($\alpha > 0$), but fertility is independent of mortality ($\lambda = 0$), then equilibrium levels exist for population and wages, but they depend sensitively on mortality conditions (m_t) which are exogenously determined and subject to change. Consequently, the equilibrium wage does not depend solely on institutionally determined parameters; it is itself a dependent variable in the analysis.

An exogenous change in mortality will eventually entail a compensating change in fertility, but only after a new level of wages has been established. Consider, for example, the centuries before and after the Black Death; they illustrate, one can argue, an exogenous long-run increase in mortality (see Lee 1970 and 1973). The present specification of the fertility control system suggests that population will fall, causing the real wage to rise, which in turn causes fertility to rise; this continues until fertility reaches the higher level of mortality, after which time the system will remain in equilibrium at the new levels of population and wages.

Such a system provides some control over material welfare in the face of a fluctuating demand for labor or mortality, but the control is evidently imperfect.

4. Constant Equilibrium Wage (CEW): If there is a preventive check ($\alpha > 0$) and if in addition fertility compensates perfectly for variations in mortality ($\lambda = 1$), then the equilibrium wage will be constant. It equals $\exp(-\mu/\alpha)$, and thus depends solely on the parameters of the fertility control equation. This system, and this system alone, allows us to interpret the equilibrium wage as an institutionally determined parameter. Since this interpretation is a central tenet of the population theory of classical economists, we may infer that the CEW specification of the model corresponds to classical population theory.

We may also see this in another way. Combining equations (1) and (3) of the previous section, we find that when $\lambda = 1$, $P^*/P = \mu + \alpha \ln(w)$; thus the rate of population growth depends solely on the real wage, *and is independent of mortality.* This expresses the classical view that: "The actual progress of population is . . . determined by the relative difficulty of procuring the means of subsistence, and . . . is little affected by unhealthiness or healthiness . . ." (Malthus 1970: 262).

We note that the preventive check alone is insufficient to establish the classical conclusions (nor would the addition of the positive check

161

help in this regard); a further check on fertility, tying it closely to mortality (so that $\lambda=1$) is required.

We have discussed the following four systems:

$\alpha=0$, $\lambda=0$:	Constant Fertility	(CF)
$\alpha=0$, $\lambda=1$:	Constant Population	(CP)
$\alpha>0$, $\lambda=0$:	Mortality Dependent Equilibrium Wage	(MDEW)
$\alpha>0$, $\lambda=1$:	Constant Equilibrium Wage	(CEW)

The properties of each system are summarized in Table 4–1.

5. Fixed Hearths: The last system specified in the table, "Fixed Hearths," has not yet been discussed; it does not correspond to any specification of α and λ. We assume that the number of hearths (houses) in an area is fixed by convention, and that title to one of these is required for marriage (see Braun, Chapter 8). This assures a constant number of couples. If we further assume, for simplicity, that average marital fertility is constant, then this system yields a constant annual crop of babies, say B, independent of total population size. How large will the equilibrium population be under these circumstances? If e_0 is the expectation of life at birth, then the total population will be given by Be_0. If e_0 changes, say from 25 years

TABLE 4–1. PROPERTIES OF FERTILITY CONTROL SYSTEMS

System specification	Population		Wage	
	Size	Equilibrium	Level	Equilibrium
CF $\alpha=0$, $\lambda=0$	Mortalility	N.E.	Mortality Demd. for L	N.E.
CP $\alpha=0$, $\lambda=1$	Constant	N.E.	Demd. for L	N.E.
MDEW $\alpha>0$, $\lambda=0$	Mortality Demd. for L	Mortality Demd. for L	Mortality Demd. for L	Mortality
CEW $\alpha>0$, $\lambda=1$	Demd. for L	Demd. for L	Demd. for L	Constant
Fixed hearths	Mortality	Mortality	Mortality Demd. for L	Mortality Demd. for L

Note: "Demd. for L" signifies "demand for labor"; "equilibrium" refers only to stable equilibrium; N.E. indicates nonexistence.

to 35 years, then equilibrium population size will change proportionately, in this case by 40 percent. This system thus provides only imperfect protection against mortality change. Furthermore, it does not enable a population to expand or contract with the demand for labor, since the number of hearths is fixed. To the extent that changed production relations lead to changed numbers of hearths, the system may be approximated by the MDEW specification with $\lambda = 0$ and $\alpha = -\overline{m}_t/\beta$.

Another model which we have not discussed is the "Moving Standard" model, according to which the conventional living standard is revised on the basis of prevailing wage rates. This model may be appropriate for changes which have taken place in the past century; however, its application to preindustrial Europe is often tautological (see Lee 1970), and the phenomena it is envoked to explain may be more adequately accounted for by the MDEW model.

E. EXTENSIONS OF THE MODEL

We have so far assumed that σ_t had no time trend, and hence, that there was no irreversible economic progress. We now remove that assumption by respecifying the population-wage relation as follows:

$$w_t = \exp(\sigma + \rho t + \epsilon_t)P_t^{-\beta} \tag{6}$$

Here the demand for labor is shifting outward at the constant rate ρ, and ϵ_t represents fluctuations about this trend. Wages will be constant (except for ϵ_t) only when population is growing at the steady state rate ρ/β. This specification will be useful for estimation and testing.

It is also of interest to develop an equation expressing the behavior of population when it is out of equilibrium. Substituting from Equations (1) and (6) into Equation (3), we find the differential equation in P. The solution to this is:

$$P_t = e^{(rt - a/b + (\ln P_0 + a/b)e^{bt})} \tag{7}$$

where $r = \rho/\beta$; $a = \mu - \rho/\beta + \sigma\alpha + m(\lambda - 1)$; and $b = -\alpha\beta$.

This equation may be used to simulate the path of population size over periods in which mortality is constant and the demand for labor is increasing at a constant rate. Paths of wages and fertility may be derived using Equations (1) and (6). When mortality is changing dis-

163

cretely, we may simulate population, fertility and wages by splicing together the appropriate segments of their paths as implied by Equation (7). We will do this below in the next part to simulate these variables for eighteenth-century England under various hypotheses.

II

ESTIMATED STRUCTURAL RELATIONS

A. INTRODUCTION

In this part we apply the previous model to data from England, 1250 to 1700 and 1705 to 1784. The data series are controversial and of very poor quality; thus some readers may prefer to view the following estimates and tests as merely illustrative, although I myself consider it possible to draw some substantive conclusions.

Since a previous paper (Lee 1973) analyzed the period 1250 to 1700, we will concentrate on the eighteenth century.

Controversy over the role of population in eighteenth-century England centers on the question: "Did the Industrial Revolution create its own labor force? Or did the vagaries of disease and the weather produce an additional population that either stimulated an Industrial Revolution or had the luck to coincide with one independently generated ?" (Habakkuk 1965: 157). However, as Habakkuk points out, the controversy is often reduced to the empirical question whether variation in the birth rate or the death rate was responsible for change. Thus according to Drake: "With reliable population statistics, the mechanism of change would have been at once apparent" (Drake, 1969: 2). But this view is mistaken. To answer Habakkuk's question requires more than reliable statistics; for one may accept the *fact* that mortality declined while rejecting this decline as an explanation for population growth. Marshall wrote: "The obvious temptation is to assert that the death rate was not only the variable, but also the determining, factor in the increase of population . . . But, clearly, the forces that prevent a birth rate from falling may be as significant as those that make it rise" (Marshall 1965: 248). And in a similar vein, Deane and Cole wrote: "In conditions of demographic equilibrium birth and death rates tend to fluctuate directly and not inversely; so the question remains why the fall in the death rate was not accompanied by a decline in fertility" (Deane and Cole 1962: 134).

These authors, like Malthus, argued not that exogenous variation in mortality was altogether absent, but rather that such independent variation was an inadequate explanation for population change.

It should be clear that these issues are closely related to the discussion of the first part, and in particular to the values of the parameters λ and α. If $\lambda=1$ and $\alpha=0$, corresponding to the CEW specification, then the demand for labor alone can affect population growth; mortality is irrelevant, as Marshall and Deane and Cole suggest. On the other hand, if α and λ both are 0, corresponding to the CF specification, then only mortality can affect population growth; the demand for labor is irrelevant. But these are not the only possibilities. Under the MDEW specification, with $\alpha>0$ and $\lambda=0$, both mortality and the demand for labor may be effective sources of population change. And in this case the allocation of responsibility for population change between the two is not a simple task.

To explain an historical instance of population change, we must first evaluate the structural relations (the parameters of the equations) and then consider the interaction of this structure with the historical course of exogenous disturbance (e.g., mortality change). Neither the structure by itself, nor the disturbance by itself, can furnish an adequate explanation.

In this part we attempt to determine the general nature of the population control system as described by α and λ, and the production constraints within which it operated, as described by β and ρ.[4] Having thus established the structural relations, we discuss the extent to which changes in mortality or the demand for labor was responsible for population and wage change in each period.

B. DATA

The data series used for 1250 to 1700 are discussed elsewhere (Lee, 1970 and 1973). For the eighteenth century, our demographic series are derived from Rickman's abstracts (Mitchell and Deane 1962) following Ohlin (1955); and the real wage series is derived from Gilboy's data (Gilboy 1934) following Deane and Cole (1962: 19). We realize there are acute difficulties with each of these series; some of these difficulties are discussed in the appendix. By limiting our analysis to the period 1705–1784, we avoid some of the more severe problems. We have also experimented with different series to determine the sensitivity of our results to the choice of data.

C. TESTING AND ESTIMATION

1. *Assumptions.* We assume that exogenous variation in fertility is small (relative to that in mortality and wages) and that all variation in

[4] Actually ρ describes an exogenous exponential shift in the demand for labor.

165

mortality is exogenous. Subsequent parts relax these assumptions and investigate the extent to which they are justified.

2. *Discrete Form.* We begin by converting the continuous form of Equations (1), (3) and 6 to discrete form. Let $\{P_t\}$ be a series of observations of population size at ten year intervals. Let $\{w_t\}$, $\{f_t\}$, and $\{m_t\}$ be series of average values of real wages, CBR, and CDR over the ten-year intervals t–1 to t. Equation (1) is unchanged:

$$f_t = \mu + \alpha \ln(w_t) + \lambda m_t. \tag{8}$$

The average level of the wage over the interval will be related to the midpoint population size. Assuming a constant rate of growth within the interval, the midpoint population is given by $\sqrt{P_t P_{t-1}}$; its logarithm is given by the average of the logarithms of the end-points. Thus Equation (6) takes the form:

$$\ln(w_t) = \sigma + \rho t - (\beta/2) \, [\ln(P_t) + \ln(P_{t-1})]. \tag{9}$$

The rate of growth of population is given by the difference of the logarithms of the end-points, divided by the length of the interval.

With decadal observations, Equation (3) takes the form:

$$\ln(P_t) - \ln(P_{t-1}) \equiv 10(f_t - m_t). \tag{10}$$

Equations (8) to (10) constitute the system in discrete form. It will be noted that this system is overidentified.

3. *Summary of Results.* The equations were estimated using ordinary least squares (OLS) on the structural Equations (8) and (9), and using two stage least squares (TSLS) on the complete system. The results are summarized in Table 4–2.

4. *Discussion of Parameter Estimates.* The parameters α and λ of the fertility control equation determine important properties of the system as a whole. The estimated values of these parameters, for both periods, indicate that α was significantly greater than zero, so that fertility was positively related to the real wage; and that λ was closer to zero than to one, so that fertility did not compensate for variations in mortality. Thus the MDEW (Mortality Dependent Equilibrium

166

TABLE 4–2. PARAMETER ESTIMATES

Period and method	β	ρ(%)	λ	α λ Unconstrained	α λ=0
1250–1700 TSLS	1.10 (.16)	.10 (.044)	.23 (.20)	.0103 (.0052)	.0135 (.0048)
1705–1789					
OLS	1.29 (.35)	.60 (.017)	−.38 (.17)	.0366 (.0081)	.026 (.0086)
TSLS	1.87 (.60)	.85 (.27)	−.60 (.25)	.049 (.013)	.026 (.0086)

(Standard errors in parentheses)

Source: Lee, 1970 and 1973.

Wage) specification is appropriate for both periods.[5] It will be recalled that in this specification, both the actual and the equilibrium values of population and wages depend with considerable sensitivity on mortality levels, while the demand for labor is also capable of inducing change.

The wage-population equation describes the production relations within the context of which the population control system operated. The estimates of β for both periods, which are not significantly different from one another, suggest sharply diminishing returns to labor; indeed the estimated elasticities are too large to be consistent with a straightforward neoclassical interpretation.[6]

The estimates of ρ are of particular interest. In the period 1250 to 1700, there was apparently very little change in the demand for labor; we have estimated a shift parameter of *at most* .1 percent per year. In the eighteenth century, however, the estimated shift increases to between .6 and .85 percent per year. This change in the shift parameter is the most striking difference between the two periods.

The steady state rate of population growth (i.e., the rate consistent with constant wages) is given by ρ/β. For 1250–1700 this was about .09 percent per year; more rapid growth would cause deteriorating wages, as in the sixteenth century. For 1705–1784, ρ/β was about .45 percent per year, or five times as great.

[5] For alternative methods of estimating these equations and for formal testing procedures, see Lee, 1970 or 1973.
[6] They are inconsistent with a Cobb-Douglas production function, but could arise from a Constant Elasticity of Substitution production function.

167

D. SIMULATIONS UNDER VARIOUS HYPOTHESES

The explanation of actual change in population, fertility and wages may be approached through simulations, substituting estimated parameters in Equation (7). We may then simulate the time paths of these variables under several hypotheses: (1) The demand for labor shifted at the constant estimated rate, $\hat{\rho}$, but mortality remained constant at the level of 1705–1714; (2) the demand for labor remained constant at its level in 1705, but mortality varied as observed; and (3) the demand for labor shifted as estimated, and mortality varied as observed.[7] These simulations help us to assess the extent to which the variations in population, fertility and wages in the eighteenth century were a systematic response to the increasing demand for labor which was part of the industrial revolution, and to what extent they were "fortuitous," due to the effect of "vagaries of disease and the weather" on mortality.

The results of such simulations are shown in Figure 4–1, together with the original data series. Inspection shows that neither the increasing demand for labor, nor the exogenously varying mortality can adequately explain eighteenth-century population and wage changes. We must consider the two together to derive a satisfactory explanation. More specifically, the shift in the demand for labor determines the equilibrium levels for fertility and wages, and the equilibrium time-path for population, while changes in mortality determine the timing and amplitude of fluctuations about the equilibrium level or trend. These results may be compared to those in the period 1250 to 1700, where exogenous change in mortality did appear to account for virtually all the variation in population and wages (see Lee 1973).

In this part we have estimated and tested the set of structural relations comprising the population control system, and made an initial attempt to assess the sources of disturbance. To do so we have had to make some simplifying assumptions about both structural parameters and the sources of exogenous variation. In the remainder of the chapter we relax these assumptions and examine in a more systematic way the sources of disturbance.

---

[7] All simulations assume that fertility is independent of mortality ($\lambda = 0$), and that mortality is independent of the real wage ($\gamma = 0$ in the notation of the third part). The first assumption is roughly consistent with our estimates, but the second is not consistent with the short run elasticity we estimate in the third part. Including an endogenous component of mortality would have little or no effect on simulations 2 and 3; in simulation 1 it would lead to larger population and lower wages, thus reinforcing the general conclusions we will draw below.

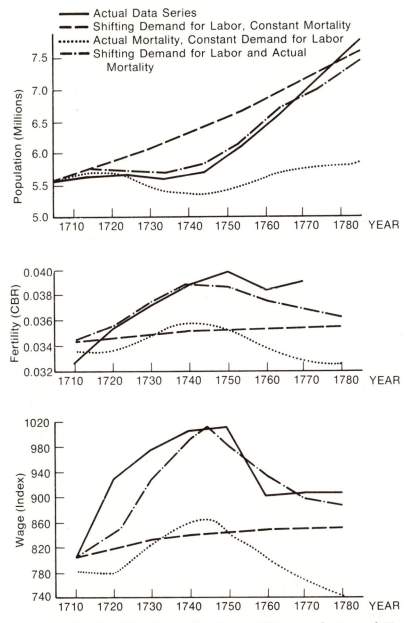

Figure 4–1 Simulated Population, Fertility and Wages under Several Hypotheses: England, 1705–1784

III

MORTALITY AND WAGES: A TIME SERIES ANALYSIS

A. INTRODUCTION

It is sometimes thought that the positive check controlled population size in preindustrial Europe: growing populations pressed on limited resources; real wages fell; and mortality rose to reduce the rate of growth. The operation of this mechanism would depend on a negative relation between mortality and material well-being. Was there such a relation? Numerous empirical studies appear to show that there was: by exhibiting the coincidence of peaks in grain prices and burials on the local level (Goubert 1960); by calculating the correlations of short run fluctuations in the crude death rate and a harvest index on the national level (Thomas 1941); and by showing a negative association of age-specific mortality and social class cross-sectionally.

On the other hand, the empirical work reported in the second part revealed a positive correlation of mortality and wages in both periods studied.[8] This result is consistent with the views of those historians who have attempted to explain high wages by high mortality. Thus Mathias wrote: "high real wages . . . in some periods tend to reflect conditions in the aftermath of plague and endemic disease, as in the fifteenth century" (1969: 6). Phelps Brown and Hopkins (1957) suggest that low mortality due to independent epidemiological changes might account for the declining real wage of the sixteenth century. Eversley (1967: 216) attributes the high wages of the 1730s and 1740s in part to the high mortality of those years.

How are we to reconcile these apparently contradictory results? In this part we will show that the contradiction is only apparent, and that a plausible model can generate either a positive association or a negative association, or even both simultaneously, depending on the nature of the exogenous disturbance to which the system is subjected. We shall also analyze actual series of mortality and wages and show that their associative behavior is consistent with the model.

B. THEORETICAL RELATIONS BETWEEN MORTALITY AND WAGES

1. *The Model.* We must begin by recognizing the simultaneity of the relations between real wages and mortality: on the one hand, high wages led to lower mortality, *ceteris paribus;* on the other hand, high mortality led to falling population and rising wages. The next step is

---

[8] This result was not discussed in part 2. The correlation of wages and the CDR for 1250 to 1700 was plus .47 (see Lee, 1973).

to realize that there was a large exogenous stochastic component in both of these relations. Short-run variations in climate had a strong effect on harvest, and therefore on grain prices and real wages, whatever the size of the labor force. Similarly, epidemiological factors and climatic variations exercised an important effect on the death rate in the short run as well as the long, whatever the level of the real wage (Chambers 1965; Habakkuk 1965).

In order to analyze the implications of these simultaneous relations, we may use the model developed in part 1 with an additional equation expressing the negative structural relation between mortality and wages:

$$m_t = d - \gamma \ln(w_t) + \eta_t \tag{11}$$

This expresses m_t, the crude death rate, as a function of wages, plus an exogenous disturbance term, η_t (the logarithmic form for wages is solely for econometric convenience). The remainder of the model is unchanged. The real wage is expressed as a function of population size, P_t, with a shift parameter ρ which indicates a steady increase in the demand for labor, and a stochastic disturbance, ϵ_t: $w_t = e^{\sigma + \rho t + \epsilon_t} P_t^{-\beta}$. To simplify the analysis, we assume the CF specification, with $\alpha = 0$ and $\lambda = 0$. (Note that if $\lambda = 1$ then fertility would always perfectly compensate for variations in mortality, so that these would have no effect on population or wages, and the anomalous results would not arise.) The assumption of zero net migration is expressed in the following identity, closing the model: $\dot{P}_t / P_t \equiv f - m_t$.

As in Part 2, Section C, we may express this model in a form appropriate for discrete time. The result is simplified by using the identity to eliminate P, and by altering the notation. Let x_t be the deviation of $\ln(w_t)$ from its equilibrium value and y_t be the deviation of m_t from its equilibrium value. Then we find:

$$x_t - x_{t-1} = (\beta/2)(y_t - y_{t-1}) + \epsilon_t - \epsilon_{t-1} \tag{12}$$

$$y_t = -\gamma x_t + \eta_t. \tag{13}$$

All the parameters except β, expressing diminishing returns, and γ, expressing the positive check, have dropped out.

From these equations we may find the reduced form of the model, expressing each of mortality and wages as a function solely of the

171

exogenous disturbance terms, ϵ and η. Let $a_0 = 1 + \gamma\beta/2$, and $a_1 = 1 - \gamma\beta/2$. Then after several substitutions, we have:

$$a_0 x_t - a_1 x_{t-1} = (\beta/2)(\eta_t + \eta_{t-1}) + \epsilon_t - \epsilon_{t-1} \tag{14}$$

$$a_0 y_t - a_1 y_{t-1} = -\gamma(\epsilon_t - \epsilon_{t-1}) + \eta_t - \eta_{t-1}. \tag{15}$$

These equations describe a pair of simultaneous autoregressive processes with feedback. Cross-spectral analysis can be used to derive the relation between them. In particular, it may reveal any differences in the model's implications for the short run and the long run;[9] it is here that the anomalous results are observed. However, before proceeding to this analysis, it may be useful to give a brief account of spectral analysis itself.

2. *A Digression on Spectral Analysis.* The spectrum of a process x_t, denoted $g_x(\lambda)$, gives the distribution of the variance of x_t by frequency, λ (good sources are Granger and Hatanaka 1968; Fishman 1969; or Nerlove 1964). In the diagrams appearing in this chapter, frequency is expressed in cycles per century. A frequency of 20 cycles per century corresponds to a period, or cycle length, of $100/20$ or 5 years. If x is an uncorrelated random series, then its spectrum will be constant over all frequencies. If there is a tendency for x to move in cycles of frequency λ_0, then $g_x(\lambda)$ will show a peak at λ_0. For example, the spectrum of the Swedish harvest index, 1749 to 1880, shows peaks at frequencies of 7.5, 20, and 37.5 cycles per century, corresponding to periods of 13.3, 5, and 2.7 years.

However, in this chapter we do not use spectral analysis to search for cyclic tendencies in the data, but rather to study the theoretical and empirical relations between two or more series. The cross-spectral concepts used to describe these relations are the "gain," "phase angle," and "coherence." The gain, $G(\lambda)$, indicates the extent to which fluctuations in one series, say x, are amplified or attenuated as they are passed on to another series, y, at a specific frequency. It is analogous to a frequency-specific regression coefficient of y on x. The phase angle, $\phi(\lambda)$, indicates the extent to which the response of y lags or leads the fluctuations of x, at frequency λ. We measure it in fractions of a cycle; thus a phase angle of .5 indicates a negative relation of x and y; when x is at a peak, y is at a trough. The coherence, $C(\lambda)$, is analogous to the correlation between the two series at frequency λ;

[9] Here and throughout we use the terms "long term" and "short term" as synonymous with "low frequency" and "high frequency," not in the economic sense. The intent is to provide an intuitive interpretation of the spectral results.

the coherence squared, $C^2(\lambda)$, indicates the proportion of the variance of y that can be explained by x, at frequency λ.

These three functions—gain, phase angle, and coherence—may be calculated from actual data series.

We may also start with a specific model and derive from it the implied cross-spectral functions. Suppose that y and x are related as follows:

$$y_t = \sum_{j=-r}^{s} k_j x_{t-j} + \epsilon_t. \tag{16}$$

Here y may depend on past and future values of x, and also on a random variable ϵ which is assumed independent of x. The coefficients k_j are called a "filter," and they imply a specific "transfer function," $K(\lambda)$, defined as:

$$K(\lambda) = \sum_{j=-r}^{s} k_j e^{-i\lambda j} \text{ where } i = \sqrt{-1}.$$

The "gain" of the transfer function is the modulus of $K(\lambda)$; i.e., $|K(\lambda)|$. The spectra of y, x and ϵ are related by the squared gain:

$$g_y\sigma(\lambda) = |K(\lambda)|^2 g_x(\lambda) + g_\epsilon(\lambda).$$

The coherence squared of y and x gives the proportion of the variance of y which is explained by x. Thus,

$$C^2_{xy}(\lambda) = |K(\lambda)|^2 g_x(\lambda)/g_y(\lambda).$$

The filter alters not only the amplitude of the fluctuations in x at each frequency λ but also the timing of these fluctuations. This change in timing is given by the phase angle, $\phi(\lambda)$.

The models analyzed in this chapter are considerably more complex than the one we have just discussed. They involve feedback, which means we must consider two equations simultaneously; and each equation is itself more complicated than equation (16) as is illustrated by a comparison of (16) with Equations (14) and (15). Nonetheless, it is hoped that this brief discussion will be of some help for understanding what follows.

3. *The Theoretical Cross-Spectral Functions.* From the reduced form Equations (14) and (15) we may derive the theoretical cross-spectrum. The details of this derivation are given elsewhere (Lee 1972) and we do not present them here. We do present the gain, phase angle, and coherence implied by various assumptions about the quantity of exogenous variation in mortality and wages.

We begin by considering the polar cases in which all exogenous variation comes from one variable. Thus suppose that mortality is determined entirely by the wage level so that $\eta=0$. Then the gain, $G_{yx}(\lambda)$, and phase angle, $\phi_{yx}(\lambda)$, take on the following simple forms: $G_{yx}(\lambda)=\gamma$ and $\phi_{yx}(\lambda)=\pi$ (or .5 cycles) for all λ.

This says that all fluctuations in mortality are exactly one-half cycle out of phase with those in wages (i.e., there is a negative relation between the two which is the same for all frequencies). The amplitude of a fluctuation in wages is multiplied by γ as it is transmitted to mortality.

Now let us consider the other polar case, in which wages are determined entirely by population size, so that $\epsilon=0$. In this case, we have:

$$G_{xy}(\lambda)=(\beta/2)[(1+\cos\lambda)(1-\cos\lambda)]^{1/2}$$
$$\phi_{xy}(\lambda)=\pi/2 \text{ (or .25 cycles)}$$

Here wage changes lag one-quarter cycle behind mortality changes at all frequencies; one might say that they were positively related when wages were lagged suitably.[10] The gain changes with frequency. At high frequencies it is zero, so that fluctuations in mortality have no effect on wages. For a cycle of period four years ($\lambda=\pi/2$ or 25 cycles/century) the gain is $\beta/2$, and it rises steadily for longer periods, reaching infinity at $\lambda=0$.

Summarizing these two cases, we see that fluctuations in wages are passed on to mortality uniformly over the short and long run. On the other hand, high frequency fluctuations in mortality have virtually no effect on wages, while low frequency changes are highly amplified. The more general treatment, when both mortality and wages are subject to exogenous disturbance, will reflect some combination of these effects.

In order to derive numerical values for the gain, coherence, and

[10] The method does not distinguish between a lag of one-quarter cycle or a lead of three-quarters cycle; these distinctions, which are particularly tricky in empirical work, must be made on independent grounds—e.g., common sense.

TABLE 4–3. THEORETICAL CROSS-SPECTRAL FUNCTIONS

Frequency λ in cycles per century	Corre- sponding period in years	Cross-spectral functions evaluated at $\beta = 1; \gamma = .02; k = 900$		
		$C^2(\lambda)$	Lag $\phi(\lambda)$ of w behind m in a cycle	$G_{xy}(\lambda)$
50.00	2	.262	.500	.020
25.00	4	.262	.495	.020
12.50	8	.262	.486	.020
2.08	48	.284	.430	.019
1.04	96	.352	.375	.018
.52	192	.497	.322	.015
.26	384	.640	.289	.009
0.00	∞	.740	.250	.000

phase angle in this more general case, we must have rough estimates of β, γ, and of the relative magnitudes of ϵ and η. Our regression estimates suggest that $\beta \doteq 1$ to 2. We derive a value for γ from the provisional assumption that the elasticity of mortality with respect to wages is -1. We further assume that the coefficients of (exogenous) variation for mortality and wages are equal; this implies that $g_\epsilon(\lambda) \doteq 900\ g_\eta(\lambda)$, so that in absolute terms, the variance of wages is much higher than that of mortality.[11]

Table 4–3 presents values of the cross-spectral functions based on these assumptions. This table indicates that for short run fluctuations (of period less than eight years, let us say) we may ignore the effect of exogenous changes in mortality on wages. The gain, coherence, and phase shift are all very close to those of the polar case when $\eta=0$. This means that we may use cross-spectral estimates for high frequencies ($\lambda > \pi/4$ or 12.5 cycles/century) to determine empirically the values of γ and $g_\epsilon(\lambda)/g_\eta(\lambda)$.

For lower frequencies, we observe that the coherence increases, and the phase angle decreases. This reflects the stronger influence of longer run changes in mortality on population size and wages. In the limit, exogenous fluctuation in mortality dominates the system totally.

Figures 4–2 and 4–3 exhibit these calculated values for coherence and phase angle.

In addition, Figure 4–3 shows the calculated phase shift between wages and deaths. This is derived from the relation: $D_t = m_t P_t = (1/\sigma)^{1/\beta}\ e^{\ln(W_t)/\beta}$.

[11] This is less arbitrary than it may appear, for it is independent of the unit of measurement for wages; 900 is the square of the ratio of the means of the $w_t\sqrt{w}$ and the CDR.

175

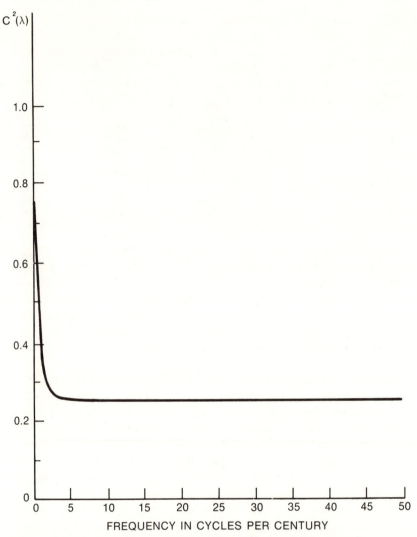

Figure 4–2 Coherence Squared of Mortality and Wages (Theoretical)

C. ESTIMATED RELATIONS BETWEEN MORTALITY AND WAGES

In this section we use the results derived above to aid the empirical analysis of mortality-wage relations. We analyze four sets of data: the series of long-run averages for 1250 to 1700 and for 1705 to 1784 which were discussed in Part II (these consist of only 9 and 8 observations, respectively); and annual series of deaths and real wages for London for 1700 to 1787, and England and Wales for 1780 to 1870.

176

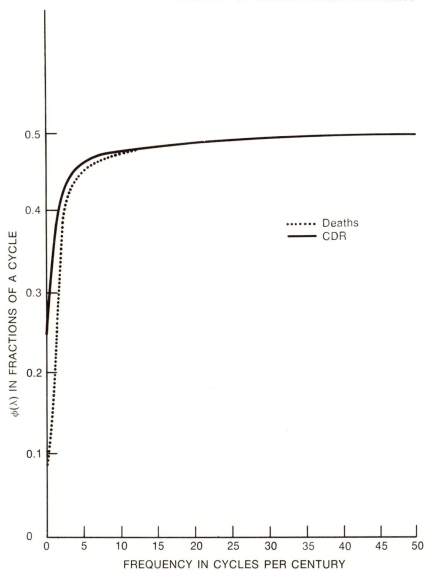

Figure 4–3 Phase Shift for Mortality and Wages

1. *Series of Long-Run Averages.* While we cannot perform a spectral analysis of the data used for the regressions, since in each case we have only 8 or 9 observations, there is a rough procedure available for determining whether most of the exogenous variation originated in mortality (σ_η^2) or in the demand for labor (σ_ϵ^2).

177

If $\sigma_\epsilon^2>0$ and $\sigma_\eta^2=0$, then the scatter of mortality against wages (with no lags) should show a negative relation.

On the other hand, if $\sigma_\epsilon^2=0$ and $\sigma_\eta^2>0$, then at each frequency the phase shift is $\pi/2$ (one-quarter cycle) and the gain is $(\beta/2)[(1+\cos\lambda)/(1-\cos\lambda)]^{1/2}$. This relationship should be examined for each frequency, since the lag depends on cycle length; however this is impossible due to the small number of observations. Visual inspection of the data for 1250 to 1700 suggests that most of the variation is contained in a "cycle" 300 to 400 years long. Under the present hypothesis, therefore, we would expect that a scatter of the log of wages against mortality lagged 100 years (one-quarter cycle) would show a positive relationship, with a slope of 65β.

For the period 1705 to 1784, most of the variation is contained in a forty-year "cycle." We thus expect that a scatter of the log of wages against mortality lagged ten years would show a positive relationship, with a slope of 6.2β.

Figures 4–4A and 4–4B show the relevant scatters for 1250 to 1700. The hypothesis that $\sigma_\eta^2>>\sigma_\epsilon^2$ is strongly supported and the slope is consistent with $\beta \doteq 1$.

Figures 4–5A and 4–5B suggest similar conclusions for the period 1705 to 1784. Here the slope is consistent with $\beta \doteq 2$.

Thus this crude procedure lends support to the assumption (implicit in the regression analysis) that most variation entered the system through exogenous change in mortality. It also suggests values of β similar to those produced by the regression analysis. However it did not enable us to estimate γ.

2. *Annual Series.* We now examine annual series of mortality and wages, for which a finer grained analysis is possible. Unfortunately we lack a national mortality series for eighteenth-century England; we have instead used the London Bills of Mortality in conjunction with the Gilboy real-wage index for the London area (Creighton 1965; Gilboy 1936).

The assumption of population closure is violated in this case; London relied on heavy immigration for the maintenance and growth of its population. Nor is it reasonable to suppose that these migratory movements were independent of wage changes, though the fact that wages in the London area moved in parallel with those in the West moderates this difficulty.

The estimated cross-spectrum of the two series is discussed below. Surprisingly, the cross-spectral estimates for mortality and the cost of living (not shown here) were more stable and had smaller variances than those for mortality and real wages.

178

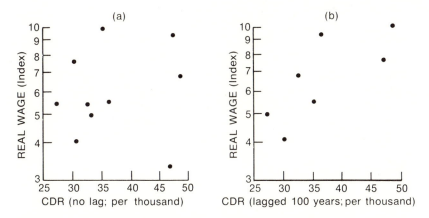

Figure 4–4 Mortality Wage Scatters for 1250–1700 (50 year averages)

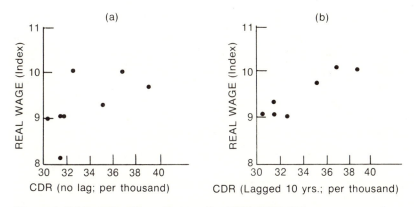

Figure 4–5 Mortality Wage Scatters for 1705–1784 (10 year averages)

Note: If all exogenous variation originates in wages, 4-4(a) and 4-5(a)
      should show negative relationships.
      If all exogenous variation originates in mortality, 4-4(b) and 4-5(b)
      should show positive relationships.

179

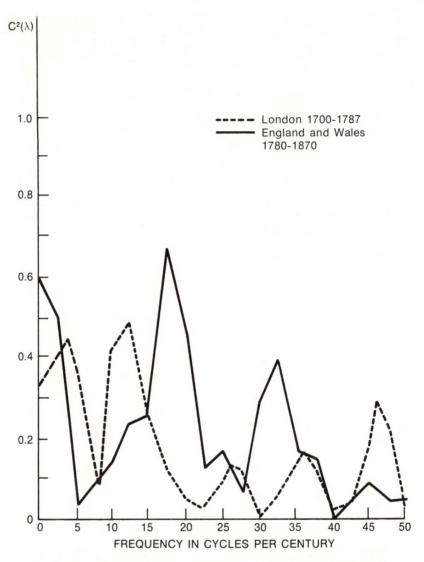

Figure 4–6 Estimated Coherence Squared Between Deaths and Wages

The estimated coherence squared is shown in Figure 4–6. We tested the null hypothesis of independence between the two series, or zero coherence at all frequencies. For the mortality and cost-of-living series, we were able to reject this null hypothesis at the 1 percent level. However for the mortality and real-wage series, we were unable to reject it for significant levels below 12.5 percent.

180

The estimated gain of mortality over wages for periods less than or equal to 8 years implied an elasticity of mortality with respect to wages of $-.6$. The gain for the cost-of-living index likewise suggested an elasticity of $+.6$.

The estimated phase angle is shown in Figure 4–6. The standard error of the estimated phase angle at any frequency depends on the coherence at that frequency. In Figure 4–6 the more reliable estimates, corresponding to estimated squared coherences of at least .2, are indicated by solid and hollow circles. In the short run, the phase shift is close to a half cycle (π) for mortality and real wages. This indicates a negative relation between the two, as expected. In the long run, for periods greater than fifteen years, the phase shift is close to zero. It is also very close to the theoretical expectation for the case in which exogenous variation in mortality is considerably greater than exogenous variation in wages. Unfortunately, the nonclosure of the London area population renders this result suspect.

About one-third of the variance of mortality is contained in the single band of frequencies centered on $\pi/20$ or a period of forty years. This proportion rises to two-thirds if we consider the other "long-run" frequency bands for which the small phase shift holds. Thus if we look at the process as a whole, the positive relation of mortality and wages dominates their co-variance. This is illustrated by a highly significant correlation of $+.26$ for mortality and wages, with no lag, over this period. With a lag, this positive correlation rises to $+.48$. Cross-spectral analysis allows us to sort out the short-run and long-run relations, and hence to detect the significant *negative* relation in the short run.

We performed a similar analysis on series of deaths and real wages for England and Wales from 1780 to 1870. The series of deaths was formed by splicing Rickman's series to the registration series (both taken from Mitchell and Deane 1962) with a suitable adjustment factor. A geometric trend was removed. For real wages, we used the Phelps Brown and Hopkins series for builders in Southern England (1956). In view of the controversy surrounding the standard of living during the Industrial Revolution, this series should be regarded with caution; however it is less misleading than a consumer price series.

The estimated phase shift is shown in Figure 4.6. As in the case of the London cross-spectrum, the phase shift is close to zero at low frequencies; however this time, deaths lag wages slightly, contrary to theoretical expectations. For the short run, we find significant coherencies for periods of six to ten years, and in this frequency range the phase shift does indicate a negative relation between mortality and

181

wages with an estimated elasticity of about −.3. However for shorter periods, where coherence is low and estimates unreliable, the phase angle suggests no consistent relation.

D. CLIMATE, MORTALITY AND WAGES

It is generally agreed that variations in climate affected both harvest and mortality (Habakkuk 1965; Dubos 1966; Le Roy Ladurie 1967; Vallin 1970). This is an important point to consider, for it bears directly on several issues in this chapter. We constructed a time-series model on the assumption that exogenous disturbances in mortality and wages (η and ϵ) were independent; might this assumption seriously bias our results? Similarly, we interpreted the estimated cross-spectrum of mortality and wages on the assumption that it reflected causal relations between the two and not their common response to climatic disturbance. Finally, it is possible that some climatic changes would have a "shearing" effect: reducing agricultural productivity and at the same time causing population growth by reducing mortality.

In this section we attempt to confront these issues in a preliminary manner. An annual rainfall series exists for England from 1727, but we have not been able to obtain it. We do have a monthly temperature series for central England (Manley 1953), which affords some insight into the effects of climatic variation. In what follows we relate the mean temperatures of January and July to deaths and real wages in England from 1780 to 1870.

We first consider mortality. The partial cross-spectrum of deaths on real wages, net of the effects of temperature, does not differ appreciably from the bivariate estimate. We cannot infer that the estimated relation between mortality and wages is causal; we can only infer that it is not due to the influence of temperature on each series.

The partial cross-spectral estimates of deaths and temperature are of interest in their own right. Figure 4–8 shows the estimated coherences for January and July. These are rather low and do not allow us to reject the null hypothesis of global independence. Nonetheless, if we restrict our attention to those frequencies for which the coherence squared is at least .2, then the phase diagram (Figure 4–9) exhibits an interesting pattern. It suggests that mortality varied directly with the July temperature and inversely with the January temperature: hot summers and cold winters were unhealthy.

We now consider the relation between temperature and real wages. Much has been written about the effect of climate on the harvest in European history; their relation was apparently complex and nonlinear,

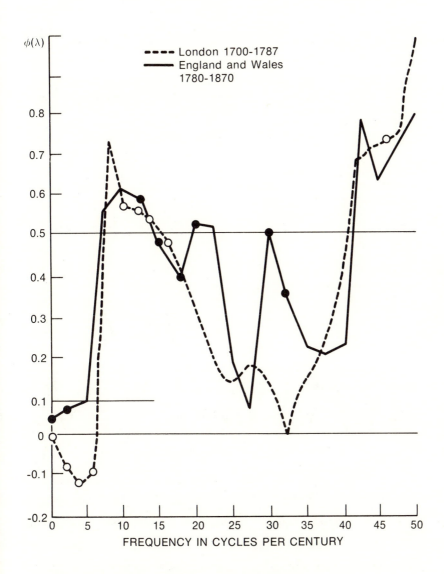

Note: ● or ○ implies $C^2(\lambda) \geqq 0.2$ at this frequency

Figure 4–7 Estimated Phase Shift Between Deaths and Wages

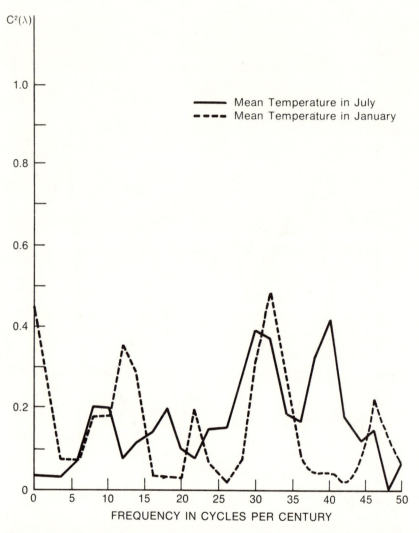

Figure 4–8 Coherence Squared of Deaths and Temperature for England, 1780–1870

with rainfall playing a more important role than temperature, in France and England (Le Roy Ladurie 1967).

The cross-spectral analysis of real wages and temperature yielded coherencies similar to those for temperature and mortality: large enough to suggest a link, but not large enough to permit rejection of the null hypothesis. The estimated phase shifts were not consistent, showing positive relations for some frequencies and negative for others.

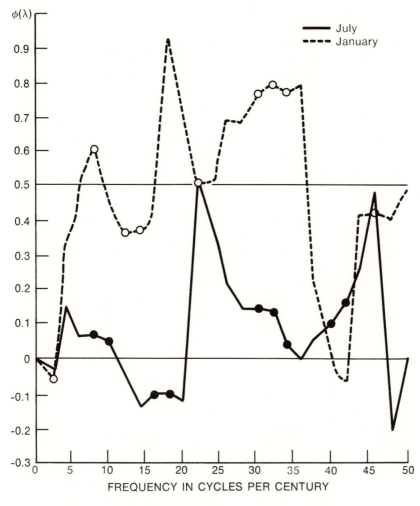

NOTE: O and ● indicate $C^2(\lambda) \geqq .2$

Figure 4–9 Phase Shift for Deaths and Temperature in England, 1780–1870

The analysis is worth pursuing with more appropriate series, but for the present, we can say nothing.

E. CONCLUSIONS

1. *General.* While the positive check did exist and operate, it would be misleading to portray mortality as the passive regulator of population size and wages. Much more important than its role as a controlling

185

factor was its role as a *disrupting* factor, causing wide swings in population and wage levels.

2. *Theoretical.* An equilibrating system such as the one analyzed here will converge to a stable state if left undisturbed; and in such a state its behavior conveys no information about its structural relations. If the system is disturbed, estimation may be possible; however, the statistical associations we observe will depend as much on the way it is disturbed as they do on the structural relations we wish to estimate.

The analysis of mortality and wages distinguished three cases: (1) Mortality is determined entirely by the real wage; exogenous variation enters the system only through wages. Then we will observe a negative association between mortality and wages. (2) Wages are determined entirely by population size; exogenous variation enters the system only through mortality. Then we will observe a positive association of mortality to wages, with wages lagging a quarter-cycle at each frequency. (3) More realistically, exogenous variation enters through both mortality and wages. Then we observe a negative association for short run fluctuations and a positive one for very long run fluctuations: what happens in between depends on the relative magnitude of the disturbances. This analysis resolves the apparent contradiction with which we introduced this part.

These theoretical results may be extended to cross-regional studies. Even if mortality depends negatively on economic well-being, we may observe a positive association between the two—provided that other geographic differences such as climate and exposure to contagion also affect mortality appreciably.

3. *Empirical.* The empirical analysis, which was performed on four sets of quite unreliable data, yielded consistent results. A dominant positive correlation of mortality and wages was found, and spectral analysis revealed that the positive relation held for long and medium run fluctuations (of period twenty years and greater), while the negative relation held only over the short run. The estimated short-run elasticity of mortality with respect to wages was $-.6$ for London from 1700 to 1787, and $-.3$ for England and Wales from 1780 to 1870.

The positive relation of mortality and wages for low frequencies allows us to infer that fertility did not perfectly compensate for mortality change (i.e., $\lambda < 1$), and that there were diminishing returns to labor ($\beta > 0$).

The dominance of the positive relation, not only at very low frequencies but also for periods so short as 20 years, indicates that exogenous fluctuations in mortality were the major source of disturbance to the system, dominating fluctuations in the demand for labor.

Further analysis showed that these results were not changed when the effect of temperature variations on mortality and wages was taken into account. We also reached the tentative conclusion that hot summers and cold winters had an adverse effect on mortality.

IV

NUPTIALITY AND MARITAL FERTILITY

A. INTRODUCTION

We have emphasized that over the long run, social control over material well-being was exercised through the regulation of fertility. If the illegitimate birth rate is low, fertility may usefully be regarded as the outcome of interaction between nuptiality and marital fertility. We have so far made little attempt to distinguish, theoretically or empirically, which of these components of fertility might be affected by such regulation.

In this part we will use time series of births and marriages to analyze the relation of nuptiality and marital fertility to mortality and wages. This analysis will provide alternate estimates for the parameters α and λ in the fertility equation of part I, as well as shedding light on a complex of issues centering on "moral restraint," "natural fertility," and the preventive check.

Malthus thought that in Europe of his day, the preventive check took the form of "moral restraint"—the postponement of marriage from prudential considerations, combined with celibacy before marriage and unrestrained fertility within marriage (1872). This hypothesis is related closely to the widely held belief that in preindustrial Europe, marital fertility was not subject to voluntary control, and was therefore relatively constant over time, if not cross-sectionally. Observed variations in a time series of births are then attributed to changes in the marriage rate and to changes in fecundity due to privation and disease. The "natural fertility" hypothesis—that marital fertility behavior did not vary by parity—is a special case of this argument.

Some studies have cast considerable doubt on the hypothesis that marital fertility was relatively constant over time. For example, Wrigley's reconstitution study of Colyton (1966) showed significant long run change in marital fertility as well as nuptiality over a three hundred year period. A number of scholars have found that short run fluctuation in nuptiality cannot account for fluctuations in birth series (Carlsson 1970; Connor 1926; Ohlin 1955; Yule 1906); one of these scholars concluded: "There is no doubt, then, that marital fertility and the marriage rate moved together, and that of the two it was, in the short run,

187

(marital) fertility and not the marriage rate that exercised the greatest influence on the birth rate" (Ohlin 1955: 162).

Our investigation of these issues will proceed in three stages. We first construct a stochastic model relating time series of births and marriages, and use spectral analysis to derive its implications under various assumptions about the variance and covariance of nuptiality and marital fertility. We next estimate the actual relations between birth and marriage series using data from England (1780–1870) and Sweden (1749–1880). Comparison with the theoretical relations enables us to test the various hypotheses. Finally, we estimate the relations between nuptiality and marital fertility, on the one hand, and mortality and wages, on the other. This provides alternative estimates of α and λ, and indicates the extent to which moral restraint is an adequate characterization of fertility control in the populations studied.

B. A BIRTH-MARRIAGE MODEL

Let f_x be the fertility rate for marriages of duration x years,[12] net of marital dissolution by death or divorce. $\sum_x f_x$ is the baptism-marriage ratio; and we define $f^*{}_x = f_x / \sum_j f_j$.

Similarly, let w_a be the distribution of female marriages by age for the average birth cohort, net of mortality, and for marriages of all orders. We define $w^*{}_a = w_a / \sum_j w_j$.

An appropriate convolution of w and f yields an approximation to ϕ_a, the net maternity function: $\phi_a \doteq \sum_x f_x w_{a-x}$. Evidently the fact that we attribute the same stream of births to a 20-year-old and 45-year-old bride causes some distortion; fortunately, this is not serious.

We now suppose that w and f are subject to stochastic disturbances θ and ϵ which cause them to fluctuate about their mean values in the following pattern:

$$w_{a,t} = w_a + u_a \theta_t$$
$$f_{x,t} = f_x + v_x \epsilon_t, \text{ where}$$

u_a and v_x represent the sensitivity of the age- and duration-specific rates to the stochastic disturbances; they are normalized to sum to the values of $\sum w_j$ and $\sum f_j$ respectively.

[12] For a more detailed exposition of the model and derivation of the theoretical results, see Lee, 1975.

188

For simplicity of exposition, let $u_a = w_a$ and $v_x = f_x$. Then births (B) and marriages (M) will be related as follows:

$$B_t = (1 + \epsilon_t) \sum f_x M_{t-x}$$
$$M_t = (1 + 0_t) \sum w_a B_{t-a}.$$

This is a simultaneous equation system with feedback. It states that current births depend on past marriages and current marital fertility, while current marriages depend on past births and current nuptiality. The problem is to untangle this model's implications for the behavior of series of births and marriages and their relations to one another. To do this, we first derive a linear approximation to the multiplicative model.

Let h_t and z_t represent proportional variations of births and marriages about their respective means (e.g., $h_t = .01$ indicates that at time t, births were 1 percent greater than their long run average number). Ignoring second order terms in deviations, the following approximation holds:

$$h_t \doteq \sum \phi_a h_{t-a} + \sum f^*{}_x \theta_{t-x} + \epsilon_t$$
$$z_t = \sum \phi_a z_{t-a} + \sum w^*{}_a \epsilon_{t-a} + \theta_t.$$

The first equation decomposes the variation in births at time t into three approximately additive sources: past variations in births (i.e., current age structure), past variations in nuptiality, and current variation in marital fertility. The second equation gives a similar decomposition for variation in the marriage series.

The variations in nuptiality (θ_t) and marital fertility (ϵ_t) are disturbances to this system. If nuptiality and marital fertility were constant (i.e., $\sigma^2\epsilon = \sigma^2\theta = 0$), then births and marriages would be completely determined and perfectly predictable, and their coherence ($C(\lambda)$) would be unity. When variations in nuptiality and marital fertility continually disturb the system, however, this is not true.

The functions ϕ, f, and w are known for various populations. For the present analysis we have based our calculations on data for Crulai (Gautier and Henry 1958) assuming them typical for preindustrial Europe; the results are not sensitive to this assumption. Spectral analysis is used to derive the theoretical relations between time series of

189

births and marriages on differing assumptions about the variation and covariation of nuptiality (θ) and marital fertility (ϵ) (for a related analysis, see Coale 1970). We then use spectral analysis to estimate the relations between actual series of births and marriages for England and Wales from 1780 to 1870, and for Sweden from 1748 to 1880. Comparison of estimated and predicted cross-spectra allows us to determine which assumptions about θ and ϵ are consistent with the data.

The reader may have noted that we implicitly assumed constant mortality. In fact I have analyzed the effect of fluctuating mortality on a birth series, using similar methods, and found that the short run behavior of the birth series was unaffected (see Lee 1974c).

C. ESTIMATED RELATIONS BETWEEN BIRTHS AND MARRIAGES

If marital fertility were constant—or equivalently $\epsilon = 0$—then all variation in births, at each frequency, would derive directly or indirectly from the variation of nuptiality. More precisely, the spectra of h and z would be related as follows:

$$g_h(\lambda) = |F^*(\lambda)|^2\, g_z(\lambda)$$

where $|F^*(\lambda)|^2$ is the squared gain function derived from the function f. Evidently, on this hypothesis, the ratio of the spectrum of h to the spectrum of z should equal the squared gain.

Figure 4–10 shows this function and also the ratio of the estimated spectra for Sweden and England and Wales.[13] We first note that the discrepancy between the theoretical and actual ratio becomes very large as we move from low to high frequencies. For fluctuations of period 10 years, the actual and theoretical already differ by a factor of about 15; for periods of 5 years they differ by a factor of 30; and for periods of 2 to 3 years, they differ by a factor of 100 to 200. This shows that the proposed explanation for variation in the series of births is strikingly inconsistent with the actual pattern of variation in the two series, particularly for short-run fluctuations.

It is also illuminating to consider the squared gain function itself. It indicates the proportion of the variance in nuptiality that will be transmitted to variation in births at each frequency. For fluctuations of period as long as 20 years, only about one-tenth of the variance is passed; for a period of 10 years only one-thirtieth is passed; for five years the proportion is one hundredth; and for two years it has fallen below one two-hundredth. For an inspection of $|F^*(\lambda)|^2$ we conclude

[13] The Swedish series are taken from Statistiska Centralbyrän, 1955. The English are based on Mitchell and Deane, 1962.

190

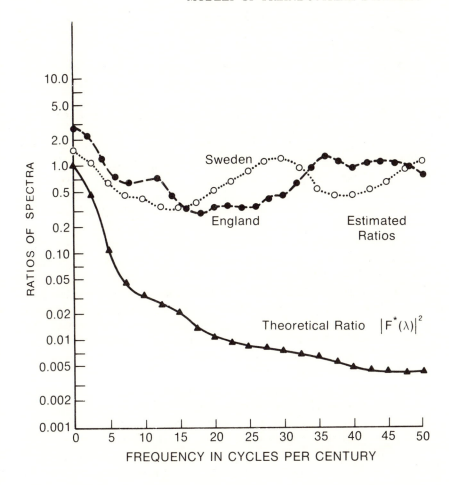

RATIOS OF SPECTRA

FREQUENCY IN CYCLES PER CENTURY

Sweden

England

Estimated
Ratios

Theoretical Ratio $|F^*(\lambda)|^2$

Note: Births and marriages are measured as proportional deviations from their mean values.

Figure 4–10 Ratios of Spectra of Births and Marriages

that the effect of short run fluctuations in marriages on births will be
almost totally damped, and longer fluctuations will be substantially
attenuated. Thus it is *in principle* impossible for nuptiality to explain
short run variation in a birth series.[14]

[14] Impossible, that is, for distributions of births by duration of marriage, and for
first births as a proportion of all births, not too unlike those of France in 1956 or
in the 18th century. This is a very weak condition.

Elsewhere we have extended this analysis, using a function f_x for monthly intervals, and shown that seasonal variations in nuptiality were even more highly damped, and have a negligible effect on the seasonality of births. This confirms the results of other studies which have compared the seasonalities of first and higher order births, and found them the same (e.g., Henripin 1954).

We may approach the question of constant marital fertility in a slightly different way by studying the theoretical and actual lags between marriages and births. The spectral analysis of the function f_x yields not only the squared gain, which we have already discussed, but also the "phase shift" or lag between fluctuations of a given frequency in marriages and those in births. The phase shift may also be calculated empirically for actual series; it is the lag (or lead) which produces the maximum correlation between the two series at a given frequency.

Figure 4–12 shows the theoretical phase shift on the assumption that marital fertility was constant. It also shows the estimated phase shift for England and Sweden. We again note a striking inconsistency between the predicted and the estimated relations: the former exceeds the latter by a factor of two or three. Consider, for example, fluctuations of period 5 years. The theoretical model predicts a lag of .28 cycles or 1.4 ($=.28 \times 5$) years; the estimated lag is about .07 cycles or .35 years. Clearly this lag is inconsistent with the hypothesized causal relation between the two.

Therefore, we reject conclusively the hypothesis that fluctuations in nuptiality account for fluctuations in births; it is inconsistent with the quantity of short run variation present in birth series, and it is inconsistent with the estimated lag of births behind marriages.

We next consider the hypothesis that fluctuations in nuptiality and marital fertility were independent (or more precisely, uncorrelated);[15] this is consistent with the view that the former resulted from choices and the latter from involuntary fecundity impairments. A natural assumption is that the variances of θ and $_\eta$ at each frequency are related by the same constant, so that $g_\theta(\lambda) = k\, g_\epsilon(\lambda)$. The constant can be estimated from the ratio of the estimated spectra of births and marriages at the higher frequencies, for these are uncontaminated by feedback or age structure. Inspection of Figure 4–11 suggests that k is roughly 1.5, or that the coefficient of variation of nuptiality is about 20 percent greater than that of marital fertility. This is a surprisingly low ratio, since nuptiality is generally thought to have been considerably more volatile. Indeed similar investigations at the parish level have indicated

[15] Of course, even if ϵ and θ are uncorrelated, h and m will still be correlated due to age structure of population and duration structure of marriages.

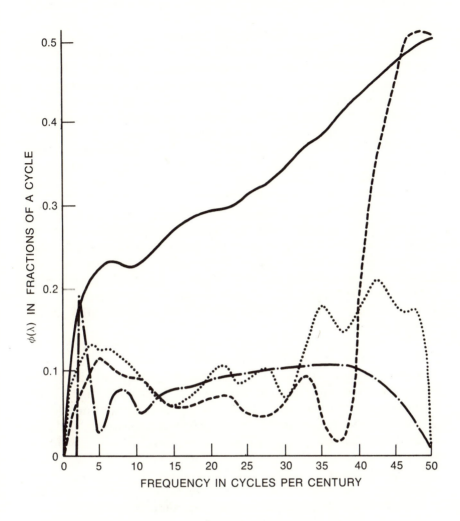

Figure 4–11 Phase Shift of Births Over Marriages

Empirical
.... England, 1780-1870
- - - - - - Sweden, 1749-1880
Theoretical
———— Marital Fertility Constant
—··— Marital Fertility and Nuptiality Correlated; Lag is 4 Months

coefficients of variation for nuptiality two to three times as great as for marital fertility.

If ϵ and θ are independent, then the ratio of the spectra of births and marriages will be given by $(1+k|F^*(\lambda)|^2)/(k+|W^*(\lambda)|^2)$. Since both $|F^*(\lambda)|^2$ and $|W^*(\lambda)|^2$ are very small at higher frequencies, this ratio will be close to $1/k$ for these frequencies, and thus be roughly consistent with the actual ratios shown in Figure 4–1.

A more critical test of this hypothesis is provided by the comparison of theoretical and actual coherence squared. Figure 4–12 shows the theoretical coherence squared under three different assumptions: that marital fertility is constant (in which case the coherence is 1.0 at all frequencies); that marital fertility and nuptiality vary independently (in which case the coherence is close to zero at most frequencies) and that nuptiality and marital fertility are correlated, with an appropriate lag (in which case the coherence declines roughly linearly with increasing frequency). Figure 4–12 also shows the estimated coherence squared of births and marriages. The contrast is conclusive: only the hypothesis of correlated variation is consistent with the actual series. More specifically, the series suggest that there was a correlation of .9 between marital fertility and nuptiality, with marital fertility lagging about four months.[16]

Since fluctuations in nuptiality were the result of conscious decisions, and fluctuations in marital fertility were very highly correlated with those in nuptiality, it seems likely that marital fertility was also subject to voluntary control. This inference is strengthened by a multivariate cross-spectral analysis of births in relation to marriages and deaths, indicating that marital fertility was much more highly correlated with nuptiality than with mortality—which one would not expect if fecundity impairment accounted for variations in marital fertility. (For a similar argument, see Carlsson, 1970.) Explanations other than voluntary control are possible (some of these were discussed in Part I), but voluntary control appears to me to be the most plausible.

In any case, this analysis has helped to justify the earlier treatment of fertility as a single variable: the major difference between fluctuations in nuptiality and those in marital fertility lies not in the factors which influenced each, but rather in the greater inertia (autocorrelation) imparted to fertility behavior by nuptiality.

[16] With continuous time, the coherence squared of the specification shown in Figure 4–13 would be .81; however the lagged relation, together with discrete time sampling, reduces it to the values shown in Figure 4–13. The actual specification used was:
$\theta_t = \tilde{\theta}_t + w_t$; $\epsilon_t = \tilde{\epsilon}_t + .667w_t + .333w_{t-1}$; $\tilde{\theta}$, $\tilde{\epsilon}$ and w are uncorrelated; $\sigma^2(\theta) = \sigma^2(\epsilon) = 1$; $\sigma^2(w) = .9$.

There is one other aspect of preindustrial population dynamics which this stochastic birth-marriage model elucidates: the occurrence of births, marriages, and age structure in cycles of a length between 25 and 35 years.

If we assume the correlated variation specification of Figure 4–12, we may calculate the implied spectrum of births and marriages. Figure 4–13 shows such a theoretical spectrum for births. It exhibits a strong peak at a period of 30 years, indicating a tendency for the birth series to move in cycles of this length. The spectrum of marriages (not shown here) looks similar. This shows that the age pattern of demographic rates amplifies a particular frequency of the random shocks to which the population is subject, causing quasi-cycles of length about 30 years. The explanation does not depend on the occurrence of a catastrophic shock and is thus free of one of the principal defects of the classical demographic analysis of such cycles.[17]

Inspection of Figure 4–13 also shows that the spectrum of births corresponds closely to the spectrum of marital fertility (ϵ) for periods of twelve years or less; it is not noticeably affected by age structure or nuptiality. This result will enable us to study causes of fluctuation in marital fertility.

D. FERTILITY, MORTALITY AND WAGES

It will be recalled that in the model of part I there occurred the equation:

$$f_t = \mu + \alpha \ln(w_t) + \lambda m_t$$

The central questions raised by this model revolved about the parameters α and λ. In this section we attempt to estimate these parameters from an analysis of short-run fluctuations, drawing on the theoretical work of previous sections.

We will first consider nuptiality. The estimated coherence squared of marriages and real wages is shown in Figure 4–14. Significant coherencies occur only for relatively high frequency fluctuations, with periods of 3 to 6 years. In this frequency range, marriages lag real wages slightly, by perhaps a couple of months. The estimated elasticity of marriages with respect to the real wage is about .5.

The coherence between deaths and marriages is plotted in Figure

[17] For a more detailed discussion, see Lee, 1975. For a similar analysis for the case in which the population is subject to control (α and β both nonzero), see Lee 1974a.

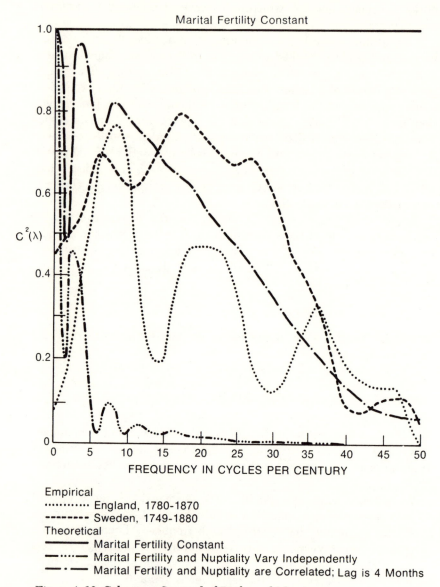

Figure 4–12 Coherence Squared of Births and Marriages

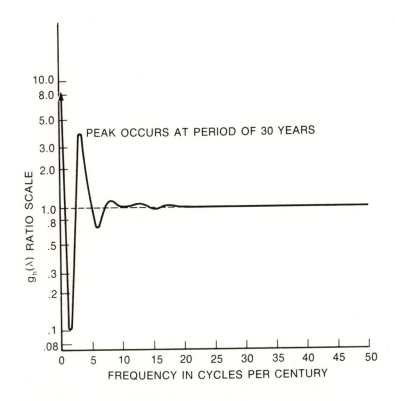

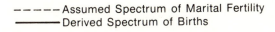
Assumed Spectrum of Marital Fertility
Derived Spectrum of Births

Assumptions:
1.Spectra of nuptiality and marital fertility equal 1.0 at all frequencies.
2. Fluctuations in marital fertility are correlated with those of nuptiality with a lag of four months.

Figure 4-13 Theoretical Spectrum of Births

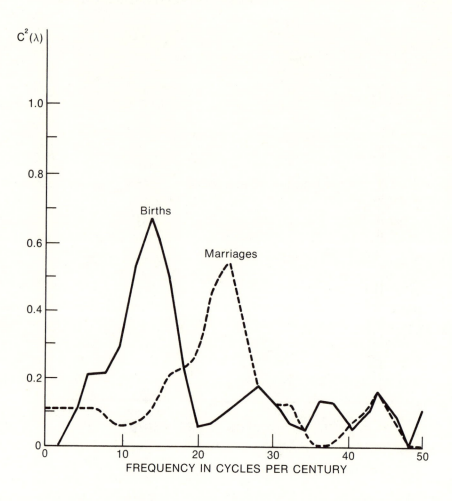

$C^2(\lambda)$

FREQUENCY IN CYCLES PER CENTURY

*For births, the estimate is partial, net of deaths. The marriage estimate is bivariate.

Figure 4–14 Estimated Coherence Squared of Births and Marriages with Real Wages, for England and Wales, 1780–1870

4–15. There is significant coherence at very low frequencies, which we are reluctant to interpret, and at high frequencies, with periods of 2 to 3 or 4 years. This latter coherence can definitely be attributed to a nuptiality-mortality association.

The phase shift indicates either a negative relation between the two, or that marriages led deaths by about a year, depending on how literally one interprets the estimates.

198

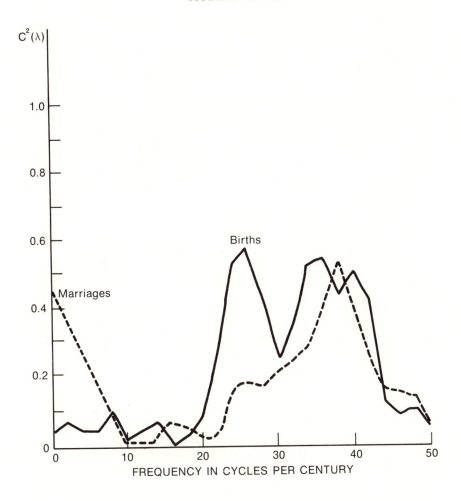

*For births, the estimate is partial, net of real wages.

Figure 4–15 Estimated Coherence Squared of Births and Marriages with Deaths, for England and Wales, 1780–1870

These results lend themselves to no simple interpretation. They do seem inconsistent with the theory that high mortality enabled the young to marry by giving them access to parental holdings and to other forms of wealth. However, nineteenth century England is not the appropriate context in which to test this theory.

We have found that only short-run fluctuations in marriages were

199

related to real wages or mortality. These high-frequency fluctuations were shown in a previous section to have virtually no effect on fertility. Any direct link between fertility, mortality, and real wages, therefore, must derive from the behaivor of marital fertility.

The coherence of births and real wages is shown in Figure 4–14. Significant values occur for periods of roughly 5 to 12 years. Recalling the theoretical cross-spectrum of the previous section (see Figures 4–12 and 4–13), we must attribute this coherence to the covariance of marital fertility and real wages; neither nuptiality nor age structure can have played a significant role.

The estimated phase shift is close to zero, implying a small lag of births behind real wages. In the frequency band where significant coherencies are observed, the estimated elasticity of marital fertility with respect to wages is about .25.

The coherence of births and deaths is plotted in Figure 4–15. It is close to zero over the low frequency range. An apparent close negative relation for periods of 5 to 10 years disappeared when wages were taken into account.

For periods of less than 5 years, the relation to mortality accounts for roughly 40 percent of the variance in marital fertility, with an estimated gain of about .35. The phase shift is close to zero indicating a positive relation between fertility and mortality. It is not clear how this is to be interpreted. Was there a mortality-morbidity-fecundity link? Then the phase shift should be one-half cycle, plus about nine months. Was there a mortality-fertility link operating through the interruption of lactation? Or a behavioral link, with couples attempting to replace children who died? Then births should lag about a year behind mortality. And all of these relations are obscured by the contribution of autonomous fluctuations in births to fluctuations in deaths via infant mortality. Perhaps analysis of monthly data, together with formal modeling, could answer these questions.

It is worth noting that this estimated relation between births and deaths is quite different for Swedish data. There we find a high coherence between births and deaths throughout the entire frequency range, with a median value of .4. The phase shift is consistently one-half cycle, so fertility and mortality were negatively related. The gain of births over deaths remained remarkably constant at .2. It is, however, possible that a multivariate analysis of the Swedish data, including a price or real wage series, would alter this pattern.

Let us now summarize these results. The estimated links among nuptiality, mortality, and real wages are such as to have virtually no effect on fertility. Fluctuations in marital fertility, however, affect fertility directly; and over the range of periods from two to twelve years, mortality and real wages account for about 45 percent of the variation in marital fertility.[18]

The results of this section are inconclusive. Taking them at face value, we are led to the following estimation of the basic equation:

$$f_t = \mu + .009 \ln(w_t) + .35m_t,$$

where the coefficient of $\ln(w_t)$ is calculated to yield an elasticity of .25.

E. CONCLUSIONS TO PART IV

1. Fluctuations in marriages are in principle incapable of causing short-run fluctuations in births. This is true for fluctuations as short as the seasonal, and as long as 10 years.

2. Marital fertility was nearly as variable as nuptiality.

3. Variations in marital fertility and nuptiality were very highly correlated with one another—which has led many observers to the erroneous conclusion that fluctuations in marriage rates explained fluctuations in births. This close correlation of marital fertility and nuptiality suggests that marital fertility may have been subject to voluntary control.

4. Marital fertility was more closely related to both mortality and the real wage than was nuptiality. Thus "moral restraint" is a poor characterization of the preventive check for the populations studied here, at least in the short run.[19]

5. The short-run relation of fertility to mortality and wages is consistent with the MDEW specification.

V

CONCLUSION

PREINDUSTRIAL societies, faced with fluctuating mortality and agricultural productivity, and sharply diminishing returns to labor, developed institutions affording them some measure of control over population size and material well-being. In this chapter we have discussed various possible population control strategies, and their implications. Using English data, we attempted to identify empirically the structural rela-

[18] This is the median coefficient of multiple determination for this frequency range.

[19] More precisely, moral restraint was an important determinant of the mean level of fertility, but marital fertility appears to have been responsible for variations in fertility.

tions defining the control system and its context of operation. We also studied the exogenous disturbances, via mortality and the demand for labor, to which the system was subject.

A. METHOD

The empirical investigation of these questions raised complicated methodological issues, for the observed statistical associations depend equally on the underlying structural relations and on the form of exogenous disturbance; explanation and analysis must take both of these into account. Examples may be drawn from each of the three empirical parts. Thus in Part II we showed that whether declining mortality explains population growth in the eighteenth century depends not only on the empirical question of whether such an exogenous decline did indeed occur but also on hypothesized structural relations: Would fertility ordinarily compensate directly for such a variation? This depends on λ. How rapidly would the "falling-wages-preventive-check" mechanism operate to equate fertility and mortality? This depends on α and β. Did an increasing demand for labor forestall its operation? This depends on ρ. In Part III we showed that an observed positive association of mortality and wages is quite consistent with a negative structural relation between the two, provided that the independent variation of mortality is considerably greater than that of wages. In Part IV we showed that although fluctuations in births and marriages are highly correlated, and this correlation appears consistent with the assumed structural relations (births following marriages with a lag), closer analysis of the structure showed that the explanation could not possibly be true.

While this chapter has been concerned with inference from time series data, similar problems arise with cross-regional studies. There are many questions which statistical analysis of accurate data will not suffice to answer, except in conjunction with carefully thought out models.

B. LIMITATIONS

Before discussing results, we should emphasize the limitations of the data. Aside from some Swedish series used in Part IV, all the data are drawn from English experience. Their reliability is very questionable, particularly with regard to long-run changes. Much of our analysis focuses on short-run changes for which the data provide an adequate basis; however, our occasional inference from observed short-run relations to unobserved long-run relations is hazardous.

202

There is also a deeper problem with the analysis, stemming from the assumptions of the model. We have emphasized the depressing effects of population growth on wages. However, we took a steady shift in the demand for labor, measured by ρ, to be exogenous. Our formulation of the model thus precluded the possibility that population growth itself played a fundamental role in causing those changes which led to an increasing demand for labor, as suggested by Eversley (1967).

C. RESULTS

Malthusian population theory provides a convenient framework for the discussion of our results. We found that sharply diminishing returns to labor did indeed characterize production, as evidenced by population-wage relations ($\beta > 0$). We also found that both the positive and the preventive checks did exist and operate (α and $\gamma > 0$), although the Malthusian versions must be qualified. Thus while mortality did react negatively to wage changes, the exogenous component of mortality change dominated the systematic component; mortality was not first a passive controlling factor, but rather an active disruptive one. And while fertility did react positively to wage change, it was not governed principally by "moral restraint" as Malthus asserted (1872). For marital fertility was nearly as variable as nuptiality; it was more highly correlated with the real wage than was nuptiality; and it was more closely correlated with nuptiality than with mortality, suggesting that voluntary control may have dominated such involuntary influences as fecundity impairment.[20] These results also cast some doubt on the hypothesis of natural fertility, though they are far from conclusive.

We have found support for three Malthusian propositions: diminishing returns, the positive check, and the preventive check. We are thus led to accept the Malthusian Dismal Theorem: Economic progress alone could not improve the condition of labor, except temporarily, unless it continued perpetually at an exponential rate. Significant improvement could come only from a change in the reproductive behavior of the population.

There are, however, other Malthusian assertions which we reject. Malthus, and later classical economists, treated the long run equilibrium wage as a socially defined parameter, variously known as "subsistence," "conventional living standard" or "natural price of labor." Our theoretical analysis showed that the long run equilibrium wage could not be a parameter unless either mortality did not vary exoge-

---

[20] The generally low level of fertility was certainly due to late marriage, but the elasticity of fertility with respect to wages was due to marital fertility, at least in the short run.

nously, or fertility compensated perfectly for such variation as occurred ($\lambda = 1$). But empirical analysis showed that neither of these conditions was met. We must conclude that societal control over the material well-being of its members was severely limited, in the long run as well as in the short run.

Malthus and other classical economists also thought that, as a matter of historical fact, variations in the demand for labor were the major cause of population change rather than differences in mortality (e.g., Malthus 1970: 262). The argument depends not only on the existence of diminishing returns and the positive or preventive check, which we have confirmed, but also on two propositions which we failed to confirm: First, the demand for labor schedule must have shifted appropriately when population changed; and second, either mortality must not have varied independently or fertility must have compensated perfectly for such variations as occurred.

We found that from 1250 to 1700, none of these conditions was satisfied, and indeed that exogenous mortality change explained the variation in population size and wages. There was very little change in the demand for labor schedule. However, from 1705 to 1784 the demand for labor schedule was shifting relatively rapidly, reflecting early stages of the agricultural and industrial revolutions. In this period, the interaction of exogenously varying mortality and steadily shifting labor demand explains quite well the behavior of population and wages; here classical analysis fares much better.

D. GENERAL

It is usual to stress the mean levels of variables under preindustrial conditions—the low productivity of labor and the high mortality. Our analysis has instead emphasized their variability. We discussed at an abstract level the demographic strategies which societies might pursue in an effort to protect their population sizes and living standards from the fluctuations of an erratic environment. We found that in England one of these strategies (the MDEW or mortality dependent equilibrium wage) was embodied in control mechanisms which did act to stabilize the return to labor. However, this strategy provided better protection from changes in the demand for labor than from changes in mortality. The former led only to temporary disequilibria, with population size reacting passively to restore the initial real wage; the latter caused the equilibrium values themselves to change, and thus deprived society of control over its living standard.

Appendix: Data for England, 1705–1784

A. DEMOGRAPHIC ESTIMATES

RICKMAN's parish register abstracts of baptisms and burials provide estimates of births and deaths for single years, at ten-year intervals, from 1700 to 1780; thereafter, these data are available annually. We assumed that the totals were representative for the decade on which each was centered; thus the estimated total for 1710 was assumed representative of the years 1705–1714. Using constant correction factors (which receive some empirical support from Razzell 1972), we interpolated population size between 1695 and 1801, years for which relatively firm population estimates are available (Glass 1965). These, together with the birth and death estimates, provide the basis for estimates of the crude birth and death rates over the periods 1695–1704, 1705–1714, ..., 1785–1794.[21]

In our treatment of these data we have followed the work of Goran Ohlin (1955) in his unpublished dissertation. Flinn's recent comprehensive review of the subject has called this study "quite the most thorough and rigorous yet made" (1970: 63).

The deficiencies of estimates derived in this way have been discussed in detail by many authors. Indeed Flinn writes: "After a century and a half of attempts to wiring acceptable information from the basic *PRA* (Parish Register Abstracts) data, the struggle has at last been abandoned as unprofitable. For many reasons, results drawn from the PRA, whether in the form of totals of population or of the vital rates, are built on such shifting sand as to make them virtually unacceptable for the purposes of modern scholarship" (1970: 20). This is a stern warning. We shall, nevertheless, argue that the data are not inadequate for our purposes.

The principal difficulties with these data are the following: (1) Were the years for which we have totals representative? Analysis of Swedish data suggests not. (2) Were the figures accurately compiled and reported to Rickman? Many errors have been found. (3) What correction should be made for underregistration? (4) Did the degree of underregistration change drastically over the period?

The first two difficulties can be resolved in a fairly satisfactory manner by comparing Rickman's decadal figures to averages centered

---

[21] In Lee 1974b, I have used these data to derive estimates of gross reproduction rates, life expectancies and age structure over the period.

on these years drawn from other sources. I have done this for the mortality series using the following burial and crude death rate series: London Bills of Mortality (Creighton 1965); Vale of Trent (Chambers 1965b); Worcestershire (Eversley 1965); a large sample of rural English parishes divided into North and South subsamples (Krause 1967). These show a good agreement concerning the timing and magnitude of changes in mortality, with one another and with Rickman's decadal series. This establishes first, that the years sampled by Rickman were not seriously atypical, and second, that errors in reporting did not cause serious distortion at the aggregate level.

In our analysis we are concerned principally with the timing and relative magnitude of *changes* in the demographic variables; the absolute levels are not crucial. For this reason, it makes little difference what correction ratios we use to go from reported baptisms or burials to estimated births or deaths, so long as these are constant over time. Most studies assume that the registration of births was about five percent less complete than that of deaths; we have followed Ohlin in assuming that 73 percent of births and 80 percent of deaths were registered. These ratios are consistent with the 1695 and 1801 population totals.

The most serious problem is the possibility that the extent of underregistration varied significantly over the century. Krause has argued that the registration of deaths deteriorated badly toward the end of the century, giving the spurious impression that mortality declined after 1780. He writes: "The system virtually collapsed between the 1790s and 1820, and statistics for both town and country became utterly misleading" (1965: 385).

It is difficult to accept Krause's view that the decline in mortality did not come until the nineteenth century, in view of the generality of the eighteenth century decline of mortality in the rest of Europe (Guillaume and Poussou 1970). Flinn also shows some skepticism of Krause's derivation of his results (1970: 28).

In any case, Krause believes that there was little change in the degree of underregistration *before* 1780 (1965: 393). We should be on relatively firm ground, therefore, if we restrict our analysis to the period 1700–1780, which we have done so far as the demographic data are concerned.

B. REAL WAGE SERIES

Following Deane and Cole (1967: 19), we have used Gilboy's data (1934) to construct a weighted average of the regional wage series, using population estimates as weights. Gilboy's cost-of-living index was then used to deflate the series, yielding a real wage series for the period 1700 to 1789.

More specifically, we took Gilboy's wage series for Lancaster laborers as representative of the North; that for London laborers as representative of the South; and an average of the series for Exeter and Oxfordshire laborers as representative of the West. Rather than using the wage levels, we used the indices. It makes a noticeable difference which year one chooses as base; we calculated the average three ways, using 1700, 1745, and 1789 as base years for the regional series.

The population estimates for the three regions (North, South, and West) were taken from Deane and Cole (1962: 103) who provide them for 1701, 1751, 1781, and 1801. We interpolated between each pair of points, assuming a constant rate of population increase. Each region's annual wage was appropriately weighted, and averaged to derive the series of national estimates. This was then divided by the annual cost-of-living index, resulting in a real wage series.

The population of the three regions comprised about 40 percent of the national population over this period. Of this 40 percent, the share of the North rose from 29 percent in 1700 to 38 percent in 1790. According to Deane and Cole (1962: 20), the evidence from areas not included in these three regions does not appear to conflict with the broad outlines suggested by this weighted average.

The annual real wage series was then used to form five-year averages for 1700–1704, 1705–1709, . . . , 1785–1789. These were in turn used to form two sets of decennial series: one centered on 1705, 1715, etc.; the other on 1710, 1720, etc. For some purposes one is appropriate, for some purposes the other.

5

Inheritance Systems, Family Structure, and Demographic Patterns in Western Europe, 1700–1900

LUTZ K. BERKNER AND FRANKLIN F. MENDELS

THE availability of land and the rules of inheritance that govern succession to it have been invoked time and again as primary factors in determining both the family structure and the demographic patterns of Western European peasant societies. It has been pointed out repeatedly that impartible inheritance and the integral transmission of the land prevents the creation of new households by maintaining a fixed number of openings on the land and therefore limits the number of marriages, encourages the emigration of children, and leads to slow population growth. Partible inheritance, on the other hand, results in fragmentation of the land and rapid population growth through local settlement and a high marriage rate (Habakkuk 1955).

The argument that assigns an independent causal role to inheritance systems in explaining population trends has a long history. Arthur Young, noting the practice of partible inheritance in certain French provinces on the eve of the Revolution, argued that partibility only led to poverty. The continuous subdivision of farms was detrimental to agricultural productivity because small farms were cultivated by peasants almost devoid of capital who could not afford to invest in the improvements that modern agriculture required. Subdividing the land at each generation expanded marriage opportunities and population growth by allowing widespread acquisition of holdings, irrespective of their economic viability for the future support of a family: "Couples marry and procreate on the *idea*, not the *reality*, of a maintenance" (Young 1969: 317).

This was probably the prevailing opinion until the argument about inheritance and population was turned around by Frederic Le Play and

We thank Joel Singer, Etienne van de Walle, Charles Tilly, and William Parish for letting us use their data. For a more recent utilization of Van de Walle's data, see Van de Walle and Hermalin, 1975. William Leugoud and Nancy Fitch assisted us in preparing this paper. Financial support was provided by a grant from the Ford and Rockefeller Foundations Program in Support of Social Science and Legal Research on Population Policy.

his followers in the middle of the nineteenth century. It was now argued that the adoption of the Civil Code in France, which strongly restricted testamentary freedom in favor of nearly equal inheritance prescribed by law was a decisive factor in explaining why the French birth rate was low. The argument was that when the peasant proprietor was faced with the prospect of being forced to divide his land among several children, he practiced family limitation to prevent economic disaster. As a result a relatively high birth rate was maintained only in those areas where division was resisted (Le Play 1871; Bertillon 1897; Brandt 1901).

Thus partible inheritance has been used to explain both population growth and population decline, depending on whether it is supposed to affect nuptiality or marital fertility. Young linked the creation of new holdings with widespread marriage, leading to population growth; Le Play claimed that the fear of reducing the size of the family holding was a major incentive to practice birth control within marriage. This shift in emphasis in the explanation of total fertility—from marriage patterns in the eighteenth century to marital fertility in the nineteenth—corresponds to the generally accepted proposition that the demographic transition in Europe was accompanied by a change from societal to individual control over fertility, and that this resulted primarily from a shift in regulation through marriage to one of individual decisions concerning family size (van de Walle 1968; Wrigley 1972; Coale 1969). "In pre-industrial Europe the chief means of social control over fertility was prescribing the circumstances in which marriage was to be permitted." (Wrigley 1969: 119). This control has been called the western "European marriage pattern" (Hajnal 1965) and rests on the norm that marriage requires an economic base which in the past usually meant land.

Since access to the land was regulated by inheritance systems, they should have played an important role in explaining regional differences in population growth in European peasant societies. Before the widespread adoption of birth control in the second half of the nineteenth century, inheritance systems should have operated primarily through their effect on nuptiality and migration. Our purpose is to examine the extent to which these propositions can be supported by exploring the theoretical relationships between inheritance, household structure, marriage patterns, and migration rates, and presenting some evidence which illustrates the real nature of these relationships.

210

I

INHERITANCE SYSTEMS

THE term "inheritance system" is rather imprecise and can refer either to the law or the custom. Inheritance *laws* are enormously complex and varied. They indicate who will share in the estate, whether strictly equal portions will be given to all the children or whether preferential and even exclusive treatment will be accorded to one of them. The relative degree of equality varies according to whether personal or real property is at stake. Closely linked to inheritance are the prescribed provisions for the widow (dower) and rules concerning marriage portions (dowry) for children who have already left home. Some inheritance laws curtail the parental power by requiring strict equality among the heirs; others give the father wide discretion in disposing of his property through a testament or presentation of gifts. Even before the introduction of national statutory laws in the early nineteenth century, most European regions had had written customary laws governing inheritance since the sixteenth century. For example, in Old Regime France there were three major types of written customary inheritance law. In central and southern France strong parental power was concentrated in the hands of the father who could use his testament to choose a single heir and transfer most of his property to him. In Normandy and the West, on the other hand, the father was forbidden to name an heir, make a will, or provide any gift to sons beyond a strictly equal portion of the inheritance. In the area around Paris, there was a legal compromise between these two extremes. All the children had a claim to the inheritance but the parents together decided how to give out the portions; the children had the option of accepting their portion as permanent or returning it to be redivided in an inheritance settlement (Yver 1966; Le Roy Ladurie 1972).

Besides the laws there are the "traditional" inheritance *customs* of the peasantry, which are the norms of the society, and may represent either an historically ingrained ideology or merely the currently accepted forms of behavior (Maspétiol 1955: 131). When the French customary laws were codified in the sixteenth century, it is indeed possible that they reflected the regional differences in popular customs at that time. But once codified they became fixed rules of law, while customs could continue to change. As legal historians have repeatedly discovered, there are often major discrepancies between the customary written law and the practices which the notaries were recording in private contracts (Gay 1953). In many regions married daughters had the option to share in the inheritance, but it was customary for them

211

to sign disclaimers when they received their marriage dowries. In southern France, where the father supposedly had tremendous powers through the right of testament often the peasants did not bother to leave a will, which meant that property was divided evenly among the children (Le Roy Ladurie 1966).

It may appear that the degree of equality of inheritance rights is directly related to the extent to which landed property becomes fragmented at every succession, but equal inheritance does not necessarily lead to the equal division of the land. Before the land reforms of the late eighteenth and nineteenth centuries, certain types of land tenure prohibited the division of holdings. Where there was a strong feudal system the manors could require impartibility and the actual inheritance customs would have little effect on the division of the land. In central Europe the lord often required the peasant holding to remain intact, so that if the inheritance customs assured equality the siblings had to be compensated by the heir who took over the farm (Berkner 1972a). A similar situation could arise from restrictive settlement laws. Where some authority—the manor, the village community, or the state—exercised and could deny the right to settle or build a house in a community the effect of partible inheritance customs was limited (Wopfner 1938; Braun 1960: 51). In general, the areas of impartibility in western Europe were those with a strong manorial control over land tenure and settlement rights (Faith 1966; Wopfner 1938).

By "inheritance system" we mean the combination of laws, customs, land tenure rights and settlement restrictions that regulate the partibility of the land at a succession. These inheritance systems may be ranked along a continuum from strict impartibility, when there is only one successor for each holding, to strictly equal partibility when all the children receive an equal fraction of their parents' real property. In between is a wide range of possibilities which we call preferential partibility, when the land may be divided among several of the children, but one of them receives a larger or preferred share of the patrimony.

II

Inheritance Systems and Demographic Patterns

In order to clarify the relationships between the systems of inheritance and demographic patterns, it will be helpful to examine their operation in an ideal-type peasant society in preindustrial western Europe. In such a society the land is entirely held by independent owner-occupiers of farms which produce approximately at subsistence level, using family labor. The amount of land held by each family is fixed at

212

inheritance and there is no land market or tenancy. For the economy to function, farm size and family composition must be mutually adjusted. The given system of transmission of the family farms (from strict impartibility to equal partibility) will correspond to a certain family and household structure, to expectations among the children concerning marriage and succession, and to a social stratification for the entire village.

In this ideal type of peasant society, let us consider the consequences of a system of absolutely impartible inheritance. There will be only one heir to the farm who is allowed to marry and stay in the household with his parents. All the peasant households go through a phase in which there is co-residence of the peasant and one married child, forming the so-called stem family (Berkner 1972b). The other children may remain in the household when they reach adulthood as long as they can contribute to the labor requirements of the farm, but they may not marry. Some of the nonheirs will be able to find local marriage opportunities: Many of the girls will marry into other households, and some of the younger sons will become established in local households which have no male heirs. But since the number of holdings does not increase, many of the children will only have a choice between remaining celibate in the family household, or emigrating from the village. Thus the pure case of impartibility will result in co-residential stem family households, celibacy, and out-migration. The higher the outmigration, the lower the celibacy within the village, if both sexes emigrate at the same rate.[1]

In the opposite case of strictly equal partible inheritance, we will find a very low frequency of households in which parents co-reside with a married child, because each child will receive a piece of land on which to establish an independent household, and the parents can detach a small plot for their own use after retirement. Because all the children receive a piece of land, all of them can marry locally and there will be no reason for emigration. Therefore, perfect partibility should lead to a high proportion of nuclear family households, high nuptiality, and low emigration.

Between the two extremes of strict impartibility and strictly equal partibility lies a diverse variety of inheritance systems which we will call preferential partibility. All of them aim at a compromise between the goal of keeping the family farm totally intact by naming only one successor and the opposite goal of providing each child with an equal portion of land. These systems operate by compensating certain chil-

[1] When migrations involve predominantly one sex, higher celibacy should result among the other from the imbalance of the sex ratio.

213

dren (especially the girls) with monetary payments instead of land or using wills and other contracts to transfer the bulk of the holding to one heir while the other children receive only small plots. Two basic aspects of systems of preferential partibility are that the inheritance law does not require that the land be divided in order to assure equality, and that peasant customs appear to be extremely flexible in the variety of compensations that are deemed acceptable. Compensation need not be in land, or even cash; it may be a provision of support until marriage, a dowry at marriage, an apprenticeship, or even an education. At times such a system may operate exactly like impartibility, and this could happen even within the stipulations of the French Civil Code which protected the rights of each child. These inheritance rights concern the division of the assessed value of the property; there is no legal reason that the portions cannot be paid in cash after the value of the estate has been determined (although a dissatisfied heir may demand partition). In many regions of nineteenth-century France, one son inherited the entire holding, and the other children agreed to be compensated in other ways (Brandt 1901). However, the arrangement could also consist of naming one child as the successor to the major part of the land, while splitting off smaller plots for some of the other children. If this happened, there followed a continuing fragmentation of the land, creating a social structure composed of a relatively stable number of large farms and an increasing number of very small ones (Zink 1969). Sometimes these small parcels were not actually farmed by the children who received them at all, but within a few years were leased or sold to the principal heir. (Dion-Salitot 1971; Pingaud 1971).

III

Intermediate Variables

The enormous amount of flexibility within a system of preferential partibility means that economic and demographic circumstances will play a major role in determining its actual operation. This also means that systems of preferential partibility do not lend themselves to firm predictions concerning household structure or population patterns. In general, we would expect to find co-residential stem families in the households of the preferred heirs, but these may represent only a small proportion of the many nuclear family households created by splitting off numerous small plots. The demographic patterns in the village will depend on whether these nonpreferred heirs actually get a piece of land, whether it is economically feasible for them to get married and

214

stay on that plot, or whether they sell their plot and emigrate. None of these things can be predicted without knowing a great deal about the relative level of economic opportunity within and outside the village.

Economic opportunity strongly affects the outcome of a system of preferential partibility, but if we consider the reality of peasant villages in the eighteenth and nineteenth centuries we see that even strict partibility and strict impartibility rarely work as in the ideal type. In the ideal-type village the fit between the inheritance system, the family, nuptiality, and migration assumes that there are fixed proportions between the total income of the family, the amount of land it holds, and the family labor it needs. In reality peasants have considerable leeway available to them for adjustment (Boserup 1965). They are also placed under the influence of many forces which compete with or mitigate the effects of the inheritance system.

Peasants produce goods not only for themselves, but also for the market. Moreover, they buy goods on the market. To this extent, the economic viability of an agricultural holding is affected not only by its size, but also by externally determined market prices. Market forces may also induce changes in agricultural specialization and thus create or remove constraints on holding size. As a result peasants are obliged to find ways of avoiding the division of the land in spite of the inheritance system, or conversely, the new crops may facilitate or encourage subdivision. The former case was described in a village of the Jura after 1870 where the development of commercial dairy-farming discouraged further subdivisions (Dion-Saletot 1971); the latter is exemplified by the adoption of the potato, which made it possible to support a family from the production of a smaller surface of land.

Inheritance was not the only way of acquiring land. There existed at least some parcels which were on the market to be bought, so that villagers could modify the land distribution created by the inheritance system through exchanges in the land market. Peasants could also rent land from others. In many regions most of the peasants were tenant farmers who rented all or parts of their holdings. The inheritance rules concerning land partibility did not affect leaseholds; thus the greater the proportion of the land that was held under a lease, the less it was affected by the inheritance system. The personal property of a tenant farmer was usually divided but since there is no link between personal property and a particular locality, there is little reason to expect a continuity of heirs in one place. Likewise, if the land was held under a short-term lease or in insecure tenancy, the children would have no expectation of succession to the farm.

The inheritance of land was not a necessary condition for residence in an agricultural village if nonheirs could reside in other people's houses as servants or lodgers or if new houses or cabins could be built in response to the demand for them. But the demand for servants and lodgers as a supplement to family labor depended on changes in the composition of the family over the life cycle and the size of the farm (Berkner 1972a). Therefore the fit between holding size and family composition did not have to be perfect. A large, undivided holding could be operated by a small nuclear family if outsiders could be hired. Conversely a small, divided holding could serve as a residence for a large, extended family if some of its members worked outside and brought in their cash income (Maspétiol 1955).

Agriculture was not the only source of support for the peasantry. Industrial or commercial opportunities could develop in the village or elsewhere in the region. When additional income from cottage industry could be earned on farms the partition of the land could continue beyond the limits set by considerations of purely agricultural viability (Mendels 1969, 1972). As a rural society becomes increasingly industrialized subsistence is no longer in direct proportion to the size of the landed property. The formation of new households will depend primarily on the conditions of labor demand in the rural industry, not on the inheritance system. When nonagricultural sources of income are available outside the village, they create an attraction that alters the assumptions made about migration patterns based on the availability of land openings. The pull of a city may increase emigration by encouraging celibate siblings to leave or heirs of small parcels to sell or rent them to the preferred heirs who remain in the village (du Maroussem 1915).

It would be a major error to view the peasant as a helpless creature forced to blindly follow the dictates of an inheritance system. As Malinowski (1964: 30) pointed out long ago, a primitive native is just as likely as a modern businessman to break the rules if it is in his interest and he thinks that he can get away with it. Recently Bourdieu (1972) has sharply warned against excessive legalism in the interpretation of peasant behavior. The inheritance system sets limits, creates problems and opportunities, and evokes certain types of behavior which conform to it or avoid its consequences. Inheritance laws and customs are things that the peasant must deal with in planning a strategy which will reach his goals; they do not determine the goals or the strategy. Historians and anthropologists usually assume that the basic peasant goals are to maintain the family property intact while providing for one's old age (Goody 1973; Habakkuk 1955). The strategy that is adopted by any individual peasant family to fulfill such goals will depend on the local inheritance system operating within certain constraints (Cole 1971). When population or economic pressures become overwhelming, peasant strategy will aim to adjust the inheritance practices or the demographic patterns. A system of strictly equal partibility will create overwhelming pressures for such a change within a few generations if mortality falls to a level where every family has more than 2 children surviving to adulthood. If a stable population grows at the slow rate of about 0.75 percent per year on the average there will be 2.5 survivors per peasant family (to the age of 30). If there is local endogamy, the number of holdings will increase at the rate of 25 percent each generation. After four generations of strictly equal partibility, the average farm size will be 1:2.44 of the size it was a century earlier. For the case of a population growth rate of 1.35 percent per annum corresponding to a doubling in 50 years of the population, there would be three survivors to the age of 30 per family. In this case the number of holdings will increase at the rate of 50 percent per generation and the average farm size will be less than one-fifth of the size it was 120 years before.[2] Such a rate of fragmentation will drive holding size below subsistence, unless equal partibility is abandoned. In fact every western European society that has continued to be a peasant society has eventually been forced to adopt some type of preferential partibility to prevent the fragmentation of land below a level of minimum subsistence.

IV

BELGIAN, FRENCH, AND GERMAN EXAMPLES

THE demographic consequence of an inheritance system will depend on the effect of that system in the past on the social structure, the proportion of the population for whom inheritance of the land is still crucial, the amount of leeway that the system allows the peasant in charting a strategy, and the effect of local or regional economic development on that strategy. This can be illustrated with some case studies of peasant societies (1) where the social structure was such that the

[2] In contemporary India, with a population doubling in 30 years and a generation length of 27 years, 100 holdings would fragment into 1,212 in 108 years, should strictly equal partibility prevail! The formula to be applied here is

$$\frac{H_1}{H_0} = \left(\frac{S_A}{2}\right)^G,$$

where H_1 is the final number of holdings, H_0 the initial number of holdings, S_A is the number of survivors to age A, and G is the number of generations of length equal to A years. Correspondence with a population growth rate is obtained by defining the length of generation as the time in which a population growing at the rate r will increase in the ratio of $S_A/2$, or $r = (\ln (S_A/2))/A$. We have used $A = 30$ in the European case (27 in the Indian case).

inheritance system had little effect on the partibility of the land and demographic patterns were largely explained by economic changes; (2) where, on the contrary, the inheritance system definitely shaped demographic patterns, especially in those areas which continued to be impartible over a long period of time; and (3) where systems of partible inheritance have themselves been shaped by demographic and economic restraints.

Flanders is an example where land partibility was largely independent of the inheritance system (Mendels, 1975). Most peasants did not actually own their farms but held three- to nine-year leases. In the eighteenth century the land became very fragmented except for the region of the Polders where subdivision of the large commercial farms was curtailed. What determined this difference was not the inheritance system, which was strictly egalitarian in both cases. The indivision of the commercial farms ultimately stemmed from the type of soils of the area in which they were located. The heavy soils of the Polders required large plows pulled by several horses which were expensive and practical only on large holdings. The sandy light soils of the interior of Flanders, however, were well suited for labor-intensive agriculture on small family farms. Moreover, many peasants in the interior supplemented their incomes by weaving linen at home. The cumulation of labor-intensive agriculture and industrial activity raised the total income that could be earned on every acre of land and consequently drove up rents. It was thus in the interest of landlords in the interior to subdivide their holdings and rent them to peasants in small parcels.

The population of the Flemish interior grew twice as fast as the population of the Polders in the course of the eighteenth century. In the interior the annual number of marriages increased with the prosperity of the linen industry while in the Polders it did not. On the other hand, in the Polders, marriages increased with the prosperity of the commercial agriculture. In both areas, therefore, marriages were noticeably responsive to changes in the market economy (Mendels 1969, 1970a, 1972).

Just as eighteenth-century Flanders is a case where equal inheritance is not an important factor in explaining either fragmentation or nuptiality, the Pays de Caux in eighteenth-century Normandy is an area where preferential inheritance explains very little about either household structure or demographic patterns. The Pays de Caux was one of the only regions in Old Regime France which had a customary law of male primogeniture and the oldest son received two thirds of the real property. But as in Flanders, peasant proprietorship was very rare; 80 percent of the villagers were tenants. There were a few commercial farms in each village, but the majority of the households were headed by agricultural wage-laborers and handloom weavers working in the cotton textile industry. There is almost no evidence of stem families even on the large farms and the rate of household formation was high due to the local opportunities in rural industry. It was the fluctuations in the market for agricultural and industrial goods, not the availability of holdings through the inheritance system, that explains population growth in this region (Berkner 1973).

However, there are peasant societies in which inheritance systems have been crucial determinants of household and demographic patterns. This is primarily true in rural societies that conform most closely to the ideal type in which the social structure is predominantly made up of independent land-holding peasants whose farm production provides at least for the subsistence of their families, and where commercialization, urbanization, and industrialization have had limited influence. As we have shown, it is unlikely that any peasant society which continued a system of strictly equal partibility could approximate the conditions of this ideal type. However, at certain points in time, such as the period immediately following the settlement of a frontier area or the resettlement of a depopulated region, these conditions could still exist before the effects of fragmentation had changed the society.

One such example is provided by a comparison of household structure in two regions of late seventeenth-century Lower Saxony which had suffered population losses earlier in the century during the Thirty Years War. Both of the regions were predominantly agrarian and similar in social structure but followed opposite inheritance practices. In the territory of Calenberg the majority of peasants held their land under a form of tenure which prohibited the division of holdings and practiced impartible inheritance, while in the nearby territories of Gottingen and Grubenhagen holdings could be divided and the peasants followed a custom of partible inheritance. There was a distinct difference in the household structure of the two regions in 1689. Stem family organization was prevalent in Calenberg, where impartible inheritance resulted in families of co-resident parents and married children in nearly thirty percent of the households. The region of partible inheritance, however, displayed little evidence (6 percent) of co-resident household of parents and married children. These divergent household patterns were also associated with different demographic patterns. In the region where holdings were divided both the number of households and the total population increased more than twice as much as in the impartible region between 1689 and 1766.

From a study of a German hamlet in Franconia (Planck 1967) in

219

which the number of holdings remained constant due to impartible inheritance, we can demonstrate that when the average number of surviving children per family is 3 (in this case 2.9 survived to age 15) in the long run every third adult must actually remain celibate or emigrate from the locality. There were 274 transfers of the 24 farms in the hamlet from 1650 to 1966, during which time 821 children survived to age 30. Over three centuries one-third of the children (274/821) could have become heirs, another third could have married these heirs if there were total hamlet endogamy, and one-third would have been excluded from local marriage or succession. In actuality, only 22 percent (180) of the descendants inherited a farm directly from their parents, only 7 percent (57) married into another local household, and the remaining 70 percent neither became heirs nor married locally. Since not all the holdings were taken over by a direct descendant and hamlet endogamy was not frequent, 311 people [3] could have been accommodated from outside the hamlet; this is almost exactly the actual number of people who immigrated into the hamlet (321). Most of these (223) came to marry an heir, and 85 percent originated from within 12 miles of the hamlet.[4] If we assume the other localities were able to accommodate this same proportion of outsiders to native adults as in this hamlet (39 percent) one-third of the adults (31 percent) would be excluded from the local marriage network.[5]

V

NINETEENTH-CENTURY FRANCE: A STATISTICAL ANALYSIS

IT is in France that we find a diversity of systems of preferential partibility both before and after the introduction of the Civil Code, and this makes it particularly difficult to predict any demographic consequences with certainty. One of the few studies that deals with this question is a detailed description of a village in Burgundy in the nineteenth and twentieth centuries. It suggests that birth control as a means of preserving the patrimony was adopted in the nineteenth century by only a small number of well-to-do peasants, but it was only one of several

[3] $311 = (274$ potential heirs $= 274$ potential spouses$) - (180$ actual heirs $+ 57$ actual spouses$)$.

[4] Seventy men and 152 women came into the hamlet to marry an heir; 49 married couples (hence 98 persons) immigrated to take over a holding.

[5] Planck (1967: 251) arrives at the same proportion in the following way. There were 570 surviving children who did not find a local opening and 14 who emigrated after taking over a farm, for a total of 584 potential heirs and spouses who left; 321 persons immigrated into the hamlet to marry or take over a holding. The difference between the inhabitants who left and outsiders who came in to marry or take over a holding is 263, 32 percent of the native survivors.

means available for preserving the family farm. Those families that limited births were able to build up and maintain their holdings, while those who did not, continued to fragment them at every succession. But toward the end of the century more families made use of monetary payments and contractual agreements to keep the farm intact (Pingaud 1971).

This choice of strategies is what the followers of Le Play had in mind when they argued that the role of the *eldest* son in a preferential inheritance system was being replaced by an *only* son in a system of equal partibility. However, this local study indicates that preferential partibility allowed such wide latitude in peasant strategies, that the variation within a department may have been as great as the variation between departments. Nevertheless, studies based on the agricultural survey of 1866 (Brandt 1901) indicate that the peasants in some departments were more likely to follow strategies aimed towards impartible inheritance than in others. In the northern departments, partibility was widespread; in Brittany and most of the southern departments, peasants were more likely to practice impartible inheritance.

We have strong reservations about the reliability of designating the "typical" inheritance practices of an area at the level of aggregation of the department. Moreover, it is impossible to control for all of the variables that interfere with the working out of the effects of the inheritance system. Nevertheless, since a recent study (Parish and Schwartz 1972) has shown that it is possible to measure differences in household complexity at the departmental level, it would be interesting to examine the relationship between the supposedly typical inheritance practices, household structure and demographic patterns.

The two measures of household complexity used as indicators of family structure in nineteenth-century France are the average number of adults (over 20) per household and the number of marital units per household for each department. Marital units per household (MUH) should be a good measure of stem families, as it indicates the prevalence of the co-residence of two married couples. Average adults per household (APH) includes both the married and the celibate adults, so it should measure the extent to which adult children remain in the parental household.

We have used the measures of MUH and APH calculated by Parish and Schwartz for 1856, the first available date, for the 67 predominantly rural and agricultural departments. Marital fertility (Ig) and proportion of women married (Im) for each department in 1856 were taken from van de Walle's calculations. For emigration, we used the measure of net departmental migration between 1866 and 1886 (Goreaux 1956);

221

a negative value indicates net outmigration, a positive value net immigration. As for farm fragmentation, we used the ratio of farms under 10 hectares to those over 40 hectares per department in 1882 (Goreux 1956); a high value indicates a high proportion of small farms, hence high fragmentation.

The table of zero-order correlations between these variables shows certain patterns of covariation. The correlation between impartible inheritance (using a dummy variable with 0 value for partible and 1 for partible or mixed practices) and fragmentation (measured 16 years later) is not significantly different from zero (Table 5–1.)

The two variables appear to be independent of each other, for in France fragmentation was not only the result of partible inheritance, but in some areas it led to the adoption of impartible practices, and in others fragmentation was related primarily to other factors such as the land tenure and market conditions. Column (1) shows that impartible inheritance practices are positively correlated with the two measures of extended family households, low nuptiality compensated by high marital fertility, and negative immigration (that is, emigration) which served to curtail population growth. However, the co-variation of the two measures of family structure is not the same. The number of adults per household (column 2) shows the same pattern as impartibility, but the number of marital units per household (column 3) is associated with *high* nuptiality not compensated by low marital fertility and is also correlated with low fragmentation of the land. Thus, while inheritance

TABLE 5–1. CORRELATIONS OF DEMOGRAPHIC VARIABLES IN 1856

	(1) Impart.	(2) APH	(3) MUH	(4) Im	(5) Ig	(6) Immig.	(7) Frag.
(1) Impartible inheritance (Impart.) 1886	—	.57	.46	−.32	.37	−.41	.12 (n.s.)
(2) Adults per household (APH)	.57	—	.61	−.40	.42	−.37	.08 (n.s.)
(3) Marital units per household (MUH)	.46	.61	—	.35	−.15 (n.s.)	−.21	−.28
(4) Proportion females married (Im)	−.32	−.40	.35	—	−.81	.30	−.47
(5) Marital fertility (Ig)	.37	.42	−.15 (n.s.)	−.81	—	−.36	.21
(6) Net immigration (Immig.) 1866–1886	−.41	−.37	−.21	.30	−.36	—	.06 (n.s.)
(7) Farm fragmentation (Frag.) 1882	.12 (n.s.)	.08 (n.s)	−.28	−.47	.21	.06 (n.s.)	—

and one measure of extended family households (APH) is correlated with the demographic variables as Le Play would have expected, the other measure of stem families (MUH) is not. Moreover, excessive farm fragmentation even though it is independent of inheritance practices, is correlated with a low incidence of stem families and *low* nuptiality.

VI

CONCLUSIONS

SOME time ago Kingsley Davis (1963: 351) dismissed inheritance systems as irrelevant in explaining demographic change because inheritance practice itself changes in response to demographic pressure. Indeed, in complex rural societies where subsistence agriculture plays a minimum role and land is actively exchanged on the market, they made little difference. In partible systems, where fragmentation is always possible, the means of dealing with demographic pressure are not rigidly defined by law or custom. Therefore peasant strategy can involve a wide range of choice. One of the choices then open to peasant strategy is to counteract the inheritance system so as to avoid the actual division of the land. However, in backward areas with subsistence family farms, it can be shown that impartibility is associated with stem family household structure, which implies high celibacy or emigration at the local level. Where strict impartibility has been enforced over long periods of time by the authorities or by rigid customs, the means to deal with population pressure are defined within the impartible inheritance system.

Historians and social scientists often seek outside explanatory forces which are (or seem to be) determined independently because they have little knowledge of their operations. Inheritance systems and practices are examples of mechanisms which are often mentioned as explaining land fragmentation, changing social structure, and population patterns. What our survey shows is not that inheritance is irrelevant, but that it cannot be assumed to always operate. The majority of today's legal profession is not primarily engaged in clarifying or enforcing the law. Rather, the function of a large number of lawyers consists in helping clients to bend, circumvent, and otherwise use the law to their best economic advantage. The same must have been true of peasants and their notaries in the past. There are circumstances where what looks like the effect of the inheritance system will in fact be the result of economic and demographic factors. To find out one has to know the local patterns of land tenure, the village economy, and of course one has to know the inheritance system actually operated in practice.

6

A Multivariate Regression Analysis of Fertility Differentials Among Massachusetts Townships and Regions in 1860

MARIS A. VINOVSKIS

AN understanding of the determinants of fertility is essential to anyone interested in American social and economic history. The number of children born has a significant impact on the family as well as the society as a whole. Yet very little progress has been made by demographic historians in ascertaining and explaining fertility differentials. The few studies that have attempted to examine American fertility patterns historically are handicapped by methodological weaknesses that minimize their usefulness for analyzing fertility differentials.

Most of the recent work in American historical demography has been concentrated on the colonial period. The lack of readily available birth rate data has forced these historians to rely mainly on the laborious but indispensable technique of family reconstitution.[1] Due to the difficulty of reconstituting all or even many of the families of an individual community, very few studies have been completed so far, and most of them are unable to yield very much information on fertility differentials at any point in time. Almost all of these studies have concentrated on small agricultural communities and very little effort has been made to analyze the demographic history of the larger commercial centers (Demos 1970; Greven, 1970; Lockridge 1970). As a result, it is very difficult to analyze rural-urban differences in fertility. Since most of the reconstitution studies end before 1800, they are also unable to yield any information on fertility differentials between industrialized and nonindustrialized segments of society. In addition, due to the small sample sizes of these studies, it is virtually impossible to analyze fertility differentials within any of these community case studies by sub-

* I would like to gratefully acknowledge financial assistance for computer time from the Harvard-M.I.T. Cambridge Project and the Harvard University Center for Population Studies. An earlier version of this paper was delivered at the American Historical Association Meeting in New York City, December 29, 1971 and at the Chicago University Economic History Workshop, May 5, 1972.

[1] For a review of recent work in American historical demography, see Greven 1967; Lockridge 1968; Vinovskis 1971. For a critical survey of the sources of historical demography, see Hollingsworth 1968.

dividing the group and still have enough subjects in each subgroup for the differences among these groups to be statistically significant.[2] Finally, most of the studies to date have omitted assembling other socio-economic characteristics of the population. This has made it even more difficult to discuss fertility differentials within the population since we are unable to distingiush significant socioeconomic subgroups within the populations under investigation.[3] As a result of these methodological limitations, most of the studies based on family reconstitution have been unable to furnish us with adequate data on or analysis of fertility differentials though they have been very useful in providing indications of the overall levels and trends of fertility before 1800.[4]

By its very nature, microlevel analysis of fertility differentials based on family reconstitution makes any interpretation of the influence of the social structure on fertility difficult.[5] A more appropriate level at which to analyze fertility differentials is among nations or subdivisions within a country. The major attempt to investigate American fertility differentials and trends historically on a macrolevel is Yasukichi Yasuba's analysis of the fertility ratios of the white population of the United States between 1800 and 1860 (Yasuba 1962). Yasuba examined changes in fertility among all of the states and territories during that period. Though his study benefits from having a broad scope, it suffers from being forced to rely on aggregative data accumulated on a state-wide basis. An underlying implicit assumption in Yasuba's research design is that the states and territories can be treated as relatively homogeneous units in analyzing demographic differences. As we shall later see, there are significant intrastate differences in demographic, economic, and social variables that are obscured by relying exclusively on interstate comparisons and which may seriously alter the interpretation of such a study.[6] In addition, Yasuba's study suffers from the lack

[2] Many of the studies in historical demography that rely on sampling fail to apply tests of significance to their data; for example, see Bloomberg 1971. For a critique of this practice, see Hareven and Vinovskis 1975.

[3] On the problems of generalizing about demographic characteristics of a larger population on the basis of family reconstitution data without taking into account the socio-economic level of the population under investigation, see Vinovskis 1971.

[4] For an interesting attempt to speculate on the general outlines of early New England demographic history on the basis of these earlier studies, see Smith 1972.

[5] It is difficult to study the effects of variations in the social structure on fertility when the focus is on the individual or the family. To analyze the determinants and consequences of the social structure on fertility, it is necessary to analyze aggregate social units rather than individuals (Blau 1969; Goldscheider 1971: 21-47).

[6] This does not mean to imply that studies at the interstate level are not useful. Ideally, one would study fertility differentials at the interstate, intrastate, and family levels to see the interactions of the variables under investigation at different social levels. Unfortunately, much of American historical demographic

of data on socioeconomic variables other than the degree of urbanization and industrialization, and a crude estimate of per capita income. Thus he ignored such potentially important determinants of fertility as religion and education. Finally, Yasuba's study is limited by the statistical procedures that he used. Most of his work is based on rank-order correlations which are effective only in measuring the association between any two variables at a time. Thus, he finds industrialization, urbanization, and income per person 10 years and older are inversely associated with fertility, but he has considerable difficulty in determining the relative importance of these factors in explaining fertility differentials since the three independent variables are highly correlated among themselves.[7]

Wendall Bash studied fertility ratios of New York towns from 1840 to 1875. By analyzing fertility ratios at the town level rather than at the state level, Bash was able to ascertain significant demographic differences within the state. Bash's analysis, however, is also limited by the small number of socioeconomic variables and the statistical procedures used. He used only four independent variables: (1) population density; (2) land value; (3) value of dwellings; and (4) percent foreign-born. Furthermore, the study's usefulness is limited in that it depends entirely on the analysis of variance—a procedure which underutilizes the data (Bash 1963).

The present study is an analysis of fertility differentials among

---

analysis has been carried out at different levels without any explicit consideration of the underlying assumptions in each situation.

[7] Yasuba did attempt to deal with this problem by standardizing the states with respect to one socioeconomic variable and then examining the rank-order correlation between fertility and urbanization. This is a very crude approximation since he could only standardize for one socioeconomic variable at a time. Thus, though the states may be standardized on one measure, they were not necessarily identical on a second index of socioeconomic development. Furthermore, given the small number of cases investigated, Yasuba continually has a problem of finding high correlations in order to be statistically significant (Yasuba 1962: 173-177).

Since this paper was originally written, Colin Forster and G.S.L. Tucker have reexamined the problem by using multiple regression analysis (Forster 1972). However, the effort by Forster and Tucker, though an improvement on Yasuba's work, is inadequate for several reasons. First, though Forster and Tucker have improved upon Yasuba's measure of land availability by calculating the number of white adults per farm (adult-farm ratio), their measure also lacks conceptual clarity. Second, all of the economic historians who have analyzed fertility differentials have ignored such potentially important factors as the educational level of the population. Finally, though the use of multiple regression analysis by Forster and Tucker is a significant improvement on the statistical techniques employed by Yasuba, they do not make full use of its potential by restricting themselves to only three independent variables. In addition, the particular measures of land availability and urbanization Forster and Tucker have used raises the possibility of multicollinearity in their regression analysis. For a critique of their work as well as a different perspective on this issue, see Vinovskis 1972.

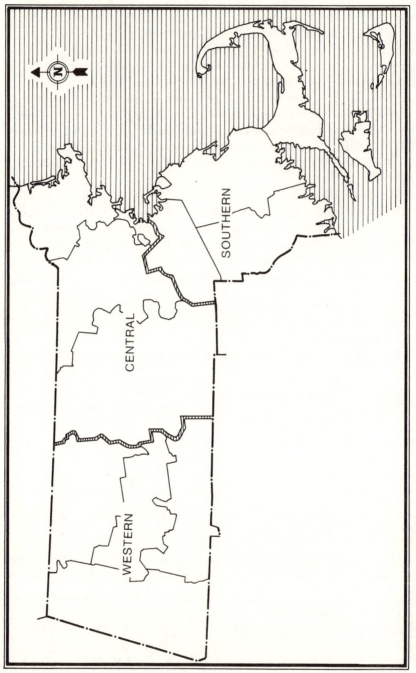

Figure 6–1 Regions of Massachusetts

Massachusetts townships in 1860 that attempts to avoid the limitations of the earlier studies by assembling sixteen socioeconomic variables and using multiple regression analysis.[8] In order to test for the possibility of significant intrastate fertility differentials, Massachusetts was divided into three geographic subregions: Central Massachusetts (Suffolk, Essex, Middlesex, and Worcester counties), Western Massachusetts (Hampshire, Hampden, Franklin, and Berkshire counties), and Southern Massachusetts (Norfolk, Bristol, Plymouth, Barnstable, Dukes, and Nantucket counties).[9]

I

DEVELOPMENT OF MASSACHUSETTS BETWEEN 1790–1860

BEFORE turning to the analysis of fertility differentials in 1860, it is necessary to consider the demographic and socioeconomic trends in the Commonwealth between 1790 and 1860. Though it is only possible to sketch the main developments, it is important to understand the forces at work over time in that society as well as to place the demographic experience of Massachusetts in a broader context.

Any investigation of fertility differentials and trends in Massachusetts is hampered by the lack of adequate birth records. Though a statewide vital events registration system was begun in 1842, it did not provide accurate information on births by 1860 (Gutman 1956). Consequently, it is necessary to construct an index of fertility from the federal censuses. Though a variety of indices of fertility can be calculated from the censuses, the most useful is the white refined fertility ratio—that is, the number of white children under 10 years of age per 1,000 white women between the ages of 16 and 44. Unlike annual birth rates, white refined fertility ratios measure fertility over a decade.[10]

The federal censuses of the early nineteenth century are not detailed enough for the computation of refined fertility ratios for the black

[8] This chapter is part of a larger analysis of fertility differentials and trends in Massachusetts from 1765 to 1860 (Vinovskis 1975a). The determinants of fertility differentials in 1860 are not necessarily the same as the determinants of change in fertility over the hundred year period (Vinovskis 1974, 1975, 1976a). In other words, in this chapter we are seeking to account for the existence of fertility differentials at a point in time rather than trying to account for changes in fertility during the previous years.

[9] The particular regions were chosen in order to keep the number of towns in each region roughly equal and to reflect actual regional differences in economic and social development as much as possible (Vinovskis 1975a).

[10] For a discussion of the accuracy and usefulness of using fertility ratios rather than birth rates, see Vinovskis 1975; Yasuba 1962: 23-41. There have been a number of different terms used to describe the number of children under ten years of age per woman between the ages of 16 and 44. Throughout this paper we shall refer to this child-woman ratio as the refined fertility ratio.

population. Therefore, this investigation of fertility focuses only on the white population of Massachusetts. This limitation does not seriously impair the analysis since blacks made up a very small percentage of the total population between 1790 and 1869.[11]

Yasuba found wide geographic differentials in the white refined fertility ratios between 1800 and 1860. Generally, the white refined fertility ratios were higher in the newer states and territories than in the older areas and higher in the South than in the North. The older states in New England had the lowest fertility ratios in 1800 and continued to have throughout the period. Massachusetts had the lowest white refined fertility ratio in the United States between 1820 and 1850 and the second lowest fertility ratio in 1800, 1810, and 1860 (Yasuba 1962).

The white refined fertility ratio declined in the United States from 1,844 in 1800 to 1,308 in 1860—a decline of 29.1 percent. The white refined fertility ratio in Massachusetts declined 39.3 percent over that same period, but unlike the trend in the United States, it rose slightly in the decade 1850 to 1860. It is also interesting to note the demographic split in New England between the states of Massachusetts, Rhode Island, and Connecticut and those of Maine, Vermont, and New Hampshire. Whereas in the first three states the white refined fertility ratios declined by 39.3, 39.0, and 38.5 percent between 1800 and 1860, in the second group the ratios declined by 43.9, 47.8, and 47.2 percent (Yasuba 1962).

Just as there were significant geographic differences among the states and territories, there were similar differences in the white refined fertility ratios among the Massachusetts regions. Throughout this period, Central Massachusetts had the lowest fertility ratios while Western Massachusetts had the highest until 1840 when its white refined fertility ratio dropped below that of Southern Massachusetts. There was a steady decrease in the white refined fertility ratios in all three regions of Massachusetts except for the decade 1850–1860 when there was an increase in fertility ratios in both Central and Western Massachusetts. The greatest percentage change over the entire period occurred in Western Massachusetts which had the highest fertility ratio in 1800. Thus, there was a convergence of the interregional white refined fertility ratios during the 60 year period—just as there was a similar convergence among the New England states (see Table 6–1).

We have already noted the wide differentials among regions in Massachusets in the white refined fertility ratios and the downward

[11] The percentage of blacks in Massachusetts between 1790 and 1860 was never above 1.5 percent of the total population.

TABLE 6–1. TRENDS IN WHITE REFINED FERTILITY RATIOS WITHIN
MASSACHUSETTS REGIONS, 1800–1860

	1800	1810	1820	1830	1840	1850	1860
Central	1,358	1,355	1,221	996	924	802	870
Western	1,741	1,582	1,409	1,162	1,052	891	919
Southern	1,455	1,404	1,251	1,096	1,082	967	951
Massachusetts	1,477	1,521	1,269	1,064	987	857	896

Source: U.S. Censuses, 1800–1860

trend in those ratios between 1800 and 1860. We cannot be certain, however, that these differentials and trends are due to changes in the birth rate since they may be accounted for by the differentials and trends in mortality of children under 10 years of age. For example, a large rural-urban differential in mortality rates and an increase in those rates between 1790 and 1860 might account for the changes in the white refined fertility ratios. In fact, Yasuba, on the basis of very fragmentary evidence speculated that there were significant rural-urban mortality differences and that there was an increase in mortality rates before 1860 as a result of urbanization and industrialization. Yasuba concluded, however, that though the differentials in the white refined fertility ratios and their decline over time did overstate the extent of changes in the birth rate, the large decline in the white refined fertility ratio could not be explained by the rise in mortality (Yasuba 1962: 73–101).

Since Yasuba's estimates of mortality were based on such fragmentary data and such questionable Massachusetts life tables as Edward Wigglesworth's table of 1789 and E. B. Elliott's table of 1855, it was necessary to investigate in more detail the trends and differentials in mortality rates. It was particularly difficult to obtain mortality rates for children since death rates are the most underregistered during the first year of life. On the basis of recalculating mortality data for Massachusetts during these years it appears that Yasuba and other demographers have greatly exaggerated the rural-urban differences in mortality rates for Massachusetts before 1860. Though there were rural-urban differences in Massachusetts mortality rates, these differences were relatively small and were found mainly between townships under and over 10,000 population. Furthermore, though there were considerable yearly fluctuations in mortality between 1790 and 1860, the overall death rate remained relatively stable. Thus, though the differentials and trends in white refined fertility ratios may overstate differences in

231

the birth rates, it is much less of a problem than suggested by Yasuba (Vinovskis, 1975; Vinovskis, 1971).

Throughout this period, Massachusetts experienced considerable population shifts. Unfortunately, this topic has never been investigated thoroughly so that we do not have accurate data on net migration for Massachusetts. Large numbers left the state in search of economic opportunities, but this was offset by immigration into Massachusetts from other states—particularly from the rest of New England. In addition, Massachusetts attracted an increasing wave of foreign immigrants after 1845. Thus in 1860, 65.4 percent of the population of Massachusetts had been born in that state and another 13.3 percent had been born outside of Massachusetts but within the United States. The remaining 21.2 percent were foreign-born and most of these were from Ireland. Central Massachusetts had the highest percentage of foreign-born in both decades while Western and Southern Massachusetts had about equal percentages. All three regions experienced an increase in the percentage of foreign-born in their populations from 1850 to 1860 (see Table 6–2).

Although it is impossible to calculate precisely the net result of the population shifts from 1790 to 1860, we can at least obtain an estimate from 1850 to 1860. In 1850 and 1860, 134,830 and 163,637 people living in Massachusetts had emigrated to the Commonwealth from other states and territories. At the same time, 199,582 and 244,503 Massachusetts-born citizens were living outside the state in 1850 and 1860. Thus, there was a net loss to the state from internal migration of the native population. This loss was offset, however, by the 164,024 and 259,496 persons who were foreign-born that resided in Massachusetts in 1850 and 1860 (Warner 1867: 290–298). The state probably gained in population from 1840 to 1860 by migration and lost popula-

TABLE 6–2. NATIVITY OF MASSACHUSETTS POPULATION IN 1850 AND 1860

	Foreign born		Born in Massachusetts		Born outside Massachusetts but in United States	
	1850	1860	1850	1860	1850	1860
Central	20.1%	24.4%	65.0%	60.6%	16.1%	14.7%
Western	11.0	16.3	72.2	68.3	16.6	15.3
Southern	11.8	16.4	79.5	74.8	8.5	8.7
Massachusetts	16.5	21.1	69.2	65.4	14.3	13.3

Source: U.S. Censuses, 1850, 1860.

232

tion in the earlier decades when the stream of foreign-born immigrants were not sufficient to offset the net loss of the native population.

The result of the declining birth rates, the stable mortality rates, and the net migration patterns was a substantial growth of the Massachusetts population between 1790 and 1860. Though Massachusetts grew at a slower pace than the rest of the country, the state nevertheless was able to increase its population by 225.0 percent during this period. Furthermore, though Massachusetts averaged an 11.4 percent growth rate per decade from 1790 to 1820, it experienced an accelerated growth rate of 24.0 percent per decade between 1820 and 1860. Particularly impressive population gains were registered in Central Massachusetts, especially in the last 40 years (see Table 6–3).

One of the most frequently cited determinants of fertility differentials is the degree of urbanization (Jaffe 1942; Robinson 1963 and 1961; Robinson and Robinson 1960). Yasuba's study found that increasing urbanization was inversely correlated with the white refined fertility ratios in the United States before 1860—particularly during the last three decades.[12] In this context it is important to realize that Massachusetts was more urbanized than the rest of the country during this period. The percentage of the population in Massachusetts living in towns over 2500 persons increased from 27.6 percent in 1790 to 77.7 percent in 1860. The population growth of larger towns (over 8000 persons) was even more rapid. The percentage of persons living in towns over 8000 people increased dramatically from 4.8 percent in 1790 to 44.0 percent in 1860 (see Tables 6–4 and 6–5).

Though the percentage of persons living in towns over 2500 people increased steadily throughout this period, Western Massachusetts remained far behind the other two regions. In addition, though both Central and Southern Massachusetts had an almost identical percentage of its population in towns over 2500 persons between 1790 and 1860, Central Massachusetts had a larger proportion of its population in cities larger than 8000 people (see Tables 6–4 and 6–5).

Just as Massachusetts was more urbanized than the rest of the nation between 1790 and 1860, it was also more commercialized and indus-

[12] Yasuba found that there was little correlation between the degree of urbanization and the decline in the white refined fertility ratios between 1800 and 1830. He did find a small positive correlation between the increase in urbanization and the decline in fertility from 1830 to 1860. Yasuba argues that it was after 1860 that the close correlation between the two variables occurred. Since Yasuba's analysis suggests that changes in urbanization became more important in explaining the decrease in fertility as the level of urbanization increased, one might hypothesize that changes in urbanization in Massachusetts would have played a more important role in explaining the decline in fertility there than in the rest of the nation (Yasuba 1962: 185-187).

TABLE 6–3. TRENDS IN GROWTH OF POPULATION OF MASSACHUSETTS REGIONS, 1790–1860

	1790	1800	1810	1820	1830	1840	1850	1860
Central	176,249	195,102	223,968	253,692	307,338	392,684	567,989	734,324
Western	89,972	106,317	112,182	119,496	129,229	138,820	167,476	181,743
Southern	112,566	121,426	135,890	150,099	173,841	206,196	259,047	314,999
Massachusetts	378,787	422,845	472,040	523,287	610,408	737,700	994,514	1,231,066

Source: U.S. Censuses, 1790–1860.

TABLE 6–4. PERCENTAGE OF POPULATION OF MASSACHUSETTS REGIONS
LIVING IN TOWNS OVER 2,500, 1790–1860

Central	35.2%	42.0%	47.0%	46.9%	51.7%	62.4%	74.7%	83.6%
Western	0	2.7	9.9	12.9	19.7	26.7	46.9	50.0
Southern	37.7	41.9	43.8	44.0	51.0	63.0	73.8	80.7
Massachusetts	27.6	32.0	37.2	37.8	44.5	55.9	69.9	77.7

Source: U.S. Censuses, 1790–1860.

TABLE 6–5. PERCENTAGE OF POPULATION OF MASSACHUSETTS REGIONS
LIVING IN TOWNS OVER 8,000, 1790–1860

Central	10.3%	17.5%	20.5%	22.1%	27.4%	40.4%	49.3%	57.6%
Western	0	0	0	0	0	6.1	7.2	9.0
Southern	0	0	0	0	0	14.6	25.2	30.2
Massachusetts	4.8	8.1	9.7	10.7	13.8	27.1	36.8	44.0

Source: U.S. Censuses, 1790–1860.

trialized. Massachsetts took an early lead in manufacturing with the development of the factory system which gradually replaced household manufacturing. Simultaneously with the development of manufacturing was the increasing commercialization and specialization of the rest of the economy (Clark 1929; Hazard 1921; Kirkland 1948; Morison 1921; Tryon 1917; Ware 1931; Zevin 1971).

There were significant regional differences in the economic development of Massachusetts—particularly between Western Massachusetts and the other two regions. Western Massachusetts was much more involved in agriculture than the other two regions.[13] Central Massachusetts led the other two regions in the percentage of persons engaged in manufacturing. Because of its heavy involvement in shipping and fishing, Southern Massachusetts led the other two regions in the percentage of persons engaged in commerce with Western Massachusetts coming a poor third. Though differences between the regions persisted in

[13] The data on the percentage of persons engaged in agriculture, manufacturing, and commerce are not really adequate because the censuses from which they were calculated changed in their definitions of the various occupations during this period. An attempt was made to make these figures as comparable as possible to each other by combining several minor occupational groupings in 1840 and 1855 to approximate the general divisions in 1820. Though the absolute levels of employment in any given census year may not be accurate, the relative percentages as well as the trends are probably an accurate reflection of the shifts in the Massachusetts economy during these years.

235

both the percentage of persons engaged in agriculture and manufacturing, the trends in those occupations in all three regions were nearly identical (see Table 6–6).

Unfortunately, it is very difficult to obtain reliable estimates of changes in most cultural variables over time. For example, we have no accurate estimates of church membership or attendance between 1790 and 1860. We can estimate changes in the amount of education per capita between 1826 and 1860 for Massachusetts residents. The changes in education are very important for our analysis of fertility since many demographers emphasize the role of education in determining fertility levels (Adelman 1963; Friedlander and Silver 1967; Heer 1969; Westoff and Potvin 1966). In fact, some family planning advocates in the less-developed countries today assume that increases in the level of education will result in decreased fertility (Berelson 1969; Davis 1967).

Most American historians have simply assumed that there was a significant increase in per capita education between 1820 and 1860—largely as the result of the well-publicized reform efforts of men such as Horace Mann and Henry Barnard. Recently Albert Fishlow has challenged this analysis by arguing that the amount of education per capita remained relatively stable between 1830 and 1860 in the New England states (Fishlow 1968).

A detailed analysis of educational trends in Massachusetts reveals a more complex pattern. The amount of education per person actually

TABLE 6–6. EMPLOYED PERCENTAGE OF EMPLOYED PERSONS IN AGRICULTURE, COMMERCE, AND MANUFACTURING IN MASSACHUSETTS, 1820–1855

		1820	1840	1855
Central	Agriculture	49.6%	35.5%	16.4%
	Manufacturing	37.4	45.9	66.0
	Commerce	13.0	18.6	17.6
Western	Agriculture	80.4	67.4	54.4
	Manufacturing	18.2	30.4	39.9
	Commerce	1.4	2.2	5.7
Southern	Agriculture	47.8	36.7	23.3
	Manufacturing	32.3	38.3	54.8
	Commerce	20.0	25.0	21.9
Massachusetts	Agriculture	57.6	42.1	24.2
	Manufacturing	30.4	40.8	58.9
	Commerce	12.1	17.1	16.9

Sources: U.S. Censuses, 1820, 1840; Massachusetts State Census, 1855.

declined between 1826 and 1860. This is a somewhat deceptive statistic because it was due to the gradual elimination of children under four in the public schools—a group who probably did not benefit very much from their school experiences at that time (May and Vinovskis 1972). If we calculate the amount of education received per child between four and sixteen or five and fifteen years of age, the amount of education did increase. In addition, there is reason to suspect that there were significant increases in the quality of education in the classrooms during this period (Vinovskis 1972).

Looking at Massachusetts between 1790 and 1860, we see a state where the birth rate is declining, the death rate remains relatively stable, there is a net population loss before 1840 from migration but a gain during the last decades as a result of immigration from abroad, a steady accelerating population growth, increased urbanization and industrialization, and an overall increase in the amount of education received by school age children.

II

Definition of Variables

Initially over fifty variables were considered for inclusion in the analysis of fertility differentials among Massachusetts townships in 1860. The number of variables were reduced to 24 by constructing indices based on 2 or more variables and by eliminating variables which were almost identical measures of a previously used factor. Though the 24 variables were satisfactory at the statewide level, it was discovered that they were inappropriate for the analysis of regions within the state. Many of the variables that were independent of each other at the state level were highly correlated with each other at the regional level—thereby introducing the problems of multicollinearity. It was decided to avoid this problem by reducing the analysis to 16 variables that were relatively independent of each other at both the state and regional levels. This reduction in the number of variables was achieved with a loss of overall explanatory power, in terms of R^2, of about 5 percent at the state level.

For purposes of this analysis, it is convenient to group the sixteen variables into seven broad categories: index of fertility, demographic factors, ethnic factors, urban development, economic development, religious factors, and educational factors (see Table 6–7).

The index of fertility used is the ratio of white children under 10 years of age to white women between the ages of 16 and 44. By using this white refined fertility ratio, rather than a crude fertility ratio based

237

TABLE 6–7. VARIABLES USED IN MULTIPLE REGRESSION ANALYSIS OF
FERTILITY DIFFERENTIALS AMONG MASSACHUSETTS TOWNS
IN 1860

I. Index of fertility
    X(1)   White refined fertility ratio under 10

II. Demographic factors
    X(2)   Number of white women per 100 white men
    X(3)   Standardized death rate, 1859–1861

III. Ethnic factors
    X(4)   Percentage of population born in Ireland
    X(5)   Percentage of population born in British America
    X(6)   Percentage of population white

IV. Urban development
    X(7)   Annual rate of population growth, 1850–1860
    X(8)   Total population

V. Economic development
  A. Industrialization
    X(9)   Assessed value of manufacturing per capita
  B. Commercialization
    X(10) LOG_{10} assessed amount of money in trade, shares, etc. per capita
  C. Agricultural development
    X(11) Percentage of population that are farmers
  D. Rate of economic development
    X(12) Percentage change in assessment of property per capita, 1850–1860

VI. Religious factors
    X(13) Church seats per 1000 persons
    X(14) Catholic church seats per 1000 persons

VII. Educational factors
    X(15) Percentage of persons under twenty in all schools
    X(16) Amount of money spent per public school student

on the number of children per total population, we can minimize some
of the differences in fertility due to variations in the age composition
of the population in the townships. Though it would have been desirable to use birth rates rather than fertility ratios, it was impossible to
do so because of the deficiencies in the state registration of births in
1860. The use of fertility ratios rather than birth rates probably does
not introduce any serious distortion into the analysis since the two
measures are usually highly correlated (Bogue and Palmore 1964;
Grabill and Cho 1965; Hareven and Vinovskis 1975; Vinovskis 1975).
The data for the white refined fertility ratios were obtained from the
federal census of 1860.

Two demographic measures are used as independent variables. First,
the number of white women per 100 white men is used as an indirect
measure of differences in marriage behavior among the towns. Ideally

one would like to have used the median age at first marriage and the proportion ever married. Though Massachusetts did collect data on the number of marriages in each town during this period, it was discovered that the data were inaccurate. As a result, it was necessary to rely on the very crude approximation offered by the sex ratio of the white population.[14]

Previous studies have pointed out the importance of infant mortality rates on the level of fertility. Since the Massachusetts data on infant mortality were of questionable accuracy, it was decided to rely on the standardized death rates for each township from 1859 to 1861. Though the standardized death rates also suffer from underregistration during these years, they are much more accurate than the infant mortality rates and they are probably a reasonable approximation of the relative level of mortality among the Massachusetts townships in 1860 (Friedlander and Silver 1967; Heer and Smith 1968; Vinovskis 1975).

Obtaining data on the ethnic composition of the population was difficult since there are no town summaries of the percentage of the foreign-born population available in the published summaries of the federal census. Rather than attempt the logistically impossible task of tabulating each individual's ethnicity from the manuscript census, an estimate was made on the basis of a straight-line interpolation of the percentage of the foreign-born population from the Massachusetts state censuses of 1855 and 1865. Since the percentage of foreign-born remained relatively stable between 1855 and 1865 in Massachusetts, this procedure probably yielded reliable estimates of the relative level of the foreign-born population in Massachusetts townships in 1860.

The Massachusetts censuses of 1855 and 1865 summarized national origins of the foreign-born population in 16 categories so that it is necessary to condense that data for analysis. At the same time, it was important to investigate the various immigrant groups in as much detail as possible. Since 71.3 percent of the foreign-born in Massachusetts in 1860 were Irish, it is not surprising that the percentage of foreign-born and the percentage of those born in Ireland were highly correlated (.71). In order to avoid the problem of multicollinearity, it was decided to use the percentage of the total population born in Ireland rather than the percentage foreign-born. In addition, persons born in British America were examined separately since they comprised the second largest group of immigrants in Massachusetts. The remainder of the foreign-born population was not analyzed in more detail because it

[14] There is considerable debate on the importance and meaning of the sex ratio data that were available. For an introduction to this debate, see Tien 1959; Vinovskis 1975.

represented such a small percentage of the total population. The proportion of the population that was white was readily available from the federal census.

Measuring the degree of urbanization is made difficult by the lack of any commonly accepted definition. Often the term is used as a broad category which encompasses such processes as industrialization or commercialization of the economy as well as population growth or concentration. In this chapter urbanization will simply be defined in terms of population size and change. Thus, the total population of the town is used as an index of the degree of urbanization while the rate of population change between 1850 and 1860 is used as an index of the rate of urban development.

Economic development is examined under four subdivisions—industrialization, commercialization, agricultural development, and the rate of economic growth. Though these four categories are interrelated, it is useful to examine them separately under the general heading of economic development. The assessed value of manufacturing per capita was used as the index of industrialization. The LOG_{10} of the assessed amount of money in trade, shares, or on hand per capita was used as an index of commercialization (the LOG_{10} was used because it makes the nonlinear relationship between the assessed amount of money in trade, shares, or on hand per capita and the white refined fertility ratio more linear and thus enables us to use the least-squares method of analysis). The agricultural development of the economy was measured by the percentage of the population that were farmers according to the federal census. The rate of economic change was approximated by the percentage change in the assessment of property per capita between 1850 and 1860.

Accurate data on religious membership at the township level did not exist for Massachusetts in 1860. Consequently, it was necessary to use an approximation that was available—the number of church seats per 1,000 persons. Since there probably is a three- or four-year lag between a sizable increase in church membership and the construction of a new church, this index reflects religious affiliation three or four years earlier. In addition, this index might also reflect differences in the relative affluence and concern about church buildings among the various denominations. Since the white refined fertility ratios also measure fertility behavior over a decade, the effect of the time lag in church construction is minimized. Since Catholics were suspected of higher fertility than the other groups, the number of Catholic church seats per 1,000 persons was also included.

Educational factors were available from the annual school reports

240

compiled by the Massachusetts Secretary of Education. The level of education in the town was measured by the percentage of persons under 20 in all schools in 1860. The quality of education was approximated by the amount of money spent per public school student.

Despite the increased cost, it was decided to collect data from all Massachusetts townships rather than sample from them. In this way it was possible to avoid worrying about problems of statistical significance due to sampling errors. Altogether, complete data on all variables mentioned above were gathered on 303 of the 330 Massachusetts townships in 1860. Though some data were available on the 27 towns not used, it was decided to omit them rather than to reduce the number of independent variables in the analysis since there did not appear to be any systematic bias introduced by the omission of these towns.

III

Statistical Procedures Employed

MULTIPLE regression analysis allows one to study the relationship between an independent variable and a dependent variable while taking into account the influence of the other independent variables on that dependent variable. Multiple regression analysis attempts to produce a linear combination of the independent variables which will correlate as highly as possible with the dependent variable. The underlying mathematical procedure is the use of the linear least-squares method which produces the smallest possible residual between the predicted value of the dependent variable from the regression equation and its actual value.

The order and manner in which variables are introduced into the regression equation affect the outcome. Selecting the best regression equation possible is difficult since there is no single, simple statistical procedure for doing this and personal judgment as well as the nature of the phenomenon being investigated must play a major role in selecting the best regression equation. One might calculate all the possible regression equations and examine their differences. However, this procedure is too expensive and wasteful of computer time—especially when there are 15 independent variables. A more sensible and economic procedure is to use stepwise regression analysis which allows the examination of a complex phenomenon and yet avoids unwarranted oversimplification. In stepwise regression, the first step chooses the single independent variable which best explains the dependent variable. On the second and subsequent steps another independent variable is entered if it is the one which is the best predictor of the remaining unexplained variance of the dependent variable. Thus, step-wise regression usually provides the best predictor of the dependent variable with the fewest independent variables. One common danger with stepwise regression is that it sometimes encourages overzealous researchers to add independent variables as long as they contribute significantly to explaining the dependent variable even though these additional independent variables may have little meaning from a con-ceptual point of view. It is also important to remember that the order in which independent variables are entered into the equation under a stepwise procedure does not neecssarily reflect their relative association with the dependent variable since independent variables are entered on the basis of their ability to reduce the unexplained amount of variance rather than the strength of their association with the dependent variable.[15]

The relationship between 2 variables is not always linear. Thus, even though the coefficient of linear correlation between 2 items may be quite low, it does not necessarily mean there is little or no association between them since that relationship might be curvilinear rather than linear. To investigate this possibility, each of the independent variables was plotted against the dependent variable and examined for non-linearity. In addition, each independent variable was transformed into LOG_{10} and then correlated with the white refined fertility ratio to see if it provided a better fit. Finally, since linear transformations using LOG_{10} cannot exhibit a positive slope at one point and a negative slope at another, it was necessary to use a polynominal of the second order as a further test of a curvilinear relationship. Thus, the independent variables were squared and correlated with the white refined fertility ratio. On the basis of these tests, it was discovered that the relationship between the white refined fertility ratio and the independent variable $X(10)$ was better described by converting the latter to LOG_{10}.

In order to check the possibility that the entire analysis was distorted by the presence of an extreme case such as Boston, another stepwise regression was calculated with Boston being excluded. Since Boston's omission did not have any appreciable effect on the equation it was included in the final runs.

In an effort to test the relative contribution of each category of fac-tors to the explanation of the white refined fertility ratio, a series of stepwise regressions were run—first with just the variables within each of the larger categories against the white refined fertility ratio; and then with each of the larger categories individually excluded while the

[15] For a very useful discussion of the alternative ways of ordering variables for regression analysis, see Draper and Smith 1966.

remaining variables from the rest of the categories were analyzed against the white refined fertility ratio.

Finally, in order to test for the possibility of significant intrastate fertility differentials, Massachusetts was divided into 3 geographic regions and each of these regions was then analyzed separately and these results were compared with those for the state as a whole.

IV

RESULTS

THE means and standard deviations of each variable for the state and the 3 regions are shown in Table 6–8; the simple correlations between the white refined fertility ratio and each of the independent variables are displayed in Table 6–9.

The simple correlations between the white refined fertility ratio and the independent variables demonstrate the complexity of trying to account for fertility differentials at the township level. The correlation coefficients usually are of the same sign and magnitude for the state and the three regions within it. The highest correlations with the white refined fertility ratio usually are the sex ratio of the white population, the total population of the township, the index of commercial development, the percentage of the population that are farmers, the number of Catholic church seats per 1,000 persons, and the amount of money spent per public school student. Though there are variations among the regions, the overall picture is one of relative similarity rather than marked differences. The region that deviates the most from the others and the state as a whole is Southern Massachusetts.

Though correlation coefficients can establish the relationship between two variables, that relationship may be caused by a third factor which has not been considered. One way to investigate this possibility is to employ multiple regression analysis which calculates the relationship between the dependent variable and any independent variable after controlling for the effects of the other independent variables on that dependent variable.[16] The most useful statistics for this purpose are the beta coefficients which indicate the relative importance of each of the independent variables in accounting for the variance of the dependent variable—the white refined fertility ratio (see Table 6–10).

Examining the signs of the correlation coefficients and the beta coefficients, we see that there are some significant differences between them. Of the 60 correlation coefficients in Table 6–9, 10 of them re-

---

[16] This also minimizes the possibility of a spurious correlation due to the use of ratio variables in the analysis. For a good introduction and discussion of the problems of using ratios in correlation and regression analysis, see Kuh 1955.

TABLE 6–8. MEANS AND STANDARD DEVIATIONS OF VARIABLES

	Massachusetts (All)		Massachusetts (Central)		Massachusetts (Western)		Massachusetts (Southern)	
	Mean	Standard deviation	Mean	Standard deviation	Mean	Standard deviation	Mean	Standard deviation
White refined fertility ratio under 10	993.88	149.83	978.87	129.77	1,026.89	175.63	979.32	143.2
Number of white women per 100 white men	101.35	8.80	101.40	8.77	99.67	9.39	103.35	7.7
Standardized death 1859–1861	16.37	7.66	16.07	5.73	14.92	3.91	18.69	12.3
Percent Irish	8.92	7.00	10.45	6.69	7.61	7.02	7.86	7.0
Percent British American	1.73	2.66	2.53	3.45	1.34	1.64	0.83	1.4
Percent white	99.43	0.96	99.64	0.54	99.13	1.26	99.45	1.0
Annual rate of population growth 1850–1860	0.83	2.60	1.27	3.15	0.13	1.66	0.92	2.3

Total population	3,811.92	10,967.56	5,261.20	16,032.63	1,787.80	2,026.29	3,779.20	4,243.3
Assessed value of manufacturing per capita	49.05	285.58	55.07	213.00	64.61	445.67	19.25	31.6
LOG_{10} assessed amount of money in trade, shares, etc., per capita	1.91	0.35	1.93	0.35	1.73	0.32	2.07	0.29
Percent farmers	8.34	5.66	7.17	5.23	12.15	5.61	5.67	3.72
Percent change in assessment of property per capita, 1850–1860	31.14	105.26	39.10	156.55	16.49	20.06	35.32	24.22
Church seats per 1,000 persons	756.60	324.44	686.49	251.63	872.74	379.35	735.66	328.50
Catholic church seats per 1,000 persons	31.00	108.69	34.79	74.61	14.67	48.64	44.57	185.18
Percent under 20 in all schools	47.35	8.30	46.19	6.82	48.91	9.23	47.46	9.20
Amount of money spent per public school student	5.79	2.44	5.78	1.93	5.60	2.93	6.02	2.59

TABLE 6–9. CORRELATION COEFFICIENTS BETWEEN THE WHITE REFINED
FERTILITY RATIO UNDER 10 AND THE INDEPENDENT VARIABLES

	Massachusetts (All)	Massachusetts (Central)	Massachusetts (Western)	Massachusetts (Southern)
Number of white women per 100 white men	−.54577	−.56543	−.67673	−.25412
Standardized death rate, 1859–1861	−.06700	−.14354	−.21433	.08308
Percent Irish	−.08851	−.10284	−.15162	.09262
Percent British American	.05565	.07934	.14411	−.00229
Percent white	−.06260	−.04657	−.13138	.16659
Annual rate of population growth, 1850–1860	.00109	.02335	.02869	.04960
Total population	−.18563	−.23523	−.38815	−.12150
Assessed value of manufacturing per capita	−.11145	−.10161	−.15938	.06313
LOG_{10} assessed amount of money in trade, shares, etc., per capita	−.27645	−.02987	−.39756	−.42521
Percent farmers	.26548	.27601	.26052	.05584
Percent change in assessment of property per capita, 1850–1860	−.01927	.00381	.00649	−.14649
Church seats per 1000	−.03300	−.10984	−.04172	−.07822
Catholic church seats per 1,000 persons	−.13118	−.21850	−.34271	−.01024
Percent under 20 in all schools	−.08235	−.09261	−.03377	−.22302
Amount of money spent per public school student	−.20635	−.41760	.05678	−.39129

verse their signs (i.e., the beta value is positive and the correlation coefficient is negative or vice versa) when calculated as beta coefficients.
This is particularly significant in the case of the percentage of the
population that are Irish. The correlation coefficients between the
white refined fertility ratio and the percentage of the population Irish
for all of Massachusetts, Central Massachusetts, and Western Massachusetts are negative while the beta coefficients are positive. In other
words, a researcher relying only on correlation coefficients would have

TABLE 6–10. BETA COEFFICIENTS

	Massachusetts (All)	Massachusetts (Central)	Massachusetts (Western)	Massachusetts (Southern)
Number of white women per 100 white men	−.45278	−.42871	−.55094	−.11141
Standardized death rate, 1859–1861	.01183	−.02350	−.01939	−.00078
Percent Irish	.09814	.14126	.24975	.36723
Percent British American	.00039	.03434	.04556	−.09390
Percent white	−.04902	−.02634	−.07786	.03439
Annual rate of population growth, 1850–1860	.03536	.12960	.11061	−.23941
Total population	−.15747	−.06766	−.08616	.00410
Assessed value of manu-facturing per capita	−.04082	.04621	−.05739	−.06583
LOG_{10} assessed amount of money in trade, shares, etc., per capita	−.23701	−.05029	−.43037	−.29053
Percent farmers	.12951	.18875	.01180	−.08569
Percent change in assessment of property per capita, 1850–1860	−.01701	.01207	.11101	−.21801
Church seats per 1,000	−.08500	−.02542	−.12489	−.05244
Catholic church seats per 1,000 persons	−.00276	−.09148	−.25153	−.02283
Percent under twenty in all schools	−.14603	−.12495	−.13558	−.21249
Amount of money spent per public school student	−.09418	−.26950	−.08993	−.40454

been misled to believe that the relationship between these variables was negative whereas in reality it is just the opposite.

Just as with the analysis of correlation coefficients, the examination of the beta coefficients reveals the complexity of trying to account for the fertility differentials among the Massachusetts townships in 1860. Of the 15 independent variables 7 differ in their beta coefficients among the 3 regions. We can generalize that for the state and the 3 regions, the sex ratio of the white population, the standardized death rate, the percentage of the population white, the total population of the township, the index of commercialization, the index of industrialization, the index of economic development, the number of church seats per 1,000 persons, the number of Catholic church seats per 1,000 persons, the percentage of persons under 20 in all schools, and the amount of money per public school student were negatively correlated with the white refined fertility ratio whereas the percentage of the population that was Irish, the percentage of the population that was British American, the annual rate of population growth between 1850 and 1860, and the percentage of the population that were farmers were positively correlated. In addition, the independent variables that had the strongest influence on the white refined fertility ratio were the sex ratio of the white population, the percentage of the population that was Irish, the index of commercial development, the percentage of persons under 20 in all schools, and the amount of money spent per public school student.

In order to ascertain the relative importance of each of the six groups of independent variables in accounting for the differentials in the white fertility ratio, two multiple regressions were calculated for each group of variables. First, each group was inserted by itself to see how much of the R^2 each group could explain by itself. Then each group of independent variables was removed one at a time from the equation in order to see how large a change in the R^2 would result from the omission of that group while all the other independent variables remained in the equation (see Tables 6–11, 6–12, 6–13, and 6–14).

For the state as a whole, the demographic and economic factors provide the best explanation of the differentials in the white refined fer-

TABLE 6–11. CONTRIBUTION OF EACH GROUP OF INDEPENDENT VARIA-
BLES TOWARD EXPLAINING THE WHITE REFINED FERTILITY
RATIO UNDER 10 FOR ALL MASSACHUSETTS

	Change in R^2	
	Inserted initially	Removed while all other categories are retained
Demographic factors	.29796	.15929
Ethnic factors	.01864	.00677
Urban development	.03576	.01832
Economic development	.12459	.07046
Religious factors	.01725	.00648
Educational factors	.05811	.02011
R^2 for all variables = .40952		

248

TABLE 6–12. CONTRIBUTION OF EACH GROUP OF INDEPENDENT VARIA-
BLES TOWARD EXPLAINING THE WHITE REFINED FERTILITY
RATIO UNDER 10 FOR CENTRAL MASSACHUSETTS

	Change in R^2	
	Inserted initially	Removed while all other categories are retained
Demographic factors	.32310	.13520
Ethnic factors	.01990	.00897
Urban development	.05882	.01361
Economic development	.08328	.02188
Religious factors	.05555	.00729
Educational factors	.21140	.05290
R^2 for all variables = .44999		

tility ratios among the townships. The remaining groups of variables contribute relatively little in the way of explanation. In Central Massachusetts the demographic and educational variables provide the most explanatory power with economic development a much weaker predictor. In Western Massachusetts the demographic, economic, and urban factors are particularly important though the urban factor's importance diminishes if you test its significance by calculating the loss in explanatory power by removing this group from the overall equation. Finally, educational and economic factors are particularly im-

TABLE 6–13. CONTRIBUTION OF EACH GROUP OF INDEPENDENT VARIA-
BLES TOWARD EXPLAINING THE WHITE REFINED FERTILITY
RATIO UNDER 10 FOR WESTERN MASSACHUSETTS

	Change in R^2	
	Inserted initially	Removed while all other categories are retained
Demographic factors	.46152	.13798
Ethnic factors	.13016	.03131
Urban development	.18478	.00978
Economic development	.21341	.11685
Religious factors	.12259	.04677
Educational factors	.00375	.01337
R^2 for all variables = .66746		

249

TABLE 6–14. CONTRIBUTION OF EACH GROUP OF INDEPENDENT VARIA-
BLES TOWARD EXPLAINING THE WHITE REFINED FERTILITY
RATIO UNDER 10 FOR SOUTHERN MASSACHUSETTS

	Change in R^2	
	Inserted initially	Removed while all other categories are retained
Demographic factors	.07013	.00865
Ethnic factors	.03589	.05151
Urban development	.02482	.02701
Economic development	.22130	.09793
Religious factors	.00727	.00302
Educational factors	.23430	.09055
R^2 for all variables = .41257		

portant for Southern Massachusetts which is the only region in which demographic factors are not very important.

Though the use of correlation coefficients, beta coefficients, and changes in R^2 have given us a good indication of the relative importance of individual variables or groups of them, we also need to consider the overall effectiveness of the resultant regression equation in accounting for the variation in the dependent variable. The most useful measure of this is R^2—the ratio between the variance of the dependent variable explained by the independent variables and the total variance of the dependent variable. Thus, if the independent variables perfectly predict the values of the dependent variable, R^2 would be equal to one. On the other hand, if the independent variables have no relationship to the dependent variable and therefore are not helpful in predicting values of the dependent variable, R^2 would be equal to zero.

For Massachusetts as a whole, R^2 for the 15 independent variables is .40952. In other words, approximately 41 percent of the variance of the white refined fertility ratio can be accounted by the independent variables. Again there are significant regional variations in R^2. Thus, R^2 for Central Massachusetts, Western Massachusetts, and Southern Massachusetts are .44999, .66746, and .41257 respectively.

V

DISCUSSION OF RESULTS

THE most striking result of this analysis of fertility differentials among Massachusetts townships is the importance of the demographic factors.

250

This group of factors is more important for Massachusetts as a whole, Central Massachusetts, and Western Masachusetts than any other set of variables. Only in Southern Massachusetts is the impact of this group of variables relatively negligible.

The most important variable in the demographic group is the number of white women per 100 white men. The negative relationship between this variable and the white refined fertility ratio is not surprising since it is an indirect measure of the marriage rate and the proportion of the population marrying. Ideally one would have liked to have data on the actual marriage rate and the proportion ever marrying, but those data were unavailable. Though the sex ratio was a significant factor in all 3 regions, it is much less important in Southern Massachusetts.

Previous studies have demonstrated a positive relationship between the infant mortality rate (or the crude mortality rate with which it is highly correlated) and the birth rate. Parents in areas of high mortality often have more children in order to insure that at least some of them will survive to adulthood and carry on the family name and take care of the parents in their old age. In Massachusetts the relationship between the white refined fertility ratio and the standardized death rate for 1859–1861 is very weak and negatively correlated in each of the 3 regions while slightly positive for the state as a whole. The relative weakness of this variable compared to other studies is not as surprising as it might appear at first glance. First the deaths are not completely registered in all Massachusetts towns and this might have introduced a slight bias (Vinovskis 1972). Second, the level of mortality was quite low throughout the state so that parents had much less worry about having at least one child survive than in the less-developed countries today. The rural-urban differences in mortality rates were relatively small in Massachusetts so that this variable had much less explanatory potential than in areas where the mortality differentials were larger (Vinovskis 1972). In addition, there is reason to suspect that people in Massachusetts often misperceived the actual extent of mortality in their communities—thus reducing the importance of the actual death rates in influencing their behavior (Vinovskis 1975).

In order to test for the possibility that the differences in fertility were really due to a large concentration of women in their most fertile ages in some of the townships, the percentage that white women between the ages of 20 and 29 were of white women between the ages of 16 and 45 years was calculated and included as an independent variable in some of the earlier regression runs. Since this variable added very little explanatory power, it was eliminated in the final runs.

251

Ethnicity was not a major determinant of fertility differentials by itself. Only in Western Massachusetts was the contribution of this group of variables significant as measured by R^2. The percentage of the total population that was born in Ireland was negatively correlated with fertility. However, as anticipated, when controlling for other factors such as urbanization, religion, etc., the relationship became positive. The percentage of the population that was born in British America was generally positively associated wtih the white refined fertility ratio and it was weak in all four areas. Similarly, the percentage of the population that was white was weak but negatively correlated. These results generally confirm the findings of other studies on the role of ethnicity though the importance of this factor was less than other scholars have suggested. Perhaps this is due to the fact that the impact of the ethnic groups was studied at the township level rather than as a group within individual communities or neighborhoods.[17]

The term "urbanization" has often been used as a catch-all for a wide variety of changes taking place within the context of cities. Due to the difficulties of measuring the various components of urbanization, historians have used population size (which is readily available in the nineteenth century) as an index of this phenomenon. As we have seen, this narrow definition is not very useful for analyzing Massachusetts in 1860 since many aspects often associated with urbanization such as increasing commercialization and industrialization were not highly correlated with the size of the township or population growth. For analytical purposes, however, we shall use urbanization in this essay to denote population size and population growth. In this sense, urbanization was relatively unimportant in explaining fertility differentials among the townships except for Massachusetts and even there it became quite insignificant if we measured its impact by the loss in explanatory power when this group of variables was removed from the equation.

The effects of urbanization on fertility were mixed at the regional level. Areas which were growing the most rapidly were positively correlated with the white refined fertility ratio (except Southern Massachusetts which was surprising strongly negatively correlated)—partly reflecting the fact that at least some of the population growth in those towns was due to the relatively high birth rates. Earlier studies have generally found that population size and fertility are inversely related to each other. This was also the case for Massachusetts in 1860. Though the direction of the association between the measures of

---

[17] For an analysis of fertility differentials using household data, see Hareven and Vinovskis 1975.

urbanization and fertility is not surprising, the strength of that relationship was much less than had been anticipated. We have been so conditioned by the emphasis on rural-urban differences in most studies that it appears strange to find that population size was not as significant in explaining fertility differentials as some of the other factors. Many of the earlier studies, however, did not look at different aspects of urbanization as we have attempted to do in this essay. In addition, many of the studies finding strong inverse relationships between population size and fertility studied societies where modernization usually did take place within the context of cities so that large rural-urban differences did develop. It is significant in this context that this investigation of Massachusetts has generally found smaller rural-urban differences for demographic indices than suggested by other demographic historians such as Yasuba (1962).

Economic development was an important determinant of fertility differentials—especially in Western and Southern Massachusetts. Furthermore, this analysis has demonstrated that it is important to examine each of the four subgroups of economic development—industrialization, commercialization, agricultural development, and the rate of economic development—separately since they are not highly correlated with each other and each one contributes somewhat differently toward explaining the fertility differentials of the Massachusetts townships. For example, the correlation between the indices of industrialization and commercialization (whether measured directly or in logarithmic form) are quite low. Perhaps this is merely a reflection of the inadequacies of the indices for those two variables. It is more likely, however, that this reflects the fact that early industrialization in Massachusetts did not always occur in the highly developed commercial centers such as Boston or Salem. Consequently, future demographic or economic investigations of New England in the nineteenth century must be careful to distinguish among the variables measuring economic development since they were concentrated in different towns within the Commonwealth.

As anticipated from previous studies, the LOG_{10} of the assessed amount of money in trade, shares, and securities per capita is negatively correlated in all 3 regions as is the assessed value of manufacturing per capita (except for Central Massachusetts where it is highly positive). The percentage of the population that are farmers is positively correlated (except for Southern Massachusetts), and so is the percentage change in the assessment of property between 1850 and 1860 per capita (again except for Southern Massachusetts which is strongly negative). The unanticipated result of this analysis is the

253

relatively weak association between the white refined fertility ratio and the index of industrialization.[18]

Religion has often been an important variable in accounting for fertility differences—especially today when the Catholic church has taken a strong stand against the use of certain types of contraceptive devices and against abortions. It is likely that churches may have played a much smaller role in the past since both the Protestant and Catholic churches disapproved of the use of contraceptive devices in the nineteenth century. To obtain an estimate of the role of religion on fertility differentials in Massachusetts in 1860 is difficult because accurate church membership is unavailable by towns. Therefore it is necessary to use a crude approximation—the number of church seats per 1,000 persons.

Except for Western Massachusetts, religious factors had relatively little impact on fertility differentials. The interest in religion, as measured by the number of church seats per 1,000 persons, is negatively correlated with the white refined fertility ratio. Similarly, the number of Catholic church seats per 1,000 persons is negatively correlated with the index of fertility. The surprising finding is the relatively weak relationship between the indices of fertility and Catholic religion except for Western Massachusetts where the two variables are strongly negatively related.

Educational factors are consistently negative in their relationship to fertility and particularly important in Central and Southern Massachusetts. Particularly important is the index of educational quality or concern—the amount of money spent per public school student. Though the educational factors used reflect levels of educational training in 1860 rather than in the 1840s when many of the parents were actually being educated, this probably does not introduce very serious biases into the analysis because the relative position among the towns on education remained quite stable during this period.

Compared to other studies of areal differences in fertility, this investigation explained a relatively modest proportion of the total variance in the white refined fertility ratios for the state as a whole (41 percent) though it is considerably more successful for some of the regions such as Western Massachusetts (67 percent). David Heer and John

[18] The index of industrialization was the per capita valuation of manufacturing activity from the 1860 Massachusetts state valuation. Another measure of manufacturing might have been the percentage of the population that was engaged in manufacturing. It is possible that if a different index would have been used, slightly different results would have been obtained. However, it is doubtful that the differences in results would be very large.

Boynton's analysis of fertility differentials among United States counties in 1960 accounted for 35 percent of the variance in fertility using eight independent variables (Heer and Boynton 1970). The one historical study of fertility differentials, William Leasure's analysis of the decline in fertility in Spain between 1900 and 1950, accounted for 17 percent of the variance in 1900, 37 percent in 1930, and 17 percent in 1950. However, since his study was restricted to only three independent variables, one would expect a somewhat lower explanatory power if all other things were equal (Leasure 1963). On the other hand, Paul Schultz's analysis of *municipios* in Puerto Rico accounted for 47 percent of the variance of the crude birth rate (Schultz 1967). In addition, David Heer and E. Turner's analysis of fertility differentials in Latin America accounted for 44 percent of the variance in fertility on a subnational basis (Heer and Turner 1965). Furthermore, most studies on the national level have explained relatively high proportions of the variance in fertility (Heer 1966).

The present study's modest explanatory power may be accounted for in several ways. By using a refined fertility ratio rather than a crude fertility ratio, differences due to age structure have been removed at the outset. When the data are recalculated for 1860 with the crude fertility ratio under 10 or 16 as the dependent variable, R^2 becomes much larger.

Second, there are serious problems of measurement and index construction in any historical analysis. We have very limited data so that it is impossible to measure precisely differences among the variables. Much more effort and attention in the historical profession must be devoted to developing and understanding various indices of social development that are readily available. Thorough scrutiny and adjustment of any of the indices used in this analysis will hopefully increase their predictive power.

There is also the question of whether all the major relevant variables were included in the analysis. For example, it would have been desirable to include per capita income data from each township, but they were unavailable for that period. Furthermore, there is also the question of whether the relationship between fertility and socioeconomic variables today is as strong as in the past. If there is a lengthy cultural lag between changes in the social structure and changes in individual behavior, one should not anticipate a high correlation between the social structure and fertility differentials during a period of rapid changes in the social structure. If adjustments to changes in the social structure are faster today than in the past because of our increased receptivity to change and our increased awareness of changes in society, the relationship between fertility and the social structure might be stronger today.

Thus, looking at fertility differentials in Massachusetts in 1860, one is struck by the relative weakness of the relationship between fertility and indices of urbanization, industrialization, and mortality rates. In addition, the regional differences within the state are significant and suggest the need for more intensive analysis of demographic and socioeconomic variables on a much smaller regional basis than has hitherto been practiced by most demographic and economic historians. The lack of larger differentials among Massachusetts towns in fertility ratios probably can be best explained in terms of the relatively high standard of living in Massachusetts throughout the nineteenth century and the gradual diminishing of demographic differences among these towns from 1790 to 1860.[19]

[19] This study has focused only on the socioeconomic determinants of fertility differentials among Massachusetts townships in 1860. For a discussion of the changes in fertility in Massachusetts townships from 1765 to 1860, see Vinovskis 1974 and 1975a.

7

Alone in Europe: The French Fertility Decline Until 1850

ETIENNE VAN DE WALLE

THE causes of the fertility decline in Europe and its connections with the great economic and social transformation of modern times have been the subject of many debates. Nowhere has the question seemed more crucial than in France, while the decline was in progress. In the Western context at least, it is only now that the transformation of the reproductive behavior of man has become the subject of academic study rather than of moral and sociopolitical condemnation. With hindsight, and from the safe vantage point of the 1970s, it seems almost odd that the issue was once so charged with emotions and that so many contemporary analyses were bent on proving that the diffusion of contraception spelled the decline of Western society. The majority of French social scientists until the Second World War deplored the decline of fertility. Official policies in most nations of the West tried to check the downward trend. The tide of opinions and policies has turned; even moderate population growth now seems excessive to many. With the passing away of the great fighting demographers of the thirties, French social science has turned to other issues than the regeneration of the race.

Today the overall logic of the demographic transition appears inescapable. The consensus takes for granted an ideal of low mortality and quasi-universal marriage, and the preservation of the standard of living and way of life that characterizes the middle of the twentieth century. These conditions are simply incompatible with completed families of eight or ten children that would be the norm in the absence of fertility control. Similarly, we cannot imagine sustained economic growth in the less developed world, unaccompanied by a drop of fertility and mortality.

Why was the decline of fertility not generally recognized in France at the time as a rational adaptation to changing circumstances? I see two reasons beyond the normal survival of established norms and values after their usefulness has ceased. First, observers failed to realize the transitory nature of the decline, and the fact that some equilibrium would eventually be found. The drop of the birth rate

257

went on for so long that it seemed that it would not stop until the population was well on its way toward disappearance or military annihilation. The impression of dropping-on-forever is lost when the regions are considered one at a time, but the birth rate was dropping in one or the other *départements* ever since the Revolution. The impression of depopulation was compounded by the fact that there was large-scale redistribution by migration, and that cries of "flight from the land" and "the French desert" became disturbingly frequent. Although the economic consequences of the slow population growth in the 19th Century may well have been negative, as Sauvy has argued (Sauvy 1969), and although natural increase was complemented by a sizable foreign migration, the decline of fertility did not lead to an overall decline of population over its long span.

There is another reason that led to misunderstanding of the meaning of the fertility decline by social scientists, moralists and politicians: a general neglect of individual motivations for the benefit of a collective point of view. The focus was on the course of population in France as a whole in contrast with that of militaristic Germany on the other side of the border. The preoccupation of individuals facing the problem of raising a family and looking at demographic shortcuts on the arduous road toward finding a job, acquiring land, or transmitting an intact patrimony by inheritance, were not judged as legitimate influences on the population. It must be said in atonement that collective interests and individual roles had once been in agreement. The nineteenth-century population was slowly emerging from a period when mortality was high, and when both the survival of family lines and the growth of the nation were precariously balanced. The conflict became acute after the economic and social progress of the century. There would be strange manifestations of the ambivalence of private behavior and public norms before it was fully resolved. None is more symbolic than the fact that one of the most oppressive laws against contraceptive freedom in Europe was voted in 1920 by a National Assembly whose members had overwhelmingly chosen small families for themselves.

The official resistance by Church and State against the decline of fertility and the means employed to bring it about must have played a significant role in the course of the birth rate in France. There were collective norms influencing individual fertility behavior; there were recognized traditions and values stressing the desirability of a large family and the sinfulness of contraception. Furthermore, ignorance and the difficulty of access to contraceptive information and implements must have resulted in many unwanted births. In the final analysis, an explanation of fertility levels and trends must take into account the complex decision-making process of couples, but also the means employed in the pursuit of goals that are only progressively perceivable in the course of the reproductive years, and the combination of successes and failures in attaining these goals.

Richard A. Easterlin has presented a convenient framework for the analysis of fertility in Chapter 2. I refer the reader to his detailed exposition. I will attempt here to adapt the scheme to the data available in the instance of France, and use it to frame various fragments of explanations that emerge from an analysis of the available data. Easterlin provides four equations in a cascade of explanatory levels of fertility. A first equation at the level of the intermediate variables presents effective fertility as the combined result of natural fertility and the extent of fertility control. In a second equation, control itself is the result of the perceived excess in the number of children and of the acceptability of the principle of fertility control as well as of the availability and acceptability of methods of control. The third equation describes the circumstances under which fertility is excess relative to the demand. And finally demand of desired children, at the level of economic calculus, is a function of their utility, their cost and the income of parents.

The scheme appears flexible and complete. In particular it provides ways to account not only for fertility levels at a given time, but also for changes through time. Using the four explanatory stages, we can describe the fertility transition as the substitution of various extents of control to natural fertility; knowledge and acceptance of efficient means of control is only acquired progressively; at the same time, the decline of mortality increases the incidence of unwanted fertility; and the utility and cost of children changes with economic development and increases in personal income. Any limitation to the application of the scheme along the lines suggested by its author is likely to be the result of the paucity of data rather than of its own lack of flexibility. We need, therefore, to discuss the nature of the available information in the French example before we turn to an adaptation of the explanatory framework.

I

THE DATA

BY a fortunate coincidence, many European countries were starting to organize periodic censuses and to develop complete and accurate vital registration systems by the very time of the onset of a fast and uninterrupted decline of fertility in their population. In most instances, therefore, the statistical record covers the entirety of what was later called the vital revolution—the sustained secular drop of mortality and fertility. Of course, there had been demographic changes before, but their scope was more limited, and their perception was obscured by the spotty and unreliable character of the evidence. In contrast, during the second half of the nineteenth, and in the early twentieth century, the extent of the drop of both mortality and fertility in Europe dwarfed previous trends, which there were abundant documents making it possible to follow the transformation. France took periodic national censuses during the nineteenth century, starting with the 1801 and 1806 enumerations. The civil registration of vital events become fully operational by 1800.

This, however, is not good enough to trace the fertility decline to its onset, for two reasons. First, the official statistics of France during the nineteenth century leave much to be desired. Population data are biased and incomplete. The early censuses do not provide information on age, and there is a systematic underestimation of the number of births at the beginning of the century in many *départements*. Simple indices of fertility and mortality, such as the crude birth and death rate, computed directly from the published data, are clearly deficient, and their trends are influenced by the improving completeness of the record with time. The data are not detailed enough to compute the more sophisticated indices that are essential to study the vital revolution, such as an index of mortality free of the influence of age distribution, and distinct indices of marital, illegitimate, and overall fertility—and second, even a full and reliable demographic record right after 1800 would miss the onset of the fertility decline in France. Indeed, it is clear that the birth rate of several *départements* had already by then reached a level that most administrative units elsewhere in Europe would only approach a century later.

These are the two facts with which the student of French fertility has to cope. The decline is uncommonly early, and the documents to investigate it are unsatisfactory at best. For the earlier period, there exists of course the wealth of parish registers that the historical demographers are now slowly analyzing. For many reasons, however, they too provide no more than a limited approach to the problem that concerns us here, and they cannot replace the official statistics of the early nineteenth century. In space, the parish monographs do not satisfactorily cover the regional variation of French fertility; and in time, as we shall point out later, their methods have not worked at their best to pinpoint the date and pace of fertility changes. Because there are no fully satisfactory ways to investigate the origins of the fertility decline in France, the statistical data of the early 1800s, deserve as thorough an analysis as we can give them although they are both too early to be reliable and too late to record the earliest signs of fertility decline. They can be standardized to provide comparable indicators for the whole century, and they cover the entire territory subdivided in its standard, almost invariable administrative units, the *départements*.

The demographic indices used in this paper are the product of an extensive reconstruction of the female population of the *départements*. This is not the place to describe these estimates lengthily. The methodology used to compute them, and the estimates themselves in full, are presented and justified in a book published recently (van de Walle 1974). Be it sufficient here to specify in brief that the female population of the *départements* was reconstructed mostly from the vital registration (more reliable in general than the censuses, although the latter provided irreplaceable information on population size), and that the resulting age distributions were matched by cohort with, and checked against, the rather unreliable published age distributions that first become available in the censuses taken from 1851 on. Each birth cohort from 1801 to 1805 and beyond was depleted by mortality (and, if required, modified by migration). The deaths since the beginning of the century were allocated either among those born during the century, or among those who made up a hypothetical age distribution for 1801, based on the birth and death rate of the time; the allocation of deaths was made according to the age pattern of model life tables (Coale and Demeny 1966). The assumptions and components of the reconstructions were then revised in stages, so as to insure the best possible fit with the information provided by the series of census age distributions after 1851. In particular, it was possible to compare the size of a birth cohort at the time of registration with the number of its survivors in successive censuses; and when the reconstructed numbers were systematically smaller, the procedure pointed to the prevalence of deficiencies in the series early in the century and led to a revision of the size of the vital birth cohort. Thus, the method provides not only sets of age distributions covering the century at five-year intervals starting in 1801, but also gave revised estimates of the number of births. Similarly, the proportions married were estimated from 1831 on with the help of marriage registration data, and the results were checked against the nuptiality of census cohorts; this led to the computation of fertility indices by marital status. And finally, it was possible to derive better estimates of mortality and migration than had previously been available.

In this chapter, we shall only use estimates covering the first half of

261

the century. This is the period for which the least information was available before our reconstruction. It is of course interesting to push the story of the fertility decline as far back in time as is possible. But there is another reason to pay special attention to the beginning of the century. The nineteenth century is characterized by the reduction of prior particularisms as a result of the development of communications, the unification of laws and policies, and administration centralization. The contrasts in language, customs and development which characterized the Old Regime, will be considerably attenuated as time goes by. Concurrently, the demographic trends could well be summed up as an evening out of differentials, particularly with respect to mortality, fertility and nuptiality. By concentrating on the first half of the century, we maximize the chances of finding associations between the sharply contrasted cultural and socioeconomic make-up of the *départements*, and their fertility history.

Despite the interest of "opening up" the demographic history of the *départements* in the first half of the nineteenth century, it remains true that the period is too late to perceive the beginnings of the fertility decline. When the century dawns the level of the birth rate appears to be surprisingly low, and declining, in a substantial proportion of the *départements*. The birth rates of Figure 7–1 are based on our reconstruction of the population of the *départements*, and the estimates incorporate a correction for the underreporting of births in the vital registration. The female crude birth rate mapped here is simply the number of female births per thousand women in the population. The female rate is normally a few points below the rate for the population of both sexes. The map shows the level reached by the beginning of the century for the shaded *départements* (that is, for those *départements* where the birth rate continues to drop unambiguously and continuously from the first decade on). It is likely that the level of the birth rate in the 18th century, prior to the onset of the long-term drop that our data already reflect and prior to the diffusion of contraception, would have only very rarely been less than 30 per thousand for an entire *département*. It is also likely that the continuous warfare of the early 1800s contributed to the low rates even in the absence of contraception—because conscription of young males and excess mortality among husbands would affect the exposure to risks of pregnancy. But the continued decline from the low levels reached from 1801 to 1810 cannot be explained in any other way than by the widescale adoption of contraception within marriage. Furthermore, family planning was not practiced just by a privileged fragment of the population, confined for example to the cities. As the rural sector comprises the overwhelming majority, we must conclude that the peasants, the small folks, were contributing to what would be, for a long time, the lowest birth rates in Europe. Indeed, the French situation was absolutely without equivalent elsewhere, and the decline of fertility would only start in the rest of Europe after 1870 except for limited exceptions.

Later in this chapter, we shall discuss the departmental data in more detail, and relate fertility levels with other demographic indices, and with various available socioeconomic indicators. However valuable the reconstruction of demographic indices for the *départements* in the nineteenth century, it has limitations for the study of the fertility decline. For one thing, it comes quite late, well after fertility has started on its way down in several regions; for another, it deals with administrative units which may not be very meaningful to study an event that occurs primarily in the family and that reflects individual motivations as well as the reactions of social groups to their special problems. Therefore, before we can turn to the limited contribution of our data to the understanding of the decline of French and European birthrates, it will be necessary to suggest broader issues and to discuss the historical and cultural context. The analysis of the correlates of the decline of fertility during the first part of the nineteenth century, which constitutes the main subject of this paper, will have to wait until the ground is cleared. In particular, we must say a word of alternative approaches and data sets that can be used to study the fertility decline in France, and specify the level of explanation on which we can hope to make contribution in the general perspective of the Easterlin framework. In this way, it will be clearer that our data can only provide a very partial handle on the problem, and that much further investigation remains to be done.

In view of the very clear evidence in Figure 7–1, including the fact that three *départements* in Normandy had birth rates close to 20 per thousand as early as 1801–1805, it is surprising that the historical demographers using family reconstitution methods have failed to provide a more decisive image of controlled fertility before the French Revolution. Incontrovertible evidence of the resort to contraception by couples who contracted marriage before the Revolution, has been found in two small urban communities within easy access of Paris, Meulan (Lachiver 1969; Dupâquier and Lachiver 1969) and Châtillon-sur-Seine (Chamoux and Dauphin 1969). More research on the Paris region is turning up further evidence (Lachiver 1973). Early decline (but not necessarily before 1789) can be documented in three villages of the Ile-de-France (Ganiage 1963), in Sainghin-en-Mélantois (Nord) (Deniel and Henry 1965), and in Boulay (Moselle) (Houdaille 1967). In view of the large number of parish monographs using the reconstitution method, the harvest is meager, perhaps understandably so. Most studies stop at the Revolution, when the parish registration ceases to function and the official *état-civil* takes their place. Moreover, most monographs are concerned with small villages and reconstitute only a small fraction of the families, so that the information must be regrouped over long periods of time, possibly hiding the crucial transition to controlled fertility. The villages are often selected for the convenience of the researcher or in view of the quality of the registers and the areas where contraception must have appeared early, Normandy and Aquitaine, have not been intensively sampled.[1] Crulai, the subject of the most famous of all parish monographs is in the Orne *département* of Normandy, but the reconstitution of families stops with the generations born in 1742 (Gautier and Henry 1958). The marital fertility of Tourouvre-au-Perche, also in Orne, has certain peculiar features that could be caused by early resort to birth control, but marriage cohorts beyond 1765 are not considered in the study (Charbonneau 1970).[2] Work is now in progress on Normandy by Chaunu and his group (Chaunu 1973). The parish registers from the Garonne valley and Aquitaine are usually too incomplete to allow large scale reconstruction.

It is tempting to look for the fertility behavior of different social strata in the parishes, in the hope of discerning an early drop among the upper classes. Unfortunately, the population of the parishes usually is not clearly stratified, and most attempts at finding lags in the dates of fertility decline by socioeconomic status have failed. It is nevertheless certain that privileged groups have resorted early to contraception. The evidence from genealogies is convincing on this point. The Dukes and Peers who constitute the upper crust of court nobility can be shown to have controlled their fertility within marriage by the beginning of the 18th century (Levy and Henry 1960). The ruling class of Geneva has a parallel history, and this suggests that comparable urban elites in France may have been contracepting well before the Revolution (Henry 1956).

If we believe in the importance of a historical perspective, it is not trivial that fertility had started to decline in a selected social group well before the movement reached the larger part of the population. It is with some reluctance that we introduce the upper classes in this

[1] The large INED study organized by Henry and his colleagues aims at representative coverage for the population of France as a whole, but not at the regional level (Fleury and Henry 1958). The study will produce valuable information for large regions (e.g., Blayo and Henry 1967).

[2] Charbonneau disclaims any interpretation of the peculiarities of his marital fertility curves by fertility control.

264

discussion, since their behavior can always be qualified as deviant and unrepresentative. Of course, the special behavior of such a narrow social stratum could not quantitatively influence the results for the *départements* shown in Figure 7–1. Nevertheless, the fertility decline in the French nobility or upper bourgeoisie is important beyond its numerical impact on départemental or national rates, for two reasons at least. First, they shaped customs and fashions and provided a living example of a way of life that others would emulate. "Vivre noblement" was the goal of the bourgeoisie, and "vivre bourgeoisement" increasingly the goal of the lower classes. And these ways of life involve a readjustment of family ideals. Second, we know a great deal more about them, through their literature and memoirs, than about any other group; we are able to comprehend their motivations, and understand the logic of their actions from their abundant testimonies.

The use of belletristic evidence is clearly hazardous, and the tendency of social historians is to rely on quantitative sources rather than on the qualitative judgment of contemporaries. This point of view was forcibly defended by Peter Laslett during the Seminar where a first version of this chapter was presented. He emphasized the untruthfulness of witnesses who were less well equipped than ourselves to assess the demographic state of their country. The classical example of possibly misleading literary allusion in this area is Shakespeare's report of the young age of Juliet, which should not be interpreted as indicating the socially acceptable age at marriage for Elizabethean England (Laslett 1965: 81).[3] But in all fairness to the Bard's reputation as a historical source, it must be granted that he never claimed to be depicting English mating customs in this play, and that there exists statistical evidence of the precocity of female marriage for the Tuscan Quattrocento, a place and time more relevant to Juliet's Verona (Herlihy 1969). It would be of some interest to know whether the Globe's spectators found it obvious, possible or surprising that an Italian girl should be married at 14 years of age.

Similarly, the use of literary evidence on fertility and the use of contraception in eighteenth-century France may be fraught with dangers, but it is the only approach we have for the study of certain problems, if not of facts, at least of mentalities. For example, when Moheau says: "They cheat nature even in the villages," the phrase may tell us little about the actual diffusion of contraception in rural France around 1780; but it indicates at least that however shocking such information, it was

---

[3] "The women in Shakespeare's plays, and so presumably the Englishwomen of Shakespeare's day, might marry in their early teens, or even before that, and very often did so. Yet this is not true . . ." (81).

meaningful to the literate upper classes to whom the book was addressed.

II

Natural Fertility and the Extent of Control

As far as the distant past is concerned, literary evidence provides an approach to the analysis of fertility changes along the lines of the first two equations of the Easterlin framework. The first equation states definitionally that the level of fertility is a function of natural fertility—that is, fertility which would prevail in the absence of voluntary control within marriage—and of the actual extent of control. In practice, it is difficult to ascertain whether a certain population lives under a regime of natural fertility or uses control within marriage to a limited extent. Henry proposed to recognize the existence of natural fertility when marital fertility by age was not different for various parities or durations of marriage (Henry 1961). The test requests unusually detailed information which is not available for large historical populations.

When Ansley J. Coale initiated a project in Princeton to investigate the fertility decline on the scale of province-sized units in Europe, he divised a measurement of marital fertility in the spirit of Easterlin's first equation.[4] Coale looked for the highest reliable record schedule of marital fertility, a schedule such that the total absence of control could be postulated. The marital fertility of the Hutterites was selected as the standard. It then became possible to compute the number of births that married women of any province under study would have had during a given period around a census, if they had been exposed to the fertility of married Hutterite women. I_g, our index of marital fertility then, was the ratio of their number of legitimate births recorded for that period over the computed number. If uncontrolled fertility were always the same in human populations, the presence of control would be revealed by divergences of the I_g ratio from 1. In fact, most European populations had I_g's between 70 and 90 percent of Hutterite marital fertility prior to the large fertility decline that took place during the nineteenth century. We started with the hypothesis that high and fairly constant levels of this kind indicated the absence of fertility control within marriage, and that predecline differences in levels could be accounted for by differing lactation customs, by health and diet, genetic or climatic differences, or differences in patterns of residence and cohabitation. The fertility decline corresponded in this view

---

[4] The indices, also used later in this chapter, have been described in Coale (1969).

to a mutation of the mentalities and the acceptance of the idea of fertility control within the family. It is possible, however, that even pre-Malthusian populations were practicing various extent of control of their fertility. In his classical work on the medical history of contraception, Himes postulated that the desire for control has always been present while efficient means were only diffused recently (Himes 1963). The historical decline of fertility in this view corresponded to a new access to contraceptive methods.

The second equation of the Easterlin framework allows for the use of either of these explanations in an explanatory scheme. Once parents perceive an excess of children, their use of fertility control will depend both on the acceptability (or utility) attaching to regulatory practices, and on the knowledge (or accessibility) of such practices. Control may not be attempted either because no excess is perceived (a condition decomposed in the third Easterlin equation), or because control is unthinkable, or because contraceptives are unknown. These analytical distinctions may appear somewhat artificial where applied to an entire population. But here is a case where literary evidence comes to the rescue by offering examples of precisely the set of mentalities and the absence of birth control technology that we associate with natural fertility. It can be argued that eighteenth-century readers could identify with a model of behavior, however alien to us, where, in Messance's words, "marriage depends on the will and control of men . . . the fertility of marriages depends on causes that are absolutely independent of the control of those who alone can contribute to it. . . ." (Messance, 1766, quoted by Bergues et al. 1960: 272).

For example, a remarkable but little-known novel of 1713, *Les Illustres Françoises (The Illustrious Frenchwomen)* provides us with a universe where natural fertility is taken for granted (Chasles 1959). From our point of view, the interest of the novel is that it describes a social class where the motivations of what we would call family planning are becoming extremely powerful, although the emphasis is still on controlling marriage rather than fertility within marriage. *Les Illustres Françoises* could be fairly described as an inventory of the problems encountered by protagonists whose marriage is determined by family status and wealth. It consists in a series of tales of love between socially mismatched individuals—cadets courting rich heiresses, elopements of younger daughters who had been tucked away in convents against their will to favor older brothers and sisters, marriages of titled noblemen with impecunious but virtuous maidens. Each individual defines himself primarily as the product of his family background. One character for example, starts his story with the following

preface. "I was born in Paris from a fairly good family of the bourgeoisie; but the quantity of brothers and sisters that we were after the
death of my father and my mother . . . only permitted us to live on
a footing corresponding to the ordinary ambition of young men. . ."
(Chasles 1959: 173). Chasles's heroes see the barriers to their marriage
as the main obstacles to happiness. When the virtue of the daughter
of a bankrupt provincial squire has finally been rewarded by a rich
marriage, the protagonist comments: "They were finally married two
years before last Easter. . . She has already had two children, and is
once again pregnant, and from the look of things her family will be
very numerous; indeed she does not wait one year between deliveries
. . . She is the happiest of women" (1959: 121–122).

The strategy of family planning reflected in many writings of the
time is one where there is no fertility control within the family, but
where the creation of new families by marriage is severely restricted.
Statistical evidence on the upper classes in France confirms that a substantial proportion of the adults spent their life in celibacy, although
the age of marriage for those who married was young—less than 20 for
women on the average among the Dukes and Peers (Levy and Henry
1960). In three genealogies, Houdaille finds that 44 percent of the
women born before 1750 and 30 percent of those born between 1750
and 1799 never married (Houdaille 1971). Not unexpectedly perhaps,
the increased proportions married towards the end of the century
coincide with a sharp drop of marital fertility. One gets the impression
that the regulation of conception within marriage allows a freer access
to marriage.

But in *Les Illustres Francoises* at least, sexual intercourse leads inevitably to conception and birth, be it in or out of wedlock. The book
contains many allusions to the inevitability of pregnancy.[5] For example,
Monsieur des Prez and Mademoiselle de l'Epine have contracted a
secret marriage. When he tries to rent a room, the landlady objects:
"And will she be able to keep it a secret, if she becomes pregnant?
Because this will happen very certainly. A woman in love does not
long receive a man in her arms ere she bears the marks" (Chasles 1959:
229). And of course: "She became pregnant toward the end of September; she told me, it did not displease me, this was natural" (Chasles
1959: 252).

The book contains only one allusion to birth control, and it deserves
quotation in full. Dupuis, an avowed rake, describes the "coup de

[5] The following expression is used as an euphemism for coitus: "Nous travail-
lâmes à faire un troisiéme . . ." (Chasles 1959: 43).

scélérat" by which he seduces a young widow (Chasles, 1959: 495–496). He refers mockingly to a couple of common acquaintance:

> This woman is really very clumsy, and he is a great innocent. . . What, is it possible that neither has the secret of making love without consequences? . . . For myself, I would have every kind of intercourse with a woman, and she would never become pregnant if I did not want it. Is there anything easier?
> Do you have that secret, the widow asked promptly? Yes, I have it,

> I said, do you need it? No indeed, she said laughing, I thank you; but would you be wretched enough to use it? Yes, I replied, I would use it, and even without scruple; provided it were in order to rescue a woman from the state where I would have put her myself, I loved her, and her reputation deserved to be preserved. (Chasles 1959: 495–496).

Incidentally, Dupuis betrays his ignorance by confusing contraception ("she would never become pregnant") and abortion ("to rescue a woman from the state. . ."). And when the widow finally becomes pregnant, as all mistresses eventually do in Chasles's book, she reminds him of his promise, and he has to confess his ignorance, and his scoundrel's ploy. Strangely enough, even when confronted with the consequences of their liaison (and there will be several children before it is over), her reaction is one of relief: "I shall not love you the less for it, she told me while kissing me, and I shall esteem you more" (1959: 500). It is clear that she had a strong moral aversion to birth control, whereas he had not the necessary knowledge to use it.

Much of Chasles's interest derives from the fact that he is unusually blunt, at a time of refined writers. But it is not uncommon for other seducers to claim that they know a way of avoiding the unwelcome consequences of an affair. Since seduction scenes are abundant in the literature, the contraceptive skills of men are sometimes advertised in the extramarital context. One could quote several poems in this vein from Saint-Pavin's sodomic sonnets to Voltaire's poetic description of coitus interruptus. But extramarital relations are only one context in which the child must be avoided. There is little direct evidence on the methods used to prevent an excessive number of births within marriage, because the literature rarely discusses the later years of matrimony. Madame de Sévigné's letters to her daughter constitute a famous exception. Mme. de Grignan had one miscarriage and four births between November 1669 and September 1674, and her mother was understandably concerned about her failing health. There is, however, not the shadow of an allusion to contraception in the Marchioness's letters; [6] she recommends separate sleeping arrangements and the use of continence. Mr. de Grignan resented the intrusion of his stepmother in his marital affairs, and he was upset when "the advice of the doctor won over the advice of the confessor" (Sévigné 1862).

Our best indication on the growth of contraceptive practices among married couples comes from Church sources, from St. François de Sales to Father Féline (Bergues et al. 1960, Chapter VII). The latter stated clearly that the crime of Onan "was very common among spouses" (1960: 227). Noonan has noticed that there was increasing concern among the French clergy at the beginning of the 19th century. "The restored Church in France had some awareness of confronting a new situation. The French clergy realized that widespread practice of birth control was a new problem" (Noonan 1965: 397). The evidence of statistics confirm that contraception was becoming ever more important at the time, but does not tell us which of the variables in the second Easterlin equation was operative. Was it an increased acceptability of the idea of control, coinciding with a decline in Church authority? Was it a diffusion of contraceptive knowledge? Was excessive fertility felt more intensely for reasons to be discussed presently?

In the wider perspective of the fertility decline and the wide-scale adoption of fertility control by rural populations after 1800, it is almost certainly significant that there existed a small but influential social class well acquainted with family planning for a reasonably long time. One could argue that the role of the upper classes in this matter was that of a barometer: They responded early to economic and social pressures that were eventually to be felt by the society at large. A more interesting hypothesis, however, is that the behavior of the elites was imitated, and that contraception was diffused from their midst. This is approximately what Sauvy says: "Yet it was [the delicate libertines of the eighteenth century] who caused this demographic revolution which spread from France, together with the Revolution, over the whole world. That brilliant and corrupt aristocracy introduced forbidden practices (initially *douches, the condom,* and *coitus interuptus*) from the world of prostitution into that of irregular unions and adultery, and from there to the marriage chamber. . . Contraception spread fast among middle class families wishing to preserve or improve their eco-

---

[6] Although she has been often maligned on the subject, for instance by Himes (1963: 190), who attributes a spurious quotation to her, or by Ariès (1954) who stretches the interpretation of two unclear texts without regard for their context.

nomic level, and even amongst peasant families wanting to avoid divisions of land (especially in Gascony)" (Sauvy, 1969: 362).

If so, the mechanism of transmission remains mysterious. The explanation of the population transition by the cultural diffusion of implements and methods is not generally favored by modern sociologists. They argue that coitus interruptus, the technique usually held responsible for the decline, can be reinvented by any couple with sufficient motivation to avoid a pregnancy. Whereas it can be argued that some spread of information on contraception occurred together with progress in knowledge on the physiology of reproduction, it is not necessary to believe in the autonomous diffusion of any "funestes secrets" (in Moheau's phrase) to claim that the upper classes' early acceptance of fertility control may have influenced the behavior of the lower classes in this matter. What may have been diffusing is more subtle than contraceptive methodology: the small family ideal, as practiced by prominent members of society; the moral or religious acceptability of practices designed to realize this ideal; rational attitudes toward the control of one's fate and one's body, including the view that Nature is not an intrinsic part of God's design, but can be reshaped and influenced.

III

Excess Fertility and Economic Motivation

THE initial motivations for using birth control within marriage must probably be sought in the peculiar set of family settlements, inheritance systems, and status seeking goals of the aristocracy and the upper bourgeoisie; but the equivalent for the French nobility of Banks's work on the Victorian middle class is still to be written. The closest to that model is Blacker's analysis, unfortunately only published for the section that relates to the bourgeoisie (Blacker 1957a, 1957b). There is, however, an increasing amount of historical work on the aristocracy of selected areas, and these studies illuminate the process of transmission of property across the generations, a topic that is at the very heart of the problem that concerns us here (e.g., Forster 1960; Meyer 1971). Economic opportunities of the nobility depended greatly on inherited wealth, and the regulation of fertility was one of the ways in which noble families could influence their status.

The nobility came close to the ideal of the stem family described by Le Play, the permanent haven based on indivisible property and parental authority to which members could return in times of trouble. It has been said that the decaying mores of the eighteenth century spread

271

by the materialistic philosophy of the time "exerted an unfavorable influence on the inheritance system by leading to the forgetting of the virtues that inspire good testaments" (Le Play 1864). Indeed, an inheritance system that left patrimonies intact required virtuous participants to survive, and this may have led to its downfall. Forster showed for the nobility of Toulouse that the smooth transmission of the patrimony required a great deal of family loyalty on the part of younger sons and daughters, precisely because the law recognized that they had rights (Forster 1960). They were entitled to a legal share in the family estate at the death of their father. The transmission of half of the patrimony, including the paternal domain, usually took place in the marriage contract of the eldest son, by donation to the first son to be born from the new union. This was an effective way of eluding the common law, since the siblings would have no claim on what had never belonged to their father. But the other children were still entitled to enough of the unsettled portion of the estate to represent a serious burden on family fortunes.

There was a way out, and it was customary to obtain the renunciation of future claims in return for a dowry or a pension. Furthermore, the law excluded from a legal portion any member of the family who entered the clergy. The older son and perhaps a daughter would be privileged, but the cadets had to be bought off with a commission in the army or a position in the Church. Their price was not necessarily cheap, although there would be those who, because of loyalty to the family, would agree to spend their life in a convent or to pine away as an old maid in a room of the family castle. The number of children would necessarily multiply the number of quarrels and law suits. There were few openings leading to a successful career for younger sons, since they were barred from demeaning occupations such as commerce or industry. And careers in the army or the Church required an initial investment, sometimes of considerable magnitude. The plight of younger sons generally was recognized at the time, and the tucking away of daughters in convents was increasingly deemed scandalous.

In that context, the early motivations for family planning must be sought. Preventing marriage is a clumsy and unpopular way of regulating the transmission of property between generations. Of course, there are problems in accepting the explanation. How does the French system compare to other systems of inheritance in the nobility? Many of the features that have been described would apply almost literally to the English peerage whose fertility declined much later. Is it possible that the English had many more opportunities for their young sons than the French, in trade or in agriculture which were not there supposed to be demeaning occupations? And finally, any explanation will have to integrate mortality and its trends.

Under a regime of high mortality, the reproduction of individual families is necessarily balanced precariously. The titled nobility has great vested interest in reproduction, in continuity, and therefore it should find high fertility rather important. The ideal would be that precisely one male and one female child per family get married each generation, and survive to the mean age of child-bearing—the demographic concept of a net reproduction of one. Thus each peerage would be transmitted, the name would be eternal, and the hassle with self-seeking cadets and daughters devoid of religious vocation could be avoided. With the level of mortality of the French dukes and peers, a Net Reproduction Rate (NPR) of 1 would require about four births per woman on the average. But this would ensure the survival of the group, and not of individual families, and a performance well in excess would be necessary to maintain a reserve army of potential heirs. A decline of mortality would change the problem. If the trend of mortality in the British peerage is a guide, mortality was declining during the eighteenth century. Was this sufficient to exert a pressure on succession, and to trigger a reaction on the side of fertility? A large number of family lines became extinguished, and it is difficult to understand why fertility declined so much, and why there were so many childless women among the French dukes and peers—35 percent for the second half of the eighteenth century, as against 9 percent one century earlier (Levy and Henry 1960). The moralists of the time put the blame on luxury—what we now would call hedonism. One would like to believe instead that the aristocracy was behaving rationally, and that the fertility decline was an adaptation to changed circumstances. But one cannot exclude the possibility that economic self-interest and a concern for the health, beauty, and social availability of women was becoming more important than the collective survival of the lineage.

This incursion into the area of motivation brings us under the coverage of Easterlin's two last equations. In the remainder of this chapter, we shall abandon the rather speculative description of the upper classes and address ourselves to the data on the French *départements*, described earlier, which refer to a period when the diffusion of the fertility decline was reaching an ever-increasing area of the country. These data allow us an indirect investigation of the interrelationship set out in the equations of the Easterlin framework, although considerable caution is in order. The interrelations are stated in terms of individual families and personal motivations. In contrast, we shall deal with ecological correlations between characteristics of the *départe-*

ments, and cannot infer from them that individuals are reacting in one way rather than another. For example, when we find a statistical association between a high proportion married and a low marital fertility among the *départements,* this does not necessarily mean that those persons who regulate their fertility are also marrying earlier and more in any *département* than those who do not. Although the inference is not implausible, it could only be drawn from individual fertility histories. The only meaning of the finding is that younger or more frequent marriage predominates in those areas where marital fertility is lower, and older or less frequent marriages in areas where the fertility of unions has remained high. Furthermore, this tells us little about causality. Has age at marriage come down because fertility declined, or has fertility declined because marriages were taking place earlier, or have both variables yielded to common influences? We can sometimes tell because of the chronological sequence of changes, but causal inferences are always hazardous. We must also beware of the fallacy of believing that a correlation between levels at a point in time signifies that there were past trends. For example, the fact that mortality and fertility are related in the early nineteenth century does not necessarily mean that fertility has come down in response to lower mortality. These limitations of our tools limit singularly the value of our deductions and hypothesis. I shall nevertheless present an interpretation of the change of fertility, and illustrate it with correlations and regressions derived from the French example.

The départemental data distinguish between overall fertility (I_f), and marital (I_g) or illegitimate (I_h) fertility. Furthermore an index of the proportion married, I_m is also available. The value of the indices is that a distinction can be made between strategies of family formations, to an extent impossible with only an overall fertility measure. A certain level of overall fertility in a *département* can be reached (assuming that illegitimate fertility is negligible for our purpose) either by contraception within the married state, or by restrictions on the proportions married at the childbearing ages. I_m, the proportion married at those ages, reflects both the age at marriage and the practice of permanent celibacy. We compare two areas with comparable general fertility, where this result is attained by a very different combination of marriage and fertility control strategies (see Table 7–1). Manche appears on Figure 7–1 as an area of low birth rates already at the beginning of the century, but it will preserve a relatively high marital fertility in combination with late marriage and low proportions ever-married. In contrast, Lot-et-Garonne combines very early marriage with very low marital fertility.

274

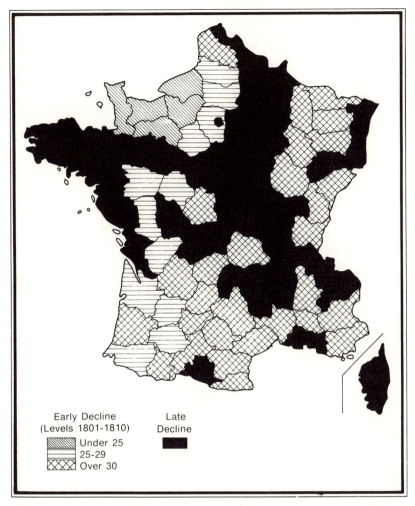

Figure 7–1 Female Crude Birth Rates in Departments with Early Decline, 1801–1810

We present in Table 7–2 some simple linear correlation coefficients between indices of general fertility (I_f), marital fertility (I_g), illegitimate fertility (I_h), and standardized proportions married (I_m) in each of the census years between 1831 and 1851. Eighteen hundred and thirty-one is as far back as we are able to reconstruct marital status in France. Before then, the only fertility measure available is the crude birth rate (a measure closely associated with I_f), and we cannot isolate marital fertility.

275

TABLE 7–1. OVERALL FERTILITY (I_f), MARITAL FERTILITY (I_g), ILLEGITI-
MATE FERTILITY (I_h) AND PROPORTIONS MARRIED (I_m), AGE
AT FIRST MARRIAGE AND PROPORTIONS EVER-MARRIED.
MANCHE AND LOT-ET-GARONNE, 1831 AND 1851.

	Manche		Lot-et-Garonne	
Variable	1831	1851	1831	1851
I_f	.238	.225	.225	.204
I_g	.567	.491	.351	.291
I_h	.021	.025	.031	.024
I_m	.398	.430	.605	.656
Age at first marriage [a]	27.3	26.6	23.3	22.0
Proportions ever-married [b]	.83	.84	.92	.92

[a] Singulate mean age at marriage, computed from the proportions single.
[b] Proportions ever married in the cohorts of women born in 1801–1805 and 1821–
1925 respectively, computed from the proportions married in post-1951 censuses.

TABLE 7–2. ZERO-ORDER CORRELATION COEFFICIENTS BETWEEN OVERALL
FERTILITY (I_f), MARITAL FERTILITY (I_g), ILLEGITIMATE
FERTILITY (I_h), AND PROPORTION MARRIED (I_m). THE 86
Départements of FRANCE, 1831, 1836, 1841, 1846, AND 1851.

	r at the same date with:		
	I_g	I_h	I_m
I_f in 1831	.717	.141	−.151
1836	.758	.060	−.219
1841	.769	.134	−.231
1846	.769	.102	−.205
1851	.760	.089	−.198
I_g in 1831		−.261	−.774
1836		−.237	−.767
1841		−.194	−.772
1846		−.197	−.753
1851		−.195	−.754
I_h in 1831			.363
1836			.191
1841			.245
1846			.198
1851			.159

The most remarkable association revealed in Table 7–2, is the highly significant negative correlation between marital fertility and the proportions married. Spengler has commented on a similar finding later in the century, and concluded that "in France the population has always (since 1860 at least) sought to limit natural increase, either by deferring and/or avoiding marriage, or by limiting fertility within the married state" (Spengler 1938; 73).

The correlation coefficients between I_f and I_g in Table 7–2 are highly significant, whereas those between I_f and I_m are low, although of constant negative sign. In other terms, marital fertility appears to be the main determinant of general fertility (and of the birth rate) in the beginning of the nineteenth century, and is only tempered by the influence of the proportions married to a minor extent. The sharp contrast of strategies is not everywhere as evident as for Manche and Lot-et-Garonne. And finally, changes in I_f between 1831 and 1851 are highly correlated with changes in I_g ($r=.761$), but only weakly correlated with changes in I_m ($r=-.246$) during the period. (Changes in I_g and I_m are significantly associated during the period: $r=-.325$. In other terms, the largest increases in proportions married tend to occur in those areas where marital fertility has dropped most.)

Now that we have discussed the interrelations between our dependent variable, we can return to the Easterlin framework. The reader will remember that Equation 5 analyzes the circumstances under which excess fertility is perceived by individuals: the number of previous births must be numerous, and child mortality must have been low enough to insure the survival of enough children to exceed the desired number. A decline in mortality, therefore, may initiate a decline in fertility. There are reasons to believe that mortality might also enter the reasoning at the regional level of aggregation. Areas where mortality had declined are also those where population pressure may be felt if fertility remained high and there was no migration; where mortality remained high, or where the population had made use of the opportunities to move out of its *département* of birth, fertility too might remain high without bringing about intolerable pressure on the land or the institutions. The crucial importance of the level of mortality is generally acknowledged. Furthermore, it has been argued that the difference in the timing of the fertility decline in France and in England can be accounted for by their respective dates of urbanization. In France, ". . . families had to reduce the number of births at an early state. This was so, because the opportunities in the cities were rather limited and, in turn, rural/urban migration did not provide an adequate outlet" (Friedlander 1969: 363).

When we go beyond these theoretical insights, it is difficult to disentangle the lines of causation. As we shall show presently, there is a striking correlation between the birth rate and the expectation of life at birth in the beginning of the century. We are not so concerned by the fact that high fertility may be leading to high infant mortality; although the relation is measurable and significant in several studies, its magnitude is not such that it would produce the kind of ecological correlation that we find for the French *départements*. More disturbing is the possibility that fertility and mortality are moving down together under the influence of common causes. If it were possible to demonstrate the antecedence of the mortality decline, we could logically argue in terms of causation. Unfortunately, our data cover the nineteenth century only, and right from the beginning both vital trends are oriented downward. The example of Germany, however, must inspire caution. Both fertility and mortality seem at a plateau during the beginning of the century, and start their decline at about the same time. Knodel has shown that there was no systematic tendency for mortality to start its decline earlier (Knodel 1973). The movements were related, but not subordinated. There was no evidence of the lag that could be expected if the population had to realize that new mortality conditions were now allowing lower fertility for the same net reproduction.

A similar argument can be made about the meaningfulness of a relation between migration and growth (or fertility). Is the population controlling its fertility to avoid the pressure that leads to migration away from home? Or is no migration the result of an absence of growth independently achieved?

Confronted with a range of possible interpretations, some of which are not exclusive, we can do no more than present the linear correlation coefficients between the expectation of life at birth and net migration on one hand, the fertility on the other. In the process of reconstructing the female population of the *départements*, it became possible to obtain some estimates of the mortality and net migration of the period. No estimates of mortality are available for the four most urban *départements*, Bouches-du-Rhône, Rhône, Seine and Seine-et-Oise, so that the following analysis is restricted to 82 units. The estimate of mortality is the expectation of life at birth, and it is free of the influence of age distribution.[7] It reflects more than the mere child mortality that we expect to be associated with the perception of excess fertility. Unfortunately, in some *départements*, infant mortality contains an impor-

---

[7] The computation of e_0^0 is explained in van de Walle (1973). The registered number of deaths for a 5-year period is distributed according to a model age-schedule of mortality and related to the reconstructed population.

278

tant component of children who came as nurslings and died far from their place of birth. This factor, highly related to the vicinity of large cities such as Paris or Lyon, confuses the relationship. Our index of mortality has largely eliminated the nursling factor.

Table 7–3 gives the correlations between mortality and overall fertility, measured first by the birth rates, and after 1831 by the index I_f. The coefficients cover a range of dates, since some lagging should be expected, and since the indicators of mortality and fertility reflect lasting conditions and differentials. I show also for comparative purposes the level of the correlation with I_g, marital fertility, at two points in time, but if the interpretative model suggested above has some validity, we should expect a relation between overall fertility, as it results from the interaction of marital fertility and the proportions married, and mortality, rather than between marital fertility and the latter. The cor-

TABLE 7–3. Zero-Order Correlation Coefficients between Expectation of Life at Birth and Various Measures of Fertility: Crude Birthrate (CBR), Overall Fertility (I_f), and Marital Fertility (I_g) during the First Half of the Nineteenth Century, 82 *Départements* of France, Selected Dates.

Variable	Expectation of life at birth in:					
	1801–1805	1811–1815	1821–1825	1831–1835	1841–1845	1851–1855
CBR in						
1801–1805	−.380	−.600	−.714	−.650	−.768	−.660
1811–1815	−.474	−.648	−.768	−.653	−.694	−.591
1821–1825	−.366	−.590	−.760	−.644	−.724	−.677
1831–1835	−.305	−.434	−.697	−.631	−.706	−.672
1841–1845	−.262	−.373	−.657	−.579	−.715	−.648
1851–1855	−.276	−.376	−.662	−.592	−.708	−.638
I_f in						
1831	−.327	−.389	−.624	−.522	−.580	−.637
1836	−.254	−.375	−.601	−.529	−.621	−.657
1841	−.230	−.375	−.614	−.529	−.652	−.675
1846	−.276	−.408	−.657	−.562	−.671	−.688
1851	−.286	−.412	−.673	−.588	−.685	−.699
I_g in						
1831	.039	−.033	−.219	−.253	−.361	−.451
1851	.071	−.126	−.309	−.340	−.500	−.563

Note: Coefficients are underlined when fertility and mortality refer to the same dates.

TABLE 7–4. ZERO-ORDER CORRELATION COEFFICIENTS BETWEEN NET MIGRATION, 1806–1846, AND OVERALL FERTILITY (I_f) AND MARITAL FERTILITY (I_g), 1831, 1836, 1841, 1846, 1851, 82 *Départements* of France.

	r between net migration, 1806 to 1846 and	
Year	I_f	I_g
1831	.134	.229
1836	.176	.267
1841	.220	.299
1846	.222	.319
1851	.207	.304

Note: Positive coefficients indicate a direct association between out-migration and fertility, or an inverse association between in-migration and fertility.

relations are all significant: the higher mortality in a *département*, the higher also fertility. (The negative signs in Table 7–3 reflect the fact that our index of mortality is expectation of life rather than mortality.) The correlations tend invariably to go up with time; the crude birth rate in 1801–1805 is more highly associated with the expectation of life at birth in 1841–1845 than with that of the same period. The lags might suggest that it is fertility that influences mortality. More plausibly, one might argue that the characteristics that led to a decline of the birth rate led also, with some delay, to the decline of mortality. In other terms, the correlations are strikingly high, but do not really confirm the hypothesis.

Table 7–4 gives the correlation coefficients between net migration and fertility. The estimate of net migration encompasses the period 1806 to 1846, for women only.[8] The correlation coefficients with general fertility are small, but positive: the more out-migration and the less in-migration, the higher fertility. The increase with time of the correlation might indicate that migration influences fertility, in conformity with the model given above; but the association is hardly significant. Marital fertility is more highly correlated than general fertility. The meaning of that finding is somewhat unclear. Is it possible that the *départements* with a mobile population are also more open to outside influences and to the transmission of ideas, including the idea of family planning? The evidence does not permit us to answer the question.

[8] The net-migration index is the ratio of the population of 1806 to the population that is computed by subtracting the births and adding the deaths from and to the population of 1846 (females only).

IV

Socioeconomic Correlates of Fertility

THE last equation in the Easterlin framework decomposes the demand for children as a function of the utility of children, their "price" relative to other economic goods, and the income of the parents. At the macro-economic level, one could argue that the economic indicators in large geographical units such as the *départements* might be significantly related to fertility. We cannot demonstrate the exact nature of the relationship involved, but might identify some broad hypotheses relating fertility to economic variables. In particular, it is possible to obtain data pertaining to incomes and prices, and to other phenomena that may influence them; foremost among these is urban or rural living, which would be expected to modify two of the equation's variables, the subjective value of children or their objective cost.

The first half of the nineteenth century is much less well endowed with social and economic statistics than the subsequent period. The more detailed population censuses begin with the 1851 one. Moreover, agricultural and industrial censuses and surveys are a phenomenon of the second part of the century. Nevertheless, new sets of data—new in the sense that they had been almost inaccessible before—are now being opened up, and a wealth of socioeconomic information is revealed in unexpected places, such as the military archives (LeRoy Ladurie and Dumont 1971). In this section, we want to make use of yet another neglected source of information: the taxation data of the time.

References by contemporary social scientists such as Lavergne and Villermé, who used the taxation data by *département* as a proxy for income or as indicators of economic development, led us to this source. Lavergne thought that average direct taxation per head or per hectare gave a good reflection of the respective wealth of the *départements*, and used them extensively in his classical study of French agriculture (Lavergne 1861). At the time, the taxation data were considered as the only usable indicators of income. They were easily available on a regular basis. At least some information was published yearly by *département*, in the *Comptes Généraux de l'Administration des Finances*.

There were four categories of direct taxes: the land tax (*contribution foncière*); the personal tax (*contribution personnelle et mobilière*); the tax or doors and windows (*contribution des portes et fenêtres*); and the tax on licenses (*contribution des patentes*). Of those four, two seem of doubtful relevance for our purpose. Although the second category was conceived first as a tax on revenues from labor and nonagricultural incomes, its main component was a tax on the letting value of furnished houses. As for the tax on doors and windows, it was another kind of

281

land tax on buildings only. We shall restrict our discussion of direct taxes to the land tax, making up a very large proportion of the total, and to the tax on licenses. The latter was regarded by contemporaries as a fair indicator of the extent of commercial and industrial development of the *département*.[9]

The reader will perhaps forgive us if we go somewhat into the genesis of our research, since an understanding of the mechanism of taxation may spare future students of the same data some of the faulty inferences of which the present author was at first guilty. Early in this study, highly significant correlation coefficients (r's generally in the neighborhood of $-.7$) between the land tax per head and marital fertility (I_g) at all dates were found. It was then tempting to infer that marital fertility was low in the *départements* with the highest income. Taxation per head in Normandy, for example, was considerably heavier than in the Breton *départements*. The land tax regroups both the tax on buildings and on property without buildings, but the high overall correlation persisted even after elimination of the urban *départements* with high real estate values. The finding seemed to suggest a clear association between the importance of rural incomes and the control of fertility. On the other hand, r's of $-.7$ seemed almost too high to be true, and we set out to look for possible flaws in the argument. Could there be, for instance, an influence of population growth (and therefore of fertility) on the amount of tax paid by individuals in various regions?

The history of the land tax is of some interest in this connection. When the Old Regime toppled in 1789, the tax system was one of its most unpopular features, and the Constituent Assembly resolved that a new land tax based on the taxable net revenue of property would provide the bulk of the State's income. As there were not usable estimates of what the land's revenue might be, it was decided that a global sum for France voted yearly by the Assembly, would be apportioned among the *départements* in such a way that their proportionate share would be the same as that of the provinces they were replacing. As the provinces had not all been taxed according to the same system, this was clearly unfair. The shares of 14 overburdened *départements* were alleviated in 1791, and those of 52 *départements* in 1821. But the political difficulty of increasing the share of a *département* was judged insurmountable, and the areas that had been paying little under the monarchy (e.g., the *départements* of Languedoc and Corse) continued to pay less than the others.

[9] "Sans regarder le produit plus ou moins élevé de l'impôt des patentes, ainsi que le nombre plus ou moins grand de ceux qui l'acquittent, comme la mesure exacte de l'état de l'industrie, nous croyons néanmoins que ce double renseignement peut en donner une connaissance générale . . ." (Benoiston de Chateauneuf et Villermé 1843: 48). See also France, Ministère des Finances 1839: 70.

The readjustment of 1821 was to be the last one before 1891 (when the house tax became rated), and the taxation law of 1821 established the principle of the fixity of départmental shares. Whenever the tax was raised, it was raised proportionately everywhere, in the form of so-called *centimes additionnels*. It is important to understand that the land tax (as well as the *contributions personnelle et mobilière* and *des portes et fenêtres*) is a tax of apportionment (i.e., apportioned from a national total fixed by law). Of the direct taxes, only the *Patente* is rated locally according to a tariff. As time went by, therefore, the taxation load represented the economic situation of the *départements* less and less. In particular, differential population growth related to a constant quota would systematically bias the meaning of per capita taxation figures. Thus, when interpreting the negative correlation between taxation per head and fertility, we cannot discount the following line of causation: Lower fertility means less population growth and, the burden being stable for the *département*, higher taxation per head.

Fortunately, the unfairness of taxation led to numerous efforts at correction, and although none succeeded after 1821, in the process of attempting reform the administration produced several estimates of land income and value. The adjustment of 1821 itself was the result of a series of inquiries into rents and land prices over a period of years, and drew upon the early results of the *cadastre* that was being established since 1808. The results of the 1821 inquiry have been used here as our benchmark for the beginning of the century; they give the average net revenue of land, buildings included. But considerable more detailed estimates were also collected between 1851 and 1854 (Ministère des Finances 1879). They were the result (as of 1851) of the direct assessment by agents of the administration in each commune, and were checked against current sales and rents. The 1851 benchmark includes for each *département* an estimate of both revenue and sale value of lands and buildings; the average sale value of various types of land is indicated, as well as the average sale value of houses, distinguished from that of factories and manufacturers.

We have already recorded Benoiston de Chateauneuf and Villermé's opinion that the license tax (*contribution des patentes*) was a fair indicator state of industrial and commercial development in the départements. In this instance, the mode of levying was rated—although by no means proportionally to industrial or commercial gains. Before 1880, the license tax consisted of a fixed amount depending on the class of profession and the size of the locality. Detailed classification of the classes of occupations does not seem available for the period under study at the départemental level, so that we cannot distinguish industry from commerce, or even from the professions. This of course detracts

283

considerably from the interest of the information. In 1837, a date for which an unusual number of tabulations are available, the license on industrial establishments (iron works, glass making, foundries, steel mills, paper mills, spinning mills, etc.) represented 3 million francs on a total of 29 collected from the license tax, or only about 10 percent. The number of industrial licensees was 33,638 out of a total of 1,290,231 —less than 3 percent. Because the rate depended on the size of the locality, and because there were more important commercial and industrial establishments in the larger cities, the average license fee and the total amount by *département* or per head are very highly related to the degree of urbanization. The fraction of the population which pays the license tax, however, is more related to the degree of economic advancement of the *départements;* in a way, it offers an index of the extent to which even rural populations have developed secondary or tertiary sectors of activity. As such, the number of licenses per 1,000 persons in the population will be used here as a supplement to the land value index.

Table 7–5 presents the zero-order correlation coefficients between the demographic indices and the economic ones. There is of course a high degree of correlation between the land revenue measures in 1821 and 1851 ($r = .860$) and even between the land revenue at both dates and both the amount and number of license fees per 1,000 inhabitants (all the r's being close to, or above .6). All the indicators measure to some extent the prosperity of the départements during the first half of the century. And the regional variation in that prosperity is closely related to the variations of fertility. Most striking is the negative correlation between marital fertility (I_g) and land revenue. It is stronger than the negative correlation between revenue and overall fertility (I_f) or than the positive correlation between revenue and the proportion married (I_m). The use of partial correlations shows that the relation between land income and I_f or I_m is almost entirely accounted for by their own relationship with I_g.

Illegitimate fertility (I_h) is highly and positively correlated with the amounts paid in license fees. The correlation of I_h with land revenue disappears when the returns of the *patente* per head are kept constant. This reflects the fundamental association between illegitimacy and urbanization, rather than income. Similarly, there is little genuine association between the number of licenses per 1,000 inhabitants and I_h once the factor of urbanization is accounted for. And finally, marital fertility (I_g) does not appear to be influenced by urbanization to a significant extent. (Using another index of urbanization than the license tax, for example, the agglomerated population in towns of more than 2,000 inhabitants, yields essentially similar results.)

284

TABLE 7–5. ZERO-ORDER CORRELATION COEFFICIENTS BETWEEN THE CRUDE BIRTHRATE (CBR), OVERALL FERTILITY (I_f), MARITAL FERTILITY (I_g), ILLEGITIMATE FERTILITY (I_h), PROPORTION MARRIED (I_m), AND LAND REVENUE AND LICENSE TAX, DURING THE FIRST HALF OF THE NINETEENTH CENTURY, 86 *Départements* OF FRANCE, SELECTED DATES.

| | Land revenue per person | | Patente, 1837 | |
	1821	1851	Amount per person	Number per person
CBR in				
1801–1805	−.066	−.168		
1806–1810	−.129	−.241		
1811–1815	−.193	−.230		
1816–1820	−.227	−.226		
1821–1825	−.217	−.202		
1826–1830	−.302	−.303		
I_f in				
1831	−.456	−.463	−.034	−.286
1836	−.444	−.462	−.071	−.305
1841	−.396	−.411	−.012	−.275
1846	−.345	−.355	−.020	−.251
1851	−.294	−.310	.015	−.240
I_g in				
1831	−.628	−.669	−.263	−.553
1836	−.583	−.620	−.213	−.500
1841	−.552	−.593	−.198	−.481
1846	−.533	−.574	−.202	−.479
1851	−.512	−.561	−.200	−.479
I_h in				
1831	.339	.373	.765	.473
1836	.350	.392	.795	.457
1841	.292	.357	.802	.407
1846	.306	.376	.829	.420
1851	.305	.408	.843	.429
I_m in				
1831	.484	.536	.258	.524
1836	.453	.469	.057	.442
1841	.465	.490	.141	.451
1846	.462	.488	.110	.440
1851	.469	.498	.089	.450

A relationship of illegitimacy and urbanization is not surprising, and the correlation of land income with marital fertility is more interesting because it was less expected. If ecological correlations reflect the personal motivations chartered in the Easterlin framework, one would expect more income to be associated with a higher demand for children rather than a lower one. The prevailing relationships might however be the result of a change in the subjective value of children and their objective cost, compensating the increase in income; but if so, the change does not appear to have gone together with urbanization.

If we treat the correlations in a more legitimate way, by considering that marital fertility and rural income in the data analyzed really characterize *départements* rather than people, we must find an explanation to account for the fact that the poorest areas are those that have maintained high levels of marital fertility.[10] The forces at play may be non-economic. It is possible for example that the richest areas were also those where development had occurred on a wide front, including better communication systems, secularization of attitudes, and rationalization of outlook. The puzzle remains, because it is difficult to associate our income variables with indicators of communication or of secularization. We have tried to relate fertility to literacy, but the correlation is not significant. An index of religiousness fares only just a little better; but it is not a very good one, and none seems available at the time. A. d'Angeville thought that the contributions paid in the *départements* for the diffusion of the Catholic faith between 1827 and 1834 would provide a good indicator of catholicism, if related to the total amount of direct taxes (Angeville 1969). There is a weak correlation, rising from $r = .262$ with I_g in 1831 to $r = .292$ with I_g in 1851; but it seems to be by way of I_m, the proportions married being lower in more Catholic areas.

V

CONCLUSION

By 1851, the fertility decline had established clear regional differentials in France. Distinguishing between marital and overall fertility is an indispensable refinement, since the proportions married and the fertility of marriage were so clearly inversely related. Once this is established, the most significant correlates of overall fertility indices are the expectations of life at birth, while the land revenue per head of population correlates most highly with marital fertility. Both of these sets of correlations are negative. It is in the high mortality departements that the birth rate is high; the richest *départements*, as far as landed income is concerned, are those where birth control has made the most inroads, or has affected fertility first.

[10] In good logic, we should also explore the other line of causation: namely that areas of high fertility have remained poor. Although marital fertility changes a great deal during the first half of the century, the income ranking of the *départements* remains rather stable between 1821 and 1851. We would of course like to be able to show that, say pre-Revolutionary, income levels explain nineteenth-century fertility differentials, rather than have eighteenth-century fertility levels explain income differences in 1851. But the sequence seems more likely even in the absence of data.

Lest the high expectation of life of a *département* be attributed to its income characteristics, we must hasten to specify that land revenue per head and mortality show no significant correlation. Taken together, these two characteristics account for a large portion of the variance in both overall or legitimate fertility. The adjunction of other variables, such as the number of *patentes* or the index of Catholicism, does little to increase the explanatory power of our multiple regressions. (See Table 7–6; missing data led to the exclusion of Bouches-du-Rhône, Corse, Rhône, Seine, and Seine-et-Oise.)

On the face of it, we end up with an "explanation" of the fertility decline along the line of population transition theory, with a major role played by the decline of mortality and with an independent influence of income. Unfortunately, we cannot assert that mortality declined before fertility; all we know is that their levels are geographically related during the first half of the century. Nor can we find a satisfactory explanation for the role of rural income; the factors stressed by demographic transition theory are primarily urbanization and industrialization, which show no clear relation to fertility in the French *départements* at the time. It is possible that the meaningful relations are obscured by the use of large aggregates such as the *département*, and that one should expect no more than gross indications with purely descriptive validity. Thus, our data may show no more than that a region such as Brittany preserved high fertility associated with rural poverty and high mortality in the early nineteenth century, in contrast with Normandy, which behaves differently on all these counts. As a description, this is interesting; but it explains nothing.

An explanation of the exact timing and determinants of the fertility decline should follow quite different paths. It should investigate individual couples, classified according to a series of cultural, social, and

TABLE 7–6. MULTIPLE CORRELATION COEFFICIENTS BETWEEN OVERALL FERTILITY (I_f) OR MARITAL FERTILITY (I_g), AND EXPECTATION OF LIFE AT BIRTH, RURAL INCOME PER HEAD, NUMBER OF *patentes* PER 1,000 INHABITANTS, AND AN INDEX OF CATHOLICISM, 81 *départements*, SELECTED DATES.

Year	I_f	I_g
1831	.736	.738
1836	.818	.701
1841	.778	.673
1846	.767	.707
1851	.664	.775

economic characteristics. A series of cohorts should be followed throughout the historical sequence of the fertility transition. The fertility behavior of classes of people should be related to their background. Although the French historical demographers are attempting to do this kind of research more and more, the French sources are far from ideal. It should be possible to select other regions of Europe where fertility is clearly still uncontrolled in the nineteenth century and where it starts to drop within range of a full fledged vital statistics and census system. For instance, there are communes in Belgium where the detailed population registers of the time have been preserved, and where annual lists of inhabitants are available in combination with detailed indexed vital records and a host of other statistics—starting at a time when marital fertility was close to 90 percent of Hutterite fertility. Although the determinants of the fertility transition may have varied from one region of Europe to another, they happened close enough in time to be necessarily related. It is time that some attention be given to other data than the French parish records when the passage to controlled fertility is analyzed.

But France will remain the tantalizing puzzle: Why did it, alone in Europe for more than fifty years, embark on the first wide-scale decline of marital fertility? Even departmental data contribute some insight to the solution of the problem, by providing the general background of the changes.

8

Protoindustrialization and Demographic Changes in the Canton of Zürich

RUDOLF BRAUN

I

INTRODUCTION

REGIONAL case studies in early industrialized European countries—for example in England, Germany, France, and Switzerland—indicate that it was by no means the technical and organizational changes of the factory system and the whole range of socioeconomic changes generally ascribed to the term "Industrial Revolution" which first brought a sustained and incisive population growth. Already in the period preceding the Industrial Revolution changes in generative patterns, family functions, family structures, and family cohesions together with a considerable population growth could be observed among those people who earned their living wholly or partially by cottage industry. These changes were so marked and evident that numerous contemporary writers described this phenomenon, and, in trying to find its causes, emphasized the interrelation with the new mode of life created by the employment and earning possibilities of the putting-out industry. Hence, from the point of view of the general topic of this reader "The Relationship among Early Industrialization, Shifts in Fertility and Changes in Family Structure" it seems inevitable to broaden the scope of the term "Early Industrialization" so that the period of cottage industry preceding the Industrial Revolution will be included. Moreover, this chapter will be concerned primarily with the cottage industry, because essential preconditions of the epoch-making caesura of the "Industrial Revolution" were molded by a complicated net of causes and effects in the environment of the so-called protoindustrialization.[1] This refers particularly to the whole set of demographic aspects.

Our empirical investigation will concentrate on a Swiss canton, Zürich, belonging to those parts of eastern Switzerland, where in the seventeenth and especially the eighteenth century the textile industry

---

[1] The term "protoindustrialization" was invented by Franklin Mendels; see his unpublished dissertation, University of Wisconsin 1969: Industrialization and Population Pressure in Eighteenth Century Flanders. Richard and Charles Tilly use the term in their article of 1971.

operating on the putting-out system expanded fast. Later these regions became the seedbed of the Swiss factory industry. The canton of Zürich is well suited, indeed, for the purpose of comparison, because it experienced a regional distribution of cottage industry which was not uniform; certain parts of the canton became highly industrialized, whereas in other parts the putting-out system could gain no foothold. This situation gives us the possibility of comparison within the same sociopolitical framework and thus provides methodological advantages by reducing the intervening variables.

We mentioned before that the cottage industry of eastern Switzerland became the cradle of the Swiss factory industry and of the Industrial Revolution, if this term is suitable at all for the Swiss experience. This continuity certainly would provide an ideal basis for comparing the demographic changes connected with cottage industry with those which took place when the new technical and organisational system of factory production developed. However, we decided that we will only touch upon this transition from cottage to factory industry—a transition which lasted in the textile regions of eastern Switzerland up to the twentieth century marked by some distinct breaks. The paper will omit the reasons why such limitation of our topic seemed necessary.

Before discussing the empirical investigation, let us make some general observations. To begin with, birth, marriage and death as well as family (or household) functions, structures and cohesions are determined by a whole set of interrelated and interdependent sociocultural, economic, legal, and political factors and relationships: laws governing property, tenurial and agricultural systems, the use of land; villeinage and compulsory labor service of various kinds; legal or customary regulations of socioeconomic units like communities or villages; attitudes, patterns, norms, and expectations as regards the appropriate choice of marriage partnership; the existence of more or less closed marriage circles; legal or customary rules as far as material preconditions for marriage and the founding of a household are concerned; the binding of political rights or rights of using collective property to certain immovables like houses or chimneys; rights of testamentary preference; regulations of tax and military duties; economic cycles and labor demands; the special age composition and population density caused by previous events like severe mortality of warfare or pestilence—these and other factors determined the generative paterns and all the other demographic relevant factors and components. Only the aggregate of these factors, which may have cumulative or opposing effects, will determine the direction of developments and changes (group specific and/or regional distinctions have to be recognized in analyzing the composition of the aggregate) . To avoid the danger that our formulation might suggest a one-sided cause-and-effect relationship, let us emphasize that this is by no means our intention: It is obvious that, for example, generative patterns or family structures might influence changes of inheritance laws or customs, laws governing property, tenurial systems and the use of land or even economic cycles and labor demands. We are dealing with complex mechanisms of causes and effects. Yet these complex interdependences are responsible for the fact that the subject of historical demography is so fascinating.

One glance at the population movements of preindustrial times indicates that already in these periods substantial and sustained population growth was possible, if a set of favorable preconditions and circumstances promoted such developments. H. J. Habakkuk (1963), among others, analyzed the composition of these favorable preconditions and circumstances and pointed out that in these preindustrial times changes of the composition regularly led to a backswing, i.e., a stagnation or decline in population. The population had to be kept in line with the available resources (available resources were not independent variables but determined by social, cultural, economic, legal, political, and climatic factors; furthermore as far as the side of consumption of these resources is concerned, a more or less wide scope of flexibility existed).

The preindustrial processes of population decline or stagnation rested on factors which Habakkuk with reference to Malthus divided into "preventive" and "positive" checks. All factors which intentionally determined the generative patterns (age of marriage, frequency of marriage, marital fertility, forced celibacy, and so on) belonged to the "preventive checks." Such "preventive checks" were related directly to individuals and families, but they were only effective in social groups with a "certain institutional support" and "a certain standard of living" as well as with certain legal and material preconditions (to these preconditions we have to add the sociopsychological foundation which supported these "preventive check" mechanisms) (Habakkuk 1963: 611). These institutional, legal and material criteria referred not only to individuals and families, but also, by the same token, to social groups, village settlements or communities which were endeavoring to keep population growth in line with resources, inasmuch as these criteria formed mechanisms which prevented the settlement of newcomers and pushed surplus population out of their realms. Our empirical investigation will demonstrate that these "preventive checks" were, as mechanisms, effective in those farming regions where cottage industry was absent. In addition, our empirical data will illustrate that those institutional, legal, and material criteria which had the effects of

291

"preventive check" mechanisms were at the same time also responsible for keeping off cottage industry. This was likewise a preventive measure, because the opening of the door to the putting-out system would have caused a disruption of the traditional socioeconomic structure and a break-up of the traditional and balanced village or community settlements.

As regards the "positive checks" of preindustrial periods, "population was brought into line with resources by means of variations in deaths. Mortality rose, and this cut the population back to size both directly by the increase in deaths and indirectly by terminating marriages and so reducing births." [2] One need hardly say that socioeconomically underprivileged people, the poor of the towns and the countryside, were particularly at the mercy of the effects of these "positive checks." This was caused not only by the level of their standard of living and the way they had to find their livelihood, but also, closely connected with these aspects, by the fact that they traditionally lacked the institutional, material, and legal support of the "preventive checks," as well as the internalized behavioral paterns and the psychological adjustment which were part of these mechanisms.

Our empirical investigation will illustrate that most of the people who earned their living wholly or partially by the cottage industry belonged to these poor and underprivileged classes or to those who were forced by the "preventive check" mechanisms (especially by testamentary obstacles) to leave home and seek their livelihood elsewhere with the help of the putting-out system. Furthermore, our investigation will make it evident that the cottage industry could gain a foothold and expand in those regions and communities where the beforementioned criteria of the "preventive checks" were lacking or too weak to function as effective barriers, i.e. to prevent the settlement of newcomers and to push the surplus population out of their realms. The result was that those parts (in comparison with the nonindustrialized farming regions) were marked by a considerable population growth and an increase of density, despite the fact that their natural resources (quality of soil, orographical characteristics, and so on) could in no way match those of the agricultural parts.

These few general remarks about mechanisms which determined the preindustrial population movements must suffice. We will encounter these mechanisms in our empirical section and analyze them in more concrete terms. We may recall that the preindustrial population movements were marked by the characteristic that periods of growth were

[2] Habakkuk 1963: 608; we may add that malnutrition and other disease of poverty led to a higher number of sterile women.

followed regularly by those of stagnation or decline. A permanent and at the beginning even accelerating population growth could only be observed when industrialization started. The literature has labeled this phenomenon as "Demographic Revolution." Despite intensive research endeavours, however, the interdependences and the network of causes and effects between Industrial Revolution and Demographic Revolution still remain to be clarified. There exists certain proof that in England, at least in the regions of cottage industry, a considerable population growth preceded the Industrial Revolution. The same phenomenon can be recognized in the eighteenth century for all regions of continental Europe where cottage industry or protoindustry generally played dominant roles as sources of livelihood. Hence, does this mean that the beginning of the Demographic Revolution has to be placed in the period preceding the Industrial Revolution? Or must this first phase connected with protoindustry be interpreted as a process of growth rather preindustrial in nature? In other words, would this process of growth preceding the Industrial Revolution again have been followed by the backswings which had been experienced in previous centuries? Or could protoindustry with all its socioeconomic implications and effects really have been able to guarantee a permanent population growth? Was it not the Industrial Revolution with all its new potentialities for increasing productivity, new employment, and earning possibilities, new consumption patterns, needs, pretensions of life and hopes for the future as well as the whole range of socioeconomic, cultural and sociopsychological aspects of human life which were brought into flux during this epoch-making caesura, which made the Demographic Revolution possible, that is a permanent and for a long time accelerating population growth? Yet, this question leads to another: How far was the protoindustry with all its implications and effects, especially those which can be ascribed to demographic aspects, part of the forces which made ready and cranked up the Industrial Revolution? After all it seems obvious that the demographic habitus of a society influences the course and the dynamic of economic changes. Thus, is it possible or even required from this point of view to interpret the population growth connected with cottage industry preceding the Industrial Revolution as a legitimate part of the Demographic Revolution?

We do not claim to answer these questions, but they will guide us in the following empirical section devoted to the case of the canton of Zürich and might serve here as vindication for our decision to concentrate on protoindustrialization.

II

THE CASE STUDY OF THE CANTON OF ZÜRICH

AT the end of the eighteenth century, Switzerland belonged to the proportionately most industrialized countries on the European continent. The chief emphasis lay on the textile industry; watchmaking came second. In 1779, Professor L. Meister of Zürich drew attention in a striking turn of phrase to the importance of this early cottage industry: "The free city-state of Geneva rests largely on the points of clock-hands . . .; several Swiss cantons on bales of silk and cotton." [3] Zürich was among those cantons that relied on bales of silk and especially of cotton. A few general remarks must suffice to depict the environment in which this textile cottage industry developed. First, a brief account of the political and constitutional background is necessary.

Under the *Ancien Régime* the Swiss Confederation consisted of thirteen loosely connected entities which in all essentials were sovereign bodies, the so-called cantons (*Stände*) or districts (*Orte*). To this union of states there also belonged subject territories known as common dominions (*Gemeine Herrschaften*), which were governed and administered by the different cantons in turn, as well as associated districts (*Zugewardte Orte*), that is territories which were not subject but were connected with the Confederation only by a treaty of protection. Thus under the *Ancien Régime*, Zürich, a member of the ancient thirteen-canton Confederation, was a city-state with limited sovereign powers. Toward the close of the eighteenth century it had an area of 1,700 square kilometers (656,371 square miles) and not quite 180,000 inhabitants (see Table 8–1). However, only some 5 percent of the population [4] enjoyed full rights of citizenship; the remainder were rural subjects. The latter had, as far as the canton Zürich was concerned, no share in government, were hindered in their economic life by the city's monopolies, and were distinguished from the privileged burghers by various other socioeconomic restrictions: educational barriers, sumptuary laws, limitations on entry to professions, and so on.

In short, a small group of privileged burghers,[5] on the one hand, and the rest of the population squeezed into a sociopolitical and economic strait-jacket, on the other, composed the set-up from which the textile

[3] Preisschriften 1774: 16. Much of the material in this essay, incidentally, comes directly from Braun 1966, chs. I and II. It overlaps with the portions selected and translated by David Landes in Braun 1966. See also Braun 1965 for an extension of the analysis to the nineteenth and twentieth centuries.

[4] The absolute number of the burghers steadily declined; it was 7755 in 1671, 6,593 in 1756, and 5,577 in 1790; see Schellenberg 1951: 22.

[5] In 1790 only 59.3 percent of the 9,400 city-dwellers belonged to families of burghers; ibid.

TABLE 8-1. POPULATION OF THE CANTON OF ZÜRICH, 1634-1870 (PERCENTAGE GROWTH)

Districts	1634–1671	1671–1700	1700–1762	1762–1771	1771–1792	1792–1812	1812–1833	1833–1836	1836–1870
Zürich	+24.3%	−2.1%	+35.7%	−7.0%	+6.4%	−4.7%	+36.9%	+18.6%	+16.8%
Knonau	+41.3	−5.6	+35.9	−4.8	+16.7	+8.6	+20.2	−7.8	+6.1
Horgen	+52.0	−8.4	+50.8	+5.6	+16.0	+4.9	+9.1	+8.9	+16.3
Meilen	+59.9	−15.8	+82.6	−4.3	+19.3	+5.4	+10.5	−2.0	+6.0
Hinwil	+45.4	−4.4	+86.1	−0.1	+30.1	+12.0	+19.6	−5.3	−1.0
Uster	+43.6	−2.7	+72.4	−6.2	+13.9	+15.9	+18.4	+1.3	+3.9
Pfäffikon	+76.5	−1.4	+92.4	−15.7	+32.5	+11.8	+13.2	−6.0	−2.7
Winterthur	+52.0	+20.6	+27.5	−8.1	+7.5	+10.6	+18.3	+5.0	+8.5
Andelfingen	+63.2	−9.7	+14.9	−13.6	+16.3	+2.3	+25.4	−0.4	+8.6
Bülach	+41.9	−6.9	+25.3	−15.5	+14.9	+7.2	+18.6	−1.0	+12.3
Regensberg	+34.1	+2.3	+5.1	−15.7	+14.9	+17.0	+21.8	−4.7	+7.2
Average	+45.3	−2.4	+42.7	−7.7	+16.2	+7.3	+19.7	+2.1	+8.3
Average of the farming districts [a]	+46.2	−4.8	+15.1	−15.0	+15.4	+8.8	+21.9	−2.0	+9.4
Average of the highland districts [b]	+55.2	−2.8	+83.6	−7.3	+25.5	+13.2	+17.1	−3.3	+0.1

[a] Farming districts: Andelfingen, Bülach, Regensberg.
[b] Highland districts: Hinwil, Uster, Pfäffikon.

industry of Zürich developed producing silk, wool, and—especially since the end of the seventeenth century—above all cotton goods on the domestic or putting-out system. In the seventeenth century a commercial group, among them Protestant refugees, a particularly entrepreneurial element, increasingly gained sociopolitical influence, not only operating out of their own guilds but also holding more and more of the important positions of various craft guilds. Thus, economic restrictions became especially rigid (more than other cantons, e.g. Bern, experienced). As far as the cottage industry with its putting-out system was concerned, only burghers were allowed to purchase raw materials for the textile production and to trade finished or half-finished goods. The entire product had to be marketed through the burghers of Zürich. Hence, the rural population could only perform limited and subordinated functions in the production and trade system of the textile industry.

Toward the close of the eighteenth century, about one-third of the total population of the canton of Zürich was employed partially or wholly in various branches of this textile industry. It did not, however, extend into all parts of the canton, as Figure 8–1 shows. While the hilly and mountainous regions and the lake areas were highly industrialized, the farming districts of the flatter parts of the canton were purely agrarian.[6]

We might, to begin with, have a look at those farming regions where the cottage industry could gain no foothold, despite the fact that they were situated mostly nearer the city of Zürich, the center of the putting-out system, and had advantages in terms of transportation and communication facilities. How can this absence of cottage industry be explained?

The nonindustrialized farming regions were marked by the traditional socioeconomic framework of closed village settlements and the three-field system of cultivation—a setup which was based on the comprehensive and binding interdependence of the villagers as a socioeconomic unit. The peasant community was closely knit together by a net of legal and customary rights, obligations and servitudes, which determined the activities of life. No man could use and till the land as he pleased. Methods and timing of work and the allocation of fields were fixed for each down to the smallest detail. Hence, it was very hard for an exogenous putting-out industry to gain a foothold in a so

---

[6] In 1787 about 34,000 cotton handspinners and 6,500 cotton looms were counted in the region of the canton of Zürich. In addition, 2,500 silk-looms were operating. The wool goods production and framework knitting (hosiery) were insignificant; see Bodmer 1960: 227 and 211.

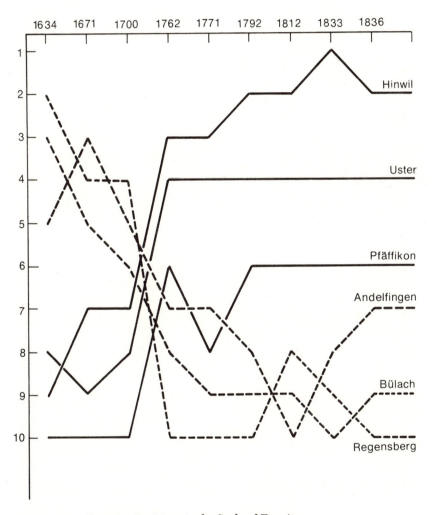

Figure 8–1 Changing Positions in the Scale of Density

Figure 8–2 The Cottage Industry of the Canton of Zürich at the end of the Eighteenth Century

rigidly ordered socioeconomic unit, as long as the latter retained its vitality. In such a firmly articulated and close-knit collectivity, industry had little play. Industrialization would have destroyed not only the material but also the human bases of such a community. As a result, the village settlements had to take steps, with all the means at their disposal, to prevent an uncontrolled diffusion of industry. Their field servitudes, crop rotation, common pasturage, their laws governing property and the rights of using common property, as well as their legal and customary regulations in general, were of great service in this connection.

Some factors had the effect of barriers in keeping out industry: First, the general right of using the common property and being a member of the community was the strongest obstacle for the entry and the settlement of newcomers and provided legitimation for claiming a so-called *Einzugsgeld* (fee of settlement for newcomers); the more common property the community had, the higher was the settlement fee, which had to be confirmed by the city council. Especially after the middle of the seventeenth century, the *Einzugsgeld* was raised periodically.[7] But this fee of settlement would hardly have been an effective obstacle. Much more important was the fact that there existed or was introduced a *numerus clausus* concerning the right of using the common property and being a member of the community. This fixed number of rights was vested in the houses (or chimneys) and not in persons or families. The effect was twofold: it kept newcomers out and prevented too great an expansion from within. The newcomers not only had to pay the fee of settlement but also had to gain possession of a house with its vested right of using the common property and being a member of the community. Moreover, the *numerus clausus* of these rights was used as legitimation for setting up regulations that no new house could be built either in the village settlement or outside, unless an old one was torn down. These regulations prevented an uncontrolled expansion from within too. As a concession to the pressure from within, the community usually allowed the partition of rights of using the common property into half, third, and fourth parts, because the possession of such a right or part of it was the basis of living and community membership. This concession gave the "closed-shop" set-up more flexibility. Yet the regulations forbidding the construction of new houses in turn was a protection against an uncontrolled expansion by means of partition of the rights of using common property.

[7] In a host of sources formulations like the following are found: The community is asking the city council for a higher *Einzugsgeld* in order to keep foreigners out and not being overflowed by newcomers.

To be sure, these barriers were not primarily erected to keep out industry, but to guarantee the traditional livelihood of the members of the agrarian community bound together as an economic entity and a social union. Unfitted for changes toward agrarian reforms (new cultivation methods, new crop rotations, and so on), the closed village settlement and the traditional three-field system of cultivation were at this time a rather unproductive and in many ways outdated kind of subsistence farming, based on the working power of the family members, employing hired hands sparingly, and loaded with tax obligations. For the foregoing reasons, such communities were all the more eager to protect the livelihood of their members by setting up and enlarging safety measures against the entry and settlement of newcomers as well as an expansion from within. The mechanism of these safety measures was an agrarian kind of protection; nevertheless it had, by the same token, the effect of keeping out of the realm of the community those individuals and families who earned their living by working for the exogenous textile industry. We must emphasize again that such a population would have endangered the traditional socioeconomic unit in its balanced interdependences as a whole. This was manifested in communities which were still run on a three-field system, with common land and pasturage, with compulsory field use, and even with prohibitions on building. But these forms no longer corresponded to reality. For one part of the population they had, for one reason or another, become obsolete. In short, these communities lacked the strong institutional, legal, and material means (and probably the spirit of collectivity as well) to maintain the comprehensive and obligatory union of the villagers as a socioeconomic entity. These communities, most of them situated in the spurs of the hill and mountain regions, could not keep cottage industry out. Being hindered by the unadaptive three-field system of cultivation, the socioeconomic adjustment of these communities to the new exogenous earning opportunities proved to be very painful and costly—costly in terms of socioeconomic disruption and disorganization.

The above-mentioned barriers or safety measures have to be evaluated as institutional, legal, and material elements of traditional mechanisms, "preventive" in their nature, by which population growth could be kept in line with resources. Before providing a detailed analysis of these "preventive checks" in operation, a glance at global data with the help of maps and diagrams will show some of the effects of these mechanisms.

Table 8–2 shows the relatively slow population growth of the farming regions in the period from 1671 to 1792 compared with the sub-

TABLE 8-2. POPULATION OF THE CANTON ZÜRICH, 1634–1836 (ABSOLUTE NUMBER AND DENSITY)

Districts	1634 absolute Population	1634 Density per square km	1671 absolute Population	1671 Density per square km	1700 absolute Population	1700 Density per square km	1762 absolute Population	1762 Density per square km	1771 absolute Population	1771 Density per square km	1792 absolute Population	1792 Density per square km	1812 absolute Population	1812 Density per square km	1833 absolute Population	1833 Density per square km	1836 absolute Population	1836 Density per square km
Zürich [a]	15,209	—	20,511	—	20,081	—	27,246	—	25,351	—	26,973	—	25,720	—	35,216	—	41,775	—
Knonau	5,061	45	7,100	63	6,699	59	9,107	81	8,672	77	10,124	90	10,996	97	13,216	117	12,180	108
Horgen	6,152	59	9,932	95	9,100	87	13,724	131	14,495	139	16,814	161	17,642	169	19,245	184	20,956	201
Meilen	5,941	78	9,139	119	7,693	100	14,049	183	13,447	176	16,040	209	16,904	221	18,671	244	18,305	239
Hinwil	4,485	25	8,684	49	8,304	46	15,455	86	15,437	86	20,086	112	22,490	126	26,893	150	25,463	142
Pfäffikon	5,452	34	8,106	51	7,996	50	15,382	96	12,960	81	17,166	107	19,187	120	21,714	135	20,408	127
Uster	4,570	41	6,567	59	6,391	57	11,017	98	10,334	92	11,767	105	13,641	122	16,153	144	16,360	146
Winterthur	9,041	36	13,469	53	16,240	64	20,704	82	19,019	75	20,450	81	22,614	90	26,748	106	28,072	111
Andelfingen	7,170	43	11,788	71	10,646	64	12,233	74	10,571	64	12,292	74	12,574	76	15,771	95	15,716	94
Bülach	8,962	48	12,686	69	11,806	64	14,792	80	12,492	68	14,353	78	15,385	83	18,243	99	18,061	98
Regensberg	7,330	46	10,093	64	10,325	65	10,854	68	9,148	58	10,515	66	12,304	77	14,985	94	14,280	90
Total and average	79,373	48	118,075	71	115,281	70	164,563	99	151,926	92	176,580	107	189,457	114	226,855	137	231,576	140

Sources: Data for the years 1634, 1671, 1700, 1762, 1792, 1812, 1833 and 1836 are provided by G. Meyer von Knonau, 1837; data for the years 1700, 1762 and 1771 by Waser, State Archive of Zürich, B X 27. The areas of the districts and the whole canton are measured with omitting the lake; see: Schweizerische Arealstatistik, Lieferung 184, Bern, 1912 S. 24.
[a] District of the city.

stantial increase of population in the industrialized communities. The farming districts Andelfingen, Bülach and Regensberg had a rate of growth during these 120 years of only 4.3 percent, 13.1 percent, and 4.2 percent, whereas the industrialized districts Hinwil, Pfäffikon and Uster experienced one of 131.3 percent, 111.8 percent, and 79.2 percent according to these data.[8] Table 8–1 shows that the period from 1634 to 1671 was marked by a rather dramatically fast population increase both in the flatter agrarian parts as well as the mountainous regions, which later became strongholds of cottage industry. We will deal with this demographic phenomenon in Section III but might mention here that drastic population decreases caused by plagues in the years 1611, 1628–1629 and 1635–1636 made, so to speak, room for such a pre-industrial population growth.

Figure 8–1 illustrates contrasting growth patterns. Figures 8–3 and 8–4, dealing with long-distance migration, demonstrate one of the mechanisms which were responsible for the regional differences in population movement. Figure 8–3 portrays long-distance migration around 1660, that is at a time when the cottage industry was in its earliest stage. The map shows very little difference between the various regions of the canton. Less than a century later (1734–1744), when the cottage industry still had not reached its peak (the quarter of a century after 1744 experienced the most rapid industrial growth), the picture had changed: the industrialized regions of the canton participated significantly less in the migration to North America. These results could be confirmed by other migration data, that is the mercenary migration or the short-lived migration of servants. Statistical data of 1780, for example, dealing with the origins of the 1,936 servants working at that time in households in the city of Zürich, show that scarcely a handful were coming from the industrialized regions; the overwhelming majority had their origins of birth in the farming regions of the canton of Zürich or the neighboring farming districts.[9] Clearly, such data indicate that in the farming regions mechanisms were at work which pushed surplus population, single persons, and whole families out of their communities, whereas the industrialized regions, traditionally marked with the same emigration movements, in the course

[8] Source: Meyer von Knonau 1837; for the following maps see Kläui and E. Imhof 1951, plates 35, 37, and 40.

[9] See State Archive of Zürich, B IX 85; we are, of course, well aware of other factors, which played a role in long distance migration. Considering the attraction of the mercenary employment, you have to take into account the agrarian and pro-toindustrial cycles and factors like protoindustrial labor demands, wages, food prices, and other indications. In protoindustrial boom years, the mercenary service could hardly compete with protoindustrial earning possibilities.

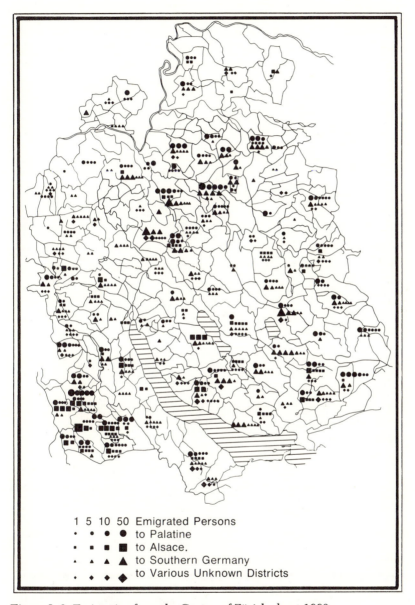

1 5 10 50 Emigrated Persons
· • ● ⬤ to Palatine
· ▪ ■ ◼ to Alsace.
▪ ▴ ▲ ▲ to Southern Germany
· ◆ ◆ ◆ to Various Unknown Districts

Figure 8–3 Emigration from the Canton of Zürich about 1660

Figure 8–4 Emigration from the Canton of Zürich to North America, 1734–1744

of industrialization increasingly lost this push-force and even developed a certain pull-force of immigration. A short look at the socioeconomic structure of these industrialized regions will help to explain this phenomenon.

To be sure, the various industrialized regions of the canton of Zürich cannot be treated as a unity; each had its own legal, institutional, economic, and social characteristics; even geography and to some extent climate were different. Each of these regions brought to the assimilation of the putting-out system its own circumstances. Yet even so, the same factors played a role, though in different composition and with different weight and patterns. The same forces impeded or promoted the process of industrialization. All of these industrialized areas were marked by the fact that they no longer had, or never had, any firmly ordered economic collectivity in the sense of the three-field system. Their legal, economic, and social structure was no longer, or had never been, an organic unit with the vitality and the strength to block the incursion of industry. Let us select the Highland as an example of one distinct industrial area.

The Highland is a hilly and mountain area which, at the beginning of industrialization still was sparsely settled. The upper regions, with a harsh climate, soil of a poor quality, and bad orographical characteristics, were barely opened up. Thus, the tenurial and agricultural forms as well as the forms of settlements were quite unlike those of the farming areas. There were few village settlements but scattered hamlets, homesteads, and crofts. There was no common property (land), or none worth mentioning, to be protected; thus, there were few, if any, legal provisions to prevent settlement or to prohibit the building of new houses, and the few there were little effective. There was also no economic union which could be endangered by cottage industry. The so-called *Egartenwirtschaft* was the dominating system of cultivation in this area of scattered hamlets, homesteads and crofts, lacking the rigid order which governed the tilling of fields and the rotation of crops down to the last detail. Pastureland was plowed, and the fields were used, with varying crop rotation, for two or three years. After this period the fields were once more given over to pasture and new ones plowed up.[10] The peasant in this area, therefore, did not know the economic constraint of villages with a vital three-field system. Rather he had the free disposition of his land. He could use and till it as he

[10] In this area one found also a kind of three-field system, but without control of the fields by a collectivity; every hamlet, homestead or croft governed its own field distribution. To be sure, the outline of these two "models" is to a certain extent "idealtypical."

Figure 8–5 Districts (1834)

wished. In other words, whereas the village peasant had to work within the collectivity and derived his security from it, the Highland farmer had much more free play. He was to a certain extent an entrepreneur, with the economic values and spirit of the entrepreneur. The specifically material characteristics of his farm enterprise—its considerable independence, its flexibility and adaptability—were in harmony with the markedly individualistic character of the Highland farmer, whereas the institutional, legal and material features of the closed village settlements and the three-field system of cultivation, marked by the lack of adaptability, went along with the spirit of the villagers bound by tradition and collective thinking and rather hostile toward changes.

As a result, the Highland experienced a fruitful symbiosis between agriculture and the exogenous putting-out industry, especially in the course of the eighteenth century. Industrialization did not take place at the expense of agriculture. On the contrary, large areas of the Highland were stimulated by the cottage industry: waste land was drawn into cultivation and settled; better use was made of the already cultivated terrain; the livestock was improved; new crops were introduced; and so on. In short, in the Highland the cottage industry promoted to a certain extent agrarian reforms. Moreover, for the first time, whole areas of the upper and higher parts of the Highland were actually opened up and settled, as a comparison of Figures 8–2 and 8–3 indicates. These hamlets, homesteads, and crofts, new-founded in a marginal region of steep and cleft woodlands, could never have been established on a purely agricultural basis; the earnings of the putting-out industry were essential for their existence. Indeed, many of these new settlements were primarily founded as places to live and work for the cottage industry and not for agricultural purposes. And many of these settlements had to be given up in the course of the nineteenth century, when cottage industry (hand-loom weaving at this time) decreased. They again became woodland, and still are today.

As we pointed out above, cottage industry managed to penetrate not only the Highland, where the *Egartenwirtschaft* system dominated, but other regions as well. The areas around the Lake of Zürich belonged to these industrialized districts. These areas were ones of thoroughfare by water and land, where the local population traditionally rendered service to travellers and helped with transit-trade; offering opportunity of employment and even a kind of limited entrepreneurial activities, being open to trade and communication with the city of Zürich, and having a long established viticulture, these lake areas displayed a remarkable socioeconomic dynamism and adaptability in the course of

307

industrialization. Here too a fruitful symbiosis was possible between putting-out industry, agriculture and, as a *specificum* of this region, trade. This was also the district where most of the middlemen of the putting-out system lived, conducting often this kind of limited entrepreneurial activity side by side with thoroughfare services, business, and trade.[11] Also the hill areas on the left side of the lake, where the economy could be increasingly based on livestock, brought rather favorable conditions to meet and to be integrated with cottage industry. This kind of agrarian economy was stimulated by industry too. Only in those farming areas which could not keep out industry but were unfitted for adjustment did industrialization take place at the expense of agriculture and of socioeconomic disruption and disorganization generally.

We were able to give only a rapid and very rough sketch of the different circumstances which opened the door to the putting-out system. Figure 8-2, picturing the distribution of the cotton industry of Zürich at the time of its first prime toward the end of the eighteenth century (1787), shows that there was not a circular net around Zürich as center of distribution. Rather the most intensively industrialized areas were situated in parts far off from Zürich, in the pre-Alpine zones, although these peripheral districts were drawn into the putting-out system only later and suffered from extremely unfavorable transport conditions. Particularly the Highland had inconceivably bad communications. To bring the raw material in, distribute it, and carry the finished goods back was a rather difficult task. For this reason the Highland was only slightly touched by the first expansion of cottage weaving. The transport of the warp yarn and rolls of cloth would have been too hard. As a result, until the collapse of hand spinning in the first years of the nineteenth century, the mountainous parts of the canton of Zürich remained mainly dependent on spinning and not weaving. Figure 8-2 documents clearly that weaving was concentrated at this time in the industrialized areas around the Lake which were more open to trade and communication.

Though every district brought its own preliminary conditions to meet and be integrated with cottage industry, they all shared the common feature that their socioeconomic structure as well as their legal and institutional framework furthered—or at least could not hinder and prevent—the growth of cottage industry and were at the same time able to adjust to this new source of earnings. This common feature also helps to explain the fact that the industrialized districts not only lost

[11] This group of middlemen proved to become pioneers in factory production after the Helvetic Revolution opened the way for the rural population to engage independently in production and trade; see Rudolf Braun 1967.

their push-force of emigration in the eighteenth century but also managed to maintain in their realm a rather dramatically increasing population. Once the putting-out system brought earning opportunities, the people could find a place to live and work in these districts, because they lacked the strong mechanisms of the pure farming districts, which kept newcomers out and allowed only a limited expansion from within. In addition, the adjustment quality of the traditional sources of livelihood in the industrialized districts were responsible for the above-mentioned symbiosis which further enlarges the living-space; these traditional resources were not hampered but rather stimulated and promoted by industry.

Yet these aspects touch only the surface of the relationships among early industrialization and demographic changes. In attempting now to analyze changes in marriage patterns, fertility, family structure, family phases, and family cohesion during the course of early industrialization, we will limit the field of our investigation to the Highland, disregarding the other industrialized districts of the canton of Zürich. These results, however, will be placed against the contrasting background of the pure farming districts.

When cottage industry is being discussed, the peaceful image is often conjured up of the peasant who tills his fields, tends his cows, and in times when there is no work to be done, busies himself with domestic industry. To begin with, this picture does not do justice to the socioeconomic conditions of early industry in the Highland. The great mass of people who first and foremost founded their existence on industrial earnings were drawn from the margins of a peasant community. They were people who possessed very few resources in the form of land and property; indeed, often they had not a scrap of ground to call their own. The socioeconomic conditions of this rural back country could not offer sufficient working and earning possibilities for all. When industrialization started, there was a disproportion between labor supply and demand. Able-bodied men with their families could not make enough during the working season to tide them over. A high proportion of the population hardly earned enough for the most vital and elementary necessities of life. Many men went abroad temporarily or permanently to seek work. Fathers had to leave their families behind in the most abject poverty; children who were barely ten years old were sent out to fend for themselves. The expanding cottage industry found in such individuals workers who grasped eagerly at the new source of earnings.[12]

[12] For a detailed illustration of this situation see the first chapter in Braun 1960 where a host of contemporary sources portray the misery and poverty of these people.

It is important to emphasize this background of misery, poverty, and forced migration in search for necessities. The people in the Highland who first and foremost founded their existence on cotton spinning traditionally lacked the security of a firmly rooted peasant environment. Rather they were used to a marginal and roving existence. They were familiar with the fact that the bare need to make a living tore families apart, drove children out of home, forced fathers to leave their families, or uprooted the whole family. It is no exaggeration to state that for these people the cottage industry proved to become a medium which could guarantee a rooting in the land of their ancestors, permanent settlement in a home, as small and scanty as it might be, and the united family.

This we have to bear in mind, when we investigate the smallest and most natural community, the family. First, what changes did industrialization bring in the requirements for marriage and the founding of a family?

Let us begin with the contrasting environment of a peasant society. In a peasant society an engagement of marriage may have nothing of the character of an intimate, private understanding between two "lovers." In a peasant marriage contract, the economic unit, with its human and material requirements, is the dominant consideration. Personal preferences have a lower priority. The main point is to maintain the organic cohesion of the enterprise. The unstable equilibrium between the work and consumption requirements of a peasant family and the size of its holdings must be assured. The result is a set of peasant marriage customs to which the individual members of the family must conform.

The classical portrayals of such peasant marriage contracts and marriage customs are to be found in the novels of Jeremias Gotthelf, describing the milieu of the wealthy peasant proprietors of the Emmenthal (canton of Berne). Referring to the Zürich farming districts, a contemporary observer of changing marriage patterns during the course of industrialization, J. C. Hirzel, wrote in 1792 as follows: "It thus became a custom to leave the holdings together and pass them to the sons alone, and these in turn limited their marriages so that the farm would always be capable of supporting the family. . . . As a result we see that the population of the fertile Wehntal [belonging to the nonindustrialized, pure farming districts] has increased only little. A peasant reckons this way: my farm can feed no more than one, at most two sons; the others may have to remain unmarried or seek their fortune elsewhere" (Hirzel 1792: 129).

Hirzel is describing here the so-called *Anerbenrecht*, that is the right

310

of testamentary preference. The tendency to give preference to one heir and to limit the fragmentation of the land was strengthened in the Zürich countryside in the seventeenth century by the development of fixed rights to using common property and to being a member of the community as well as of regulations forbidding the building of new houses—in short, by the erection of the above-mentioned barriers, which we characterized as "preventive check" mechanisms. Clearly, the inheritance and marriage customs described by Hirzel were an interrelated part of these "preventive checks." These behavioral patterns, values, and customs corresponded with the institutional, legal, and material elements of the "preventive check" mechanisms of the peasant community. In the Highland, however, as we have seen, this feature was not prominent. Peasant marriage customs of a kind promoted by *Anerbenrecht* probably were most lacking there even before industrialization.

The earning possibilities generated by the putting-out industry of Zürich, however, created an entirely new situation. For those men who stemmed from a peasant milieu—and we are here speaking only of them—there were now entirely new possibilities of marriage and founding a household. Industrial earnings could make a substantial contribution to a peasant enterprise. With this transformation of the basis of peasant existence, the circumstances of inheritance rights were transformed. Hirzel was well aware of this transformation. He wrote that where manufacturing earnings slip in, the peasant alters his above-cited calculation as follows: " 'I have three to four sons; each one gets some herbage, at least enough for a cow, a bit of field, and so on. This should go a long way toward maintaining the household, and the working of this small property will leave enough time to earn the rest through manufacture.' In the end, people found that it was even enough to have a corner in the house for a spinning-wheel or a loom and enough land for a vegetable garden." Hirzel went on to tell us of "a brave and worthy farmer" whom he had come to know that year (1792), "who is cultivating only one-eighth of the holding of his grandfather and yet is living happily and well" (Hirzel 1792: 104). In his Letters on Switzerland (1791) C. Meiners wrote: "The increased and sure income offered by the combination of cottage manufacture with farming hastened and multiplied marriages and encouraged the division of holdings, while enhancing their value; it also promoted the expansion and embellishment of houses and villages. Thanks to the prospects which were opened to the farmer by his labor and that of his children, he no longer set early and anxious limits to the fecundity of his marriage. Previously fathers and sons avoided dividing fairly large

311

and, even more, modest holdings, for they were concerned that each piece be able to nourish its holder. This fear vanished entirely with the diffusion of manufactures and cottage industry; and now the sons redivided the parcels received from their fathers, themselves the product perhaps of several divisions, because people are convinced that even a small field is enough to feed a diligent holder along with wife and children" (Meiners 1791: 47).

Both Hirzel and Meiners observed that marriages were more numerous and concluded at an earlier age in those peasant areas where there was cottage industry. J. C. Hirzel even tried to establish the fact of increased marriages statistically.[13] Yet, it must be emphasized that such marriages could no longer be called peasant marriages, for without the possibility of earning money in industry, they would never have been concluded. As far as the Highland was concerned, cottage manufacture was a by-occupation for the very smallest part of the peasants (we are not speaking here of the landless cottage worker mentioned above; we will examine these people later), but was the foundation and precondition for their marriages and made it possible for them and their families to survive and be rooted in a fractional farm holding. This comes out clearly in the synodal address of Salomon Schinz, pastor of the Highland community of Fischenthal, in the year 1818: "Such a population density would never have arisen in this raw district if the substantial earnings from manufacture had not facilitated and promoted their nourishment and increase and thus doubled the number of people in half a century. If all these people are to remain here, this source of income, which in fact created them, is absolutely indispensable. Even the landowners of the middle class could not survive without these earnings, for they have piled up large debts on many parcels, either through costly purchases, or the frequent division of holdings and the consequently indispensable construction of new dwellings, or through buying out the inheritance claims of other family members— debts whose interest could not possibly be paid with the output of the soil, but only with the earnings yielded by the spinning wheel and shuttle. All of this has inevitably brought on many a disaster; when cotton earnings have diminished, the false appearance of well-being has vanished from these districts. Really comfortable landowners in my community, and also in Bäretschweil, Bauma, Sternenberg are rare; indeed, there are only a few people who can boast that only half of their lands are mortgaged. The man who has only four Gulden to pay

[13] Hirzel 1792: 77; he chose as an example the community of Fischenthal, situated in the Highland, and offered the following annual averages of marriages concluded: 1641–1670: 42; 1671–1700: 81; 1701–1750: 113; 1751–1760: 165.

in interest on a small parcel, big enough for a cow in summer and winter, can still make it. But any serious misfortune to his cow or his land can throw him into the class of poor, and if he has a ruthless creditor, into the class of homeless. And this latter class is frightfully numerous. Over 1,360 persons in my commune must live exclusively from earnings in manufacture, and 200 households have no real property, while many have neither livestock nor chattels—their spinning wheel or loom or indispensable household articles excepted—and even the latter are lacking to the poorest" (Schinz 1818: 8).[14]

With these changes, described by contemporary observers over and over again, often with similar formulation, a whole complex of customs necessarily began to change again. Alongside the altered laws of inheritance, there developed a new attitude toward marriage. A contract of marriage was no longer a settlement or treaty that determined the fate of a human and economic community down to the smallest detail. For the marriageable daughters and sons of the peasantry, these changes meant a widening of the scope of their personal pretensions. Matrimony could now be enveloped in a much more intimate aura. It had the chance to become a reciprocal commitment of two people, who hoped to realize individual happiness through it.

Let us now examine this development more closely in that class of the population who were not from a secure peasant milieu, i.e., those poverty-stricken people grasping eagerly at the new industrial earning possibilities. It was pointed out above what the possibilities of industrial earnings meant for these people. Since the beginning of the eighteenth century, the demand for labor of the putting-out industry of Zürich had accelerated, and the broadest layers of the population of the Highland had placed their fate in the hands of the putters-out, trusting blindly to the flimsy, weak cotton thread which provided their living. "Carelessly they get married without consideration, if they can manage to support wife and children; they blindly trust that the good industrial earnings will continue forever," wrote J. J. Nüscheler in an essay about "The Revision of the Matrimonial Laws in the canton of Zürich" (Nüscheler 1831: 17). With pastoral indignation Salomon Schinz sketched how, in the milieu of Fischenthal cottage workers, a girl entered into matrimony: "Raised at the wheel or the loom, without knowledge of other housework or field work; almost daily in bad company until deep into the night, and when work is over, spending the daily pay or part of it for sweets or drink, indulging every lust and not

---

[14] It has to be noted that 1817/1818 was a year of famine; moreover, the breakdown of the hand spinning with all the grave socioeconomic consequences had just occurred.

scorning for the purpose any means, however shameful, even embezzle-ment of the materials to be worked up or theft of wares from the house of her parents, and then entering into marriage, when compelled by necessity, often with a youngster equally light-minded and poor, own-ing between them neither bed nor household utensils—. . . what kind of results can be expected from such penniless marriages, where the people concerned owe the shopkeeper for the very clothes on their backs?" (Schinz 1818: 11). A colleague of Schinz, the pastor of Wild-berg, made the same observation that in these circles marriages were contracted without any thought to material considerations: "These people, who have two spinning wheels but no bed, contract early mar-riages fairly often" (Hirzel 1816: 16). Numerous other contemporary sources could be cited which were concerned with this phenomenon. "Beggar weddings" is the term generally used in these sources, and quite often they call for laws to prevent such marriages. In holy zeal, Johann Schulthess, Professor of Theology and member of the Board of Church and Education, wrote that "the State and the Church may, by all means, not consent to such beggar weddings." Being a clergyman, he had, of course, the Bible at hand to support this statement: "He who does not support his relatives, and especially his closest household members, who no longer believes in God, says the apostle; yes, indeed, he is wickeder than a heathen" (Schulthess 1818: 52). A host of others were playing the same tune. Hence local authorities were eager to find ways and means to act in this direction. In April 1813, to mention only one example, the local controlling body for good conduct (the so-called *Stillstand*) of Wetzikon (a Highland community) ordered "that early marriages of poor people may, if possible, be prevented by the pastor; therefore, the beginning of a love affair and engagement should be brought to the attention of the pastor by the members of this con-trolling body." Knowing about life, the pastor of this community wrote resignedly at the end of this protocol: "Who wants to take care of a basket of fleas?" (cited by Meier 1881: 461).

The fact that the new customs of engagement, marriage, and found-ing a household were, nearly without exception, evaluated negatively in these contemporary sources, has to be explained by the nature and therefore the bias of these sources. Our critics, with their paternal sense of responsibility as part of their function and of their social back-ground as burghers, had only the material side of these beggar wed-dings in mind. Their sharp condemnation of the new marriage customs reflected this point of view, which derived especially from the experi-ences of crisis and famine years. The passage of time and our historical awareness permit us to place the personal-human aspect in the foreground. In so doing, we cannot only illuminate more clearly the change in ways of life but also, in contrast to the sources, we can assess differently and more positively these pathbreaking innovations.

To begin with, it must be emphasized that it is not industrialization that altered the customs and usages of matrimony. Industrialization simply gave to a large segment of the rural population the material possibility of starting new ways. With industrialization these people could individualize courtship and marriage. This development must be viewed against a background of the larger Western tendency toward individualism, which got its decisive push in the late Renaissance and the Reformation. A transformation of the erotic consciousness is implicit in this development. A privileged layer of the urban bourgeoisie copies and takes over already developed forms of a courtly aristocratic way of life. With the dissolution of the baroque unity of life, the erotic consciousness is isolated from this heightened universal context and secularized; imbued by Pietism with a new warmth, an ego-centered Eros arises. In the first half of the nineteenth century, bourgeois love receives its outer and inner mold, which still today, dissolved and recast as the "dreamboat" of romantic love, sings to us from every radio and record player. It is in this context, sketched here with a few catch words, that we must view the transformation that was triggered by the availability of income from industry. Along with urban fashions and the luxurious tastes of the city, a spiritual-emotional attitude and its external manifestations penetrated the manufacturing population of the Zürich countryside.

Putting-out industry gave girls and boys the material prerequisites for marriage, and this possibility did away with any hesitation or fears that the young might have about knowing and getting to love each other. With no material considerations to stand in the way, one could yield to the attraction of the other sex. "The young lad," wrote Johann Schulthess, "begins, as soon as he is confirmed—as though it were a veritable initiation ceremony—to steal after one or more girls." These maidens, however, the writer continued, "knowing that they cannot get a man any other way, open their chambers to these night boys and abandon themselves to the certain or uncertain hope that, in case of pregnancy, they will not be abandoned to shame." "This picture," protested Schulthess, is not "the fantasy of an ivory-tower scholar; oh no, it is drawn from life." Reared in the countryside, he tells us that "he had witnessed as a young boy many an example of this scandalous behavior, which had become much more serious and common in the four decades since." Schulthess referred to the inspection records of the rural pastors and cited from them a report: "The so-called practice of

315

bundling (*zu Licht gehen*) gets to be looked upon as a right and a freedom, and to be considered as nothing sinful. Marriage is always the sequel of pregnancy" (Schulthess 1818: 54 ff,).

Once again it would be wrong to see the form of courtship known as bundling—*z'Licht go*, as it is called in the Zürich countryside—as a product of the means of existence offered by the putting-out industry. Bundling goes back to preindustrial times and arises essentially from the circumstances of small peasant and village life. Only with the coming of home industry was bundling taken over by a much larger population.

The contemporary sources are full of complaints about the bundling customs in the industrial areas. J. C. Nüscheler, who for seventeen years was chairman of the Matrimonial Court, wrote that toward the close of the eighteenth century the bundling pattern became not only increasingly common between engaged couples but also between two lovers who did not think of marriage, and despite the fact that such premarital intercourse was forbidden and should have been fined (Nüscheler 1831: 29 ff.). Johann Schulthess pointed out the distinction of the moral code between industrialized and farming regions. In the industrialized areas where early, careless marriages, and beggar weddings became common, so he stated, premarital intercourse, bundling, adultery, and prostitution were also in use, whereas in the farming areas with the so-called *Anerbenrecht* chastity and pure morals still dominated (Schulthess 1818: 53 ff.).

Yet the moral code of bundling and premarital intercourse among the industrial workers, though distinct from that of the farming communities, was nevertheless subject to social control. This is indicated by the custom of the so-called *zu Ehren ziehen* (literally translated: to take him by his honor), that is the moral obligation of the lover to marry his sweetheart in case of pregnancy. This *zu Ehren ziehen* is quite frequently mentioned in the contemporary sources, but negatively evaluated as a pattern which helps to break down the moral restraint against premarital intercourse and to fortify the habits to get married only when pregnancy motivates such a step. Certainly, these behavioral patterns as regards premarital intercourse and marriage were stimulated by the new industrial earning possibilities which "dematerialized" marriage contracts and the decision of founding a household. The "dematerialization" of marriage contracts had the effect that the partnership was less bound together by property motivations and therefore could become more humanized and fragile. To put it bluntly, marriage became more a matter of human relations and less that of a property holding. The complaints, often stated in the contemporary

316

sources, about an increase of divorces in the industrial areas, have to be seen from this angle. This leads us to the aspects of family structure, family cohesion, and marital fertility.

As was pointed out above, already in the eighteenth century concerned men, conscious of the dramatic increase of population in the industrialized regions, were writing articles on the subject. People everywhere related this demographic phenomenon, often in dramatic terms, to the growth of cottage industry. We have quoted Johann Schulthess, who spoke of a "torrent of people" and cites the expression of a deceased pastor, "These people came with cotton and must die with it" (Schulthess 1818: 39). Even more vivid was the observation of a rich peasant and village official with whom Uli Brägger, The Poor Man Of the Toggenberg, conversed in 1793: "The cotton industry, like a foul pile of dung, has produced and given birth to all this vermin, this crawlin' and proud beggar pack" (Brägger 1945: vol. III, 157).

Some of these contemporary observers even took the trouble to prove statistically the relationship between cottage industry and population increase, comparing the population growth patterns of industrial districts with farming districts. Gerold Meyer von Knonau, for example, who stated that "industry had created an artificial population," went on to prove this fact by comparing the communities of the Highland district Hinwil with those of the farming district Bülach (Meyer von Knonau 1867: V).[15] In 1792 J. C. Hirzel did the same comparison for an industrial community of the Lake district, Wädenswil, and a farming community of another district nearer the city of Zürich. He also gave data about the number of cottage workers in these two communities: 1,965 or one fourth of the population in Wädenswil, and 176 or $\frac{1}{22}$ of the population in the farming community, Regensberg, mentioning that 44 of the 176 had taken up industrial work only in the last two years (Hirzel 1792: 121ff.).

Contemporary observers agreed that the surplus of births and the increase in population in the industrialized areas primarily rested on two causes: the habit of marrying earlier and an increased frequency of marriages. Some writers also thought that marriages were becoming more fecund among industrial workers. C. Meiners, for example, advocated this view: "The prospect of industrial earnings by himself and his children leads to the habit that the countryman will no longer set untimely and anxious limits to the fertility of his marriage" (Meiners 1791: 47). This motive about the children's earning capacities was often brought up to support the opinion of more fertile marriages

---

[15] For a comparison of the growth pattern of these two districts see Table 8–1.

among the industrial classes. J. C. Hirzel must have shared the same opinion before he investigated statistically these matters in the Highland community of Fischenthal and came to the conclusion that most probably not an increase but a decrease of the marital fertility must have taken place. He was so surprised at this result that he did not trust his data and reflected the possibility of incomplete records for the earlier times (Hirzel 1792: 77).

We will come back to this question in Section III, but have to draw attention to the fact that the industrial population cannot be viewed here as a whole; we have to make distinctions.

In those places where the industrial population was still able to keep something of its peasant holdings or, especially true for the Highlands, was acquiring new land, other circumstances prevailed than among the landless cottage workers. It is striking how property in the soil leads to the preservation of kinship ties even in putting-out circles. The practice of *Rastgeben* (allowances from children to parents) could not assume among propertied families those forms that it did among the families of landless cottage workers. Wherever a mountain peasantry established itself on the basis of industrial earnings, the children were obliged to devote their efforts to the common economy. They could not abandon the task of earning the costs of the property by spinning and weaving. How much of this customary compulsion determined the fate of the daughters, especially, is known to us from the accounts of an old woman silk weaver. She reports that her family counted on her earnings as a matter of course. "Only wait until your daughter grows up," the neighbor said to her father, "then you can put some money aside." Naturally one gave up the money earned in this way to the family and used it for the common household or those of the brothers. The sister of the informant wove at home until her fortieth year, putting all her earnings into the common pot. In such a familial economic unit, the bonds between parents and children, determined as they were by material forces, were strong, and no restrictions were placed on the fecundity of a marriage. Children, especially daughters, were desired. The above-mentioned neighbor of our informant himself had seven daughters.

If then we are justified in expecting from propertied marriage at the least a stable rate of fertility, this is not true for the marriages of landless cottage workers. Children were less welcome in such circles, even though they were already able to defray their own upkeep at a tender age. The parents were not unhappy to see them leave and board out with strangers. As hard and "inhuman" as we may find this today, the parents were also not unhappy to have their children die. When Uli

318

Brägger was cured of a dangerous illness, his father said to him: "God has heard your entreaties. . . . I, however, I'm willing to admit, did not think as you did, Uli, and would have considered myself and you fortunate if you had passed away" (Brägger 1945: vol. I, 126). Johann Schulthess wrote: "Hence so many parents who not only think about it, but wish loudly and openly for the death of their children. You can hear—I'm speaking now as a witness—a needy woman murmur against heaven because a child of a well-to-do neighbor has died: 'I am not so lucky,' she says. 'If one of my children fell off the bench, instead of his breaking his neck, two of them would spring up in his place.' And another woman, a gleaner, walking next to her pastor in the street and holding the hand of a lively child hardly recovered from the smallpox, says without shame in front of both of them: 'Oh, if it had only died of the smallpox' " (Schulthess 1818: 57).

This attitude toward children was determined, on the one hand, by purely external motives. The small child keeps the mother from her work. But for her, time is money. Once the child grows up and can pay for his own upkeep, it enters into the customary *Rast* (allowance) relationship. On the other hand, the inconceivably bad housing also played a role. The sharp increase in population, combined with local prohibition on construction, gave rise to a housing situation in which any increase in the size of the household necessarily had the effect of an unbearable burden.

Yet the attitude of the industrial population toward offspring and child-rearing cannot be explained from these external and material aspects alone. Property holding is, on the one hand, a matter of origin but, on the other, also a symptom of certain behavioral patterns and values. Industrial earnings provided the possibility not only of dividing property holdings but also of keeping up or even newly acquiring property holdings as well. Thus, it was a question of habits and values going hand in hand with family structure and family cohesion whether the industrial workers relied more and more (or had had to rely entirely from the beginning) on their industrial earning capacities, or used the industrial basis for the upkeep and even new acquisition of property holdings. The attitude toward the allowance system—the *Rast*—might give us some indications about the mechanism of the external and internal factors.

Rast (rest) meant originally only a certain amount of daily or weekly work load which the cottage worker was setting for himself as a goal in the endless task of spinning or weaving, or was setting as a required working load for his children before they were free to play. Later the content of this term was enlarged; among the industrial population it became the meaning for maintenance allowance: the children had to earn a certain amount of money per day or week for their maintenance; the surplus of their earnings was at their disposal. Moreover, the habit developed among the poorest industrial workers that the children left the family at a very early age, often not even ten years old, and settled with their spinning wheel somewhere else and paid as boarders the maintenance money. This practice was likewise called *Rast:* taking *Rast* (the child) and giving *Rast* (the landlady).

We emphasized above that among those families who were still firmly rooted in their own soil and property, despite the fact that industrial earnings were part of their livelihood, the *Rast* system in its developed form was not found. The children turned their earnings as a matter of course over to the economic unit of the family. The maintenance of the property had priority over individual happiness. Thus the sister of the above-mentioned informant, who lived in the house until her fortieth year, had no savings of her own. We have to recognize, however, that these were spiritual and emotional ties to the family and its property holding which lacked the three-field system kind of institutional and legal strait-jacket; these Highland families, half peasants and half cottagers, were not villagers, but lived on scattered homesteads. Many of them had traditionally an Anabaptist background which was, at least to some extent, responsible for these behavioral patterns and values as regards family loyalty and family cohesion. Some matrimonial patterns of this milieu were hardly different from those of the farming milieu; the question of who got married and at what age was likewise less an individualistic decision than a family agreement.

As soon as this spiritual and emotional tie to the family property and the soil changed, forms of the allowance system necessarily developed. Unquestionably, such a tendency became stronger with the growth of industrialization. The relationship of cause and effect cannot, however, be established in general terms, but depended in each case on the particular circumstances. Johann Conrad Nüscheler provides us with a very instructive example. On inquiring about the reason for unused and neglected holdings, he "generally" received the following answer: "My wife and I are getting old. We can't work as much as before. We also have three children, two of whom pay us each week an allowance of thirty *Batzen* (a small coin). Only the one daughter still helps us in our work. We work only as much as we can and have to, and make out our living with what the two other children give us. It would be very hard for us to find workers and day laborers, or to support a boy and a maid: board and wages are much too high. Thank God, we can make out quite well with what the children give us" (Nüscheler 1786:

38ff.). The example shows how far the process had developed in the course of a generation. For not only had the children lost their interest in their peasant holding, but in the resignation of the parents one can see that the pride of the peasant in his own land had disappeared. The source throws light on the inner composition of the family. The strongest ties to parents and farm were those of the daughter who was still working in the enterprise. The other children had merely an allowance relationship, i.e., they paid their thirty *Batzen* maintenance and no longer had any obligation to work. They had become boarders in their own family. If, in this family, still peasant, though to be sure only partially so, the changes had been able to proceed so far in a generation, we shall not be surprised by the development of the *Rast* system among those people who had had no land or property for generations; we are referring to those landless and migrant people who had to found their existence first and foremost on industrial earnings. In these circles it became not only common for the children to pay their parents their weekly maintenance allowance as soon as they were able to do industrial homework (at the age of five usually) "and to think that they have bought thereby complete independence" (Hirzel 1792: 146), but even the loosest family tie was broken, and the children went out and boarded in the homes of strangers.

The contemporary sources are full of complaints about this malpractice "which destroys the natural relationships between parents and their children" (Hirzel 1816: 15) and is responsible for "the neglect of the holy obligations of the parents" (Hirzel 1816: 15). In 1777 the State Church came out with a pastoral letter against the *Rast* system, and two years later (1779) the City Council released a mandate concerning the *Rast*. This mandate ordered that a child who had not finished school could not take *Rast* in the home of strangers. Children out of school but not yet confirmed were allowed to take *Rast* outside their families, but only in the same community and with the permission of their parents and their local pastors. They were obliged to attend religious supervision and Sunday school.[16]

The social consequences of this *Rast* system are obvious: It stamped the attitude toward marital fertility and offspring; the material motivations as well as the spiritual and emotional motives of rearing children were undermined in such a milieu. Drawing into account the inconceivably bad housing conditions in some communities as an outcome of obsolete regulations on construction, we might get a better understanding of the fact that these parents were glad to see their

[16] See Hirtenbrief über die Erziehung der Kinder auf dem Land, Zürich 1777: 47; and for the mandate see State Archive of Zürich: III AAb1.

children take *Rast* in the homes of strangers and to have them "out from under their feet." [17] In such a milieu the inner cohesion of the family was weakened to such an extent that it seems hard to speak of a parent-child relationship. Only for a short period of infancy had these *Rast*-children, as they were called, the privilege to be "integrated,"—at least in a physical sense, in their families. It is no surprise that when with the mechanization of spinning the factory system was innovated, these *Rast*-children provided the pool of children who were sent out of the home to take work and board at the factory enterprise (see Braun 1965: chapter I).

One is tempted to blame all these nuisances on industrialization, for it brought, along with its demands for labor, the material possibility of loosening family ties in such a way. And yet one must keep in mind where these people had to seek their bread before industrialization. If the father was earning his and his family's upkeep in Swabia, the daughter was working as a domestic in Zürich, the oldest son was fighting as a mercenary in Dalmatia, and the mother was trying to tide the rest of the family over at home, one can hardly speak of an inner or outer family togetherness. That was the fate of poor, small peasant families, especially in the Highland: day workers, laborers, and tolerated squatters. How about the propertied ones? Those children who had no inheritance rights either gave up the idea of founding a family and remained as valets and maids on the farm, or they were compelled to leave and make their fortune elsewhere. The critics of the eighteenth century found it easy to forget these aspects of preindustrial peasant life. They tended to place only a negative value on the social consequences of industrialization and to sing the praises of peaceful rural life. They did not want to see that many were enabled for the first time by protoindustrialization to remain in their homeland. However, the unfavorable social consequences of the *Rast* system are in no way to be gainsaid or depreciated. We are simply trying to present a balanced view of the system.

Moreover, the critics did not want to see that outdated rules on construction or on freedom of movement and other limitations of the activities of the rural subjects helped to promote malpractices such as taking *Rast* in the home of strangers by children. In areas, for example, where no construction regulations forced industrial workers to live together in one room with one or two other families—in those areas the *Rast* system in its grossest form was much less in use. To be sure, in this milieu, too, the giving and taking of *Rast* among children and their

[17] Visitationsakten (inspection reports) Wetzikoner Kapitel 1771-1772; see State Archive Zürich: E I21.

parents had developed, but the children stayed at home and the industrial family unit at least lived together in a physical sense. To a lesser degree, however, this kind of *Rast* tended also to weaken the family cohesion, or was a symptom of weakened cohesion. In addition, the earlier and more frequent marriages had the effect of shortening the years of family togetherness. These effects and the enhanced scope of independence in relation with the industrial earnings (for the children more possibilities of becoming independent, and for the parents less obligations) strengthened the tendency toward a nucleus family structure among industrial workers, with separate households and strong property separation (if they had any). In the Highland a typical form of house-construction developed in the course of industrialization, which manifests this kind of nucleus family separation: A chain of tiny little cottages were built wall to wall growing like the segments of a vascular plant. They were designed for a nuclear family earning its living with industrial homework. Only those families which were firmly rooted in property holdings, despite their dependence on industrial earnings, lacked these characteristics. But, as mentioned above, their religious background has to be recognized in evaluating their different behavioral patterns.

III

Some Final Remarks and General Conclusions

In attempting to reach some general conclusions, we are well aware that our present statistical data are in many regards insufficient and very scanty. Nevertheless, together with the qualitative empirical evidence we have, it might serve as a basis for discussing the key questions of our introductory section.

To begin with, let us have a look at the overall population movement in the course of the seventeenth and eighteenth centuries. During the seventeenth century the canton of Zürich was struck four times by the Black Death, namely 1611, 1628–1629, 1635–1636, and 1668. The plague catastrophe of 1611 was exceptionally severe, whereas the epidemic of 1668 was (with the exception of one district) a minor one, and proved to be the last time Zürich had to suffer from this contagious disease. Between the periods of epidemic the canton of Zürich experienced a high rate of population growth with relatively minor regional differentiations. Nevertheless, for the canton of Zürich as a whole to recover from the population setback caused by the plague took more than half a century. According to the research of Johann Heinrich Waser, one of the pioneers of demographic and socioeconomic

323

statistics of Switzerland which was done in 1780, the population of Zürich declined 42.9 percent in the period between 1610 and 1634. By 1678 the population had increased, according to Waser's data, to 133,228, i.e. still not quite the number of the year 1610 (138,932). Though lacking data for the following decade, we might guess that in the late 1780s Zürich finally had reached again the level of 1610, because these years were marked by neither epidemics nor famines. The 1790s, however, were times of famine and starvation, causing another severe population setback; in 1700 the population dropped to 115,281, that is a decrease of 13.5 percent since 1678.

Clearly, the population movement of the seventeenth century was characterized by traditional features, that is severe setbacks caused by epidemics or famines and starvations. As a result of these setbacks a rather remarkable population growth took place in plague-free periods and in years of good harvest. Johann Heinrich Waser, who recorded over centuries all the plague epidemics as well as times of famine with which the canton of Zürich was struck, made the following interesting observation as regards the demographic development and generative pattern: "Despite the heavy death rate caused by epidemics, I evaluate the damages brought about by famine and starvation as at least as severe as the former, not only because of the loss of people as such, but also as regards their effects. As soon as a pestilence is overcome, the survivors—like those who have escaped from a shipwreck—are cheerful and gay. The deceased have made room for the surviving people and left them considerable legacies. It is hard to find servants, because there is much open employment; the houses and estates are falling much below their real value; everybody is finding enough work as well as plenty of food; thus, whoever is able to marry will marry. . . . We might, therefore, state that the losses caused by pestilence can be compensated within a decade. Damages brought by famine and starvation, however, have more severe consequences, because after these catastrophes the impoverished, worn-out and discouraged people are in want of the dearest necessities of life and will need years to recover. Whoever is not in the highest degree careless will think twice before he gets married. And due to the fact that children will not be considered a blessing of God but rather a burden of married life, the population will increase very slowly." [18]

[18] See State Archive Zürich, B X 27; Waser provides statistical evidence that it was possible, indeed, to close severe gaps caused by plague within a decade. He refers to a parish, Sennwald, outside of the realm of the canton of Zürich, which was diminished by the Black Death of 1628–1629 from 609 to 144 souls, but could increase its population within five years up to 330; 75 people, however, were foreigners, among them 30 women, who married native men. The very fast recovery

Mortality and fertility data of one parish, Birmensdorf, might illustrate the growth pattern of the seventeenth century; this example supports Waser's remarks (see Table 8–3).[19] The exceptionally high rate of growth during plague-free periods is further manifested in Table 8–1: the growth rate for the canton of Zürich as a whole between 1634 and 1671 is 48.8 percent, despite the fact that the years 1635–1636 and (though not severe) 1668 were marked by plague epidemics. The regional growth rates of this period show two noteworthy features. First, there are relatively minor regional differentiations. Neglecting Hinwil with a growth rate of 93.6 percent, the growth rates of all the other districts vary between a low of 34.9 percent (Zürich) and a high of 64.4 percent (Andelfingen). Second and more important, we find no growth patterns showing a striking difference between the flatter parts of the canton and the hilly and mountainous regions, which later became industrialized.

Finally, a look at the population density in the year 1671 displays differentiations varying from a low of 49 (Pfäffikon) to a high of 119 (Meilen). The most densely populated districts (Meilen and Horgen) belong to the lake area; the flatter regions, which during the eighteenth century remained agrarian (Andelfingen, Bülach, and Regensberg) follow next; the hilly and mountainous districts of the Highland (Hinwil, Pfäffikon and Uster) still have, together with Winterthur, the lowest density.

These references suggest the following demographic posture for the seventeenth century. Up to the last quarter of the century the generative patterns were determined by mortality, for example, by severe setbacks caused by the Black Death. In no parts of the canton did preventive check mechanisms have to bring the population into line with resources. There was not only "plenty of room" in the canton itself but

---

from the plague epidemic of 1635–1636 might be illustrated by three parishes of the canton of Zürich, belonging to the fruitful agrarian region of the northern part: Within a decade these parishes had reached again the level of 1634 as the following data show:

	1634	1637	1643	1646	1659
Stammheim	1,716	1,429	1,670	1,754	1,812
Ossingen	655	558	693	714	756
Marthalen	703	680	769	840	862

see Schnyder 1925: 36

[19] See Max Baer 1926: 12 ff.; In the period 1667–1673 the average mortality was 2.8 percent and the average natality 4.4 percent; in the period 1768–1775 both the average mortality and natality were 2.9 percent. Birmensdorf became slightly industrialized during the eighteenth century; in 1780 about one-twelfth of the population was engaged with spinning or weaving. We are well aware that data from only one community are insufficient.

TABLE 8–3. MORTALITY AND NATALITY DATA OF BIRMENSDORF (DISTRICT OF KNONAU)

Year	Mortality	Natality
1635	7.8%	4.7%
1636	2.3	4.3
1637	1.7	5.3
1638	1.6	5.5
1639	4.0	5.0
1640	2.5	5.0
1641	1.4	4.9
1642	3.9	6.2
1643	2.1	5.0
1644	2.3	5.0
1689	2.8	3.9
1690	2.9	1.6
1691	2.2	2.3
1692	3.3	2.3
1693	7.1	2.1
1694	5.5	1.9
1695	2.0	2.9
1696	1.1	4.0
1697	3.1	4.0
1698	2.0	3.3
1699	2.1	1.9
1700	3.0	2.4
1701	2.4	3.6
1702	2.4	3.1
1703	2.1	2.6
1704	2.0	4.0
1705	4.9	4.2
1706	2.8	4.4
1707	2.9	4.5
1708	1.9	4.6
1740	2.5	2.7
1741	2.6	3.7
1742	2.4	2.4
1743	2.3	3.0
1744	5.2	3.4
1745	3.9	3.1
1746	3.1	3.3
1747	2.1	2.5
1748	2.9	4.8
1749	2.9	3.6
1750	3.3	3.3
1751	2.0	3.9
1752	3.0	3.1
1753	3.2	3.0
1754	3.3	3.6

also, due to the effects of the Thirty Years' War, after the Peace Treaty of Westphalia, attractive migration opportunities to neighboring states. We might, therefore, assume that the frequency of marriage as well as marital fertility were relatively high and the age of marriage low. At the end of the third quarter of the century, however, it seems that the population was approaching a certain level of saturation in regard to the still traditional resources. This was true particularly, in the flatter agrarian districts. An indication of this phenomenon is the fact that the communities of these districts, in connection with other endeavors of a closed shop policy, now increased their efforts to get from the city council the confirmation for higher fees of settlement for newcomers. As far as the hilly and mountainous districts are concerned, the cottage industry was still quite undeveloped at this time and could not contribute significantly as an exogenous factor to the traditional resources. Hence, population pressure started to build up, manifested in the milieu of misery, mentioned in Section II, with its forced streams of migration in search for a livelihood. The so-called "Descriptions of all Paupers of the Canton of Zürich," that is, books where the recipients of alms and their personalia were recorded, show that the *miseria* of these regions was alarming even before the time of famine and starvation of the 1790s.[20] Judging from the population decrease between 1671 and 1700, mainly caused by the famine years, we have to assume that in all parts of the canton a high proportion of the people lived on the edge of poverty at this time. The rate of decrease was highest in Meilen (15.8 percent), a lake district, followed by an agrarian district of the flatter part (Andelfingen = 9.7 percent) and again by a lake district (Horgan = 8.4 percent).[21] Families belong to the positive checks; that is, the death rate is highest among the poor people.[22] We might therefore assume that throughout the canton of Zürich the mortality of the poor people was exceptionally high during the 1790s. This is relevant for the social composition of the society.

Turning now to the eighteenth century, the demographic features changed drastically, especially as regards the regional differentiations. This is illustrated by the sharply different growth rates as well as

[20] Such "Descriptions" exist for the years 1649, 1660, 1680 and 1700; see State Archive sub F I 354–357; a comparison between 1680 and 1700, i.e. before and after the time of famine and starvation, is especially instructive.

[21] See Tables 8–1 and 8–2. It must be emphasized, however, that these rates of population decrease between 1671 and 1700 are a rather insufficient and questionable indication for the proportionate death toll caused by these famine years of the 1790s in regard to the various districts. Differentiations of the growth rate, e.g. between 1671 and 1690, can significantly distort the picture.

[22] It might be mentioned that the Black Death was also to a certain degree related to the socioeconomic position, i.e. the poor had to suffer more than the rich.

changes in the population densities. Comparing the growth rate between 1671 and 1792 we get the following scale: [23]

Hinwil	= 131.3%		Winterthur	= 51.8%
Pfäffikon	= 111.8%		Knonau	= 42.6%
Uster	= 79.2%		Bülach	= 13.1%
Meilen	= 75.5%		Andelfingen	= 4.3%
Horgen	= 69.3%		Regensberg	= 4.2%

Taking from Table 8–1 the average growth rate of our three Highland districts on the one hand and of the three farming districts on the other, we get a more detailed picture of the different growth patterns of these two regions after 1700: [24]

	Highland	Farming
1700–1762	84.5%	15.6%
1762–1771	−7.5%	−15.0%
1771–1792	26.6%	15.4%
1792–1812	12.9%	8.4%
1812–1833	17.1%	21.7%

The above data show that during the first half of the century the two growth patterns were very distinct, leveling off in the second half and reversing in the first half of the nineteenth century, when cottage industry declined and the factory system developed.

The population density for the period 1671–1792 changed as follows:

1671	*1792*
Meilen	Meilen
Horgen	Horgen
Andelfingen	Hinwil
Bülach	Pfäffikon
Regensberg	Uster
Knonau	Knonau
Uster	Winterthur
Winterthur	Bülach
Pfäffikon	Andelfingen
Hinwil	Regensberg

[23] Compare this scale with the data of Table 8–4 about the degree of protoindustrialization of the various districts.

[24] H = average growth rate of the three Highland districts: Hinwil, Pfäffikon and Uster. F = average growth rate of the three farming districts: Andelfingen, Bülach and Regensberg.

Comparing the two scales we see that the three Highland districts ascend, whereas the three farming districts descend: Hinwil gains seven positions, Pfäffikon five, and Uster two; Andelfingen and Regensberg lose five positions and Bülach three. Meilen and Horgen, the two lake districts, still hold first and second place. Figure 8–1 provides a detailed picture of the changes of the scale for our three proto-industrialized Highland districts and the three farming districts after 1634. According to our census years, the most drastic changes took place between 1700 and 1762; there is empirical evidence that the crucial period was approximately between 1740 and 1765, especially during the boom period of the Seven Years' War.

The average density of the three farming districts in the year 1671, that is, at a time when the setbacks caused by previous plague epidemics were more than compensated: 1634 = 46 per square kilometer and 1671 = 68 per square kilometer. In the year 1792 the average density had only risen to 73 per square kilometer. The average density of the three protoindustrialized Highland districts rose in the same period from 53 to 108. Even the districts with the most mountainous backwood communities, Pfäffikon, was more densely populated in 1792 than the farming districts. This serves as an indication of how greatly the developing cottage industry enhanced the "living space" of the Highland communities, that is, added to the traditional resources—combined or exclusively—new ones, whereas the resources of the farming districts stagnated. Yet, we might recall from Section II that it needed special legal preconditions for the utilization of these enhanced earning potentialities. The farming districts in turn had to apply legal and customary checks to protect their limited resources.

In short, with the development of protoindustry, distinct regional features of population growth occurred during the first half of the eighteenth century. It is difficult to analyze the set of interrelated demographic variables—mortality, fertility, nuptiality, and migration—which were responsible for these regional differentiations of growth patterns. We do not have sufficient empirical evidence for such a task. Nevertheless, we might venture some tentative conclusions.

As regards mortality, the eighteenth century was much less marked by population setbacks caused by epidemics or famines. Plague had vanished. The occasional epidemics of dysentery and smallpox were more local in nature and caused relatively minor ravages.[25] With the exception of 1770–1771, times of severe famine and starvation were also lacking. To be sure, there were years of good and bad harvest as well

[25] Epidemics of dysentery were recorded for the years 1709, 1712, 1744, 1763, and 1768; small pox epidemics for the year 1715 and in the late 90s; see Brunner and Senti 1937: 6f.

TABLE 8–4. DISTRIBUTION OF COTTON INDUSTRY 1787 [a]

Districts	Number of cotton handlooms	Number of cotton spinners	Number of people per cotton handloom [b]	Number of people per cotton spinner [b]
Knonau	12	4,584	844	2
Horgen	1,647	3,288	10	5
Meilen	1,253	2,315	13	7
Hinwil	659	8,308	30	2
Pfäffikon	452	6,254	38	3
Uster	1,997	2,754	6	4
Winterthur	210	2,203	97	9
Andelfingen	8	470	1,537	26
Bülach	14	765	1,025	19
Regensberg	5	556	2,103	19

Source: State Archive of Zürich : A 76

[a] The district of Zürich has been left out; it is a special case.

[b] These population data are not for the year 1787 but 1792 (see Table 8–1).

as times of dearness and depression, but they were less Europe-wide phenomena. Moreover, improved state-controlled food provision and storage, as a result of a new—we might call it "cameralistic"—understanding of governmental functions, helped in the eighteenth century to ease such times of want as long as they were regional in nature.[26] Whether there was a stronger resistance against illness and disease among the lower classes due to their protoindustrial earnings and enriched diets, has to remain an open question. Some empirical evidence supports such an assumption.[27]

Although the eighteenth century experienced severe population set-

[26] These improved mechanisms of food supply were, of course, not unrelated to the protoindustrial development. Industrial earning potentialities enhanced the buying capacity of the people of the countryside. This was true not only for the cottage workers but also for the peasants, because the consumer demands of the former gave the latter selling opportunities, brought them closer to the market, and stimulated their market orientation within the limits of the still traditional agrarian structure. A host of new functions, tasks, and obligations of the state, which developed or enhanced during the eighteenth century, are relevant, to mention only a few: food storage, price control, new measurement against epidemic disease, new training of midwives, public health generally, the invention and propagation of special meals for the poor in times of want, and so on. These aspects are especially relevant for changing mortality features of the lower order of society.

[27] For these aspects of diet and nutrition of the cottage workers see Rudolf Braun 1960: 90 ff; we might mention that it was mainly due to the famine of 1770–1771 that in the canton of Zürich potatoes became a component of the daily menu and soon provided the basic diet for the cottage workers, particularly in times of dearness and depression.

330

backs, it would be incorrect to speak of a fundamental change of mortality patterns inasmuch as the lower order of society was still especially vulnerable to traditional positive checks; a high proportion of the population remained caught in the Malthusian circle. The population decreases in the period 1762–1771 serve as an indication. Both positive checks were operating during this period, namely epidemics of dysentery in 1763 and 1768 and the famine of 1770–1771; the latter caused not only a sharp increase in the death rate but also a sharp decline in the birth rate in the early 1770s.[28]

The absence of severe population setbacks helps to explain the more rigid closed shop policy of the farming communities in the eighteenth century. Not being willing or able to change their socioeconomic structure to provide more "living space" for the people, they had to apply legal preventive checks. This created push forces: migration as servants, maids, or mercenaries became means to postpone marriage or to remain single; short or long distance migration in order to find a new place for settling and living. We have to assume that these forms of migration were the most effective means to hold the population in line with the limited resources. In addition, there are indications of postponed marriage and forced celibacy among those remaining at home; at least there is evidence of such behavioral patterns among the wealthier peasant families.[29]

By contrast, the demographic posture of communities with proto-industrialization seemed to be marked by little or no push forces provoking migration, a high frequency of marriage and a relatively low age of marriage due to the lack of motivations to postpone wedlock. Marital fertility could have been slightly higher than that of the farming communities as a result of the lower age of marriage; empirical evidence, however, is insufficient to prove this point.[30]

To return to the questions raised in our introductory section, this

[28] We have to emphasize that the data of 1771 are rather inaccurate due to the fact that this census was connected with an account of food stock. This helps to explain the fact that among the four districts with exceptionally high population decreases are all three farming districts: the farming communities had to hide more food stock and hence were more opposed to the census. We are not in a position to provide curves of birth and death rates for the eighteenth century. Data for several Highland communities, however, show from 1768 to 1771 a sharp increase of the death rate and from 1770 to 1773 a sharp decline of the birth rate.

[29] See Oertli-Cajacob 1974; Benken is situated in the agrarian district Andelfingen.

[30] The average household size of the farming community Marthalen was e.g. 1771 4.7 and that of the industrialized highland community Fischenthal 1771 5.5; see State Archive sub B IX. See also T. R. Malthus, 1872: Book II, Chapter V ("Of the Checks to Population in Switzerland"). Malthus, using the data provided by M. Muret, describes similar contrasting demographic patterns: Leysin, a pastoral parish in the Alps, with a high degree of preventive checks on the one hand, and parishes in the hilly region of the Jura, where protoindustry (watch making) was common, without such preventive checks.

case study suggests the following conclusions. Just like other regions of continental Europe where protoindustrialization played a dominant role as a source of likelihood, the industrial districts of the canton of Zürich experienced a considerable population growth during the eighteenth century.[31] This demographic phenomenon well preceded the so-called "Industrial Revolution" or the "breakthrough into modern economic growth." The different population development of the farming districts supports the fact that the growth pattern was clearly linked to protoindustrialization. It seems, however, incorrect to use the label "Demographic Revolution" to characterize this phenomenon. The reasons are twofold: First, as we pointed out, similar demographic features could be recognized during the seventeenth century after plague epidemics and in famine-free periods. At that time cottage industry was still quite undeveloped. Distinct regional differentiations of growth patterns, however, were lacking. Secondly, the population swingback caused by the famine of 1770–1771 demonstrates that a sustained population growth was still not guaranteed by the economic circumstances of protoindustry. The decrease of the birth rate as a result of this famine indicates that society, in the farming districts as well as in the industrialized districts, still reacted in a traditional way.

Yet the population development of the eighteenth century brought demographic transformations, which were new and have to be labeled as protoindustrial in nature. Due to the different growth patterns of the peasants and the cottage workers, the proportion of people in the countryside who had little or no property and depended for their living mainly or exclusively upon protoindustry rose drastically.

This brought fundamental changes in the social composition of society; changes in terms of property, income, wealth, and occupational distribution; changes in the protection of property rights and status privileges of all kinds; a new comprehension and style of rule; new forms and mechanisms of approbation to political functions and power, to social circles or economic resources—to mention only a few aspects and dimensions. Part of these transformations was a need of developing new values and behavioral patterns—and of reinterpretation of old ones—related to these and other fields of political, legal, social, and economic life and actions. Furthermore, coming back to the steadily

[31] The same phenomenon can be found in other rural areas in Western and Central Europe which experienced protoindustrial developments. See Wolfram Fischer 1973. Fischer mentions: Ulster, Yorkshire, Lancashire, Brittany, Flanders, Montjoie, Alsace, and many strips along the Rhine down to the Low Countries, Lombardy, Piedmont, parts of Westphalia, Saxony, Lusatia, Bohemia, Silesia and Lower Austria. A demographic comparison of these protoindustrialized rural areas would be a rewarding task.

growing number of people who based their life upon protoindustrial earnings, we tried to illustrate what a wide range of transformations took place as a result of or closely related to their new protoindustrial existence: the developing of new pretensions, new hopes, expectations, fears for the future, and so on; the need for new values, behavioral patterns, and wants in regard to work, leisure, feeding of themselves, their family and kinsmen, consumption patterns, outlook on life and death as well as a host of other aspects of human life—including those which are (directly or indirectly) of demographic relevance like courtship customs, sexual behavioral patterns or those toward birth and child-rearing, family cohesion, and so on.[32] Again, we have to consider aspects of reinterpretation of traditional values, patterns, needs, expectations, and whether these reinterpretations actually fitted the position and situation of these people or if they were merely nationalizations of their posture.

Our sources illustrated how contemporaries belonging to sociopolitical privileged groups and rooted in a traditionally secure milieu observed developments with great concern; they were conscious of the fact that these transformations would have a great impact upon social conditions, economic circumstances, and the future of the state. Proposals to cut to size the "dangerously" growing number of these propertyless people by legal means, i.e. by preventive matrimonial laws, became more numerous and intrusive. People were haunted by the specter of pauperism; it vanished only when the breakthrough to modern economic growth was accomplished around the middle of the nineteenth century.

These changes connected with protoindustry have to be evaluated as crucial factors in the process of socioeconomic development and modernization generally. This brings up a whole set of aspects and relationships. It is not even possible to touch on these complex questions. Some effects are obvious, for example, the importance of these changes for the creation of a potential industrial labor force—a growing number of people who were willing and able to base their existence upon industrial earnings with all its insecurities and to adapt their whole life to these new circumstances. A host of effects, however, are more hidden or less directly related but of equal importance; for example, changes in the civil law, particularly concerning protection of individual property, or changes of the tax system as a reaction to or motivated by these transformations. If the term "Demographic Revolution" should be applied at all, it has to take notice of and refer to these sketchy outlined aspects of transformation, and has to include the

---

[32] For detailed illustration of these and other transformations, see Braun 1960.

fact that the growth of these people rooted in the protoindustrial milieu could hardly have been sustained without the before-mentioned economic developments and social, legal, and political changes, which in turn were related to and influenced by this demographic phenomenon.

The eighteenth century and demographic problems in connection with protoindustrialization are, indeed, a fascinating topic because they get to the roots of processes, which lead right up to questions of pressing importance of the present, especially in regard to the relationship between industralized and non- or less-industrialized nations.

It is to be hoped that the case study of the protoindustrializing canton of Zürich might illustrate the relevance of a more qualitative approach to demographic problems—a remark, which intends in no way to denigrate the more quantitative approach; the two are complementary: both have to supplement and support each other and to serve as mutual stimulations for new lines of questioning.

9
Questions and Conclusions

CHARLES TILLY

WHAT changes a population's fertility? What keeps it constant? We have not arrived at a simple reply, a single explanatory model, or even at a standard list of determinants. Yet the net effect of the explorations in this book is to narrow considerably the range of plausible explanations, as compared with those which are being seriously proposed today. That is true on the side of general explanations. As I read them, our chapters raise significant doubts concerning the whole range of arguments in which the diffusion of new contraceptive aspirations, techniques, and information is the major mechanism of fertility change. In my view, they provide strong support for arguments balancing the costs of contraception and child care against the changing life chances of children. It is also true on the historical side. The book weighs, it seems to me, against the interpretation of fertility changes in Europe and America as resulting from changing enthusiasm for children and for family life. They call attention to a variety of social arrangements which maintained some sort of balance between the incentives and opportunities to marry and have children, on the one hand, and the carrying capacity of the environment, on the other. The book's tendency, then, runs against Malthusian, ideological and technological theories. It runs toward theories emphasizing the rational pursuit of long-run individual, household, family or community objectives.

Before discussing the general questions and conclusions which merge from the entire book, let me review the character of each chapter separately.

I
RICHARD EASTERLIN, "THE ECONOMICS AND SOCIOLOGY OF FERTILITY

EASTERLIN integrates an analysis of the determinants of desired number of children with an analysis of the extent and effectiveness of fertility control. The first follows the main lines of recent economic writing on fertility, to which Easterlin himself has been a significant contributor.

335

The second is more adventurous, for it places a variety of insights and arguments from sociology and other disciplines within a formal economic framework. Easterlin performs the synthesis by postulating a natural fertility level which is more or less known and more or less fixed over the span of a household's fertility decisions, and then by treating the demand for fertility regulation as a function of its cost and of the discrepancy between desired number of children and the number of children surviving under natural fertility.

A significant part of Easterlin's contribution is conceptual. It places the available arguments concerning fertility decisions in a single framework. Yet it has theoretical and empirical implications. For example, Easterlin shows that a relationship between fertility level and household income is likely to have two components: one affecting the demand for children and the other affecting the supply; economists have neglected the supply side of this relationship. He shows that in a variety of circumstances a maximizing household will end up with more than its preferred number of children—not because of bad luck or inefficiency but because fertility regulation costs something. More unexpectedly, he points out the considerable possibility of excess demand for children because of high mortality. That is an important result; it strengthens a weak point of the existing economic literature, ties together a number of historical observations concerning the impact of mortality changes on fertility, and helps explain not only the apparent resistance of many poor populations to reducing fertility but also the occasional long-run *rise* in fertility as incomes increase.

In Easterlin's scheme, the major sources of change in fertility are changes in income, in the cost of children relative to goods, in the cost of fertility regulation, and in tastes. The change in tastes, I think, poses the greatest difficulties. It is not clear why the taste for expensive consumer goods should grow faster than, say, the taste for highly educated children. Easterlin theorizes that over a long period of rising incomes, each generation establishes a subsistence "floor" to its indifference curves below which no substitution of children for goods provides any satisfaction, and that as a consequence of forming its tastes in a period of rising welfare each generation sets that floor higher than the previous one; but why shouldn't it work the other way round: a fertility floor below which people would rather starve than go childless? I suspect that the theory needs a greater emphasis on the direct costs and opportunity costs of children in terms of household labor. It needs more ample allowance for shifts in the labor-intensiveness of child care as a result of changes in the desired characteristics of offspring. It needs recognition that the extent to which having children insures the

336

continuity of the household depends on how much employment is available outside the household.

II

E. A. WRIGLEY, "FERTILITY STRATEGY FOR THE INDIVIDUAL AND THE GROUP"

THE continuity of the household commands a major part of Wrigley's attention. His chapter pursues two profound questions: How is it possible for a population to be self-regulating? How do varying mortality conditions affect the appropriate fertility strategy for the survival of the household, family, kin group or entire population? With respect to self-regulation, there is the possibility of individual or small-group rationality compounded by some mediating mechanism into the interest of the group as a whole; there is also the possibility of a large-group rationality which strongly constrains individuals and small groups but does not necessarily produce individual benefits for all of them.

The rationality may be conscious or unconscious. Wrigley suggests that in the transition from preindustrial to industrial social organization, western populations moved from (1) an unconscious group rationality which tended to hold total population between the environment's carrying capacity and the minimum size for survival to (2) a conscious individual rationality which gave no guarantee of an optimum for the population as a whole. In the preindustrial stage, the importance of inheritance committed the individual to the family and the family to the community as a whole. But the advent of industrialism snapped the links.

The bulk of Wrigley's analysis deals with the impact of mortality on preindustrial problems. Via a set of model populations, he shows that under conditions of high mortality (roughly speaking, with a life expectancy at birth of less than forty years) the effort to product a single surviving heir of a given sex will tend to result in very large completed family sizes, yet will frequently fail. In the hypothetical high-mortality populations under discussion, a significant minority of households will have more than one heir to provide for, but a larger minority will have none at all. The situation provides strong incentives to high fertility. As mortality declines, however, the effect of a high-fertility strategy changes drastically. If the opportunities to be transmitted to the succeeding generation remain limited, a high-fertility strategy becomes disastrous at levels much above the threshold of forty years' life expectancy. The children have no place to go; the household is stuck with them.

337

Even in prosperous western countries most populations have only passed the mortality threshold in the last century or so. To the extent that they were, indeed, strongly concerned about heirship, a large minority of western households have probably been in a situation of excess demand for children through most of history. But other households had too many children. The balancing occurred through such institutions as arranged marriage, farming out of excess children, and temporary sharing of housing. The essential institutions, Wrigley speculates, were formed through an essentially evolutionary process. Those groups which adopted them survived, while other groups destroyed themselves through over- or underpopulation. The institutions, however formed, constituted a group rationality which strongly constrained individual rationality.

Amid these more general hypotheses, Wrigley observes the specific mechanisms linking individual behavior to collective welfare. He points out that early marriage of sons whose fathers have died has very stringent limits as a survival strategy for a high-mortality population as a whole. The distribution of deaths is such that a large proportion of males will be too young to marry at the deaths of their fathers, while another large proportion will still have to live long years of celibate adulthood while their fathers are alive. The alternative of a standard age of marriage will be costly, however, since it does not permit the matching of family formation to fluctuations in the availability of niches within the group. For example, as Wrigley observes, the rule that every couple should begin marriage in its own dwelling implies either the tuning of marriage to variations in the housing supply or the maintenance of a housing stock larger than the population's average requirements. Temporary co-residence of households—especially the expectation that newlyweds will lodge with the parents of the bride or the groom—allows an escape from both alternatives. Thus a series of social arrangements which have often seemed traditional, and therefore nonrational, begin to take on meaning as collective adaptations to poverty and high mortality. Among those social arrangements are many which provide incentives to high fertility.

Despite the sureness of his steps, Wrigley's bold march through the past leaves questions strewn along the path. Explanations of social arrangements in terms of their functions or their survival value are notoriously hard to falsify; they turn easily to useless tautology. To take Wrigley's arguments concerning particular institutions as a program for research requires an enormous cost-benefit analysis of historically existing arrangements and their theoretical alternatives or a grand comparison of populations which survived with others which disappeared. Although Wrigley's analysis of the promotion of high fertility by high mortality is illuminating and persuasive for the hypothetical cases considered, it remains to match the models with historical instances and to determine what proportion of the total population was caught up in the grim contest among a relatively fixed set of local niches, deaths of occupants of those niches, and births to other occupants. In the case of Europe, we must ask whether the cities and wage-labor did not long offer an escape for the surplus population: an escape to misery or death, perhaps, but an escape which increased the play in the local system. Like all really effective theoretical enterprises, Wrigley's analysis increases the need for close observations to match the hypothetical relationships with the world which actually happened.

III

LUTZ BERKNER AND FRANKLIN MENDELS, "INHERITANCE SYSTEMS, FAMILY STRUCTURE AND DEMOGRAPHIC PATTERNS IN WESTERN EUROPE (1700–1900)"

BERKNER and Mendels want to trace the effects of inheritance customs—especially the degree of partibility—on nuptiality, migration, and overall fertility level. Their chapter complements Wrigley's, since it examines the character, extent, and effectiveness of constraints which Wrigley's models take for granted. Since historians often argue that partible inheritance accelerates the fragmentation of holdings, the building up of population pressure and general impoverishment of peasants, the chapter also touches an important element in historical interpretations of change in the western countryside.

Like Wrigley, Berkner and Mendels assume that people would generally rather marry locally than emigrate or remain single. More so than Wrigley, they assume that the variations in nuptiality which accompany different inheritance systems significantly affect the associated levels of fertility. Much more than Wrigley, they inquire into the conditions promoting the appearance of diverse forms of compound household. They conclude that the tendency of partibility to promote fragmentation of holdings is genuine but weak, and that inheritance arrangements have relatively strong, direct effects on household composition. Partibility does not have the devastating divisive effects which simple arithmetic leads us to anticipate because local endogamy tends to reconsolidate fragmented holdings, because much of the land peasants work is leased rather than owned, because under high mortality there are few surviving heirs, and because the principals involved often go to great lengths to avoid subdividing holdings which are already at the minimum required to support a household.

This last observation involves fertility and strategies of heirship most directly. Berkner and Mendels conclude that in western Europe a strong pressure for preferential partibility grew up—regardless of the legal and customary constraints—wherever the maintenance of intact holdings was important to the welfare of succeeding generations. The preference could operate through enforced celibacy of some children remaining on the land (see Bourdieu 1962), through preferential marriage or through out-migration of "surplus" children, but in one way or another it required that some potential heirs modify their rightful claims. Because all of these arrangements were costly, peasant households working within any inheritance system had a strong incentive to restrict births once they had the desired complement of heirs.

Berkner and Mendels check out some of the implied relationships via a straightforward cross-sectional regression analysis of characteristics of French departements in 1856. It reveals the expected association between impartible inheritance and complex households, between impartible inheritance and high marital fertility, between impartibility and out-migration, between partibility and female nuptiality, as well as the negative associations between farm fragmentation and both household complexity and female nuptiality. As Berkner and Mendels say, relationships estimated at such a high level of aggregation cannot clinch the case; they simply provide the warrant for further investigation of the same hypotheses. The major contribution of their work is its portrayal of inheritance arrangements, marital fertility, migration, and household composition as mutually dependent parts of a general effort to assure the continuity of peasant households and families.

IV

RONALD LEE, "MODELS OF PREINDUSTRIAL POPULATION DYNAMICS"

LEE's major effort goes into formulating, estimating, and testing simple but precise models of preindustrial population control systems. At the request of other members of the seminar, Lee includes a more extensive methodological discussion—especially concerning the logic of cross-spectral analysis—than he would ordinarily address to fellow econometricians. The central models state the alternative relationships among temporary fluctuations in wages, mortality, nuptiality, fertility, and total population. They begin with wages and mortality exogenous to the system, then successively incorporate them into the system.

The main arguments Lee considers are fairly straightforward: diminishing returns to labor, mortality change as a determinant both of wages and of population size, fluctuations in marriages as the chief source of fluctuations in births, and so on. To be more exact, Lee consistently examines both such general arguments and the main alterna-tives to them; his method is frequently to define a parameter whose various possible values correspond to competing arguments, then to estimate the parameter with the best time-series data available. The best data are often not very good, so that Lee allows us to regard the estimates as solid evidence or as proposals for more detailed research. Even with superb data, the estimation and testing of these apparently straightforward hypotheses would be complicated; some of Lee's most valuable observations concern the effects of varying assumptions built into the models. For example, he shows that "an observed positive association of mortality and wages is quite consistent with a negative structural relation between the two, provided that the independent variation of mortality is considerably greater than that of wages."

Both the theoretical results and the empirical ones comment effec-tively on available ideas concerning historical fluctuations in fertility. On the theoretical side, Lee demonstrates that even in principle chang-ing nuptiality can only be a weak, partial determinant of fertility fluc-tuations. The fact that they frequently co-vary closely happens, in his view, because they *both* responded to the changes in opportunity repre-sented in his models by real wages. (Lee does not deny any relation-ship between nuptiality and fertility; he regards the characteristic marriage pattern as strongly affecting a population's average fertility.)

On the empirical side, he finds evidence that fluctuations in wages and mortality are negatively related in the short run, and positively related in the long run. The finding is consistent with the idea that death rates rise in times of hardship, but that over a longer run the labor shortage induced by high mortality levels tends to push the wages up. His estimates also suggest that the demand for labor in England was relatively constant from the thirteenth to the seventeenth century, but began shifting upward and significantly affected the whole population control system in the eighteenth. He cautiously proposes that the shift marks the movement from social arrangements which stabilized the return to labor but were vulnerable to exogenous fluctua-tions in mortality into social arrangements broadly corresponding to the supply-demand interdependence of wages and labor envisaged by the classical economists.

Clearly the work does not end there. Lee's inquiry leads in three important directions: toward the compilation of more and better series suitable for the estimation and testing of the same models; to-ward the clearing up of uncertainties, ambiguities, and conflicts in the findings; toward the deliberate pursuit of his many suggestions. It also stands as a strong injunction to model the relations surrounding fertility very carefully before plunging into statistical analysis for the purpose of estimating those relations.

V

MARIS VINOVSKIS, "FERTILITY DIFFERENTIALS AMONG MASSACHUSETTS TOWNS AND REGIONS IN 1860"

MARIS Vinovskis follows a somewhat different philosophy. His large cross-sectional analysis begins with a substantial list of variables each of which has an arguable relationship with fertility differentials, puts a great deal of effort into the measurement of those variables over a set of geographic units, and then employs an extensive statistical procedure to search for strong, persistent relationships. The approach is much less deductive than Lee's, and probably more vulnerable to spurious interpretations of the statistical results. Vinovskis reduces the likelihood of spurious interpretations by being exceedingly careful in attaching meaning to the estimated relationships.

Massachusetts and the United States have been somewhat neglected in general discussions of the demographic transition; they were, after all, major cases of early fertility decline. As Vinovskis shows in his preliminary sketch, Massachusetts was generally the lowest-fertility state of the United States during the first half of the nineteenth century; in each of the three Massachusetts regions he distinguishes, a sharp fertility decline was already under way by 1810 and continued unabated to 1850. A large part of the chapter goes into portraying the regional trends in the first half of the century, and in providing both backgrounds and justification for the individual variables to be employed in the statistical analysis.

The multivariate analysis itself compares Massachusetts towns and regions in 1860, a year for which exceptionally rich census data are available at the local level. Using a stepwise regression procedure which follows a variance-reduction criterion, it estimates the association of fifteen variables with the white refined fertility ratio. At the statewide level, lower fertility is most strongly associated with a low sex ratio, a low proportion Irish, a large town population, high commercialization, a low proportion in farming and a low level of schooling. Some of these may simply represent regional effects, since the associations greatly weaken within regions; that is notably true of town size and proportion in farming. Nevertheless, the overall pattern is consistent wtih arguments which associate low fertility with involvement in urban-industrial-commercial life. The obvious next step is to model the relationships more explicitly and tightly, then to estimate and test the models.

VI

Etienne van de Walle, "The French Fertility Decline until 1850"

If Lee's chapter displays the special strengths of the econometrician who is capable of stating and verifying his arguments precisely, and Vinovskis' chapter the virtues of the historian who knows his site, van de Walle's chapter exemplifies the comparative advantage of the demographer. His study of France belongs to a massive series of studies of the European fertility decline initiated by Ansley Coale. Van de Walle has reported the general procedures and findings in a monograph. Here he takes the extensive technical and substantive results of that largely descriptive work for granted, and pushes on to a preliminary survey of explanations for the great demographic changes in a nineteenth-century France.

The discussion acknowledges the possible significance of inheritance customs, changing employment opportunities and other variables the chapters in this book single out for attention. But it emphasizes the diffusion of contraceptive knowledge, and the decline of moral opposition to contraceptive practice. The diffusion process, in van de Walle's view, probably began with the eighteenth-century elite, and moved steadily down the hierarchy of class. Partly because he is dealing with large aggregates (in the nineteenth century the average French *département* had close to half a million people) and partly because even at the aggregate level he lacks convincing measures of the relevant communications flows, van de Walle is not able to carry the diffusion explanation to a direct test. Instead, he carries out a simple but extensive correlational analysis of associations of fertility level with various indicators of social structure over all but the most urban *départements* at numerous census years from 1801 to 1851. Although each of the statistical analyses is cross-sectional, van de Walle fortifies his interpretations by looking at lagged relationships and examining the changing pattern of relationships over time.

The analysis reveals substantial and persistent relationships between low fertility and lack of out-migration, high levels of wealth, high nuptiality, and low mortality. Van de Walle interprets the findings as showing a lag of mortality on fertility rather than the other way round, and prefers the conclusion that both respond to some third set of variables. That interpretation may hold for the crude birth rates, but the analysis of the standardized fertility measures appears to produce results consistent with a lag of fertility on mortality. The findings as a whole fall into the sort of pattern predicted by population-pressure arguments such as Dov Friedlander's. It will take both multivariate

343

modeling of the relationships and their examination at a smaller scale than the department to tell us whether the resemblance is more than superficial.

VII

RUDOLF BRAUN, "EARLY INDUSTRIALIZATION AND DEMOGRAPHIC CHANGES IN THE CANTON OF ZÜRICH"

THE final chapter does not undertake the explicit multivariate modeling, but it does bring down the scale of analysis very effectively. Braun examines the uplands behind Zürich during the time when the city was becoming the center of an important network of rural and small-town industry. Like Vinovskis and van de Walle, Braun emphasizes the complexity of the processes he is portraying. But this time the complexity is historical and cultural. Braun wants us to understand how the specific institutions of landholding, community membership, deployment of labor and so forth affected the responses of local populations to changing opportunities.

The contrast between peasants and proletarians in the Zürich region is a case study in collective vs. individual controls over fertility. For example, Braun shows that the lowland peasant communities legally imposed a *numerous clausus:* a fixed number of households permitted to live within their confines. That is an extreme (but not unique) version of the inelastic supply of niches which figures so importantly in Wrigley's arguments. Again, Braun argues explicitly that as industry spread through the uplands inheritance customs shifted significantly and people began taking advantage of the "entirely new possibilities of marriage and founding a household."

In consonance with other studies of rural industry in Europe, Braun shows the great rise in population densities as the previously marginal agricultural areas in the uplands turned to textile production in the eighteenth century. Although the direct demographic evidence is thin, Braun makes a good case for two related developments: the slowing of out-migration and the rise of nuptiality. He emphasizes the role of declining age at marriage in a presumed general rise of fertility. The evidence at hand, however, does not allow him to make a sure distinction between the effects of changes in nuptiality and changes in marital fertility.

In terms of Easterlin's setting of the problem, there are some intriguing indications that the relative cost of children actually declined as industry expanded and the possibilities of remunerative employment for youngsters proliferated inside and outside the household. Braun hints that at times there was even a positive economic incentive to breed children for the wages they brought in. Although contemporaries regarded the apparent increase of nonmarital sexual activity as evidence of the moral decay brought about by economic change, Braun's observations raise the possibility that the declining relative cost of having children—inside or outside marriage—played its part.

Braun's analysis brings out the way changes in family structure and fertility behavior can occur through the expansion and adaptation of well-established institutional forms instead of a sharp rejection of the old ways. One example is the widened use of the old institution of bundling—*zu Licht gehen*—as the context for premarital sexual experience. Another is the expansion of *Rastgeben/Rastnehmen,* an arrangement which originally set the quota for the child's contribution of labor to the household. By extension, the conventional price of that labor set the return parents expected from another household to which they farmed out a surplus child. Finally it came to be the amount a child owed the parents from wages earned elsewhere. In Braun's analysis, the evolution of *Rast* led to a situation in which the child's obligations to the household of origin dwindled to that single customary payment, in return for which the child was free to dispose of his time, person and remaining wages. If that is correct, Braun has identified one of the major mechanisms by which the expansion of wagelabor promotes nuptiality and the establishment of nuclear family households.

VIII

OVERVIEW

THESE rich, varied chapters suffice both to show that multiple analytic styles are competing for attention in historical studies of fertility, and to identify some of the gaps and inconsistencies in the literature. Two kinds of analysis which are prominent in the literature are not directly represented in this collection: the broad, discursive treatment of major population trends and the preparation of demographic estimates for small populations via some type of collective biography. (That is not because this group rejects those ways of dealing with demographic problems; Easterlin, for example, has written a number of broad interpretations of American population history, Wrigley is one of the pioneers of family reconstitution, and each of the other contributors has several styles of analysis at his command.)

In retrospect, it is especially disappointing that none of the chapters directly reports work in collective biography. Family reconstitution and related procedures are absorbing a great deal of energy, producing important results and posing urgent technical and logical questions for the field. At the center of the difficulty is the effort to arrive at estimates of vital characteristics of large, whole populations through the tracing of those individuals or families within smaller populations—such as single villages—who remain in place and visible. At the present, any of three outcomes seems possible: (1) the development of record-linkage procedures which are sufficiently capacious and accurate to permit the tracing of large, mobile populations; (2) the development of means for detecting, estimating, and correcting the biases and uncertainties introduced by reliance on different kinds of subpopulations; and (3) a shift away from the effort to estimate general demographic parameters to the analysis of differentials within well-enumerated populations. The essays do not explicitly address these choices.

With that important exception, the essays raise all the major current issues in the historical study of vital processes. Some questions recur over and over: How much preindustrial populations were self-regulating and how; what determines the alternative responses to population pressure; to what extent the forms of urbanization, industrialization, and commercialization which prevailed before the growth of large-scale industry had reliable effects on nuptiality and fertility; what were the loci and mechanisms of the long-run fertility decline in western countries; what were the demographic processes involved in the transformation of populations from agrarian to urban-industrial.

Despite great variation in the relative weights attributed to tastes, costs and income, the papers as a whole substantiate the utility of Easterlin's categories for the analysis of the western fertility decline. The major difficulties, I think, are two: first, that Easterlin's formulation seems to assume that a couple are making decisions with a view to their own present resources and future satisfactions, whereas we have encountered a number of cases where a household or a kin group appears to make collective decisions with respect to its own continuity or the welfare of its senior members; second, that children are a potential source of income as well as a good to be consumed. The difficulties are not insuperable. Yet how they are met will significantly affect our ability to connect contemporary analyses of fertility decisions with historical studies of changing fertility.

Taken together, the essays offer an interesting commentary on the economic theory of fertility. The hesitations concerning Easterlin's formulation just mentioned apply to the economic treatment as a whole. While the decisions of couples in the light of the costs and benefits of children to them are a reasonable starting point, with respect to the problems which show up in this book the existing literature gives too little place to returns from children other than the satisfactions to be gained from direct interaction with them and from vicarious participation in their accomplishments. It also slights the participation of compound households, kin groups, and communities in the crucial decisions. We may admire the humanity of economists who emphasize the pleasure children provide. In addition to pleasure we need room for the incentives of pensions, patrimony and pecuniary return.

Our authors are uncertain of the value of "natural fertility" as a foil for the analysis of actual fertility. If they are uncertain about the natural-fertility baseline model, they are even more dubious about the empirical hypothesis of a recent transition from "natural" to "controlled" fertility. Yet the essays in the volume implicitly provide strong support for Easterlin's proposal to integrate the supply side into models of household fertility decisions.

There is some division of opinion about how to do it. Easterlin proposes to sum up the essential processes through the relationship between natural and desired fertility in combination with the cost of fertility regulation. Wrigley, Braun, Berkner, and Mendels, on the other hand, call attention to the collective controls over opportunities to marry and to engage in intercourse. The collective controls are awkward to handle either as constraints on natural fertility or as costs of fertility regulation; they may well have to be modeled separately. Lee, for his part, raises doubts that varying access to marriage is a significant regulator of fertility. On conceptual, theoretical and empirical grounds, the essays lead to conflicting conclusions concerning the significance and character of collective controls. By the same token, they make it clear that the question is crucial. We have an opportunity to submit the competing models to three different kinds of scrutiny: (1) econometric analyses of the covariation of vital events and the relevant social conditions such as employment opportunities, availability of farmsteads, and so on; Lee provides a number of leads for further efforts in this direction; (2) demographic measurement and analysis of the relationships of the vital processes in particular historical populations, on the basis of models which specify the probable demographic outcomes of different types of controls; in different ways Wrigley and van de Walle show as our opportunities in this regard; (3) search for historical evidence concerning the supposed control processes themselves; Berkner, Mendels, and Braun indicate what the historical record contains. In disagreeing, our authors help fashion the means of resolving the disagreement.

A similar division of opinion arises in the discussion of preindustrial population control systems. Most of the authors assume or confirm that many western populations, especially peasant populations, were self-regulating in the sense that their arrangements for marriage, sexual relations and childbirth kept their total numbers near some equilibrium above the minimum required for group survival but well below the maximum the environment could support. Lee offers the strongest dissent; he finds the entire preindustrial population strongly influenced by the exogenous component of mortality fluctuations—that is, the portion of changes in mortality which cannot be attributed to shifts in the real wage. He challenges the role of marriage in any such control system. And he assembles evidence against the long-run equilibrium wage set by social convention. It may be that one side or the other is wrong. It may also be that Lee's analysis applies to long, large swings in mortality and the self-regulation hypothesis applies in a shorter run. It will take close analysis of substantial time series to resolve the question. As in the case of collective controls, the best strategy for confronting the disagreement concerning the extent of homeostatic processes in preindustrial populations will combine econometric, demographic, and historical testing of the same models.

Our authors make telling observations on the grand question of the demographic transition. A pervasive theme of the essays is the change in fertility which occurs as a consequence of pursuing the same family objectives under shifting conditions of mortality and employment: The fertility strategy appropriate for assuring an heir differs greatly from one level of mortality to another; the availability of employment for children affects the number of children desired without necessarily changing general attitudes toward children, and so on. The essays (even Braun's, which makes the most of the changes in life-style associated with industrial activity) stress continuities in the fundamental behavior patterns behind varying levels of fertility.

In that regard, they minimize the importance of ideological and attitudinal changes as prerequisites of the fertility decline. To take one small instance, Easterlin suggests in passing that the concomitance of changes in marital and nonmarital fertility need not count as evidence against household-economic arguments: it is likely that fertility-control innovations originate and become widely available in response to demand from married couples, but once available help the unmarried to restrict births as well. The demand for fertility control among the unmarried is already high but ineffective; when it becomes high and effective among the married, the unmarried also benefit.

More generally, the papers lead to the conclusion that the "demographic transition" is simply one of several competing theories about the usual demographic effects of large increases in per capita income. In Easterlin's neat summary, the fundamental variables are:

1. demand for children, as outcome of
   a. tastes
   b. income
   c. prices
2. potential supply of children, as outcome of
   a. natural fertility
   b. survival prospects
3. costs of fertility regulation
   a. subjective
   b. market

In his argument, the three sets co-determine actual fertility. All three clusters of variables surely shift as large changes in per capita income occur. If important alterations in health conditions occur, either exogenously or as an indirect consequence of income changes, both components of the potential supply of children should change as well.

The regularities within such a system may be very great. Yet there is no reason to think that the changes have to be highly synchronized. There is no reason to expect an invariant sequence running from high, variable mortality and high, stable fertility to low, invariable mortality and low, fluctuating fertility via a transition in which mortality decline leads the way. One of Easterlin's competitors to the demographic-transition model has fertility responding strongly and early to economic growth, thereby producing a substantial rise in actual fertility. Lee's analysis of eighteenth-century England contains the nucleus of a theory featuring mortality changes and shifting demand for labor. Instead of seeking general explanations for "the" demographic transition, the papers suggest, we should consider the demographic-transition idea one of the several available theories concerning the dynamics of large-scale demographic transformations.

One of the possibilities which arises from the discussion in this book is a sequence running from peasant society to proletarianization to *embourgeoisement;* in such a hypothetical sequence, peasant social arrangements effectively tune fertility to mortality, but restrict it nonetheless. Proletarianization tends to raise fertility. But the acquisition of property and the investment in children's futures among all classes of the population, in this argument, checks fertility more decisively than

349

ever before. To the extent that proletarianization is the dominant process we should not be surprised to find fertility remaining high as "modernization" proceeds. In this version, the fertility side of the demographic transition traces the expansion of capitalism from western Europe to the rest of the world.

I do not say that my co-authors make such an argument. I simply say that their own analyses make such an argument plausible. Their general teaching is this: The search for recurrent sequences may make some historical sense and may be of some heuristic use, but it is an unprofitable way to go about building general explanations of fertility change. From this point of view, the most valuable historical analyses isolate the relationships among the variables involved in well-documented instances of shifts in fertility. The essays in this book show that available historical evidence can, indeed, help us to assess the validity of general explanations of demographic change.

Contributors

Lutz K. Berkner is Associate Professor of History at the University of California, Los Angeles. He received his Ph.D. from Harvard University, and has been a fellow of the American Council of Learned Societies and the Shelby Cullom Davis Center for Historical Studies at Princeton University. He has published several articles on the history of the peasant family in Europe, including "The Stem Family and the Developmental Cycle of the Peasant Household: An Eighteenth-Century Austrian Example" (1972) and "Inheritance, Land Tenure and Peasant Family Structure: A German Regional Comparison" (1976).

Rudolf Braun, since 1971, has been Professor of History at the University of Zürich. He received his Ph.D. from the University of Zürich, and has taught at the University of Berne and the Free University of Berlin. In 1969–1970 he was a Fellow of the Center for Advanced Study in the Behavioral Sciences. His publications include *Industrialisierung und Volksleben* (1960) and *Sozialer und kultureller Wandel in einem ländlichen Industriegebiet im 19. und 20. Jahrhundert* (1965; awarded the Silas Marcus Macvane Prize, Harvard University, 1968) and *Sozio-kulturelle Probleme der Eingliederung italienischer Arbeitskräfte in der Schweiz.*

Richard A. Easterlin is Professor of Economics at the University of Pennsylvania, where he received his Ph.D. His publications include *Population Redistribution and Economic Growth, 1870–1950* (1957, 1960); "Toward a Socio-Economic Theory of Fertility: A Survey of Recent Research on Economic Factors in American Fertility" (1969); "Toward a More General Economic Model of Fertility Determination: Endogenous Perferences and Natural Fertility" (1976); and "Population Change and Farm Settlement in the Northern United States" (1976). He has served as Vice-President of the Economic History Association, and is currently President-Elect of the Population Association of America.

Ronald Lee is Associate Professor of Economics, and a Research Associate of the Population Studies Center at the University of Michigan. He received his Ph.D. in Economics from Harvard. His publications include "Population in Preindustrial England: An Econometric Analysis" (1973), "Estimating Series of Vital Rates and Age Structures from Baptisms and Burials: A New Technique, with Applications to Pre-industrial England" (1974), and "Natural Fertility, Population Cycles, and the Spectral Analysis of Births and Marriages" (1975). He edited the volume *Population Patterns in the Past* (1977).

Franklin F. Mendels, since 1974, has been Associate Professor of History at the University of Maryland, Baltimore County, where he teaches European economic history and historical geography, European peasant history, historical demography and principles of economics. He has taught at the University of California, Los Angeles, and the University of Quebec, after receiving his Ph.D. in Economics from the University of Wisconsin. He has published several articles on the economic, social, and demographic antecedents and consequences of the growth of part-time peasant industry ("proto-industrialization") in early modern Europe, and is currently preparing a book on that subject.

Charles Tilly is Professor of Sociology, Professor of History and Director of the Center for Research on Social Organization at the University of Michigan. Among the books he has authored or co-authored are *The Vendée* (1964), *Race and Residence in Wilmington* (1965), *History as Social Science* (1971), *Subsidizing the Poor* (1972), *An Urban World* (1974), *Strikes in France* (1975), *The Formation of National States in Western Europe* (1975), *The Rebellious Century* (1975), and *From Mobilization to Revolution* (1977).

Maris A. Vinovskis is Associate Professor of History and a Faculty Associate of the Institute for Social Research, University of Michigan. He received his Ph.D. from Harvard University and has taught previously at the University of Wisconsin. His publications include *Demographic Changes in America from the Revolution to the Civil War* (1977) and a number of articles. He was co-editor of *The Survival Equation: Man, Resources, and the Environment* (1971) and is co-editing a volume in the MSSB series, *Demographic Processes and Family Organization in Nineteenth-Century American Society.* He is currently completing a study of nineteenth-century Massachusetts educational development and is doing an analysis of the politics of abortion in the 94th Congress.

Etienne van de Walle is Professor of Demography and Director of the Population Studies Center at the University of Pennsylvania. He received his Ph.D. from the University of Louvain, and served as research associate of the Institut pour la Recherche Scientifique en Afrique Centrale in Rwanda and Burundi (1957–1961). He was a member of the research staff at Princeton's Office of Population Research (1962–1973) and a Fellow of the Woodrow Wilson International Center for Scholars (1976). His publications include *The Demography of*

352

Tropical Africa (1968; co-authored with William Brass, et al.) and *The Female Population of France in the Nineteenth Century* (1974).

E. A. *Wrigley* is a director of the SSRC Cambridge Group for the History of Population and Social Structure and a Fellow of Peterhouse, Cambridge. His publications include *Industrial Growth and Population Change* (1961), and *Population and History* (1969), and, as editor, *An Introduction to English Historical Demography* (1966), *Nineteenth Century Society* (1969), and *Identifying People in the Past* (1972).

Bibliography

Adelman, Irma, 1963. "An Econometric Analysis of Population Growth." *American Economic Review* 53: 314–339.

Ågren, Kurt, et al. 1973. *Aristocrats, Farmers, Proletarians. Essays in Swedish Demographic History*. Studia Historica Upsaliensia 47. Uppsala: Scandinavian University Books.

Andorka, Rudolf, 1972. "Un exemple de la faible fécondité légitime dans une région de la Hongrie. L'Ormànsàg à la fin du XVIIIᵉ siècle et au début du XIXᵉ: contrôle des naissances ou faux-semblants?" *Annales de Démographie Historique 1972*, 25–53.

d'Angeville, Adolphe, 1969. *Essai sur la statistique de la population française*. Introd. Emmanuel Le Roy Ladurie. Paris: Mouton.

Ariès, Philippe, 1954. "Deux contributions à l'histoire des pratiques contraceptives. II. Chaucer et Mme. de Sévigné." *Population* 9: 629–698.

——— 1971. *Histoire des populations françaises et de leurs attitudes devant la vie depuis le XVIIIᵉ siècle*. 2d ed. Paris: Le Seuil.

——— 1975. *Essais sur l'histoire de la mort en Occident du moyen âge à nos jours*. Paris: Le Seuil.

Baer, Max, 1926. *Medizinisch-statistische Ergebnisse aus züricherischen Kirchenbüchern des 17. und 18. Jahrunderts*. Zurich: Gutzwiller.

Banks, J. A. 1954. *Prosperity and Parenthood*. London: Routledge.

Basavarajappa, K. G. 1971. "The Influence of Fluctuations in Economic Conditions on Fertility and Marriage Rates, Australia, 1920–21 to 1937–38 and 1946–47 to 1966–67." *Population Studies* 25: 39–53.

Bash, Wendall H. 1963. "Changing Birth Rates in Developing America: New York State, 1840–1875." *Milbank Memorial Fund Quarterly* 41: 161–182.

Becker, Gary S. 1960. "An Economic Analysis of Fertility." Pp. 209–213. In *Demographic and Economic Change in Developed Countries*. Princeton University Press. Universities-National Bureau Conference Series, 11.

——— 1965. "A Theory of the Allocation of Time." *Economic Journal* 75: 493–517.

Becker, Gary S., and H. Gregg Lewis, 1973. "On the Interaction between the Quantity and the Quality of Children." *Journal of Political Economy* 81: 279–288.

Behrman, S. J., et al. eds. 1969. *Fertility and Family Planning. A World View*. Ann Arbor: University of Michigan Press.

Ben-Porath, Yoram, and Finis Welch, 1972. *Uncertain Quality: Sex of Children and Family Size*. Santa Monica: The Rand Corporation. R-1117-NIH/RF.

Benoiston de Châteauneuf et Villermé, 1843. *Rapport d'un voyage fait dans les cinq départements de la Bretagne pendant les années 1840 et 1841*.

355

Mémoires de l'Académie des sciences morales et politiques. Paris: Didot. Vol. IV.

Berelson, Bernard, 1966. "KAP studies on Fertility." Pp. 655–668. In Bernard Berelson (ed.), *Family Planning and Population Programs*. Chicago: University of Chicago Press.

———— 1969. "Beyond Family Planning." *Science* 163: 533–543.

Bergues, Helene, et al. 1960. *La prévention des naissances dans la famille. Ses origines dans les temps modernes*. I.N.E.D. Travaux et Documents. Cahier no. 35. Paris: Presses Universitaires de France.

Berkner, Lutz K. 1972a. "Rural Family Organization in Europe: A Problem in Comparative History." *Peasant Studies Newsletter* 1: 145–155.

———— 1972b. "The Stem Family and the Developmental Cycle of the Peasant Household: An Eighteenth-Century Austrian Example." *American Historical Review* 77: 398–418.

———— 1973. "Family, Social Structure, and Rural Industry: A Comparison of the Waldviertel and the Pays de Caux in the eighteenth century." Ph.D. Dissertation, Harvard University.

———— 1975. "The Use and Misuse of Census Data for the Historical Analysis of Family Structure." *Journal of Interdisciplinary History* 5: 721–738.

———— 1976. "Peasant Household Organization and Demographic Change in Lower Saxony (1689–1766)." In Ronald Lee (ed.), *Population Patterns in the Past*. New York: Academic Press.

Bertillon, Jacques, 1897. *Le problème de la dépopulation*. Paris: Colin.

Blacker, John G. 1957a. "Social ambitions in the bourgeoisie in eighteenth century France, and their relation to family limitation." *Population Studies* 11: 46–63.

———— 1957b. "The Social and Economic Causes of the Decline in the French Birth Rate at the End of the Eighteenth Century." Uupublished Ph.D. Dissertation, University of London.

Blake, Judith, 1967. "Reproductive Ideals and Educational Attainment among White Americans, 1943–1960." *Population Studies* 21: 159–174.

———— 1968. "Are Babies Consumer Durables? A Critique of the Economic Theory of Reproductive Motivation." *Population Studies* 22: 5–25.

Blaschke, Karlheinz, 1967. *Bevölkerungsgeschichte von Sachsen bis zur Industriellen Revolution*. Weimar: Böhlhaus.

Blau, Peter, 1969. "Objectives of sociology." Pp. 51–52. In Robert Bierstedt (ed.), *A Design for Sociology: Scope, Objectives, and Methods*. Philadelphia: The American Academy of Political and Social Science.

Blayo, Yves, and Louis Henry, 1967. "Données démographiques sur la Bretagne et l'Anjou de 1740 à 1829." *Annales de démographie historique 1967*: 91–171.

Bloomberg, Susan E., et al. 1971. "A Census Probe into Nineteenth-Century Family History: Southern Michigan, 1850–1880." *Journal of Social History* 5: 26–45.

Bodmer, Walter, 1960. *Schweizerische Industriegeschichte*. Zürich: Verlag Berichthaus.

Bogue, Donald, 1969. *Principles of Demography*. New York: Wiley.

Bogue, Donald, and James A. Palmore, 1964. "Some Empirical and Analytical Relations among Demographic Fertility Measures, with Regression Models for Fertility Estimation." *Demography* 1: 316–338.

Borrie, W. D., 1970. *The Growth and Control of World Population*. London: Weidenfeld and Nicolson.

Boserup, Ester, 1965. *The Conditions of Agricultural Growth. The Economics of Agrarian Change under Population Pressure*. Chicago: Aldine.

Bourdieu, Pierre, 1962. "Célibat et condition paysanne." *Études rurales* 5/6: 32–135.

——— 1972. "Les stratégies matrimoniales dans le système de reproduction." *Annales, E.S.C.* 27: 1105–1127.

Bourgeois-Pichat, Jean, 1965. "Les facteurs de la fécondité non dirigée." *Population* 20: 383–424.

——— 1967a. "Relation between Foetal-Infant Mortality and Fertility." Pp. 68–72. In *Proceedings of the World Population Conference: 1965*. Vol. II. New York: United Nations.

——— 1967b. "Social and Biological Determinants of Human Fertility in Non-Industrial Societies." *Proceedings of the American Philosophical Society* 3: 160–163.

Brägger, Uli, 1945. *Leben und Schriften des armen Mannes im Toggenburg*. Samuel Voellmy (ed.). Basel: Birkhauser.

Brandt, Alexandre de, 1901. *Droit et coutumes des populations rurales de la France en matière successorale*. Paris: Librairie de la Société du Recueil général des lois et arrêts.

Braun, Rudolf, 1960. *Industrialisierung und Volksleben: die Veränderungen der Lebensformen in einem ländlichen Industriegebiet vor 1800 (Züricher Oberland)*. Zürich: Rentsch.

——— 1965. *Sozial und kultereller Wandel in einem ländlichen Industriegebiet im 19. und 20. Jahrhundert*. Zürich und Stuttgart: Erlenbach.

——— 1966. "The Impact of Cottage Industry on an Agricultural Population." Pp. 53–64. In David S. Landes (ed.), *The Rise of Capitalism*. New York: Macmillan.

——— 1967. "The Rise of a Rural Class of Industrial Entrepreneurs." *Journal of World History* 10: 551–566.

Brunner, H., and A. Senti, 1937. "Ansteckende krankheiten in Zürich." *Sonderdruck aus den Zuricher Statistichen Nachrichten*. Heft 3: 6f.

Bumpass, Larry L., 1973. "Is low fertility here to stay?" *Family Planning Perspectives* 5: 67–69.

Bumpass, Larry L., and Charles F. Westoff, 1970. "The 'Perfect Contraceptive' Population." *Science* 169: 1177–1182.

Burmeister, Edwin, and Rodney Dobell, 1970. *Mathematical Theories of Economic Growth*. New York: Macmillan.

357

BIBLIOGRAPHY

Cain, Glen G. 1971. "Issues in the economics of a population policy for the United States." *American Economic Review Papers and Proceedings* 61: 408–417.

Cain, Glen G., and Adriana Weininger, 1967. "Economic Determinants of Fertility: Preliminary Results from Cross-Sectional, Aggregative Data." Unpublished paper.

Caldwell, John C. 1968. *Propulation Growth and Family Change in Africa.* New York: Humanities Press.

Cantril, Hadley, 1965. *The Pattern of Human Concerns.* New Brunswick: Rutgers University Press.

Carlsson, Gösta, 1966. "The Decline of Fertility: Innovation or Adjustment Process." *Population Studies* 24: 413–422.

——— 1970. "Nineteenth-century fertility oscillations." *Population Studies* 24: 413–422.

Carr-Saunders, A. M. 1925. *Population.* London: Oxford University Press.

Chambers, J. D. 1965a. "Population Changes in a Provincial Town: Nottingham 1700–1800." Pp. 308–353. In David V. Glass and D.E.C. Eversley (eds.), *Population in History.* Chicago: Aldine.

——— 1965b. "The Rural Domestic Industries during the Period of Transition to the Factory System with Special Reference to the Midland Counties of England." *Second International Conference of Economic History, Aix-en-Provence 1962.* Paris: Mouton. Vol. II: 429–555.

Chamoux, Antoinette, and Cécile Dauphin, 1969. "La contraception avant la Révolution française: L'example de Châtillon-sur-Seine." *Annales, E.S.C.* 24: 662–684.

Charbonneau, Hubert, 1970. *Tourouvre-au-Perche au XVIIe et XVIIIe Siècle.* I.N.E.D. Travaux et Documents. Cahier no. 55. Paris: Presses Universitaires de France.

——— 1973. Ed., *La population du Québec, études retrospectives.* Montréal: Editions de Boréal Express.

Chasles, Robert, 1959. *Les illustres Françoises.* Vols. I and II. Ed. Fr. Deloffre. Paris: Les Belles Lettres.

Chaunu, Pierre, 1973. "Réflexions sur la démographie normande." *Mélanges publiés en l'honneur de Marcel Reinhard.* Paris: Société de Démographie Historique.

Chayanov, A. V. 1966. *The Theory of Peasant Economy.* Homewood, Illinois: Richard C. Irwin.

Clark, Colin, 1967. Population Growth and Land Use. New York: St. Martin's Press.

Clark, Victor S. 1929. *History of Manufactures in the United States.* 3 Vols. New York: McGraw-Hill.

Coale, Ansley J. 1967. "Factors Associated with the Development of Low Fertility: An Historic Summary." Pp. 205–209. In *Proceedings of the World Population Conference: 1965.* Vol. II. New York: United Nations.

——— 1969. "The Decline of Fertility in Europe from the French Revolu-

358

tion to World War II." Pp. 3–24. In S. J. Behrman et al. (eds.), *Fertility and Family Planning: A World View.* Ann Arbor: University of Michigan Press.

———— 1970. "The Use of Fourier Analysis To Express the Relation between Time Variation in Fertility and the Time Sequence of Births in a Closed Human Population." *Demography* 7: 93–120.

———— 1971. "Age Patterns of Marriage." *Population Studies* 25: 193–214.

———— 1973. "The Demographic Transition." Paper Presented at the Plenary Session of the International Union for the Scientific Study of Population Meeting. August 27-September 1, Liege.

Coale, Ansley J., and Paul Demeny, 1966. *Regional Model Life Tables and Stable Populations.* Princeton: Princeton University Press.

Coale, Ansley J., et al. 1965. *Aspects of the Analysis of Family Structure.* Princeton: Princeton University Press.

Cohen, Joel E. 1975. "Childhood Mortality, Family Size and Birth Order in Pre-Industrial Europe." *Demography* 12: 35–55.

Cole, John W. 1971. "Estate inheritance in the Italian Alps." Research Reports No. 10. Department of Anthropology, University of Massachusetts. Amherst: University of Massachusetts.

Coleman, James S. 1968. "Modernization: Political Aspects." Pp. 395–402. In *International Encyclopedia of the Social Sciences.* Vol. 10. New York: Macmillan.

Collver, Andrew O. 1965. *Birth Rates in Latin America: New Estimates of Historical Trends and Fluctuations.* Institute of International Studies Research Series No. 7. Berkeley: University of California Press.

Condran, Gretchen A. 1973. "Taste formation variables and the economics of fertility." Unpublished Ph.D. Dissertation, University of Pennsylvania.

Connor, L. R. 1926. "Fertility of Marriage and Population Growth." *Journal of the Royal Statistical Society* 89: 553–566.

Corsini, Carlo A. 1971. "Ricerche di demografia storica nel territorio di Firenze." *Quaderni storici* 17: 371–378.

Cowgill, Donald Olen, 1956. "The Theory of Population Growth Cycles." Pp. 125–134. In Joseph J. Spengler and Otis Dudley Duncan (eds.), *Population Theory and Policy.* Glencoe: Free Press.

Creighton, Charles, 1965. A History of Epidemics in Britain II. Cambridge: Cambridge University Press.

Cutright, Phillips, 1972. "The Teenage Sexual Revolution and the Myth of an Abstinent Past." *Family Planning Perspectives* 4: 24–31.

Davis, Kingsley, 1963. The Theory of Change and Response in Modern Demographic History." *Population Index* 29: 345–366.

———— 1967. "Population Policy: Will Current Programs Succeed?" *Science* 158: 730–739.

Davis, Kingsley, and Judith Blake, 1956. "Social Structure and Fertility." *Economic Development and Cultural Change* 4: 211–235.

Deane, Phyllis, and W. A. Cole, 1969. *British Economic Growth 1688–1959; Trends and Structure.* Cambridge: Cambridge University Press.

BIBLIOGRAPHY

Demeny, Paul, 1968. "Early Fertility Decline in Austria-Hungary: A Lesson in Demographic Transition." *Daedalus* 97: 502–522.

Demos, John, 1970. *A Little Commonwealth: Family Life in Plymouth Colony.* New York: Oxford University Press.

Deniel, Raymond, and Louis Henry, 1965. "La population d'un village du Nord de la France, Sainghin-en-Mélantois, de 1665 à 1851." *Population* 28: 563–602.

Deprez, Paul, 1965. "The demographic development of Flanders in the Eighteenth century." Pp. 608–630. In David V. Glass and D.E.C. Eversley (eds.) *Population in History.* London: Edward Arnold.

Dion-Saletot, Michèle, 1971. "Endogamie et systéme èconomique dans un village français." *Sociologia ruralis* 11: 1–18.

Drake, Michael, 1969a. *Population in Industrialization.* London: Methuen.

————— 1969b. *Population and Society in Norway, 1735–1865.* Cambridge: Cambridge University Press.

Draper, Norman R., and Harry Smith, 1966. *Applied Regression Analysis.* New York: Wiley.

Dubos, René J. 1966. "Problems in Bioclimatology." Pp. 289–300. In Jack Bresler (ed.), *Human Ecology.* Reading, Massachusetts: Addison-Wesley.

Dûpaquier, Jacques, 1968. "Sur la population française au XVIIᵉ et au XVIIIᵉ siècle." *Revue historique* 23: 43–79.

————— 1974. *Introduction à la démographie historique.* Paris: Gamma.

Dûpaquier, Jacques, and Marcel Lachiver, 1969. "Sur les débuts de la contraception en France, ou les deux malthusianismes." *Annales, E.S.C.* 24: 1391–1406.

Durand, John D. 1967. "Demographic transition." Pp. 32–45. In the *International Union for the Scientific Study of Population, Proceedings of the Sydney Conference. (August 21–25, 1967).* Canberra: National University Press.

Dyke, Bennett, and Jean Walters MacCluer, eds. 1973. *Computer Simulation in Human Population Studies.* New York: Academic Press.

Easterlin, Richard A. 1968a. "Economic Growth: An Overview." Pp. 395–408. In *International Encyclopedia of the Social Sciences.* Vol. 4. New York: Macmillan.

————— 1968b. *Population, Labor Force, and Long Swings in Economic Growth: The American Experience.* New York: Columbia University Press.

————— 1969. "Towards a Socio-Economic Theory of Fertility: A Survey of Recent Research on Economic Factors in American Fertility." Pp. 127–156. In S. J. Behrman et al. (eds.), *Fertility and Family Planning: A World View.* Ann Arbor: University of Michigan Press.

————— 1970. "An Approach to Fertility Analysis for LDC's." Paper prepared for a meeting (June 29-July 3, 1970) of the United Nations *Ad Hoc* Committee on Experts on Programs in Demographic Aspects of Economic Development. New York.

————— 1972. "The American Population." Pp. 121–183. In Lance E. Davis, et al. (eds.), *American Economic Growth: An Economist's History of the United States.* New York: Harper & Row.

——— 1973. "Relative Economic Status and the American Fertility Swing." Pp. 170–223. In Eleanor B. Sheldon (ed.), *Family Economic Behavior: Problems and Prospects.* Philadelphia: J. B. Lippincott.

Eblen, Jack Ericson, 1972. "Growth of the Black Population in *ante bellum* America, 1820–1860." *Population Studies* 26: 273–289.

——— 1974. "New Estimates of the Vital Rates of the United States Black Population during the Nineteenth Century." *Demography* 11: 301–319.

Engerman, Stanley, and Eugene D. Genovese, eds. 1975. *Race and Slavery in the Western Hemisphere. Quantitative Studies.* Princeton: Princeton University Press.

Espenshade, Thomas J. 1971. "A New Method for Estimating the Level of Natural Fertility in Populations Practicing Birth Control." *Demography* 8: 526–536.

——— 1972. "The Price of Children and Socio-Economic Theories of Fertility." *Population Studies* 26: 207–221.

Eversley, D.E.C. 1965. "A survey of population in an area of Worcestershire from 1660–1850 on the basis of parish registers." Pp. 394–419. In David V. Glass and D.E.C. Eversley (eds.), *Population in History.* Chicago: Aldine.

——— 1967. "The Home Market and Economic Growth in England, 1750–1780." Pp. 206–259. In Eric L. Jones and G. E. Mingay (eds.), *Land, Labour and Population in the Industrial Revolution.* London: Arnold.

Faith, Rosamund J. 1966. "Peasant Families and Inheritance Customs in Medieval England." *Agricultural History Review* 14: 77–95.

Fischer, Wolfram, 1973. "Rural Industrialization and Population Change." *Comparative Studies in Society and History* 15: 158–170.

Fishlow, Albert, 1968. "The American Common School Revival: Fact or Fancy?" Pp. 40–67. In Henry Rosovsky (ed.), *Industrialization in Two Systems: Essays in Honor of Alexander Gershenkron.* New York: Wiley.

Fishman, George S. 1969. *Spectral Methods in Econometrics.* Cambridge, Massachusetts: Harvard University Press.

Fleury, Marcel, and Louis Henry, 1958. "Pour connâitre la population de la France depuis Louis XIV. Plan de travaux par sondage." *Population* 13: 663–686.

——— 1965. *Nouveau manuel de dépouillement et d'exploitation de l'état civil ancien.* Paris: INED.

Flinn, M. W. 1970. *British Population Growth, 1700–1850.* London: Macmillan.

Fogel, Robert, and Stanley Engerman, 1974. *Time on the Cross.* 2 vols. Boston: Little, Brown.

Forster, Colin, and G.S.L. Tucker, 1972. *Economic Opportunity and White American Fertility Ratios: 1800–1860.* New Haven: Yale University Press.

Forster, Robert, 1960. *The Nobility of Toulouse in the Eighteenth Century: A Social and Economic Study.* The Johns Hopkins University Studies in

361

Historical and Political Science. Baltimore: The Johns Hopkins University Press.

France, Ministère des Finances, 1839. *Compte genéral de l'administration des finances rendu pour l'année 1838.* IIe Part. Paris.

—— 1879. "L'enquête de 1851 sur les revenus territoriaux de la France continentale." *Bulletin de statistique et de législation comparée VI:* 110–129, 185–199.

Freedman, Deborah S. n.d.a. "Consumption Aspirations as Economic Incentives in a Developing Economy—Taiwan."

—— n.d.b. "Consumption of Modern Goods and Services and their Relation to Fertility: A Study in Taiwan."

—— 1970. "The Role of Modern Durables in Economic Development." *Economic Development and Cultural Change* 19: 25–48.

Freedman, Ronald, 1961–62. "The Sociology of Human Fertility." *Current Sociology* 10/11: 35–68.

—— 1963. "Norms for Family Size in Underdeveloped Countries." *Proceedings of the Royal Society.* B.159: 220–245.

—— 1965. "The Transition from High to Low Fertility: Challenge to Demographers." *Population Index* 31: 417–444.

Freedman, Ronald, et al. 1959. *Family Planning, Sterility, and Population Growth.* New York: McGraw-Hill.

Freedman, Ronald, et al. 1965. "Stability and Change in Expectations about Family Size: a Longitudinal Study." *Demography* 2: 250–275.

Freedman, Ronald, and J. Y. Takeshita, 1969. Family Planning in Taiwan: An Experiment in Social Change. Princeton: Princeton University Press.

Freedman, Ronald, et al. 1972. "Trends in Family Size Preferences and Practice of Family Planning: Taiwan, 1965–1970." *Studies in Family Planning* 3: 281–296.

Friedlander, Dov, 1969. "Demographic Responses and Population Change." *Demography* 6: 359–381.

—— 1970. "The Spread of Urbanization in England and Wales, 1851–1951." *Population Studies* 24: 423–443.

—— 1973. "Demographic Patterns and Socioeconomic Characteristics of the Coal-Mining Population in England and Wales in the Nineteenth Century." *Economic Development and Cultural Change* 22: 39–51.

Friedlander, Stanley, and Morris Silver, 1967. "A Quantitative Study of the Determinants of Fertility Behavior." *Demography* 4: 30–70.

Frisch, Rose E. 1974. "Demographic Implications of the Biological Determinants of Female Fecundity." Research Paper No. 6, Harvard Center for Population Studies.

Ganiage, Jean, 1963. *Trois villages de l'Ile de France.* I.N.E.D. Travaux et Documents. Cahier no. 40. Paris: Presses Universitaires de France.

Gaunt, David, 1973. "Historisk demografi ellet deomografisk historia? En översikt och ott debattinlägg om ett tvärvetenskaplight dilemma." *Historisk Tidskrift:* 382–405.

Gay, Jean Lucien, 1953. *Les effets pécuniaires du mariage en Nivernais du XIVᵉ au XVIIIᵉ siècles*. Paris: Domat-Montchrestien.

Gautier, Etienne, and Louis Henry, 1958. *La population de Crulai, paroisse normande. Etude historique.* I.N.E.D. Travaux et Documents. Cahier no. 33. Paris: Presses Univérsitaires de France.

Geertz, Clifford, 1963. *Agricultural Involution: The Process of Ecological Change In Indonesia.* Berkeley: University of California Press.

Gendell, Murray, 1967. "Fertility and Development in Brazil." *Demography* 4: 143–157.

Georgescu-Roegen, Nicholas, 1970. "The Economics of Production." *American Economic Review, Papers and Proceedings* 60: 1–9.

Gilboy, Elizabeth, 1934. *Wages in Eighteenth Century England.* Cambridge, Massachusetts: Harvard University Press.

——— 1936. "The Cost of Living and Real Wages in Eighteenth Century England." *Review of Economics and Statistics* 18: 134–143.

Glass, David V. 1962. "Family Limitation in Europe: A Survey of Recent Studies." Pp. 231–261. In Clyde V. Kiser (ed.), *Research in Family Planning.* Princeton: Princeton University Press.

——— 1965. "Gregory King's estimate of the population of England and Wales." Pp. 159–220. In David V. Glass and D.E.C. Eversley (eds.), *Population in History.* Chicago: Aldine.

Glass, David V., and Roger Revelle, eds. 1972. *Population and Social Change.* London: Arnold.

Goldberg, David, and Clyde H. Coombs, 1962. "Some Applications of Unfolding Theory to Fertility Analysis." Pp. 105–129. In *Emerging Techniques in Population Research Analysis.* New York: Millbank Memorial Fund.

Goldscheider, Calvin, 1971. *Population, Modernization, and Social Structure.* Boston: Little, Brown.

Goodman, Leo A., et al. 1974. "Family Formation and the Frequency of Various Kinship Relations." *Theoretical Population Biology* 5: 1–27.

Goody, Jack, 1973. "Strategies of Heirship." *Comparative Studies in Society and History* 15: 3–20.

Goreux, L. M. 1956. "Les migrations agricoles en France depuis un siécle et leur relation avec certains facteurs économiques." *Etudes et Conjoncture* 11: 327–376.

Goubert, Pierre, 1960. *Beauvais et le Beauvaisis de 1600 à 1730.* Paris: SEVPEN.

Gould, P. R. 1963. "Man against His Environment: A Game Theoretic Framework." *Annals of the Association of American Geographers* 53: 290–297.

Grabill, Wilson H., and Lee Jay Cho, 1965. "Methodology for the Measurement of Current Fertility from Population Data on Young Children." *Demography* 2: 50–73.

Grabill, Wilson H., et al. 1958. *The Fertility of American Women.* New York: Wiley.

Granger, C.W.J., and M. Hatanaka, 1964. *Spectral Analysis of Economic Time Series*. Princeton: Princeton University Press.

Greven, Philip J., Jr. 1967. "Historical demography and colonial America." *William and Mary Quarterly*. Series 3. 24: 439–459.

———— 1970. *Four Generations, Land and Family in Colonial Andover, Massachusetts*. Ithaca, New York: Cornell University Press.

Griliches, Zvi, 1974. "Comment." In Theodore W. Schultz (ed.), *Economics of the Family. Marriage, Children and Human Capital*. Chicago: University of Chicago Press.

Guillaume, Pierre, and Jean Pierre Poussou, 1970. *Démographie historique*. Paris: A. Colin.

Gutman, Robert, 1956. "The Accuracy of Vital Statistics in Massachusetts, 1842–1901." Unpublished Ph.D. Dissertation, Columbia University.

Habakkuk, John, 1955. "Family Structure and Economic Change in Nineteenth-Century Europe." *Journal of Economic History* 15: 1–12.

———— 1963. "Population Problems and European Economic Development in the Late Eighteenth Century." *The American Economic Review* 53: 607–618.

———— 1965a. "The Economic History of Modern Britain." Pp. 147–158. In David V. Glass and D.E.C. Eversley (eds.), *Population in History*. Chicago: Aldine.

———— 1965b. "English Population in the Eighteenth Century." Pp. 269–284. In David V. Glass and D.E.C. Eversley (eds.), *Population in History*. Chicago: Aldine.

———— 1965c. "Historical Experience of Economic Development." Pp. 112–138. In E.A.G. Robinson (ed.), *Problems of Economic Development*. New York: St. Martin's.

———— 1971. *Population Growth and Economic Development since 1750*. Leicester: Leicester University Press.

Hajnal, John, 1965. "European Marriage Patterns in Perspective." Pp. 101–146. In David V. Glass and D.E.C. Eversley (eds.), *Population in History*. Chicago: Aldine.

Hanke, Gerhard, 1969. "Zur sozialstruktur der ländlichen Siedlungen Altbayerns im 17. und 18. Jahrhundert." Pp. 219–269. In *Gesellschaft und Herrschaft. Forschungen zur sozial- und ländesgeschichtlichen Problemen vornehmlich in Bayern. Eine Festgabe für Karl Bösl zum. 60 Geburtstag*. Munich: Beck.

Hareven, Tamara K., and Maris A. Vinovskis, 1975. "Marital Fertility, Ethnicity, and Occupation in Urban Families: An Analysis of South Boston and the South End in 1880." *Journal of Social History*, 9: 69–93.

Hausen, Karen, 1975. "Familie als Gegenstand." *Historischer Sozialwissenschaft* 1: 171–209.

Hawthorne, Geoffrey, 1970. *The Sociology of Fertility*. London: Collier-Macmillan.

Hazard, Blanche Evans, 1921. The Organization of the Boot and Shoe

364

Industry in Massachusetts before 1875. Vol. 23. Harvard Economic Studies. Cambridge, Massachusetts: Harvard University Press.

Heer, David M. 1966. "Economic Development and Fertility." *Demography* 3: 423–444.

——— 1968. "Economic Development and the Fertility Transition." *Daedalus* (Spring): 447–462.

——— 1969. "Educational Advance and Fertility Change." Paper presented at the International Union for the Scientific Study of Population (September), London.

Heer, David M., and John W. Boynton, 1970. "A Multivariate Regression Analysis of Differences in Fertility of United States Counties." *Social Biology* 17: 180–194.

Heer, David M., and D. O. Smith, 1968. "Mortality Level, Desired Family Size and Population Increase." *Demography* 5: 104–121.

Heer, David M., and Elsa S. Turner, 1965. "Areal Differences in Latin American Fertility." *Population Studies* 18: 279–292.

Henripin, J. 1954. *La population canadienne au début du XVIIIᵉ siècle: nuptialité, fécondité, mortalité infantile.* Paris: Presses Universitaires de France.

Henry, Louis, 1956. *Anciennes familles génévoises.* I.N.E.D. Travaux et Documents. Cahier no. 26. Paris: Presses Universitaires de France.

——— 1961a. "La fécondité naturelle: observations-théorie-résultats." *Population* 16: 625–636.

——— 1961b. "Some Data on Natural Fertility." *Eugenics Quarterly* 8: 81–91.

——— 1963. "French Statistical Research in Natural Fertility." Pp. 333–350. In Mindel C. Sheps and J. C. Ridley (eds.), *Public Health and Population Change.* Pittsburgh: University of Pittsburgh Press.

——— 1967. *Manuel de demographie historique.* Geneva: Droz.

——— 1968. "Historical Demography." *Daedalus* 97: 385–396.

Herlihy, David, 1969. "Vieillir à Florence au Quattrocento." *Annales, E.S.C.* 24: 1338–1352.

Hill, Russell C., and Frank P. Stafford, 1971. "The Allocation of Time to Children and Educational Opportunity." Discussion Paper No. 32. Institute of Public Policy Studies. University of Michigan.

Himes, Norman E. 1963. Medical History of Contraception. New York: Gamut Press.

Hirzel, J. C. 1792. *Beantwortung der Frage: Ist die Handelschaft, wie solche bey uns beschaffen, unserem Lande schädlich, oder nützlich, in Absicht auf den Feldbau und die Sitten des Volkes?* Zürich: Naturforschende Gesellschaft.

Hirzel, Joh. 1816. *Rede über den physischen, ökonomischen und sittlich-religiösen Zustand der östlichen Berggemeinden des Kanton Zürich.* Zürich: Ulrich.

Hollingsworth, T. H. 1969. *Historical Demography.* London: The Sources of History.

365

Hoover, Edgar M. 1971. "Basic Approaches to the Study of Demographic Aspects of Economic Development: Economic-Demographic Models." *Population Index* 37: 66–75.

Horska, Pavla, 1972. "Au sujet des différences interregionales dans le développement démographique en Bohème." Pp. 353–361. In *Annales de Démographie Historique 1971*. Paris: Mouton.

Houdaille, Jacques, 1967. "La population de Boulay (Moselle) avant 1850." *Population* 22: 1055–1084.

———— 1971. "Analyse demographique de deux ouvrages de généalogie sur les descendants de Mme. de Sévigné, Bussy Rabutin et Jean Racine." *Population* 26: 953–955.

Hurault, Jean, 1965. "La population des indiens de Guyane Française." *Population* 20: 801–828.

Imhof, Arthur E. 1975. Ed. *Historische Demographie als Sozialgeschichte. Giessen und Umgebung vom 17. zum 19. Jahrhundert*. Darmstadt. Selbstverlag der Hessischen Historischen Kommission Darmstadt und der Historischen Kommission für Hessen.

———— 1976. *Aspekte der Bevölkerungsentwicklung in der nordischen Länden 1720–1750*. 2 Vols. Bern: Francke Verlag.

Inkeles, Alex, 1969. "Making Men Modern: On the Causes and Consequences of Individual Change in Six Developing Countries." *American Journal of Sociology* 75: 208–255.

Jaffe, A. J. 1942. "Urbanization and Fertility." *American Journal of Sociology* 48: 57.

Jantke, Carl, and Dietrich Hilger, eds. 1965. *Die Eigentumslosen. Der deutsche Pauperismus und die Emanzipationskrise in Darstellung und Deutungen der zeitgenossischen Literatur*. Munich: Karl Alber.

Johnansen, Hans Christian, 1975. *Befolkninksudvikling og familie struktur: det 18. ar hundrede*. Odense: Odense University Press.

Jones, E. L. ed. 1967. *Agriculture and Economic Growth in England, 1650–1815*. London: Methuen.

Jones, E, L., and G. E. Mingay, eds. 1967. *Land, Labour and Population in the Industrial Revolution: Essays Presented to J. D. Chambers*. London: Arnold.

Jones, Eric L., and S. J. Woolf, eds. 1969. *Agrarian Change and Economic Development: The Historical Problems*. London: Methuen.

Kantner, John F., and Melvin Zelnik, 1972. "Sexual Experience of Young Unmarried Women in the United States." *Family Planning Perspectives* 4: 9–18.

Kellenbenz, Hermann, 1965. "Ländliche gewerbe und bäuerliches Unternehmertum in Westeuropa vom spätmittelalter bis ins XVIII Jahrhundert." In *Second International Congress of Economic History, Aix-en-Provence, 1962*. Paris: Mouton. Vol. II: 377–428.

Kelley, Allen C. 1976. "Demographic changes and American economic development: past, present and future." In U. S. Commission on Population Growth and the American Future, *Economic Aspects of Population*

Change. Vol. II. *Commission Research Reports*. Washington, D. C.: Government Printing Office.

Keyfitz, Nathan, 1965. "Political-Economic aspects of urbanization in south and southeast Asia." In Philip M. Hauser and Leo F. Schnore (eds.), *The Study of Urbanization*. New York: Wiley.

—— 1971. "How Birth Control Affects Births." *Social Biology* 18: 109–121.

Kirk, Dudley, 1946. *Europe's Population in the Interwar Years*. Geneva: League of Nations.

—— 1971. "A new demographic transition." Pp. 123–147. In National Academy of Sciences, *Rapid Population Growth*. Baltimore: Johns Hopkins University Press.

Kirkland, Edward Chase, 1948. *Men, Cities, and Transportation, 1820–1900*. 2 Vols. Cambridge, Massachusetts: Harvard University Press.

Kisch, Herbert, 1959. "The textile industries in Silesia and the Rhineland: a comparative study in industrialization." *Journal of Economic History* 19: 541–564.

Kläui, Paul, and Eduard Imhof, 1951. *Atlas zur Geschichte des Kantons Zürich*. Zürich: Oroll Füssli.

Klíma, Arnost, 1965. "The Domestic Industry and the Putting-Out System (Verlags-System) in the Period of Transition from Feudalism to Capitalism." *Second International Congress of Economic History, Aix-en-Provence, 1962*. Paris: Mouton Vol. 477–482.

—— 1974. "The Role of Rural Domestic Industry in Bohemia in the Eighteenth Century." *Economic History Review* 27: 48–56.

Knodel, John, 1968. "Infant Mortality and Fertility in Three Bavarian Villages: An Analysis of Family Histories from the Nineteenth Century." *Population Studies* 22: 297–318.

—— 1973. *The Fertility Decline in Germany*. Princeton: Princeton University Press.

Köllmann, Wolfgang, 1959. "Industrialisierung, Binnenwanderung und 'Soziale Frage.'" *Vierteljahrschrift für Sozial- und Wirtschaftsgeschichte* 49: 45–70.

Krause, J. T. 1965. "The Changing Adequacy of English Registration, 1690–1837." Pp. 379–393. In David V. Glass and D.E.C. Eversley (eds.), *Population in History*. Chicago: Aldine.

—— 1967. "Some Aspects of Population Change, 1690–1790." Pp. 187–205. In E. L. Jones and G. E. Mingay (eds.), *Land, Labour and Population in the Industrial Revolution*. London: Arnold.

Kuh, Edwin, and John R. Meyer, 1955. "Correlation and Regression Estimates When the Data Are Ratios." *Econometrica* 23: 400–416.

Kuznets, Simon, 1966. *Modern Economic Growth: Rate, Structure and Spread*. New Haven: Yale University Press.

—— 1973. "Population Trends and Modern Economic Growth." Paper prepared for the United Nations Symposium on Population and Development (June 4–14) Cairo.

Lachiver, Marcel, 1969. *La population de Meulan du XVIIe au XIXe siècle (vers 1600–1870)*. Paris: SEVPEN; Démographie et societés XII.

——— 1973. "Fécondité et contraception dans la région parisienne. (XVII–XIXe siécles)." In *Mélanges publiés en l'honneur de Marcel Reinhard*. Paris: Société de Démographie Historique.

Langholm, Sivert, 1976. "On the Scope of Micro-History." *Scandinavian Journal of History* 1: 3–24.

Lapham, Robert J., and W. Parker Mauldin, 1972. "National Family Planning Programs: Review and Evaluation." *Studies in Family Planning* 3: 29–52.

Laslett, Peter, 1965. *The World We Have Lost*. London: Methuen.

——— 1972. Ed. *Household and Family in Past Time: Comparative Studies in the Size and Structure of the Domestic Group over the last Three Centuries in England, France, Serbia, Japan and Colonial America*. Cambridge. Cambridge University Press.

Lavergne, Léonce de, 1860. *Economie rurale de la France depuis 1789*. Paris: Guillaumin.

Leasure, William J. 1963. "Factors Involved in the Decline of Fertility in Spain." *Population Studies* 16: 271–285.

Le Bras, Hervé, 1973. "Parents, Grand-Parents, Bisaieux." *Population* 28: 1–38.

Lee, Ronald, 1971. "Econometric Studies of Topics in Demographic History." Unpublished Ph.D. Dissertation, Harvard University.

——— 1972. "Population in Eighteenth Century England: An Aggregate Time Series Analysis." Paper presented at the Cliometric Conference (April), Madison, Wisconsin.

——— 1973. "Population in Pre-Industrial England: An Econometric Analysis." *Quarterly Journal of Economics* 87: 581–607.

——— 1974a. "The Formal Dynamics of Controlled Populations and the Echo, the Boom and the Bust." *Demography* 11: 563–585.

——— 1974b. "Estimating Series of Vital Rates and Age Structures from Baptisms and Burials: A New Technique with Applications to Preindustrial England." *Population Studies*. 28: 495–512.

——— 1975. "Natural Fertility, Population Cycles and the Spectral Analysis of Births and Marriages." *Journal of the American Statistical Association*. 30: 295–304.

——— 1977. "Methods and Models for Analysing Historical Series of Births, Deaths and Marriages." In Ronald D. Lee (ed.), *Population Patterns in the Past*. New York: Academic Press.

Leibenstein, Harvey, 1967. *Economic Backwardness and Economic Growth*. New York: Wiley.

——— 1973. "The Economic Theory of Fertility Decline." Discussion Paper no. 272. Harvard Institute of Economic Research, Harvard University.

——— 1974. "The Interpretation of the Economic Theory of Fertility: Promising Data or Blind Alley?" *Journal of Economic Literature* 12: 457–479.

Le Play, Frédéric, 1864. *Le réforme sociale en France.* 2 Vols. Paris.

——— 1871. *L'organisation de la famille.* Paris: Téqui.

Léridon, Henri, 1973. *Natalité, saisons et conjoncture économique.* I.N.E.D. Travaux et Documents. Cahier no. 66. Paris: Presses universitaires de France.

Lerner, Daniel, 1968. "Modernization: social aspects." Pp. 386–395. In International *Encyclopedia of the Social Sciences.* Vol. 12. New York: Macmillan.

Le Roy Ladurie, Emmanuel, 1966. *Les paysans de Languedoc.* Paris: SEVPEN

——— 1967. *Histoire du Climat depuis L'An Mil.* Paris: SEVPEN

——— 1972. "Système de la coutume: structures familiales et coutumes d'héritage en France au XVIe siècle." *Annales, E.S.C.* 27: 825–846.

——— 1973. "Un concept: l'Unification microbienne du monde (XIVe-XVIIe siecles)." *Revue suisse d'histoire* 23: 627–696.

Le Roy Ladurie, Emmanuel, and Paul Dumont, 1971. "Quantitative and Cartographical Exploitation of French Military Archives, 1819–1826." *Daedalus* 100: 397–441.

Levi, Giovanni, 1971. "Migrazioni e popolazione nella Francia del XVII e XVIII secolo." *Rivista Storica Italiana* 83: 95–123.

Levine, David C. 1974. "The Demographic Implications of Industrialization. Study of Two Leicestershire Villages, 1600–1851." Unpublished Ph.D. Dissertation, Cambridge University.

Levy, Claude, and Louis Henry, 1960. "Ducs et Pairs sous l'Ancien Régime. Caractéristiques démographiques d'une caste." *Population* 15: 807–830.

Lewis, Edward E. 1963. *Methods of Statistical Analysis in Economics and Business.* Boston: Houghton Mifflin.

Lindert, Peter, 1973. "The Relative Cost of American Children." Paper EH-73–18, Graduate Program in Economic History. University of Wisconsin, Madison.

Livi Bacci, Massimo, 1965. "Il declino della fecondità della popolazione italiana nell'ultimo secolo." *Statistica* 25: 359–452.

——— 1968. "Fertility and Nuptiality Changes in Spain from the Late 18th to the Early 20th Century." *Population Studies* 22: 83–101, 211–234.

——— 1971a. *A Century of Portuguese Fertility.* Princeton: Princeton University Press.

——— 1971b. "Una disciplina in rapido sviluppo: la demografia storica." *Quaderni storici* 17: 279–298.

Lockridge, Kenneth A. 1966. "The population of Dedham, Massachusetts, 1636–1736." *Economic History Review* 19 (2d ser.): 318–344.

——— 1968. Comments on Pierre Goubert's paper, "French Research in Demographic History, 1500–1800." Delivered at the American Historical Association Meeting (December 29), Washington, D. C.

——— 1970. A New England Town—The First Hundred Years: Dedham, Massachusetts, 1636–1736. New York: W. W. Norton.

369

BIBLIOGRAPHY

Lorimer, Frank, 1954. *Culture and Human Fertility*. Paris: UNESCO.

Mackensen, Rainer, 1967. "Theoretical Considerations Regarding Differential Transition." Pp. 37–46. In *International Union for the Scientific Study of Population, Proceedings of the Sydney Conference (August 21–25, 1967)*. Canberra: National University Press.

Malenbaum, Wilfred, 1970. "Health and productivity in poor areas." Pp. 31–54. In H. E. Klarman (ed.), *Empirical Studies in Health Economics*. Baltimore: Johns Hopkins University Press.

Malinowski, Bronislaw, 1964. *Crime and Custom in Savage Society*. Paterson, New Jersey: Littlefield, Adams.

Malthus, Thomas Robert, 1872. *An Essay on the Principle of Population*. New York: Kelley.

Mandle, Jay R. 1973. *The Plantation Economy: Population and Economic Change in Guyana, 1838–1960*. Philadelphia: Temple University Press.

Manley, Gordon, 1953. "The Mean Temperature of Central England, 1698–1952." *Quarterly Journal of the Royal Meteorological Society* 79: 242–261.

du Maroussem, Pierre, 1915. "Du retour à la terre." *La Réforme Sociale*: 70: 295–300.

Marshall, T. H. 1965. "The Population Problem during the Industrial Revolution: A Note on the Present State of the Controversy." Pp. 247–268. In David V. Glass and D.E.C. Eversley (eds.), *Population in History*. Chicago: Aldine.

Maspétiol, Roland, 1955. "Sociologie de la famille rurale de type traditionel en France. Pp. 129–140. In *Sociologie comparée de la famille contemporaine. Colloques internationaux du Centre National de la Recherche Scientifique*. Paris: Editions du CNRS

Mathias, Peter, 1969. *The First Industrial Nation*. London: Methuen.

Matras, Judah, 1965. "The social strategy of family formation: some variations in time and space." *Demography* 2: 349–362.

Mauldin, Parker W. 1965. "Fertility Studies: Knowledge, Attitude, and Practice." *Studies in Family Planning* 7: 1–12.

May, Dean, and Maris A. Vinovskis, 1972. "A Ray of millennial Light: Early Education and Social Reform in the Infant School Movement in Massachusetts, 1826–1840." Paper presented at the Clark University Conference on the Family and Social Structure (April 28), Worcester.

McElroy, Marjorie B. 1969. "Household expenditure patterns in rural South Vietnam." Unpublished Ph.D. Dissertation, Northwestern University.

Meier, F. 1881. Geschichte der Gemeinde Wetzikon, Zürich: Lesegesellschaft Oberwetzikon.

Meillassoux, Claude, 1975. *Femmes, greniers et capitaux*. Paris: Maspero.

Meiners, C. 1791. *Briefe über die Schweiz*. III. Teil. Tübingen: Cottaische.

Meister, Leonhard und Pestalozzi, and Johann Heinrich, 1781. *Ueber die Aufwandgesetze; Sammlung einiger Schriften, welche bei der Aufmunterungsgesellschaft in Basel eingeloffen sind, über die Frage: In wie fern ist es schicklich dem Aufwande der Bürger, in einem kleinen Freystaate,*

370

dessen Wohlfahrt auf die Handelsschaft gegründet ist, Schranken zu setzen? Basel: Flick.

Mendels, Franklin F. 1969. "Industrialization and Population Pressure in Eighteenth-Century Flanders." Unpublished Ph.D. Dissertation, University of Wisconsin.

———— 1970a. "Industry and Marriages in Flanders before the Industrial Revolution." Pp. 81–93. In Paul Deprez (ed.), *Population and Economics: Proceedings of Section V of the IV Congress of the International Economic History Association. 1968.* Winnipeg: University of Manitoba Press.

———— 1970b. "Recent research in European historical demography." *American Historical Review* 75: 1065–1073.

———— 1972. "Proto-industrialization: the first phase of the process of industrialization." *Journal of Economic History* 32: 241–261.

———— 1975. "Agriculture and Peasant Industry in Eighteenth-Century Flanders." Pp. 179–204. In William N. Parker and Eric L. Jones (eds.), Economic Issues in European Agrarian History. Princeton: Princeton University Press.

Merlin, Pierre, 1971. *L'Exode rural.* I.N.E.D., Travaux et Documents. Cahier no. 59. Paris: Presses universitaires de France.

Messance, ————, 1766. *Recherches sur la population, des généralités d'Auvergne, de Lyon, de Rouen, at de quelques provinces et villes du royaume, avec des réflexions sur la valeur du bled tant en France qu'en Angleterre depuis 1674 jusqu'en 1764.* Paris: Durand.

Meyer, Jean, 1971. *La noblesse bretonne.* Paris: Flammarion.

Meyer, Gerold von Knonau, 1837. *Die Volkszählung des Kantons Zürich am 9., 10. und 11. Mai 1836—ein Nachtrag.* Zürich: Orell Füssli.

Michael, Robert T. and Robert J. Willis, 1973. "The 'Imperfect Contraceptive' Population and Economic Analysis." Preliminary draft prepared for presentation at the Population Association of America meeting (April 26–28), New Orleans.

Mincer, Jacob, 1963. "Market Prices, Opportunity Costs, and Income Effects." Pp. 67–82. In *Measurement in Economics: Studies in Mathematical Economics and Econometrics in Memory of Yehuda Grumfield.* Stanford: Stanford University Press.

Mitchell, B. R., and Phyllis Deane, 1962. *Abstract of British Historical Statistics.* Cambridge: Cambridge University Press.

Mols, Roger, 1954–56. *Introduction à la démographie historique des villes d'Europe du XIVᵉ au XVIIIᵉ siecle.* 3 Vols. Louvain: Université de Louvain.

Momsen, Ingwer Ernst, 1969. *Die Bevölkerung der Stadt Husum von 1769 bis 1840.* Kiel: Geographische Institut.

Morison, Samuel Eliot, 1921. *The Maritime History of Massachusetts, 1783–1860.* Boston: Houghton Mifflin.

Myers, George C., and John M. Roberts, 1968. "A Technique for Measuring

Preferential Family Size and Composition." *Eugenics Quarterly* 15: 164–172.

Nag, Moni, 1968. *Factors Affecting Human Fertility in Nonindustrial Societies: A Cross-Cultural Study*. New Haven: Human Relations Area Files Press.

Namboodiri, Krishnan N., 1972. "Some Observations on the Economic Framework for Fertility Analysis." *Population Studies* 26: 185–206.

Nerlove, Marc, 1964. "Spectral Analysis of Seasonal Adjustment Procedures." *Econometrica*. 32: 241–286.

——— 1974a. "Toward a New Theory of Population and Economic Growth." Pp. 527–545. In Theodore W. Schultz (ed.), *Economics of the Family. Marriage, Children and Human Capital*. Chicago. University of Chicago Press.

——— 1974b. "Household and Economy: Toward a New Theory of Population and Economic Growth." *Journal of Political Economy* 82: S200–S218.

Noonan, John T. 1965. *Contraception*. Cambridge, Massachusetts: Harvard University Press.

Nortman, Dorothy, 1971. "Population and Family Planning Programs: A Fact-Book." *Reports on Population/Family Planning* 2: 1–48.

Notestein, Frank, 1953. "Economic Problems of Population Change." Pp. 3–31. In *Proceedings of the 8th International Conference of Agricultural Economists (August 15–22, 1952)*. New York: Oxford University Press.

Nüscheler, J. C. 1831. *Ueber die Revision der Matrimonialgesetze im Kanton Zürich*. Zürich: Friedrich Schulthess.

Nüscheler, J. K. 1786. *Boebachtungen eines Redlichen Schweizers aus väterlandischer Liebe entworfen, zum allgemeinen Nutzen des löblichen Kantons Zürich zusammengetragen von G. L. C.* Zürich: n.p.

Oechsli, Frank William, and Dudley Kirk, 1975. "Modernization and the Demographic Transition in Latin America and the Caribbean." *Economic Development and Cultural Change* 23: 391–419.

Oertli-Cajacob, C. 1974. "Demographische Entwicklung der Gemeinde Benken 1634–1833." Unpublished Master's Thesis, University of Zürich.

Ohlin, Goran, 1955. *The Positive and the Preventive Check*. Unpublished Ph.D. Dissertation, Harvard University.

——— 1961. "Mortality, Marriage and Growth in Pre-Industrial Population." Population Studies 14: 190–197.

Öhngren, Bo, 1974. *Folk i rörese, Samhallsutveckling, flyttningsmönster och folkrörelser i Eskilstuna*. 1870–1900. Studia Historica Upsaliensa, 55. Uppsala: Almquist & Wiksell.

Olusany, P. O. 1969. "Modernisation and the level of fertility in western Nigeria." Pp. 812–824. In *International Union for the Scientific Study of Population, International Population Conference*. Vol. 1. London.

Parish, William L., and Mosche Schwartz, 1972. "Household complexity in nineteenth-century France." *American Sociological Review* 37: 154–171.

Pavlik, Zdenek, 1967. "Les problemes de la révolution demographique." Pp.

56–59. In *International Union for the Scientific Study of Population, Proceedings of the Sydney Conference*. Canberra: National University Press.

Pellicani, Luciano, 1973. "La rivoluzione industriale e il fenomeno della proletarizzazione." *Rassegna Italiana di Sociologia* 14: 63–84.

Petersen, William, 1969. *Population*. Toronto: Collier-Macmillan.

Phelps Brown, E. H., and S. V. Hopkins, 1956. "Seven Centuries of the Prices of Consumables with Builders' Wage Rates." *Economica* 23: 296–314.

———— 1957. "Wage-Rates and Prices: Evidence for Population Pressure in the Sixteenth Century." *Economica* 24: 289–306.

Phillips, Llad, et al. 1969. "A Synthesis of the Economic and Demographic Models of Fertility: An Econometric Test." *The Review of Economics and Statistics* 51: 289–308.

Pingaud, M. C. 1971. "Terres et familles dans un village du Châtillonnais." *Etudes rurales* 42: 52–104.

Pitié, Jean, 1971. *Exode rural et migrations intérieures en France*. Poitiers: Norois.

Planck, Ulrich, 1967. "Hofstellenchronik von Bölgental 1650–1966: Strukturwandlungen in einem Fränkischen Weiler." Pp. 242–267. In Heinz Haushofer and Willi Boelcke (eds.), *Wege und Forschungen der Agrargeschichte. Festschrift zum 65. Geburtstag von Günther Franz*. Frankfurt am Main: DLG Verlag.

Polanyi, Karl, et al. 1957. eds. *Trade and Market in the Early Empires*. Glencoe: Free Press.

Pollard, Sidney, and David W. Crossley, 1968. *The Wealth of Britain*. London: Batsford.

Pool, D. I. 1970. "Ghana: the attitudes of urban males toward family size and family limitation." *Studies in Family Planning*: 12–17.

Poussou, Jean-Pierre, 1971. "Les mouvements migratoires en France et à partir de la France de la fin du XVe siècle au début du XIXe siècle: Approches pour une synthèse." *Annales de Démographie Historique 1970*. Paris: Mouton.

Preisschriften der Aufmunterungsgesellschaft in Basel, 1774. "Inwiefern ist es schicklich, dem Aufwande der Bürger, in einem kleinen Freystaate, dessen Wohlfahrt auf die Handelschaft gegründet ist, Schranken zu setzen?" (Winners of the prizes: L. Meister, J. H. Pestalozzi, Anonymus). Variaband (Gal. XVIII).

Pressat, Roland, 1969. "Interpretation des variations à court terme du taux de natalité." *Population* 24: 47–56.

Price, Jacob M. 1969. "Recent Quantitative Work in History: A Survey of the Main Trends." In *Studies in Quantitative History and the Logic of the Social Sciences* (Middletown, Connecticut: Wesleyan University Press; *History and Theory*, Beiheft 9).

Pŭrs, J. 1965. "Struktur und Dynamik der industriellen Entwicklung in

Böhmen im letzten Viertel des 18. Jahrhundert." *Jahrbuch für Wirtschafts-geschichte* No. 1: 160–196; No. 2: 103–124.

Razzell, P. E. 1967. "Population growth and economic change in eighteenth and early nineteenth-century England and Ireland." In Eric L. Jones and G. E. Mingey (eds.), *Land, Labour and Population in the Industrial Revolution.* London: Arnold.

——— 1972. "The Evaluation of Baptism as a Form of Birth Registration through Cross-matching Census and Parish Register Data." *Population Studies* 26: 121–146.

Reinhard, Marcel R., et al. 1968. *Histoire générale de la population mondiale.* Paris: Montchrestien.

Requena, Mariano B. 1969. "Chilean Program of Abortion Control and Fertility Planning: Present Situation and Forecast for Next Decade." Pp. 478–487. In S. J. Behrman, et al. (eds.), *Fertility and Family Planning: A World View.* Ann Arbor: University of Michigan Press.

Roberts, G. W. 1957. "Some Demographic Considerations of West Indian Federation." *Social and Economic Studies* 6: 262–285.

——— 1969. "Fertility in Some Caribbean Countries." Pp. 695–711. In *International Union for the Scientific Study of Population, Proceedings of the Sydney Conference.* Canberra: National University Press.

Roberts, John M., et al. 1971. "Preferential Pattern Analysis." Pp. 242–268. In Paul Kay (ed.), *Explorations in Mathematical Anthropology.* Cambridge, Mass.: MIT Press.

Robinson, Warren C. 1961. "Urban-Rural Differences in Indian Fertility." *Population Studies* 14: 218–234.

——— 1963. "Urbanization and Fertility: The Non-Western Experience." *Milbank Memorial Fund Quarterly* 41: 291–308.

Robinson, Warren C., and David E. Horlacher, 1971. "Population growth and economic welfare." *Reports on Population/Family Planning* No. 6: 1–39.

Robinson, Warren C., and Elizabeth H. Robinson, 1960. "Rural-Urban Fertility Differentials in Mexico." *American Sociological Review* 25: 77–81.

Romaniuk, Anatole, 1968a. "The demography of the democratic republic of the Congo." Pp. 241–341. In William Brass, et al. (eds.), *The Demography of Tropical Africa.* Princeton: Princeton University Press.

——— 1968b. "Infertility in Tropical Africa." Pp. 214–224. In J. C. Caldwell and C. Okonjo (eds.), *The Population of Tropical Africa.* New York: Columbia University Press.

Rosovsky, Henry, and K. Ohkawa, 1961. "The Indigenous Components in the Modern Japanese Economy." *Economic Development and Cultural Change* 9: 476–501.

Ross, John A., et al. 1972. "Findings from Family Planning Research." *Reports on Population/Family Planning* 12: 1–47.

Rutstein, Shea, 1971. "Development and Infant and Child Mortality in Taiwan." Unpublished Ph.D. Dissertation, University of Michigan.

374

Ryder, Norman B. 1967. "The Character of Modern Fertility." *The Annals of the American Academy of Political and Social Science* 369: 26–36.

Ryder, Norman B., and Charles F. Westoff, 1971. *Reproduction in the United States, 1965.* Princeton: Princeton University Press.

Saelfeld, Diedrich, 1966. "Die produktion und intensität der Landwirtschaft in Deutschland und angrenzenden Gebieten um 1800." *Zeitschrift für Agrargeschichte und Agrarsoziologie* 14: 137–175.

Sanderson, Warren, and R. J. Willis, 1971. "Economic Models of Fertility: Some Examples and Implications." Pp. 32–42. In National Bureau of Economic Research, *51st Annual Report.* New York: National Bureau of Economic Research.

Santini, Antonio, 1971. "Cicli economici e fluttuazioni demografiche. Nuzialità e natalità in Italia, 1863–1964." *Quaderni Storica* 17: 554–586.

——— 1972. "Techniques and methods in Historical Demography (17th and 18th Centuries)." *Journal of European Economic History* 1: 459–469.

Sauvy, Alfred, 1969. *General Theory of Population.* New York: Basic Books.

Schellenberg, Walter, 1951. *Die Bevölkerung der Stadt Zürich im 1780— Zusammensetzung und regionale Verteilung.* Affoltern am Albis: J. Weiss.

Schinz, Salomon, 1818. *Das höhere Gebirge des Kanton Zürich, und der ökonomischmoralische Zustand der Bewohner, mit Vorschlad der Hülfe und Auskunft für die bey mangelnder Fabrikarbeit brotlose Uebervölkerund.* Synodalrede Zürich: n.p.

Schnyder, Werner. 1925. "Die Bevölkerung der Stadt und Landschaft Zürich vom 14. bis 17. Jahrhundert." In *Schweizer Studien zur Geschichtswissenschaft.* Vol. XIV. Zürich: Leemann.

Schön, Lennart, 1972. "Västernorrland in the Middle of the Nineteenth Century. A Study in the Transition from Small-Scale to Capitalistic Production." *Economy and History* 15: 83–111.

Schulthess, Johann, 1818. "Beherzigung des vor der Züricher Synode gehaltenen Vortrags," Zürich: n.p.

Schultz, T. Paul, 1967. *A Family Planning Hypothesis: Some Empirical Evidence from Puerto Rico.* Santa Monica: Rand Corporation.

——— 1969. "An economic model of family planning and fertility." *Journal of Poltical Economy* 77: 153–180.

——— 1971. "An Economic Perspective on Population Growth." Pp. 148–174. In The National Academy of Sciences. *Rapid Population Growth.* Baltimore: Johns Hopkins University Press.

Schultz, Theodore W. 1973. "The Value of Children: An Economic Perspective." *Journal of Political Economy* 81: S2-S13.

——— 1974. ed., *Economics of the Family. Marriage, Children and Human Capital.* Chicago: University of Chicago Press.

Schweizerische Arealstatistik. 1912. Hg. eidg. statischen Bureau. Lieferung 184. Bern: Stampfli.

Scott, Joan W., and Louise A. Tilly, 1975. "Women's Work and the Family in Nineteenth-Century Europe." *Comparative Studies in Society and History* 17: 36–64.

BIBLIOGRAPHY

Ségalen, Martine, 1972. *Nuptialité et alliance. Le choix du conjoint dans une commune de l'Eure.* Paris: Maisonneuve et Larose.

Sévigné, Mme. de, 1862. *Lettres.* Edited by Monmerqué. Paris: Machette.

Sheps, Mindel C., and Jane A. Menken, 1971. "A Model for Studying Birth Rates Given Time Dependent Changes in Reproductive Parameters." *Biometrics* 27: 325–343.

——— 1973. *Mathematical Models of Conception and Birth.* Chicago: University of Chicago Press.

Shorter, Edward, 1971a. "Illegitimacy, Sexual Revolution and Social Change in Modern Europe." *Journal of Interdisciplinary History* 2: 237–272.

——— 1971b. "Women's Liberation, Birth Control and Fertility in European History." Paper presented at the annual meeting of the American Historical Association (December), New York.

——— 1972. "Sexual Change and Illegitimacy: The European Experience." Pp. 231–269. In Robert J. Bezucha (ed.), *Modern European Social History.* Lexington, Massachusetts: D. C. Heath.

——— 1973. "Female Emancipation, Birth Control and Fertility in European History." *American Historical Review* 78: 605–640.

——— 1975. *The Making of the Modern Family.* New York: Basic Books.

Shorter, Edward, et al. 1971. "The Decline of non-Marital Fertility in Europe, 1880–1940." *Population Studies* 25: 375–393.

Silver, Morris, 1965. "Births, Marriages, and Business Cycles in the United States." *Journal of Political Economy* 73: 237–255.

——— 1966. "Births, Marriages, and Income Fluctuations in the United Kingdom and Japan." *Economic Development and Cultural Change* 14: 302–315.

Simon, Julian L. 1962. "A Critique of the Traditional Planned Parenthood Approach in Underdeveloped Areas." Pp. 477–501. In Clyde V. Kiser (ed.), *Research on Family Planning.* Princeton: Princeton University Press.

——— 1974. *The Effect of Income on Fertility.* Chapel Hill, North Carolina: Carolina Population Center.

Singer, Joel, 1973. "Inheritance and Peasant Households in Seventeenth-Century Lower Saxony." Unpublished Senior Thesis, University of California, Los Angeles.

Smelser, Neil J. 1959. *Social Change in the Industrial Revolution.* Chicago: University of Chicago Press.

Smith, Daniel Scott, 1972. "The Demographic History of New England." *Journal of Economic History* 32: 165–183.

——— 1973. "The dating of the American sexual revolution: evidence and interpretation." Pp. 321–335. In Michael Gordon (ed.), *The American Family in Social-Historical Perspective.* New York: St. Martin's.

Smith, Daniel Scott, and Michael S. Hindus, 1975. "Premarital Pregnancy in America 1640–1971: An Overview and Interpretation." *Journal of Interdisciplinary History* 5: 537–570.

376

Spengler, Joseph J. 1938. *France Faces Depopulation.* Durham, North Carolina: Duke University Press.

——— 1966. "Values and Fertility Analysis." *Demography* 3: 109–130.

——— 1974. *Population Change, Modernization, and Welfare.* Englewood Cliffs: Prentice-Hall.

Spengler, Joseph J. et al. 1972. *Population Economics.* Durham, North Carolina: Duke University Press.

Srinivasan, K. 1972. "Need for Studies on Transition of Fertility Regulation." SEADAG Discussion Paper Presented at the Population Panel Seminar Meeting (April 6–8), Elkridge.

Statistiska Centralbyrän, 1955. *Historik Statistik för Sverige, 1720–1950.* Stockholm: Statistika Centralbyrän.

Stone, Richard, 1954. "Linear Expenditure System and Demand Analysis: An Application to the Pattern of British Demand." *Economic Journal* 64: 511–527.

Stycos, Mayone J. 1962. "A Critique of the Traditional Planned Parenthood Approach in Underdeveloped Areas." Pp. 477–501 in Clyde V. Kiser (ed.), *Research in Family Planning.* Princeton: Princeton University Press.

Sweazy, Alan, 1971. "The Economic Explanation of Fertility Changes in the United States." *Population Studies* 25: 255–267.

Tabah, Léon, 1967. "La contraception dans le tiers monde." *Population* 22: 999–1030.

Tabbarah, Riad B. 1964. "Birth Control and Population Policy." *Population Studies* 18: 187–196.

——— 1971. "Toward a Theory of Demographic Development." *Economic Development and Cultural Change* 19: 257–277.

Taylor, Carl, 1968. "Five Stages in a Practical Population Policy." *International Development Review* 10: 2–7.

Thirsk, Joan, 1961. "Industries in the Countryside." In F. J. Fisher (ed.), *Essays in the Economic and Social History of Tudor and Stuart England in Honor of R. H. Tawney.* Cambridge: Cambridge University Press.

Thorner, Daniel, 1964. "L'Economie paysanne. Concept pour l'histoire économique." *Annales, E.S.C.* 19: 417–432.

Thomas, Dorothy S. 1941. *Social and Economic Aspects of Swedish Population Movements 1750–1933.* New York: Macmillan.

Thompson, E. P. 1967. "Time, Work-Discipline, and Industrial Capitalism." *Past and Present* 38: 56–97.

Tien, H. Yuan, 1959. "A Demographic Aspect of Interstate Variations in American Fertility, 1800–1860." *Milbank Memorial Fund Quarterly* 37: 49–59.

Tietze, Christopher, 1962. "The Use-Effectiveness of Contraceptive Methods." Pp. 357–369. In Clyde V. Kiser (ed.), *Research in Family Planning.* Princeton: Princeton University Press.

——— 1972. "Teenage Sexual Revolution." *Family Planning Perspectives* 4: 6.

Tilly, Charles, 1973. "Population and Pedagogy in France." *History of Education Quarterly* 13: 113–128.

——— 1974. *An Urban World*. Boston: Little, Brown.

——— 1975. "Food Supply and Public Order in Modern Europe." Pp. 380–455. In Charles Tilly (ed.), *The Formation of National States in Western Europe*. Princeton: Princeton University Press.

Tilly, Louise A. 1972. "Materials for the quantitative history of France since 1789." Pp. 127–155. In Val Lorwin and Jacob M. Price (eds.), *The Dimensions of the Past*. New Haven: Yale University Press.

Tilly, Louise A., et al. 1974. "Women's Work and European Fertility Patterns." Working Paper 95, Center for Research on Social Organization, University of Michigan.

Tilly, Richard, and Charles Tilly, 1971. "Agenda for European Economic History in the 1970's." *Journal of Economic History* 31: 184–198.

Tryon, Rolla Milton, 1917. *Household Manufacturers in the United States: 1640–1860*. Chicago: University of Chicago Press.

United Nations, 1956. *The Aging of Populations and its Economic and Social Implications*. Populations Studies, No. 26. New York: United Nations.

United Nations Department of Economic and Social Affairs, 1965. *Population Bulletin of the United Nations, No. 7: 1963*. New York: United Nations.

Vallin, Jacques, 1970. "Table de mortalité de la population Française." *Population* 25: 847–867.

van de Walle, Etienne, 1967. "Breast Feeding, Fertility and Infant Mortality: An Analysis of Some Early German Data." *Population Studies* 21: 109–131.

——— 1968. "Marriage and Marital Fertility." *Daedalus* 97: 486–501.

——— 1974. *The Female Population of France in the Nineteenth Century. A Reconstruction of 82 Departments*. Princeton: Princeton University Press.

van de Walle, Etienne, and Albert Hermalin, 1975. "The Civil Code and Nuptiality: Empirical Investigation of an Hypothesis." In Ronald Lee (ed.), *Population Patterns in the Past*. New York: Academic Press.

van de Walle, Etienne, and John Knodel, 1967. "Demographic Transition and Fertility Decline, the European Case." Pp. 47–55. In *International Union for the Scientific Study of Population, Proceedings of the Sydney Conference*. Canberra: National University Press.

van de Walle, Etienne, and Francine van de Walle, 1972. "Allaitement, stérilité et contraception: les opinions jusqu'au XIXe siècle." *Population* 27: 686–701.

Vinovskis, Maris A. 1971a. "American Historical Demography: A Review Essay." *Historical Methods Newsletter* 4: 141–148.

——— 1971b. "The 1789 Life Table of Edward Wigglesworth." *Journal of Economic History* 31: 570–590.

———— 1972a. "Mortality Rates and Trends in Massachusetts Before 1860." *Journal of Economic History* 32: 184–213.

———— 1972b. "Trends in Massachusetts Education, 1826–1860." *History of Education Quarterly* 12: 501–529.

———— 1973. Review of Peter Knights, *The Plain People of Boston, 1830–1860. Journal of Interdisciplinary History* 3: 781–786.

———— 1974. "The Field of Early American Family History: A Methodological Critique." *The Family in Historical Perspective* 7: 2–8.

———— 1975. "Demographic Changes in America from the Revolution to the Civil War: An Analysis of the Socio-Economic Determinants of Fertility Differentials and Trends in Massachusetts from 1765 to 1860." Unpublished Ph.D. Dissertation, Harvard University.

———— 1976a. *Demographic History and the World Population Crisis. Chester Bland—Dwight E. Lee Lectures in History.* Worcester, Massachusetts: Clark University Press.

———— 1976b. "Socio-economic Determinants of Interstate Fertility Differentials in the United States in 1850 and 1860." *Journal of Interdisciplinary History* 6: 375–396.

———— 1977. "Angels' Heads and Weeping Willows: Death in Early America." *Proceedings of the American Antiquarian Society*, forthcoming.

Wachter, Michael L. 1972. "Government Policy Towards the Fertility of the Poor." Fels Discussion Paper No. 19. The Fels Center of Government, University of Pennsylvania.

Ware, Caroline F. 1931. *The Early New England Cotton Manufacture.* Boston: Houghton Mifflin.

Warner, Oliver, 1867. *Abstract of the Census of Massachusetts, 1865.* Boston: Wright and Potter.

Wascr, Johann Heinrich, 1780. "Bevölkerung des löblichen Cantons Zürich in verschiedenen Zeitaltern." In: *Schlözer's Briefwechsel VI.* Heft 32. Göttingen: Vandenhoeks.

Weintraub, Robert, 1962. "The Birth Rate and Economic Development: An Empirical Study." *Econometrica* 40: 812–817.

Wells, Robert V. 1971. "Demographic Change and the Life Cycle of American Families." *Journal of Interdisciplinary History* 2: 273–282.

Westoff, Charles F., et al. 1961. *Family Growth in Metropolitan America.* Princeton: Princeton University Press.

Westoff, Charles F., and Raymond H. Potvin, 1966. "Higher Education, Religion, and Women's Family-Size Orientations." *American Sociological Review* 31: 489–496.

Wheaton, Robert, 1975. "Family and Kinship in Western Europe: The Problem of the Joint Family Household." *Journal of Interdisciplinary History* 5: 601–628.

Whelpton, Pascal K., et al. 1966. *Fertility and Family Planning in the United States.* Princeton: Princeton University Press.

Wilkinson, R. G. 1973. *Poverty and Progress.* London: Methuen.

379

Wolfe, Barbara, 1973. "A Socioeconomic Analysis of Family Building Behavior." Unpublished Ph.D. Dissertation, University of Pennsylvania.

Wopfner, Hermann, 1938. "Güterteilung und Übervölkerung tirolischer Landbezirke im 16., 17. und 18. Jahrhundert." *Südosdeutsche Forschungen* 3: 202–232.

Wrigley, E. A. 1966. "Family Limitation in Pre-Industrial England." *Economic History Review* 19: 82–109.

―――― 1969. *Population and History*. New York: McGraw-Hill.

―――― 1972a. "Mortality in Pre-Industrial England: The Example of Colyton, Devon, Over Three Centuries." Pp. 243–274. In David V. Glass and R. Revelle (eds.), *Population and Social Change*. London: Arnold.

―――― 1972b. "The Process of Modernization and the Industrial Revolution in England." *Journal of Interdisciplinary History* 3: 225–259.

―――― 1973. Ed. *Identifying People in the Past*. London: Arnold.

Yasuba, Yasukichi, 1962. *Birth Rates of the White Population in the United States, 1800–1860: An Economic Study*. Baltimore: Johns Hopkins University Press.

Yeomans, K. A. 1968. *Applied Statistics: Statistics for the Social Scientist*. Vol. II. Middlesex: Penguin.

Young, Arthur, 1969. *Travels in France During the Years 1787, 1788 and 1789*. New York: Anchor Books.

Yule, G. Udney, 1906. "Changes in the Marriage and Birth Rates in England and Wales during the Past Half Century." *Journal of the Royal Statistical Society* 69: 88–132.

Yver, Jean, 1966. *Egalité entre héritiers et exclusion des enfants dotés: Essai de géographie coutumière*. Paris: Sirey.

Zarat, Alvin O. 1967. "Fertility in Urban Areas of Mexico: Implications for the Theory of Demographic Transition." *Demography* 4: 363–373.

Zevin, Robert Brooke, 1971. "The Growth of Cotton Textile Production after 1815." Pp. 122–147. In Robert W. Fogel and Stanley L. Engerman (eds.), *The Reinterpretation of American Economic History*. New York: Harper & Row.

Index

INDEX

Fecundity, 44, 59, 61, 71, 72, 75, 116, 157, 158, 187, 203
Féline, Father, 270
Fertility: economic analyses of, 23–32, 57–69, 335–36; French decline of until 1850, 257–88, 343–44; historical changes in and problems of, 3–55, 345–50; individual and group strategies, 135–54, 337–39; in Massachusetts 225–56, 342; models of pre-industrial England, 155–207, 340–42; sociology of, 69–133, 335–37; in Western Europe (1700–1900), 209–23, 339–40; in Zürich, Switzerland, 289–334, 344–45. See also Birth rates; Fecundity; Fertility control; Mortality rate; Population growth and decline; Sexual behavior; types of fertility: Constant, Lifetime, Marital, Natural, Nonmarital, Premodern, Total, Uncontrolled
Fertility control, 3, 6, 9, 13, 20, 21, 22, 24, 43, 44, 50, 54–55, 58, 68, 70–71, 72, 74–98, 102, 105–15, 120, 121–23, 124, 125–26, 127–29, 130–31, 132–33, 146, 148, 149, 152, 155, 156, 158–63, 187, 201–2, 203, 210, 257, 259, 263–73, 274, 277, 280, 286, 335–36, 340, 347, 348, 349. See also Contraception; Family planning programs
Fertility decline. See Population growth and decline
Fetus, mortality of, 71, 72, 73, 74
Fiscal records as sources of demographic data, 13
Fischenthal (Swiss Highland community), 312, 313, 318
Fishlow, Albert, 236
Fixed Hearths concept, 162–63
Flanders, 218; Belgian, 148
Flinn, M. W., 205
Fogel, Robert, 34
Food: prices, 113, 170, 171, 215, 346; storage, 330; supply, 10, 20, 32, 135, 137, 149, 158, 324
Foreign born population, 227, 232–33, 237, 238, 239–40, 248, 250, 252
Forster, Robert, 272
France, 6, 18, 25, 30, 35, 37, 43, 47, 48, 53, 148, 151, 183, 209, 211–12, 220–22, 257–88, 289, 340, 343–44. See also Civil Code (French); names of French towns and départements
Franconia, 219–20
Freedman, Deborah, S., 112, 116, 120

Freedman, Ronald, 77
Friedlander, Dov, 18, 35, 343

Geertz, Clifford, 31
Genealogy, 12
Genetics, fertility and, 73, 266
Geneva, 149, 264, 294
Geographic mobility. See Mobility
Geography, population growth and, 305
Germany, 151, 258, 278, 289. See also names of German states and territories
Gifts, inheritance laws and, 211
Gilboy, Elizabeth, 178, 206-7
Gotthelf, Jeremias, 310
Gottingen (territory), 219
Goubert, Pierre, 17
Governments: centralization within, 262; food storage programs, 330; population control programs of, 20, 21, 120. See also National states; Politics
Graunt, John, 6
Great Britain, 18, 25, 34, 127, 273. See also England; Wales
Griliches, Zvi, 39, 41
Gross Reproduction Rate, 149
Grubenhagen (territory), 219

Habakkuk, H. J., 26, 164, 291
Hajnal, John, 17, 126
Hallines (French parish), 29–30
Health conditions, 73, 97, 104, 109–11, 114, 116, 117, 119, 120, 132, 157, 266, 273, 330, 349. See also Medical care; Nutrition
Heer, David, 254, 255
Heirs. See Inheritance systems
Henry, Louis, 6, 12, 43, 266
Highlands (Switzerland), 305, 307, 308, 309–10, 311, 312, 313, 317, 318, 320, 322, 323, 325, 328–29. See also names of Highland districts
Himes, Norman E., 267
Hinwil (Swiss district), 301, 302, 317, 325, 328, 330
Hirzel, J. C., 310–311, 312, 314, 317
Historical demography, 6–55, 225, 260, 262, 288, 347, 348, 350. See also Demography
Holland. See Low Countries; Netherlands
Hopkins, S. V., 170
Horgan (Swiss district), 301, 327, 328–29, 330
Household composition, decisions, 6, 7, 11, 29, 38, 39, 41, 46–49, 51, 53,

384

Library of Congress Cataloging in Publication Data

Main entry under title:

Historical studies of changing fertility.

(Quantitative studies in history)
Revised versions of papers originally presented at a seminar at the Institute for Advanced Study, Princeton, during the summer of 1972.

Bibliography: p.
Includes index.
1. Fertility, Human—Congresses. I. Tilly, Charles. II. Berkner, Lutz K. III. Series.
HB901.H57   301.32′1   77–85569
ISBN 0–691–07595–6

ISBN 0–691–10066–7 pbk.